MEDIEVAL AMERICAN ART

MEDIEVAL AMERICAN ART

A SURVEY IN TWO VOLUMES

by

PÁL KELEMEN

VOLUME I

THE MACMILLAN COMPANY

NEW YORK · 1943

TO THE MEMORY
OF THE HEROIC NINETEENTH CENTURY PIONEERS
OF PRE-COLUMBIAN ARCHAEOLOGY

FOREWORD

All attempts to reduce art to science are in vain.
Science is not art, and, if a work of art can legiti-
mately convey scientific information, that is because
its material includes matters of universal scope.
—Tovey

MY INTEREST in pre-Columbian art and my manner of presenting it
may require a few paragraphs of a personal nature, as well as some
comment on the status of art-history at the time of my early studies.
When more than thirty years ago I attended my first classes in the history of
art, even the leading European universities were limited in their program.
While the painters and sculptors of the Renaissance were abundantly treated, the
masters of the Trecento had still the mist of a delayed sunrise on them. Spanish
art was not yet in the process of being discovered; on Greco no monograph was
yet published, with the exception of Cossio's pioneer work in Spanish. Cézanne
and Gauguin were anathema to every museum, and we were led to admire and
analyze the compositions of Géricault and Delacroix. The art of Byzantium,
together with the tremendous iconographic influence which took its name from
that metropolis, was the little noticed hobby of a few. The archaeology and art-
history of the Far and Near East were in their infancy, primarily because of a
national aloofness but also because of the difficulties of travel in those lands.

The field was then not so highly specialized. Systematized methods had not
been thoroughly established, and the inspiration and poetry of the subject were
still uppermost. Art-history was young, and we approached it through the
broad avenue of the humanities—philosophy, drama, literature, music.

In my native Budapest, the colleagues of Liszt were still holding the bastion
of academic music, but an enthusiastic if sparse audience applauded the compositions of Bartók and Kodály, based on the genuine folk song. After a perform-
ance of Debussy's quintette with the composer at the piano, we listened in breath-
less silence to his defense of his new music. Gordon Craig had just presented his
new ideas of décor and Max Reinhardt had begun his experiments, bringing the
stage out of the frame of the proscenium arch into the three dimensional in vast

halls and the open air. Nijinski was not yet a myth, but a young and talented solo dancer. In the home of the aging Auguste Rodin at Meudon Val Fleury, I listened to the sculptor's broad and elastic views on art in general—not only on sculpture—in an interview which made up one of my first published essays. At that time Rodin was far from generally acknowledged; his Balzac statue was refused, even as a gift, by the municipality of Paris.

Great revaluations in art-history and general esthetics were taking place. Salomon Reinach, Henri Bergson, Heinrich Wölfflin—in whose classes I sat— Benedetto Croce, Walter Pater, Bernhard Berenson, with others were reformulating the principles of art criticism. But intellectual life was shaken and disrupted by World War I. In the late summer of 1914, with Croce's "Estética" in my saddlebag, I rode out as a young cavalry officer.

After the war anything seemed possible in the political arena, and experimentation ran almost as wild in the arts. I was fortunate enough to be able to go on with my studies, but from my original thesis, "Impressionism before the 19th Century," I ventured far, going back into the formative periods of Christian art.

While in pursuit of this subject and studying illuminated manuscripts at the British Museum in 1926, I had my first taste of pre-Columbian art and made some notes on the strange monumental concepts and technical refinement manifest in the specimens on exhibit there. But involved then in my own studies, I did not follow up these impressions. My next contact with it did not come until after I had met and married an American in Italy and, some time later, made my first visit to the United States. Here, in 1932, I intended to study certain phases of Spanish art, so well represented in this country, but the tremendous artistic vitality in the civilization of pre-Columbian America encountered in the various museums soon began to absorb my interest.

By that time a few books had attempted to present the artistic side of this civilization, and an exhibit or two had awakened sporadic interest. I decided to make a comprehensive survey of these cultures from the point of view of art and was encouraged in this undertaking by scholars here. The outline of this work was formulated then and the collection of the material began. The scope of the project continually expanded as I went along.

This survey is planned to introduce to the reader generally interested in art those achievements of the pre-Columbian civilization which demand attention for their beauty and power irrespective of dates and styles.

It would be ideal if the objects could speak for themselves; but, for most people, some effort must be made to bridge the gap of centuries and to offset inherited esthetic standards. In this technological age, the investigation into the material construction of a work of art is threatening to become more important than intimacy with the spirit which created it. A broad new world of human expression cannot be opened by a "proliferation of minutiae"; the approach has to be through the emotional—the one common denominator of man's grasp at art. For centuries the colors of Titian have been enjoyed without analyzing their chemical ingredients, and the canvases of Velásquez have been awarded world renown without a knowledge of the kind of hair he used in his brushes. I have avoided as much as possible the "professional" terminology of the specialist—one cause of the general reader's diffidence toward books on archaeology and art-history—and have tried to present a humanistic subject to him in such a manner that he can perceive the beauty of its moods and follow not so much the intricate and overladen thoughts of an author as the clear and colorful line of the subject itself.

The full grandeur of a building, however, or the delicacy of a jade pectoral cannot be completely transmitted by a photograph. As my work proceeded, the vague reaction of the public to pictures in general, as well as the shortcomings of most of the pictures existing in this field, became increasingly apparent. At best a photograph is only an approximation, and for one who is unfamiliar with an object, it must be made to aid his eye and stimulate his imagination as far as possible. The straight front or exact profile view of anthropological files is not always the best means of bringing out artistic quality effectively. Consequently, the necessity arose for pictures taken from a new angle. The original position of some pieces had to be considered—for instance, a sculpture high in a carved frieze, with the top lighting of a tropical sun. Also those "artistic shots" had to be avoided in which an overlively background or overdramatic lighting reduced the object to a mere vehicle for the photographer. Several trips were undertaken to Spanish America for new photographs and first-hand observation and to Europe for comparative material.

To put into one survey all the manifestations of the artistic development of a wide range of cultures over one and a half millennia is obviously an impossibility. The production of each area is given space according to its artistic importance, proportionate, as I see it, to the general picture. Certain sites and specimens, which to the specialist may appear important, have been omitted because it was my conviction that they would not contribute appreciably to the reader's grasp of this art.

FOREWORD

"Pre-Columbian" as used in this survey stands for the time-span in the Western Hemisphere before cultural contact with the white man. While not entirely satisfactory, because it is not self-explanatory, this term is as good as anything offered so far and has the added advantage of being traditional, carrying with it long-accepted connotations. Columbus is, after all, responsible for the opening of the New World, and as long as his name is not perpetuated in that of the new continent, he deserves at least to be commemorated in the term which defines the civilization that existed here before his enterprise. "Medieval American" has a more restricted meaning and is discussed in the opening chapter.

In arranging the material, a name had to be coined for the Isthmian countries and the adjoining regions; I have called this section the Interlying Area. For the other territories of highest civilization, the accepted designations—Southwest, Mexican, Maya, and Andean—have been used. It will be found that the borders of these areas cannot be strictly adhered to, for cultural limits do not necessarily coincide with boundary lines. In general, a geographical rather than a chronological sequence has been followed, but here also other considerations have occasionally led to a change.

If I had not been warned that further delay would result in an indefinite postponement of publication, due to war conditions, I would have added more detail, elaborated certain ideas, and polished on the style. Data which in certain cases might have weighed down the text have been relegated to the Catalogue of Illustrations, where measurements, other such information, and various credits are recorded. In a few cases, the order of the illustrations within the framework of one page is not followed by the text, for, while the text pursues the logical sequence, the plate was arranged to please the eye. Often the use of a modest magnifying glass will increase the reader's enjoyment of the illustrations. The chronological chart and the map are appended for his orientation and are simplified and generalized to that end.

During the ten years in which the material was collected for this survey, I have received the help of a great number of museum directors, curators, photographers, art collectors, and connoisseurs. To name them all, from Vienna, Austria, to Lima, Peru, would not be possible in the space allowed. I hope that they will accept this general expression of my sincere gratitude.

There is a smaller group whose coöperation in this work was of a more personal kind. Professor Alfred M. Tozzer of Harvard University was the first to whom I went in the autumn of 1932 with my ideas and plans, and he, with the experience and understanding of a great teacher, put me on the right track; since then, whenever advice has been needed, he has given it unsparingly. Dr. Alfred V. Kidder, Chairman of the Division of Historical Research, Carnegie Institution of Washington, showed early interest in my project, and his far-reaching arm has facilitated my work both in the field and in the museums. The reader will appreciate, I am sure, his generosity in procuring the permission to include here material, as yet unpublished, from the famous Maya site, Uaxactun, excavated under the leadership of A. Ledyard Smith of the same Institution, thus making it known to a different circle. Director Donald Scott of the Peabody Museum, Harvard University, gave me the freedom of the rich collection and magnificent library there; it is through his kindness that it was possible to include the pictures of pottery specimens excavated at Coclé, Panama, the report of which is in press.

The manuscript was read by J. Eric S. Thompson of the Carnegie Institution of Washington. For years he has taken a most helpful interest in my work and, with his erudition and innate gentlemanliness, has stood at my side as a rare friend. Many of his criticisms have been included in the text, and all dates throughout the Maya Area are based on his latest conclusions. Dr. Wendell C. Bennett of Yale University has given much attention to the sections relating to South American cultures, and his nomenclature and chronology for the Andean Area have been used. Miss H. Newell Wardle of The University Museum, Philadelphia, furnished considerable data and identified a number of the Peruvian fabrics. The textile glossary is in great part her work. Kenneth Macgowan of the Office of Coördinator of Inter-American Affairs also has read the manuscript and, with his wide knowledge and connoisseurship, contributed toward the clarification of a number of statements.

Special privileges in handling and photographing the material under their care were given by Sir George Hill, Director of the British Museum, London, who also permitted me to use Maudslay's original photographic plates; Dr. Alfonso Caso, Director of the Instituto Nacional de Antropología e Historia, Mexico; Professor J. Antonio Villacorta C., Secretary of Education of Guatemala; Carlos A. Villacorta B., Director of the Museo Arqueológico of Guatemala; and also Dr. Emeriterio Oscar Salazar of San Salvador. Professor Jorge A. Lines of San José furnished photographs of unpublished rare material from Costa Rica. Professor Verle L. Annis of the University of Southern California, Los Angeles, placed at my disposal a great number of his excellent photographs. Frederick C. Orchard of Peabody Museum, Harvard University, and Kenneth

FOREWORD

C. Miller of the Museum of the American Indian, Heye Foundation, New York, gave countless hours and their unlimited patience in making photographs from my angle. The Harvard College Library coöperated in sending their books to me in Norfolk, saving me trips and giving me the opportunity to work in the calm of my study.

To arrange 960 photographs of different character, quality, and size into 306 plates was no light task, and Edward C. Wolf of The Beck Engraving Company, New York, brought to the work his great resourcefulness and good taste. For the last year and a half Helen B. Hartman has helped in the assemblage of the material, in editorial work, and in the typing. Her faithfulness to the cause and her growing enthusiasm were of great assistance to me. The index is principally her work.

Finally, acknowledgment of a more intimate character is due my wife, Elisabeth, my constant collaborator in the various phases of this survey. She has not only accompanied me on all my trips, sharing the frequent discomforts of primitive conditions, but, under most trying circumstances, has taken numberless photographs for me which otherwise could not have been obtained. She has helped also substantially in preparing the manuscript. Her rare artistic sense and unflagging spirit have contributed greatly toward the completion of this work. Throughout the undertaking she has exemplified that fine type of American womanhood—not faddist, not sterilely intellectual, but of constructive mind—which has helped to make and keep this country great and free.

Pál Kelemen

Boston, Massachusetts, October, 1932
Norfolk, Connecticut, November, 1942

Contents

VOLUME I

TEXT

(*cont.*)

‹ xiii ›

CONTENTS

VOLUME II

ILLUSTRATIONS

MEDIEVAL AMERICAN ART

I

Art–History and Medieval American Art

ONE of the most significant events at the close of the Middle Ages of Europe was the discovery of America. The same event marks the end of medieval American civilization. The phrase is not a paradox. As in Europe the nations in the process of formation created great art during these centuries, so also in America certain regions blossomed forth with marked individuality of culture, beginning roughly with our Christian era. Rising from an obscure archaic background, these pre-Columbian peoples went through the phases of agricultural development and subsequent economic expansion, struggled with problems of increasing population, felt the rivalry of belligerent neighbors and the stimulus of trade. With the coming of the white man, the fabulous civilization developed in isolation by the red man came to ruthless destruction. The modern world that has grown out of the transplantation of European culture on ancient American soil is not our subject here, although it has furnished enough color, variety, and material to occupy ethnologists and interest travelers since the beginning of the colonial era. The purpose of this book is to evaluate the artistically important aspects of the aboriginal cultures that made up pre-Columbian civilization.

Europe at the end of the 15th century was carrying on an increasingly rich trade with the Near and Far East. Merchants and travelers had been adding to the knowledge of the globe ever since Marco Polo and Sir John Mandeville, and by this time a constantly growing group of enlightened men was becoming more and more convinced of the existence of other lands and of other routes to Asia. With the rise of Turkish power, when the caravan termini as well as the eastern Mediterranean harbors, both important in Oriental trade, fell to the troops of the Crescent Moon, geographers, astronomers, navigators, and adventurers speculated on the possibility of a new approach to the Far East. In 1474 a Florentine physician and astronomer, Paolo Toscanelli, wrote to a canon in Lisbon, conjecturing on the lands that might be found in a western crossing of the ocean and giving a map and his opinion on possible weather and water conditions.

There is evidence that this may have reached the hands of Christopher Columbus and strengthened the conviction that drove him for years from one court of Europe to another, seeking support for his expedition. When he at last sailed on his first voyage to the west, he carried with him a letter from the Spanish Court addressed to "the most serene Prince, our very dear friend" and intended for the Great Khan of Cathay, that is, China. On landing on an island, to which the name San Salvador was given, his courageous band believed themselves in the vicinity of the Asiatic mainland, and as long as he lived, Columbus never realized that he had reached a new continent and no mere outpost of India. Certain misnomers from those days still survive among us, by which, for instance, we call the islands of the Caribbean the "West Indies" and designate the American aborigines as "Indians," when the romantic term "redskin" would be more exact.

The Europe of Columbus was just crossing the threshold of the Renaissance with a new impetus toward learning and the arts. Kings and emperors vied with one another as ambitious collectors and patrons of science. Artists were accorded wide respect and recognition. As early as the 1420's, Masolino, teacher of the pioneer Masaccio, is known to have left the Italian field for a time to execute the frescoes in a new palace at Buda (Budapest) for the Hungarian king, Matthew Corvinus. Leonardo da Vinci spent his last years in France at the Court of Francis I, where he died in 1519, the year that Cortés landed in Mexico. Titian (1477–1576) was commissioned by Charles V of the Holy Roman Empire, sovereign of the *conquistadores,* and traveled as far as Augsburg for a sitting for a royal portrait.

Silks from China, rugs from Persia, ivory carvings from India were in demand for the European market. The exotic products of distant lands were prized, however, more for their rarity, their collector's value, than for the creative art which they embodied. It is only in the past century that we have learned to view an art not our own with an interest devoid of condescension. It is significant that those practical objects upon which craftsmen of all countries and all ages have lavished so much skill and imagination are grouped nowadays under the heading "applied art" rather than as "minor arts."

When the *conquistadores* arrived on American soil, they found a highly developed civilization and sent shipments of gold, textiles, feather-work, stone sculpture, and pottery back to the Spanish king in proof of the success and worthiness of their mission. The gifts that Cortés received from Montezuma for his sovereign were publicly exhibited for the admiration of the Spanish Court and people. The presence of extraordinary specimens of pre-Columbian metal-work in Europe can be traced, to a certain degree, in the literature of the period.[122] Aside from the metal, most of which was soon melted down, these gifts from the New World passed into the curio collections of the Medici and Borgia Popes, the House of Habsburg, and aristocrats in their favor, thence to disappear, piece by piece, as the years went on.

Best in a position to appreciate the skill and beauty of this work, which had come from a civilization so different from their own, were the craftsmen, members of the medieval guilds. One of them, Albrecht Dürer, descendant of a line of Hungarian goldsmiths, wrote in his diary in 1520 on the occasion of a visit to Brussels:

"Also I saw the things which were brought to the King from the New Golden Land: a sun entirely of gold, a whole fathom broad; likewise, a moon, entirely of silver, just as big; likewise, sundry curiosities from their weapons, armor and missiles; very odd clothing, bedding and all sorts of strange articles for human use, all of which is fairer to see than marvels.

"These things were all so precious that they were valued at a hundred thousand gulden worth. But I have never seen in all my days what so rejoiced my heart, as these things. For I saw among them amazing artistic objects, and I marveled over the subtle ingenuity of the men in these distant lands. Indeed I cannot say enough about the things which were there before me." [148]

Unfortunately, the soldiers who carried out the Conquest were neither princes of culture nor craftsmen of delicate skill. They were akin to those French cavalrymen who in 1525 stabled their horses in the refectory of a convent near Milan, causing the early ruin of Leonardo da Vinci's fragile masterpiece, *The Last Supper*. Vandalism was even more rampant in the fight among the heathen, and history tells that hand-illuminated Persian and Turkish manuscripts were dumped into the river to serve as a bridge for European wagon trains. How could the New World fare better? Some observations of an astronomical, botanical, and medicinal nature made by the American aborigines were on a par with those of contemporary Europe; but the *conquistadores*—cold-blooded adventurers, some of them criminals released from prison to fill the ranks for this hazardous undertaking—had not braved the dangers of an unknown sea to admire a different civilization. They were after booty. Spain, deep in debt, sought new economic fields, untapped sources of wealth; her religion, new converts.

"The New Golden Land" gratified all these needs in undreamed of abundance. The inhabitants, with their spear-throwers and bows and arrows, were singularly defenseless against the guns and armor of the Europeans. Besides this, they were torn with inner dissension and unwisely sought to use the invaders against their old enemies. It must not be forgotten that the Spanish soldiery of that age was welded into a superb fighting machine comparable to the Roman legions of classic times. Magnificently equipped for those days, they were elastic and independent, resourceful in battle and capable of living off the land for long periods. Some of Prescott's anthropological conclusions may be outmoded, but his descriptions of the historic panorama in his *Conquest of Mexico* and *Conquest of Peru* remain unsurpassed. The orgy of pillage and enslavement continued for centuries in this world of apparently inexhaustible wealth. Millions of dollars' worth of gold was looted from the people. Bizarre and exotic jewelry, ranging from simple bracelets to complicated breast and head ornaments, was melted at once into ingots, the better for shipment. Gold dug from the slave-worked mines of America financed the building of the Armada, as well as England's defenses against it, for the booty of English privateers preying on Spanish galleons helped pay for the Queen's navy. Hundreds of tons went to the bottom of the sea, and still the golden stream poured in upon Spain.

It is difficult even to imagine what has disappeared in architecture, sculpture, and the other arts from the pre-Columbian scene. As the buildings served the rites of pagan gods, their destruction was looked upon as an essential and righteous act. The hand-written and illustrated books of the Maya, Zapotecs, and Aztecs, recording the time-count of the people, the history of their tribes, their ritual, and their legends, were burned by the first priests as works of the devil. Only a few examples now remain. The loss of the books is especially deplorable since these might also have helped to reveal the psychological development of this race which climbed so high through circumstances so different from our own. The spiritual and mental build-up of this world that was systematically devastated and reduced will never be grasped in its true proportions. Only broken bits of the mosaic can be found, which science is now busy trying to piece together into a coherent picture.

Had the *conquistadores* come over some centuries earlier, unfortified by the self-conscious power of the awakening Renaissance, the impact might have been less violent and medieval America might have contributed more to Europe.

There are two chief reasons why medieval American art is so tardily being granted its deserved position in the history of human civilization. In the first place, it developed and flowered in isolation—isolated at least from those contacts with the Eastern Hemisphere which formed the background of the white man's culture and contributed toward the formulation of our esthetic principles. We confront, in the chapter "Evolution or Influence," the various arguments concerning the origins of the race and the possibilities of connection with Asia or the South Sea—whether remote, accidental, or recurrent. In the second place, it was destroyed almost upon discovery, and only the most tenuous of living threads remain to bridge the gap for us across the centuries.

The fabric of Old World archaeology and art-history is like a vast web, stretching from the Roman ramparts of England to the delicately drawn woodcuts of Japan, from the Byzantine icons of the Russian steppes to the wondrous world of the royal tombs of Egypt. It is an enormous territory, which produced amazingly varied manifestations of artistic taste over an enormous period of time— from the fourth millennium B.C. to our present day. Yet remote as certain points lie from one another, as different as are the styles which they produced, nevertheless it is clear that details and even whole ideas were incorporated, adapted, and developed interregionally. At the time Greek art began to flourish, about 500 B.C., there were already three thousand years of cultural heritage from which to draw inspiration; highly artistic civilizations had existed in Mesopotamia, China, Egypt, and the eastern half of the Mediterranean with its islands. It might be said that in the cauldrons of all these previous cultures the Hellenistic ideal of beauty was first boiled down which reached forms and expressions that we accept and use today. The three continents, Asia, Africa, and finally Europe, contributed to the concepts, inspiration, and technical accomplishment of the arts of the Greeks, whose architecture and sculpture in turn still predominate in the style of our public buildings and whose precepts remain our general standard of beauty.

The art of awakening Christianity likewise drew upon previous periods. Egypt, through the Coptic, influenced the iconography of the new religion. The style of the Christian church grew out of the pagan basilica. Instead of medallions of the emperors, mosaics of the saints decorated the walls. The fresco was already in existence in the tombs of Egypt, the Hindu temples of India, the grave chambers of Etruria, the synagogue of Dura on the Euphrates. The technical formulae were already set, and the background of tradition was established. Only a new content was necessary to enliven the arts to serve the new faith.

Later Christian architecture underwent a similar development. Structural as well as ornamental elements of the Gothic had their proving-ground in the brick mosques of Persia.[144] What we know as the Renaissance was the revitalizing of the grandeur which had been Rome's a thousand years before.

We can trace back to prehistoric times the various contributions of different races and regions to our present culture, and we find that the art which surrounds us today was developed by cross-fertilization of ideas from other continents. Invisible threads of influence tie together and finally connect the remote corners of our geographical oblong.

The American continent was not in such a fortunate position. It is generally accepted that it was settled by waves of migratory hunters who crossed the Bering Sea from Asia while still in a very primitive state. Dr. Clark Wissler puts the final date of these migrations at the dawn of the Neolithic, or New Stone, Age.[169] But whatever the time, the great achievements of the early Bronze Age in Asia, the domestication of cattle, the cultivation of rice, the application of the wheel in transportation, and the use of the plow were all unknown here. The early Americans had to build up their civilization and art from their own spiritual resources. They had no wandering camel caravans that transported the products of an Orient into remote lands. There were no great galleys to carry obelisks and huge marble slabs incredible distances, to the wonder of an alien populace and the amazement of modern engineers. Nor were there Crusades to bring the glowing art of a tropical climate to a new growth in the north.

Even the three main periods of anthropology—Stone, Bronze, and Iron ages —find no application here. Although the pre-Columbian peoples did not advance technically much beyond the neolithic, yet they constructed architecture on a grand scale. Their tools were primitive, but their carvings are unsurpassed in India, Assyria, or Egypt. The ancient Americans never knew the smelting of iron, and what bronze they had was too soft for general practical use, yet their metal-work excited the admiration not only of Dürer but of jewelers' guilds throughout Renaissance Europe. Although fashioned on a simple hand loom, their textiles were highly complicated, and their pottery manufactured without the use of the potter's wheel can hold its own with the ceramic art of other continents. To appreciate the magnitude of this achievement, we have only to compare it with the accomplishments of the aborigines of other isolated territories, such as Australia.

Because each step of the way had to be invented of their own ingenuity, it is natural that the pre-Columbian peoples developed here a completely individual ideal of beauty, untouched by historical influences such as coöperated throughout the Eastern Hemisphere to form the white man's concept. The approach and attitude of the general observer toward medieval American art is bound to be affected by the ideals of beauty upon which he was reared; he is unable to make himself independent of the standards which he has been taught from youth and will feel the art of another civilization alien and remote. The realism which plays such an important rôle in our art was not a primary aim in medieval American art. It should be kept in mind always that the purpose here was the expression of an idea, often highly complex, in which the imitation of nature may frequently have been irrelevant.

Although there never was a complete break between Europe and Asia, only a few generations ago the arts of Asia, the Near East, and ancient Egypt suffered likewise from the differences in esthetic approach and evaluation. The exotic and bizarre were sought after, the rich and rare, but there was little attempt to grasp the spiritual content. Contact with the Orient has always existed, yet only recently were its styles digested and accepted by Europe.

This leads to the second reason for the tardy reception of medieval American art into the chapters of art-history. Not only is it built on concepts entirely different from our own, but, while the arts of Asia lived on and European eyes gradually acquired a comprehension of them, pre-Columbian civilization met a violent death with the Conquest. Those subtle ties were then destroyed that might have served to bind it to our times and interpret its language more directly to our European-trained minds. Between us and the last living manifestation of medieval American art there is a vacuum of four hundred years. Pre-Columbian America had no Plato to write a philosophy of its art, no Vasari to record the activities of his contemporaries. For a time after the Conquest, certain techniques were still practiced. The Peruvian skill in weaving was applied to imitations of Chinese and Persian fabrics, and a few mitres, stoles, and holy pictures in exquisite feather-work exist in European museums. Pagan symbols found their way into the sculptural ornament of early colonial buildings and appear in embroideries. But the vitality of such work weakened steadily.

This sunken civilization has never ceased, however, to intrigue the imagination of men, sometimes taking the form of pure romance and fantasy. The recently hypothesized Island of Mu now rivals Atlantis as a possible mother of pre-Columbian cultures. And as late as 1934 a pretentious book appeared which traced the Maya to a direct colonization from ancient Egypt. Thus, regardless of the mass of authenticated research now accumulated, misconceptions continue to be promulgated by writers who never saw an ancient American site and who would not think of tampering so arbitrarily with the arts of China or Egypt.

The unique contribution of pre-Columbian art lies in its presentation of the achievements of an isolated continent, in the fascinating mixture of primitiveness and maturity which could have been produced only under the circumstances that prevailed here. Only within the past century has a constructive attempt been made to add up the sum total of this legacy. Several branches of modern science are now coöperating in the task. Ethnology seeks clues to the ancient rites and customs through legends and practices of the living aborigines. The linguist, enlarging the map of languages, adds to the knowledge of the distribution and extension of various tribes and the areas of their influences. The geologist and paleontologist work on the correlation of existing and extinct animals with early man in America. The archaeologist, in surveying the extant material and excavating new sites, is occupied in unraveling the sequence of development in the various cultures and coördinating them in an ever-growing framework. As the most recent in the field, the art-historian endeavors to evaluate the production of these cultures in the light of esthetics, setting it among the arts of the rest of the world.

II

Historical Approach

A LARGE part of the American continents was inhabited when the Spaniards arrived on these shores. Although in north and east North America and in east and central South America the scale of living was still relatively primitive, certain areas—a broad band stretching from the Southwest to northern Chile—ranked high in the lasting character of their architecture and other arts. Without denying the ingenuity or specialized skill of the semi-nomadic peoples, it is clear that their mode of living did not foster development of artistic talent in the same degree as did sedentary life, which, with its settled routine, brought forth an intellectual level capable of producing a civilization of more enduring values. Where city-like settlements were constructed on a grand scale, a high cultural level was achieved.

Outspoken artistic cultures existed especially in five areas of medieval America. Four of them had architecture on a monumental scale. All of them used the true loom, which was known in less than one-fifth of the total territory of the Americas.[169] The first, the Southwest, comprises the region roughly covered by the states of Utah, Colorado, Arizona, and New Mexico. It was given this name by Charles F. Lummis, one of its first explorers, who published a series of books about the country in the late 19th century.[72] The second is the Mexican Area, stretching from the Rio Grande south through the states of Vera Cruz and Oaxaca. The third, or Maya Area, is comprised of the easternmost section of present Mexico, together with British Honduras, Guatemala, and parts of Honduras and El Salvador. We have given the name Interlying Area to those states that lie between the Maya and Andean areas. It includes the rest of Honduras and El Salvador, Costa Rica, Nicaragua, Panama, and Colombia. The Andean Area, the fifth, extends along the west coast of South America, including the lowlands and highlands of Peru and sections of Ecuador, Bolivia, Chile, and the Argentine. There are artistic manifestations outside these areas that warrant attention and will also be considered here, among them copper-work, shell and stone carvings of the Mound Builders, and pottery from Venezuela and Brazil.

Medieval American Art was chosen as title, because it designates the period within which all the objects and ruins presented here were created, paralleling the Middle Ages in Europe. Before the birth of Christ several preliminary phases of civilization must have existed in these areas, however, for some of the earliest pictorial representations that we find are already so highly conventionalized that the layman can recognize their significance only after explanation. It is supposed that many forms, which in later centuries appear in stone, metal, and other durable materials, were first fabricated of wood or leather.

The diverse cultures were generally contemporaneous, although each, in spite of apparently increasing intercourse, retained much of its own ancestral traditions. Our knowledge of commerce in medieval America is far from complete, but present-day research has shown that there was actual trade between various regions, although in some cases probably only sporadic. Adaptation from another culture seems to have occurred only after due consideration. In this, also, medieval Europe offers a parallel. Although her nations were much more closely connected, with wider and more varied fields of commerce, each, nevertheless, showed a distinctive artistic expression.

Geographically the five great areas of pre-Columbian America have a common feature in that at least parts of them were situated at extraordinarily high altitudes. The elevation of the Southwest ranges from 6000 to 8000 feet; the plateau of Mexico is about 7500 feet high. Although Yucatan, in the Maya Area, lies at sea level and some of the famous cities of the Great Period are also in the lowlands, evidence is accumulating to favor the claim that Maya culture first rose in the highlands of Guatemala, which reaches an altitude of 7700 feet. The Cordilleras in Colombia, equally high, had also their thriving settlements. In the Andean highlands there are architectural remains over 12,500 feet above sea level. As the American Indian is undoubtedly a relative of the early Mongolian, it is interesting to note, without enlarging upon theories, that the culture of Tibet flourished at a similarly high altitude, while nowhere in Europe or Africa does such a parallel occur.

The five areas under discussion have another common factor. All cultivated maize, a grain indigenous to America. A number of varieties are known to have been grown, acclimatized to the regional seasons,[87] with systems of artificial irrigation and dry-farming practiced where rainfall was deficient. There is evidence that certain tribes gave up nomadic life and became agriculturalists on the introduction of maize into the Southwest from Mexico.[95] This transformation may be observed only in this area, for in the others no trace of an antecedent period has yet been found. The cultivation of beans and squash was also widespread, and the Andean Area added to these the potato.

It is natural that the areas which produced the highest cultures were the first to be exploited. The presence of gold, or lack of it, gave impulse, direction, and speed to the Conquest. Really important discoveries of the precious metal were made only in the realms of the Aztec and Inca empires, although valuable finds were taken from the Isthmus and farther south. Cortés established himself as ruler of the Mexican Empire in 1521. In 1533 Pizarro founded Lima as the new capital of his domain, controlling the Andean Area. As early as 1524, Alvarado set up his first headquarters in Guatemala; and in 1540 Montejo broke the resistance of the Maya in Yucatan. Though poor in gold, this area was important for strategic reasons. In 1540 Coronado started with his expedition into the Southwest, a region which yielded them no precious metals in spite of the abundant rumors to the contrary that had led them on. It is ironical that great mineral wealth actually existed there, though the natives were ignorant of it. The difficulties met by all these Spaniards, although not always similar, were everywhere of almost superhuman magnitude.

The four hundred years which have passed since the arrival of the first *conquistadores* have seen innumerable journeyings and expeditions of soldiers, adventurers, missionaries, travelers, and scientists, all of whom have added information to our knowledge.

THE SOUTHWEST

The land of the Southwest is a region of high plateaus, of huge sandstone formations—called *mesas,* or "tables," by the Spaniards—and deep eroded canyons. The earliest culture of which there is accumulated evidence is that of a nomadic people who gradually gathered into camps of circular or oval pit-houses, sunk about three feet into the ground and presumably covered with a shelter of branches and earth. These were the Basket Makers. They began to practice primitive agriculture and used the spear-thrower as their weapon, adopting the bow and arrow only in the last stage of their separate existence. Taking advantage sporadically of the rain-carved caverns of the great canyon walls for living quarters, they began to construct rectangular masonry buildings, also at a late period. Although they made little and crude pottery, they were masters in the weaving of baskets, hence the name given them today.[38]

By the beginning of the 9th century, there are evidences of the infiltration of a new race, who brought with them a more perfected agriculture and a more integrated system of masonry. They established group settlements of adobe and wood, domesticated the turkey, cultivated cotton, and developed a superior type of pottery. Their manner of living, rapidly adopted by neighboring tribes, is called the Pueblo culture from the Spanish word for "village."

Harried by predatory neighbors, they were later forced to scatter, abandoning much of the territory that they had occupied. Many sought shelter in the natural caves or on the mesas, where they erected community houses of stone and sun-dried brick. Others apparently drew together in the valleys, constructing easily defended communal dwellings on the banks of the major rivers.[61]

With the 10th century, a higher architectural form developed, and the cultural achievement of individual localities reached a new height. In addition to the skillfully placed and tastefully executed community houses that nestled in the natural caverns, the objects connected with their daily life demonstrate a ripening artistic talent. The pottery shapes became refined, the ornamentation varied, the weaving ingenious, and the jewelry composite. For three hundred years this development continued.

During the 13th century another migratory movement took place. Between 1276 and 1299 a protracted period of severe drought occurred throughout the region, and for more than twenty years the high mesas and narrow mountain valleys bore an insufficient harvest. Year after year more of the Cliff-dwellers, as they are called, were forced to leave their mountain fastnesses and join their relatives in the valleys of the larger rivers. At the end, the cliff-dwellings were probably deserted, nor were they discovered by white men until the second half of the 19th century. The Indians through the centuries had held the abode of their ancestors in awe and left them undisturbed.

After the great drought, all the sedentary Southwest tribes continuously declined in numbers. The outlying sections were deserted, and a concentration of the population took place in the central regions. Finally, when Coronado and his resplendent band of seventy-five horsemen arrived from Mexico in 1540, they found only about eighty scattered villages, which were in northeastern Arizona and western New Mexico. It is interesting to note that four different languages were spoken, although the culture was relatively homogeneous.[61]

The conquerors entered the Southwest led on by legends of the seven fabulous cities of Cibola. The name seems to be the Spanish version of Shi-wi-nah, by which the Zuñi called their tribal range. The Spaniards visited most of the settlements still in existence at that time, but found no marvels, no wonders, no gold. The houses were constructed of chipped stone, sun-dried brick, and mud. The jewelry consisted of turquoise necklaces with pendants of shell or bone. This disappointing region was left to the zeal of the Franciscan, and later the Dominican and Jesuit, missionaries. Here the invaders did not encounter the armies of powerful allied tribes and war lords; each village fought its own battles and, taken singly, was doubtless easier to overcome.

The Spanish colonial history of the Southwest was as tumultuous as the medieval, but any detailed account of its manifestations is outside the scope of this book. Army posts were created along certain trade routes as these developed, but interest in the region, known as Nuevo Mexico, was not great, and it drew a minimum of white settlers. A political subdivision of Mexico after the break with Spain, this Indian world with its romantic landscape became United States territory in 1846. The Indians remained aloof and even today retain their ancient cultures to a remarkable degree. With the introduction of the horse and sheep, nomadic tribes, among them the Navaho, who now surpass the Pueblos in number, acquired a new cultural impulse.

We owe the establishment of the chronology of the ruins in the Southwest to a recent discovery in another branch of science. Dr. E. A. Douglass, astronomer of the University of Arizona, in studying the effect of sun-spots on the growth of trees, found that tree-ring formations in certain types of wood of the region are never repeated in similar sequence.[32] Thus, the series of rings, varying in width with the growth of the tree during wet and dry years, form a pattern which, although perhaps slightly divergent due to the position of the individual tree, is nevertheless recognizable as a sequence in all the trees of this type which have passed through the same season. If the date of the felling of one tree is known, the calendar of its lifetime can be computed through the cross-section of its rings, beginning with the final outer one. And as this pattern is constant, the calendar can be extended by comparison with the rings of other trees which began or ended at some time within the life-span of the first. Owing to the high dry atmosphere of the region, many of the prehistoric cities contain well-preserved wood which can be incorporated into the study. Sections of the roof beams of the numerous chapels and churches of the 17th century contribute an unbroken series of dates. Even charcoal from ancient fires has been found of use.[47] Thus, through painstaking correlation the tree-ring calendar of the Southwest has already been carried back well into the first century.

MEXICAN AREA

The second area offers one of the most complex pictures of pre-Columbian America. Lying between the lands on the north and the entrance to the Isthmus, it was the repository of various migrations and the scene of cultural metamorphoses. All the multitudes who moved about here during prehistoric millennia and whose circumstances are unknown to us left some imprint on the people and their art during the rotation of cultures. This archaic background is still much of a mystery and doubtless embraces several successive cultural phases that vary with the different regions considered.[151]

One of the earliest and highest cultures, as documented by its ruins, centered around the great temples of Teotihuacan not far from present-day Mexico City. The early site is said to have been occupied about A.D. 700 by the Toltecs, the first comers recognizable in a series of migratory shifts. These "skilled workers," as the Nahua name implies, are generally believed to be members of the Nahua language group. Some authorities, however, think that they may have been indigenous and Otomi-speaking. But whatever their source, the remains of their culture are extremely impressive. Evidences of flourishing trade with the Maya and Zapotecs of that day exist and of the exchange of certain cultural achievements. Sherds of pottery typical of one Toltec phase were excavated as far north as Pueblo Bonito in New Mexico.[61]

About the 10th century, the Valley of Mexico was again overrun by a more virile wave from the north, the Chichimecas, or "fur-wearers."[146] The Toltecs were subdued or driven out of the wide area which they had dominated, and their influence appears on the Late Maya horizon in Yucatan. The newcomers rapidly adapted themselves to the ways of the city-dwelling population, taking over many customs, often with a veneer of their own traditions.

The next arrivals of importance were the Aztecs, also members of the Nahua language group. It is interesting to note that all of these Nahua tribes belong to the Shoshonean linguistic stock which still extends as far north as Oregon and Montana. The early Basket Makers of the Southwest are believed to have been of the same racial entity, and the more cultured peoples with whom they later mingled are thought to have drifted northward from Mexico.[61]

Relatively few in number and primitive in culture, the Aztecs wandered about making contacts with their racial predecessors who were already living a sedentary life. As they were not at first strong enough to acquire any of the fertile agricultural districts, they settled on a marshy island of Lake Texcoco, founding what later became the famous city of Tenochtitlan. The accepted date for this event is 1325, and 1376 is identified as the year that the first Aztec king appeared. Less than one hundred fifty years later, Tenochtitlan became the Christian capital that we know as Mexico City.

Thanks to a tactically protected position, the tribe increased in number, advanced in civilization, and soon felt the urge toward expansion. They allied themselves first with neighboring populations, later with more distant peoples. Throughout the 15th century, they made constant gains in power and possessions, succeeding in subjugating many tribes, or at least in registering them as nominal allies. In the north they counted as tributaries the Otomis; in the east the Totonacs and Huaxtecs; in the south the Zapotecs and Mixtecs, and in the west the Tarascans. These peoples were generally more advanced in culture than the masters, yet were forced to yield to the better fighters. Their arts and crafts, however, retained their distinctive features.

The Aztecs exacted the characteristic products of each district as tribute and acquired a material culture of amazing variety. The market place of Tenochtitlan was, according to an eyewitness, Bernál Diaz, twice as large as that of contemporary Seville. It was surrounded with an immense portico where were sold products of all sorts: brightly colored skeins of cotton thread; pottery of all shapes and sizes, most of which was burnished and painted; ornaments of gold, silver, or semiprecious stones; fruits and vegetables, food, cooked and uncooked. Each kind of merchandise was assigned its own street or its own section. There was an herb street with apothecary shops, barber shops, and restaurants; a street for the sale of game of every known variety; places for furniture and tools; a court for the regulation of measures.

The Aztecs on the Mexican high plateau utilized in architecture the experience of their predecessors. Even though their temples were not the most magnificent in detail work, their imposing effect cannot be denied. Many of their art products were turned out in great numbers and, therefore, in quality could not show true finesse.

Special mention should be made here of the Zapotecs. A proud and self-reliant people, they developed their own system of writing and their own distinctive traditions. Although some of their towns are recorded as paying the Aztecs a tribute or indemnity of blankets, foodstuffs, and cochineal for fine red dye in the last pre-Columbian decades,[129] the extent of Aztec control is unclear and apparently did not affect their freedom in cultural matters. In general, they were able to maintain their independence until shortly before the Conquest, when the Mixtecs, a neighboring and antagonistic tribe, became dominant. Mixtec glyphs are akin to the Aztec, but the Zapotec system, much of which is still indecipherable, is believed by its expert, Alfonso Caso, to be related to the ancient Maya who dwelt south of them.[20] The geographical remoteness of the Zapotec realm may partly explain the amazing difference between their art and that of the Mexican high plateau. All but the most general history of this interesting region is still in shadow.

In 1502 Montezuma II, the ninth Aztec king, became head of a mighty confederacy, stretching from the Atlantic to the Pacific and far to the north and south. It was his fate to live at the time of the landing of the Spaniards, and to die a prisoner in their hands. Many historians and archaeologists have related the story of the conquest of Mexico, and Cortés's advance, so rapid and successful, has been ascribed to several factors. It was a weakness of Aztec rule that it had made no effort to assimilate subjugated tribes and had treated them too ruthlessly. Cortés succeeded in playing these tribes against their masters. The peculiar method of Aztec warfare, which served their religion, also worked to their disadvantage, for it aimed at killing few of the enemy and capturing as many as possible for human sacrifice. Furthermore, they were no match for such superior equipment as the gun, the steel sword, and the horse. After the terrible massacre of natives following the final attack on Tenochtitlan, their empire practically ceased to exist. The greedy search after gold gave the Spaniards unflagging impetus toward the complete subjugation of the Indian.

The tale of colonial Mexico with its quarrels among the Spaniards, battles with the Indians, pseudo-conversion of the natives, intrigues carried to Europe and back covers the viceregal period from 1521 to 1808. Then began the struggle for independence, coinciding with Napoleon's march into Spain. The government shifted back and forth between Spanish-Mexican emperors and republican presidents until 1864, when Maximilian of Habsburg, brother of Franz Joseph of Austria, was crowned Emperor of Mexico through French intervention. Three years later the magic cycle of Habsburg domination in the New World begun by Charles V ended with the execution of Maximilian at Queretaro.

MAYA AREA

The location of the cradle of the Maya is still a matter of conjecture. Their culture is among the oldest and, with its distinguishing characteristics, spans the American Middle Ages. While the other regions experienced considerable change in their population and subsequent alterations in their arts, Maya objects from the earliest sites bear the marks of their Maya origin. Even those from the last period before the Conquest in Yucatan show clearly defined artistic features that identify them as late branches of the great old tree.

In the first centuries after Christ, Maya art was already condensed and mature. From its architecture to its jade carvings, it speaks a language highly articulate, rich and often flamboyant, and compares favorably not only with products from the other four areas but with the high arts of other continents as well.

The Maya had an amazingly accurate calendar, a triumph of mathematical genius, and had developed a system for recording time by hieroglyphics that was so perfected at the beginning of the Christian era that its origin must be sought in a much earlier period. They even had a sign for zero—a device which appeared in Europe only with the adoption of the Arabian numerical system and not before the 10th century.

The numerical and calendrical symbols of the Maya have, to a great extent, been deciphered, although the correlation of their dates to those of our calendar is still a matter of discussion. In this survey, the Goodman-Thompson-Martinez system will be used, which places the dates about 260 years later than that advocated by Herbert J. Spinden. The calendrical glyphs, however, should not be confused with the ideographical which constitute about two-thirds of the body of Maya writing and are as yet unsolved.[92]

The earliest dated object known is a jade plaque unearthed in Guatemala, whose glyphs would correspond to A.D. 320. The Maya had the custom of erecting inscribed monolithic stone monuments, or stelae, at the end of various time cycles. The oldest yet found is at Uaxactun in the state of Peten, Guatemala, and bears a date equivalent to A.D. 328. This does not necessarily mean that Uaxactun is the earliest Maya city—other sites in the same region appear as old —for other methods of recording dates were doubtless used before stelae. Maya architecture frequently employed wood for beams and lintels, elaborately carved, and the possibility that earlier dates were recorded on wood should be held in mind. There are also indications of records painted on stucco. Such media would naturally disintegrate much more rapidly than stone slabs.

Although the glyphs are often of great service in dating the ruins, it must also be taken into consideration that some monuments may have been commemorative in character and marked with a year already past. A case in point is Stela 16 at Tikal, which, though bearing the earliest date in the city, is in style among the latest and most mature. Furthermore, it often happened that a date on a monument was effaced and another added.[112]

The principal Early Maya cities are scattered over several present-day Middle American states; Copan in Honduras, Tikal and Piedras Negras in Guatemala, and Palenque in Chiapas, Mexico, have remnants of highest artistic importance. The early dates of all these fall between 436 and 534, our era. Within the next two centuries more settlements appeared, the best known of which is Quiriguá, Guatemala.

Then followed a period of unprecedented prosperity in this region, generally known as the "Old Empire." City after city arose, and the population must have been numerous. In agreement with J. Eric S. Thompson, we must regard these "cities" as religious centers, occupied chiefly by priests and ruling officials.[150] The common people were agriculturists and lived scattered over the surrounding country, coming to the centers for religious festivals, the administration of justice, and for trade at the market. Ordinary houses were of wood, thatch, and adobe, which crumbled under the assault of the jungle as soon as they were deserted, but the innumerable artificial mounds which were crowned with temples and palaces are impressive even today. Although in ruins and overgrown with trees, they testify to the remarkable talent and tremendous effort of a people who had at their disposal only primitive stone implements and no beasts of burden.

The end of the 9th century marks the close of the creative period in the region. The center of Maya activity then shifted north to the Yucatan Peninsula. Here deciphered dates that go back to the 6th century would indicate that this territory previously had formed part of the Old Empire, but only as a provincial district. The cause of this shift of culture can only be surmised. There may have been pressure from aggressive outside tribes. Economic breakdown and threatened or actual famine resulting from wasteful primitive agricultural methods may have contributed to the decline. Revolts against the existing hierarchy have been suggested in explanation, as well as the ravages of plague.

Dr. Ira B. Bartle, bacteriologist, recently tested material from a number of Maya sites of this period, taking samples from the seemingly undisturbed heart of various ruins. Bacterial cultures of these specimens have revealed a spirillum of an extraordinarily virulent nature, with symptoms similar to cholera. These findings present a new angle for study. However, there is much more work to be done in this line before conclusions can be drawn.[5]

Whatever the cause, the fact remains that after six hundred years of intense activity, culture flickered out in the Old Empire and came to new flowering elsewhere. This does not necessarily mean that all the ancient centers were abandoned. There may have been a transplantation of culture such as occurred in the Eastern Hemisphere, where artistic achievements of one area traveled and bore new fruit in another without a mass movement among the populace or any wholesale catastrophe. With the acceptance and spread of the Gospel, the early Christian Syrian and Armenian communities did not migrate nor were they driven forth by any cosmic or economic upheaval; yet their powerful artistic influence is traceable in the iconography of western Europe. The cultural wave moved onward and left the region of its origin stagnant and in decline. A further parallel can be observed in the decay of Greece and the rise of Rome with its strong derivative culture, although no single event or general movement of population produced the shift of artistic vitality.

As early as the beginning of the 8th century, when the Old Empire was at the height of its power, a Maya people occupied the site of Chichen Itzá in Yucatan, erecting there a number of imposing edifices. Then, for some reason, cultural activity waned. After almost a hundred years, in the latter part of the 10th century, the Itzá appear, and with their occupation a number of Toltec traits were introduced.

About this same time, Mayapan and Uxmal, two other powerful independent city-states, seem to have risen, revived by other migrant tribes, and the three are said to have formed the League of Mayapan. This marks the start of the so-called "New Empire." The Aztecs at this time had not even reached the marshy borders of Lake Texcoco.

Like most of Europe's medieval alliances, the League was not successful for any length of time. About two hundred years later, aided by Nahua mercenaries from the Mexican plateau, the city of Mayapan campaigned against her rivals. In 1204 Chichen Itzá fell, though it remained until the Conquest a much-frequented pilgrimage center. The tribe of Itzá wandered south to the shores of Lake Peten. Diminished in number but unbroken in spirit, they established themselves on an island in the lake, as the Aztecs did when they arrived in the high plateau of Mexico, taking advantage of the protection offered by the surrounding water. Here they held out against all comers until 1697, preserving their independence not only against hostile Indians but even against the Spanish invaders for a century and a half after all the other tribes had been vanquished.[150]

In the meantime, in Yucatan, renewed struggles against the domination of Mayapan finally brought about its downfall in 1451. The cities continued fighting each other, however, soliciting the help of foreign migrating tribesmen. Natural catastrophes hastened the destruction brought about by wars. A great hurricane is reported to have swept the country, destroying whole towns and the surrounding forests. Famine and plague depopulated the once dense settlements, and the Spaniards on their arrival found a weakened life, quite different from the glory of earlier epochs.

Under Spanish rule the area was divided into governmental districts, all parts of the vast dominion of New Spain. As its control of the region was still far from complete in the 17th century, the Spanish administration concentrated on making secure its land and water communications. The Indians were enslaved and had no voice in the administration of their land. They were converted by force, and all vestiges of a former religion ruthlessly destroyed. The Inquisition was alert to prevent backsliding. Over the ancient religious centers the jungle spread. In the 18th century, when the Spanish plantations prospered, many ruined Maya sites were stumbled upon, and toward the end of the century, the Spanish crown ordered reports on the most famous spots.

With the movement for independence, the area was divided. Chiapas, Tabasco, and the Yucatan sector became border states of Mexico. Guatemala and Honduras formed independent republics. A small strip of the eastern coast, for centuries an outpost famous for its logwood and mahogany and once the stronghold of the English pirate, Wallace (whose name survives in the native version "Belize"), became an English crown colony under the name of British Honduras.

The remoteness of most of this area has delayed scientific investigation. Until the closing years of the last century, only a few undaunted travelers had brought back reliable descriptions. In the interior of Yucatan, Honduras, and Guatemala, the Spanish administration did not change completely the way of life. The vitality and traditions of the once great people persist to a certain degree. Pottery and textile techniques are similar to the old, and some pattern and color arrangements survive. In the vicinity of Nebaj in the Guatemala highlands, a calendar is still in use with the 260-day count, with many date names that have come down from medieval Maya practice. Ethnologists are seeking the key to ancient riddles among the customs of inaccessible highland villages, hoping that the relatively few internal upheavals may have left more of the past. Perhaps the remoteness of the regions where the old Maya civilization experienced its first flowering has helped to conserve its traditions, for here, where it was less tinged with Nahua culture, it also happened to escape the most ruthless pursuit of the Spaniards.

INTERLYING AREA

In the Interlying Area, between the Maya and the Andean, were several cultures with rich remains in pottery, stone, and, in most of them, metal-work. The crafts show a mixture of original traits with influence from both north and south, forming a bridge for investigators in other areas. No ruins of great architectural beauty have been found, but mounds and certain carved stone fragments hint that here, too, the people had substantial buildings. Besides the systematic destruction of the conquerors, the tropical climate is responsible for this lack of evidence, and the same circumstance can be blamed for the complete disappearance of woven materials that must have existed. The metal-work of this area, even if not of highest artistic standing, shows fine craftsmanship and in many cases amazing stylistic and technical combinations. The excellence of the pottery is not surprising, as all pre-Columbian cultures were highly advanced in the potter's art. In this survey specimens are included from the work of the Chorotegan culture in Honduras and farther south, the Guetar of Costa Rica, the Chiriqui and Coclé peoples of Panama, and the Quimbaya and Chibcha of Colombia.

The Isthmus around Panama was strongly policed by the Spaniards from the first. It was here that Balboa first sighted the Pacific in 1513. The Spaniards took great pains to explore these regions, believing that a sea passage between North and South America must exist. Stimulated by the dazzling material success in Mexico, they established a naval base in the Gulf of San Miguel on the Pacific in southern Panama, and from here, between 1525 and 1529, Pizarro and his reconnoitering flotillas set sail. Prescott's *Conquest of Peru* brings out the tremendous fighting courage and the infinite endurance of these doughty warriors. After the hazardous voyage across the Atlantic—which had been navigated for only a few years—the adventurers had still to cross the mountains of the Isthmus and, there in the wilderness, hastily construct crude ships for their advance into uncharted waters and undiscovered lands. It is hard to say which accomplishment is the more noteworthy, that of Cortés who opened the door to the New World or that of Pizarro who had greater distances and greater difficulties to overcome.

For the passage of Inca treasures across the Isthmus, terminal cities were founded, Nombre de Dios and Colon on the Atlantic and Panama on the Pacific. Here through the 16th and 17th centuries plodded mule trains laden with gold and silver. Tempted by the loot of this famous and perilous trail, Sir Francis

Drake and his successors, a whole coterie of privateers, pirates, and desperadoes, dared to land to attack and plunder the transports.

ANDEAN AREA

Among the five areas presented in this survey, archaeology is most fortunate in the Andean. The panorama of life and the arts here is the easiest to reconstruct because so much has been preserved by the arid climate.

About the middle of the great range of the Andes there is a high plateau averaging 12,000 feet in elevation, from one to two hundred miles wide, and more than two thousand miles long. West of this, bordering on the Pacific, lies a narrow sandy coastal zone, less than a hundred miles in width, with tropical vegetation appearing toward the mountains. One section is isolated from another by stretches of desert—a terrain theoretically unfavorable for the diffusion of civilization.

Nevertheless, a number of high aboriginal cultures existed here, firmly established at the beginning of the Middle Ages, for the most part in what is now Peru. Migrations, probably from the north, had brought a primitive agriculture to the coast, superseding an earlier existence of hunting and fishing. Several individual cultures arose in the region based on elaborate systems of irrigation: on the North Coast, the Mochica and later the Chimu; in the southern coastal sector, the Nazca, named after the river valley where it flourished. Between them lay the cultures of the Central Coast—Ancon, Chancay, Rimac, and Pachacamac. At the same time other regional cultures prevailed in the mountains, the most noteworthy of these being the Tiahuanaco, which prospered in Bolivia along the shores of Lake Titicaca, and to the north, in Peru, the Chavin.

Between the 5th and 6th centuries after Christ, the Tiahuanaco culture was spread, apparently by conquest, throughout the high plateau, absorbing the earlier cultures. It continued in power for about three hundred years, exerting a noticeable influence even in the coastal regions. At its decline, the highlands seem to have been under the changing sway of petty chiefs until the rise of the Incas. A certain shifting and unstable character is apparent in the art of this period. In the meantime, about the middle of the 12th century, a revival in the Nazca and Chimu cultures set in.

It is generally accepted that the Incas were not outsiders as were the Aztecs in the Valley of Mexico; they descended from one of the highland tribes that probably inhabited the valleys along the tributaries of the Urubamba River, having their principal seat near Cuzco, over 11,000 feet above sea level. Here at the beginning of the 12th century their chieftain established hegemony over a small group of tribes, laying the foundation of the later empire. His successors consolidated their position and advanced southward until a large region, including Lake Titicaca, was under their control. By the end of the 14th century the Inca Empire contained 155,000 square miles, or as much territory as Italy, Switzerland, and Bavaria taken together.[84] At the close of the 15th century, the tenth Inca governed not only what is today Peru, but also Ecuador, parts of Chile and Bolivia, and even a fraction of the Argentine, holding the various regional cultures together under a highly organized and ingenious administration.

The pre-Inca division of most of these separate peoples into groups with communal possessions was the basis of the feudalistic system of Inca administration. These groups formed the units in a bureaucratic network whose highest official was the ruling Inca, a benevolent but absolute monarch. With increasing power, the rulers became highly dynastic, and intermarriage of blood relatives was frequent among them. The chiefs of annexed territories were generally allowed to retain their aristocratic position, and their children received careful education at the Inca capital. Here, while practically hostages, they were taught the power and value of the existing system and proved, on the average, useful converts.

Owing to the vast extent of the Empire, a second capital was established at Quito, in northern Ecuador, for administrative purposes, and it was here that the last happy Inca ruler, Huayna Capac, died in 1525. His two sons, Huascar and Atahualpa, were engaged in a fratricidal war while the Spaniards were exploring along the coast of the Pacific.

The march of Pizarro into the capital of Cuzco in 1533 marked the beginning of the end of Inca grandeur. The following centuries were not without violence. As in other areas, the Indians were not subdued immediately and staged many revolts. As late as 1781, when the Revolutionary War in the United States was working toward its climax, there was a widespread rebellion. The leader of the insurrection, in the presence of his family, had his tongue cut out and was torn to pieces by horses; subsequently his body was burned and his head and limbs were exposed on poles.

When Napoleon put his own brother, Joseph Bonaparte, on the throne of Spain, the New World colonies began the movement which resulted in their independence. Not only were the colonials no longer bound to the mother country by loyalty to the dynasty, but they were embittered by the action of the new administration which set its seal of approval on the highly unsatisfactory colonial government. The American-born Spaniards, that is, the Creoles, and still more the *mestizos* of Spanish and Indian blood, were thoroughly disgusted and angered with their administrators, for the highest officials in Peru were still sent over from the mother country, appointed by the Council of the Indies from its seat in the lavish Renaissance palace at Seville, more than five thousand miles away from the life and problems of the colonies.

As early as 1810, the Venezuelan, Simon Bolívar, headed a revolutionary movement which forced out the viceregal administration and formed the first locally chosen government in Spanish America. Another uprising was led by the Argentine, José de San Martín, who did more than any other man for the liberation of his country as well as of Chile and Peru. In 1824 victory was won, breaking forever Spanish domination in the New World.

The standard of living for the aborigines, enslaved during the colonial regime, long remained in many respects below that of the pre-Conquest period. Lately the various governments have shown a growing understanding of the Indian and pride in his medieval past. Archaeological excavations and the preservation of collections in museums are promoted. Splendidly baroque buildings of colonial times and remnants from the pagan Indian centuries together color the background of modern Latin America.

III

Architecture

WHEN primitive man came out of his cave and constructed for himself a shelter, architecture—the most enduring art of mankind—had its beginning. In man's building, his powers of creation, talent for monumental expression, and quest after variety are displayed at their best.

Pre-Columbian civilization traveled a long road from its first obscure stages to the impressive structures to be discussed here. Lofty buildings characterize the architecture of most of the areas which show outstanding artistic achievement in other fields. Side by side, however, with the magnificent palace and sumptuous temple stood the primitive hut, just as in the European Middle Ages the shadow of imposing castles fell upon mud hovels.

The rise of civilization in the various regions under discussion was roughly parallel in time, so that contrasts are evident not only within one area but also in the comparison of that area with others. For instance, some architecture of a high standard, like the Maya, employed only doors in its massive façades, while the less splendid culture of the Pueblos availed itself occasionally of the window as well. The Pueblo Indian used a ladder to reach the upper stories of his house, while the oldest structures of the Maya, Mexicans, and Peruvians, in some cases as early as the 3rd century, show grandiose stairways.

THE SOUTHWEST

FRIJOLES CANYON

At a remote period in their existence, the people of the Southwest made use of hollows in the cliffs for temporary shelter and storage. Later, more complex buildings were pasted fast to the vertical rocks on the sloping talus at the foot of the cliff. *Pl. 1, fig. a* shows both the cave chambers and the remains of the talus-houses in Frijoles Canyon, New Mexico. The bored holes for securing the beam ends can be seen in the rock, indicating the height of the structures.[46] In the fore-ground lie the ruins of a semicircular community house of later date.

Seeking security from predatory tribes, the Cliff-dwellers fitted their compact group dwellings into natural alcoves far above their fields (*fig. b*). In many cases the caverns could be reached only by means of perilous hand and foot holds cut into the precipitous canyon walls. For building material they quarried a buff sandstone in pieces rather thinner but wider than an ordinary brick and con-siderably harder than the cliffs themselves.

The first simple system of chambers developed into a honeycomb conglomer-ate of community dwellings in a style that occurs nowhere else. As the population multiplied, second, third, and even fourth stories were superimposed in receding terraces upon the roofs of the old. The dark inner rooms, reached by hatchways, were used for food storage, and the high crevices, difficult of access, were built out into granaries. Round buildings—a technical problem for architects of all the ages—were erected with the same facility as square ones. Towers jutting up from the stone terraces or placed at strategic points on the table-land made excel-lent lookouts. The culture of the Cliff-dwellers reached its height between the 12th and 13th centuries.

MESA VERDE

The best known and perhaps the most beautiful examples of Cliff-dweller technique are found at Mesa Verde in Colorado. The Green Mesa, verdant with juniper and piñon trees, rises to a height of 8575 feet above the sea. On one side there is a sheer drop of a thousand feet and a view on a clear day for one hundred fifty miles; on the other, narrow gorges spread like the fingers of an open hand, dotted with shallow eroded caves, nearly all of which bear evidence of human habitation. Occasionally a site is fortunate enough to have a spring near by.

Cliff Palace (*Pl. 2, fig. a*), built into a cavern 425 feet long, 80 feet in depth, and 70 to 80 feet at its greatest height, is the largest of the cliff-dwellings in this group. The floor of the cave is uneven and the level of the ground structure varies to conform with it. There are square as well as round towers, and the doors and windows are placed asymmetrically, seemingly at individual conven-ience. The T-door occurs frequently. For the roofs or upper floors, as the case might be, staunch timbers were set, with smaller branches laid at right angles across them; brush and twigs filled the chinks, and a final cover of packed clay was added. Slots can be seen in the standing walls into which the beams were laid.

Cliff Palace contains one hundred seventeen rooms, ninety-four of which have fireplaces and the marks of fire. Out-of-door hearths are also common.[38] This great apartment house, which its tree rings place in the 12th century, shows evidence not only of additions in an improved technique but also of rebuilding. New partitions were erected, walls changed, new levels established; the first-story ceilings were braced for the additional weight of rooms to be added above. The different hatchings that appear on the plan (*fig. b*) show the various heights of the buildings. On some interiors are traces of designs, similar to those used on the pottery of the period, painted in red and brown on a white ground of smooth gypsum.[46]

Besides the square rooms where the inhabitants slept and stored their food, the circular subterranean chambers, called "kivas," so striking in the photograph, were an integral part of every cliff-dwelling. Indeed, the kiva still plays an essential rôle in the life of the modern Indians of the Southwest as the meeting place and ritual chamber of the various clans and societies in the involved tribal life. It has been suggested that they are associated in tradition with the sunken pit-houses of the earliest tribal ancestors.[61] They are usually circular and are sunk into the courtyard or open plaza, varying in size from 10 to 30 feet or more in diameter. Entrance is generally through hatchways in the timber roofs. Within there is usually a fire pit near the center of the floor, with a low wall or slab of masonry near it, serving as an air deflector, and a flue of some size extending up one wall. This vent is supposed to provide the means of access to the spirit people of the other world, whose coöperation is necessary to the successful conduct of life.

Square Tower Ruin (*fig. c*), also at Mesa Verde, creates a most artistic atmosphere, with its buildings on the narrow ledge leaned against the canyon wall.

BETATAKIN

Another site with spectacular Pueblo ruins of the Cliff-dweller type is situated in the northeast corner of Arizona surrounded today by the Navaho Indian Reservation. Its more famous groups are Betatakin, Keet-Seel, and Inscription House, the whole complex now named Navaho National Monument.

Fig. d shows the ruins of Betatakin, Navaho for "hillside house." They stand in the depths of a colossal cave, 400 feet high, 300 long, and 150 deep, carved by stream meander and wind erosion out of the side of a red sandstone cliff that forms the sheer north wall of the picturesque canyon. Tree-ring dates reveal that the cluster of almost one hundred fifty rooms within was built and occupied in the second half of the 13th century. While in most ruins the kivas are similar to those at Mesa Verde, there is no evidence here of sunken chambers and they must have been constructed at ground level. Other interesting architectural characteristics of the site are wattle and daub walls, small doorways closed with inset stone slabs, and loom-ties found in some of the chambers. Rectangular rooms are typical, as are the poles which form the roofs and extend beyond the walls. This latter feature has survived and can be seen today in the living Pueblo villages (see *Pl. 6*).[73]

CANYON DE CHELLY

Highly romantic are the ruins at Canyon de Chelly (*Pl. 3*), a name distorted from the Navaho *Tse-yee,* meaning "within the rocks." They lie in northeastern Arizona in a canyon full of quicksand, the light-colored stone of the White House standing in brilliant contrast to the red wall of the overtowering cliff.

The great drought of 1276–1299 hastened the abandonment of the cliff-dwellings, and when the Spaniards came, they found the Indians living in communal structures of stone and adobe, or sun-dried brick, built in the open around one or more ceremonial chambers. To such a settlement the conquerors gave the name *pueblo,* meaning "village." This type of architecture still prevails in the Southwest.

Castañeda, chronicler of Coronado's expedition, wrote of one such pueblo: "It is square, situated on a rock with a large court in the middle containing kivas. The houses are all alike, four stories high. One can go over the top of the whole village without . . . a street to hinder. There are terraces going all around it at the first stories. . . . These are like outside balconies and they are able to protect themselves under these. The houses do not have doors below, but they use ladders which can be lifted up like a drawbridge and so go up to the terraces which are on the inside of the village. As the doors of the houses open on the terraces of that story, the terrace serves as a street. The village is inclosed by a low wall of stone."[4]

PUEBLO BONITO

Pueblo Bonito, "beautiful village" (*Pl. 4, fig. a*), is one of twelve ruined community houses in the narrow valley of Chaco Canyon, New Mexico, and an excellent example of Pueblo architecture. The structure resembles a capital D;

some of the other settlements, apparently all striving for major security, are quadrangular or E-shaped.

Pueblo Bonito is 667 feet in length and 315 at its greatest width. It contained more than six hundred chambers and could have sheltered twelve hundred inhabitants within its walls (*fig. b*). The illustration shows clearly its amphitheater form, with its tiers of rooms, originally four or five stories high, built around a court that held about twenty kivas. Across the straight front was a double row of single-story rooms that opened on the inclosure. There was only one narrow entrance, behind which a barrier of masonry was placed in such a way that only one person at a time could enter the village.

The high wall in the rear, unbroken on the outside by any opening and still rising to more than 40 feet in places, testifies to the fortress-like character of the building. The tallest section shown in the picture was recently crushed by a fall of rock from the canyon wall, a catastrophe that must have been impending for centuries, for the ancient inhabitants had buttressed the cliff.

The masonry varies in character from the medium-sized hewn stones that compose the first story to the small flat ones in the upper walls, dressed to form a smooth outer surface.[38] Timber is used to strengthen the walls, and some of the floors have been found in place. Due to the extremely dry atmosphere, the wood remains dry and hard and so does not constitute a major weakness as in the tropical regions of Central America. The tree-ring calendar dates this structure as existing between A.D. 919 and 1130.

CHETRO KETL AND AZTEC RUIN

Some of the kivas in Pueblo settlements were very large, reaching 60 feet in diameter at Chetro Ketl, Chaco (*Pl. 5, fig. a*), and 50 at Aztec Ruin, New Mexico (*fig. b*). In both cases, the entrance was from the side, not through the roof, and there were two large fire pits and a raised masonry bench or dais around the wall, visible in the illustrations. The same type of roof was probably used at Chetro Ketl as is shown reconstructed in Aztec Ruin, the set-back in the upper section of the wall providing space for the roof beams, which were apparently supported by wooden or masonry pillars. The inner walls contain a number of recesses, in which ceremonial caches of shell, onyx, and turquoise beads were found. The name Aztec Ruin is unfortunate, since this settlement had nothing to do with the Aztec people.

Although the Spanish chronicler writes that the Pueblos boasted of never having been conquered, the danger of attack by nomadic tribes from the north and east must have been constant. Their careful accumulation of agricultural products was certainly a great attraction to those roving hunters in times of scarcity. For causes unknown a period of decline and depopulation occurred in the 14th century, doubtless connected with failing food and water supply, as well as depredations from outside.[47] Many of the large Pueblo ruins of the Southwest were already forsaken at the time of the Conquest.

There are, however, living settlements today which date back into medieval times. The Hopi town of Walpi (*Pl. 6, fig. a*) in Arizona is one of these, with its square one-family houses of chipped stone perched on a jutting rock high above the plain. The villages of Acoma and Zuñi are as ancient and represent somewhat the same type, while Taos (*fig. b*) is more like Pueblo Bonito, with two large tiered community houses of adobe standing in a broad valley.

The villages everywhere used the material most conveniently at hand for their building. Casa Grande in Arizona is constructed entirely of a mixture of adobe and gravel, which has dried to incredible hardness. Gila and Salt River settlements, having no quarries near, used water-ground boulders with a mud binder.[38]

Southwest architecture, with its living quarters arranged around the nucleus of the circular kivas, suggests the crystalline structure of a mineral. The tiered or set-back stories of the great houses, like huge massed terraces, varying in size and height, are very striking, and have at least optically something in common with the terraced substructures of the Mexican and Maya areas. The method of constructing flat roofs was probably similar in all our areas.

Pueblo architecture is the only pre-Columbian style which still survives. Pueblo customs and the crafts of pottery making and weaving also remain remarkably virile. This is perhaps because the art here, for the most part, served a more secular purpose and not a hieratic pagan religion as in the other areas. All the manifestations of ancient architecture elsewhere were extinguished during Spanish colonial occupation, so that all that is left for study there is in a state of ruin.

MEXICAN AREA

TEOTIHUACAN

In the Mexican Area the imposing remnants of Toltec temple structures stand only twenty-eight miles from the Mexican capital in the middle of a central valley. Generally called the Pyramids of Teotihuacan, they retain in their modern name the Nahua word meaning "where the gods reside." The site (*Pl. 7, fig. a*) covers a great area, but our main objectives lie along a straight avenue bordered by ruins, all accurately oriented. A great temple-base, a truncated pyramid, the highest in the entire Mexican region, rises at the right of one side. It was the custom of the pre-Columbian peoples from very early times to elevate their temples or altars on an artificial mound, a practice taken by some as an indication that the rites were first performed on hilltops.

It is unfortunate that the word "pyramid" persists in connection with this type of temple-base, because of the term's inevitable association with the pyramids of Egypt. The huge monuments on the lower Nile were built of great stone blocks to house the burial pomp of kings—gigantic tombstones, memorials to the dead. The pyramidal structures of pre-Columbian America were made sometimes of adobe or of smaller pieces of stone on a core of rubble and stood at the living center of religious activity. They served as an extraordinary and dramatic base for the temple proper, the holy of holies, which was erected on the top. It must be remembered that these ruins have changed much since the time they were in use. The temples themselves have disappeared, the masonry about them has collapsed, the facing crumbled. After such vicissitudes, with their original lines destroyed or blurred, it was only on superficial resemblance that these substructures were called pyramids.

Apparently, it was the inclination of science in the 16th to 18th centuries to explain away all the phenomena of pre-Columbian civilization with Old World parallels. It was impossible for that age to conceive of the cultures of the American continent except as transplantations from the world already known. Much that was written and sketched of these ruins in the early days was distorted by the mirage of this theory, and we still carry over, even into our scientific literature, ambiguous terms which give impetus to fantastic theories and sensational statements.

The Pyramid of the Sun (*fig. b*) is then the immense base for a temple of which nothing now remains. Built of selected or roughly dressed basaltic lava on an adobe hearting,[49] it rises 216 feet and covers about 10¼ acres of ground with its base, 720 by 760 feet. At the summit is the rectangular platform upon which stood the temple, the nerve center of the ritual. The conservation work, undertaken several decades ago, is now considered to have forced the contours of the temple-base somewhat along preconceived lines. However, nothing can detract from its imposing proportions.

<‹ 31 ›>

The structure as it stands is divided into five sections. On the west, the one great stairway, varying in outline as it ascends each division, mounts to the summit. At its foot is a tiered dais. This, together with the esplanades around the temple-base built at different levels, furnished the setting for the elaborate pageantry of the Toltec religious rites, for the great mass of the people could see very little of what was taking place in the temple itself. Prescott (1843) describes the building as "splendidly barbaric," and quotes the chronicler Boturini (1746) as stating that within, facing the east, stood "a colossal statue of its presiding deity, the Sun, made of one entire block of stone. . . . Its breast was protected by a plate of burnished gold and silver, on which the first rays of the rising luminary rested." Whether the description from this late date is accurate or not, there is no doubt that such an immense monument, eclipsing in size everything else in the Mexican Area, must once have been of utmost importance.

The Toltecs were the first people of the region to leave legendary accounts behind them and the first Nahua-speaking residents of the district. Their culture in the high Valley of Mexico is believed to date from about A.D. 700, and the ruins now visible are placed in the 9th century. However, from pottery finds and other remnants discovered on the site, it can be surmised that the spot had already been a pilgrim center for earlier inhabitants.

It was the custom of most pre-Columbian tribes of Mexico and Central America to rebuild and enlarge their temples periodically. In the former area this generally occurred at the end of a cycle of 52 years, a time which marked the coincidence of the sacred almanac of 260 days with the solar calendar of 365 days that ran concurrently.[151] Examination of the huge Pyramid of the Sun has shown that this structure also was superimposed upon other buildings, and the remnants of several series of stairways have been uncovered, buried under the fill of later additions.[76]

Left of the Pyramid of the Sun, on the same plate, can be seen the Pyramid of the Moon, which shows a similar division into four sections. Approximately half the size of the other, it stands some 140 feet high with a base that measures 426 by 511 feet. To date, it has been left unrestored.

About a mile south of these buildings along the same imposing avenue, rises the Temple of Quetzalcoatl (*Pl. 8*). Quetzalcoatl was the Mexican Wind-god, the Great Feathered Serpent. His symbol, the conch shell, runs through Mexican mythology and is also conventionalized into a fret with its many variations. In this pre-Columbian ruin we can best visualize the splendor and brilliance of a sunken culture, for nowhere else in the Mexican Area is such a large and well preserved section of substructure to be seen. Its good condition is due to the custom just mentioned of burying one temple under a new and larger one. The excavated façade (*fig. a*), measuring about 110 feet in width and 55 in height, was found at the heart of another edifice. A large portion of one side was intact, and its reconstruction was carried out by enlightened, modern, archaeological methods.

This base, faced with smooth stone blocks, has six receding terraces, with unusually deep offsets, uniform in height and ornamented in identical fashion. On the face of each is a long vertical panel, framed top and bottom with projecting cornices and featuring fierce sculptured heads of the Feathered Serpent (*fig. b*). His fangs are whitened, his eyes glittering with an inlay of obsidian. He wears a radiating leafy collar, and the body is indicated by the rattles and feathers in relief at either side, all the more admirably executed when we consider how often and how painstakingly the repetition is carried out. The other creature, somewhat less intelligible to us, is generally interpreted as a conventionalized mask of the Rain-god, Tlaloc.[151] Various shells are scattered throughout the rhythmically recurrent pattern. Below the panel, on the oblique base of the terrace, is a relief of stone showing the undulating body of the plumed snake and a series of shells.

Remnants of color were clearly visible on our first visit to the site a short time after its excavation but have faded considerably now from exposure. Especially noteworthy were the brilliant green of the serpent body and Tlaloc mask, the clear red rings in the headdress of the latter, and the enameled pink and white of the shells. The ramp of the wide steep stairway, ornamented with similar serpent heads, was stuccoed and also painted.

This magnificent façade and the ruin which has covered it stand in the center of a quadrangular inclosure, called the Citadel, the outer walls of which have been restored and show a continuous rampart. (See *Pl. 302, fig. a.*) The structure may have had military importance, but this aspect must be given secondary consideration in view of its obvious ceremonial character. Stairways give access to the top from both inside and outside. A number of small terraced platforms, each with its flight of steps, are placed symmetrically at intervals, clearly visible in *fig. a* of the preceding plate, especially the inset. They are similar in outline to the terraces of the Temple of Quetzalcoatl but have no ornamentation. Remnants of stucco in the empty panels and along the balustrades indicate that the complex was embellished with fresco decorations.

Because of the variety in Teotihuacan and the long period over which it flourished, this city holds a special place in the history of the Mexican Area. Its contribution to the arts other than architecture is also great, and the site must have been among the most grandiose of the Mexican high plateau. After the arrival of more aggressive tribes and the southward shift of Toltec influence in the 11th century, the center may have declined. Moreover, the Aztec Tenochtitlan soon rose to overshadow all other sites. At any rate, neither Cortés nor Bernál Diaz makes any mention of it, although they must have passed close to the place. Perhaps it was by that time completely abandoned and the astonishing "pyramids" looked to the *conquistadores* like natural mounds.

XOCHICALCO

The temple at Xochicalco (*Pl. 9, fig. a*), near Cuernavaca, in the state of Morelos, also belongs to the period of Toltec dominance of the Mexican high plateau. It is said to have been built about the middle of the 10th or in the early 11th century by a Nahua-speaking people.[99] The structure stands on a fortified height nearly two miles in circumference overlooking deep valleys. The entire hill is artificially graded and laid out in five terraces with ramparts. There are a number of other ruins, now only heaps of rectangular stones. A sugar factory in the vicinity drew on the site for its construction material. Such vandalism was frequently perpetrated on pre-Columbian buildings. The first generation after the Conquest, led by the priests, destroyed everything of the ancient world upon which they could lay their hands, and much has been lost because of the jealous bigotry which ran wild in those times.

The Nahua name *Xochicalco* means "in the place of flowers." We know that the pre-Columbian peoples held flowers in great esteem, assigning a special god to them. The ancient cult still survives in picturesque Xochimilco, "place where the flowers are," near the Mexican capital. An extraordinary tenderness and felicity characterize the Indian's handling of them, whether it be the gesture of a little boy making an offering of calla lilies in a church, or an old woman sprinkling her wild carnations as she proffers them for sale by the roadside. Their presence among the wares even of the most remote native markets shows that they are not gathered merely to attract the tourist's eye.

The temple structure illustrated is the only one at Xochicalco that has been reconstructed to a certain degree. The ruin shows the great feeling of the builders for linear variety and is outstanding, not only for its magnificently decorated substructure but for the evidences of a masonry temple on top—the only one besides Teopanzolco known in the Mexican Area today.[146]

The substructure, measuring 60 by 69 feet, is a single unit, unbroken by terraces, and the slanting base, which was kept as narrow as possible below the rectangular panels of Teotihuacan's Citadel, here constitutes a major element. It is nearly 9 feet high with a batter of about 15 degrees. This slant lends the impression that the building is implanted deep in the soil, giving the structure, incomplete as it is, more weight and stability than would a perpendicular line.

The foundation is crowned by a vertical frieze about 3½ feet high, overhanging it somewhat, which in turn is topped by a sharply protruding cornice, clearly visible in the photograph. Here we have a fine feature not occurring in earlier architecture. The play with architectural line, the counterbalancing of receding and jutting angles, and the contrasting of various constructional elements for the sake of variety are signs of development not only in technique but in creative imagination. The deliberate divergence from the perpendicular appears in European architecture also, but quite late; provincial rococo made considerable use of it in mid-18th century.

The low relief of stone which covers the slanting base is dominated by eight elaborate plumed serpents, ingeniously conceived and skillfully executed. A fluent unbroken line marks the upper outline of the snake bodies, forming an unobtrusive but consistent coupling of the main decorative motif. The smaller broken elements, representing the luxurious plumage, give weight and vibration to the figure. The rattles end in quetzal plumes, and the head of the snake shows fangs and a forked tongue which invite comparison with the three-dimensional serpent head on the Temple of Quetzalcoatl on the preceding plate. Contrast also the vigorous movement and rippling feathers of the undulating bodies here with the more even and static rendition in the older work.

In the spaces created by the curves of the serpents, human figures and glyphs are applied alternately in the same relief technique (*fig. b*). The glyphs remind us of those classed as Zapotec. In this case, they have been identified as referring to the ceremony of "kindling the new fire," held at the beginning of each 52-year cycle.[99] The eight plumed serpents are also associated with this occasion.

The human figures deserve special attention, since, used as they are here as sculptural ornament, they are unique in the Valley of Mexico. The nearest parallel will be found at Tajin, but stylistically they are still more suggestive of the Maya. The chief or god is seen from the front, with the head turned in profile, in a pose that will become familiar later in stone and jade carvings. In

Egyptian art this always seems a neck-breaking attitude, but here it is made to appear elastic and natural. The figure is poised and sinuous. The headdress, representing the upper jaw of a monster decorated with long feathers, is well posed despite its obvious weight. There are ornaments on the ankles, the wrists, around the neck, and in the ears. Though carved with primitive tools and composed into the space allowed by the curving serpent body, the figure is neither crowded nor distorted. Certain contours are emphasized with an extra incised line well within the edge, which slenderizes the mass and even gives a suggestion of three dimensions. The most expressive detail from a purely artistic point of view is his raised left hand, placed in front of the body and showing only four fingers. Beauty, grace, and dignity are in the gesture. Not merely an element in the tangled decoration of the temple-base, the figure is commanding. On the narrow frieze above the great snake, there was once also a relief of seated priestly figures with flowers and glyphs.

A stairway of fourteen steps leads up the west side. Its balustrade was decorated with a carved pattern suggesting serpent scales or rattles, but only a fragmentary reconstruction of this was possible. Of the temple proper, a low section of the wall remains, which, however, helps us little in picturing its original form. It also was carved with reliefs of both seated and standing figures interspersed with glyphs.

The entire edifice is faced with trachyte, a light-colored volcanic stone, in large uniform slabs laid without mortar. The carving was apparently done before the stones were set and was touched up afterwards.[99] Like most of the architecture of the Mexican and Maya areas, the structure was brightly painted; the chief colors remaining are red and green.

Artificial caverns honeycomb the limestone hill and some of the connecting underground chambers contain stuccoed painted walls. The style of decoration at Xochicalco, as well as the practice of subterranean building, would bring this site nearer the Zapotec-Mixtec region in idea than anything else on the high plateau of Mexico.

MALINALCO

In the southwest corner of the state of Mexico, separated by a mountain range from the town of Tenancingo, stand the ruins of Malinalco, looking down from a mountain ledge on the sleepy village from which the site takes its name, "the place of the dry grass." The approach lies along the rocky bed of a mountain stream and over the steep shoulder of one of the wild and barren hills which characterize the landscape, an even more spectacular location than that of Xochicalco.

Malinalco is of outstanding importance as one of the very few pre-Columbian sites discovered so far where buildings were hewn from living rock. The most notable temple (*Pl. 10, fig. a*) meets the visitor's eye at once, as it stands on a small plaza facing a deep gorge to the south. The main stairway of fourteen steep steps, the same number as at Xochicalco, and the wide balustrade are carved out of the ledge itself, an integral part of the hillside. The rock has weathered to a golden brown. Traces of paint are still visible and the ramps also show remnants of decoration on plaster.

The walls are cut to resemble the façade of a substructure with two terraces. On either side of the stairway, a large feline animal keeps guard, of one piece with the building and the low platform upon which it is seated. The upper parts of the bodies have been destroyed, probably on the occasion of later alteration, when this edifice was covered by another of the usual Aztec stone-and-mortar construction. The center of the lowest stair juts out to form a sort of podium, perhaps to accommodate some stone or pottery object, above which stood a large carving, now only a fragment, which must have represented a seated figure.

The single doorway leading into the temple proper is carved to form a round arch (*fig. b*). Hewn out of solid rock, it does not constitute a keystone arch. In this case there was no problem of construction for the support of a mass of masonry; the roof was light and perishable, probably wooden beams with a covering of grass or thatch. The top part of the arch is broken, perhaps by an earthquake or by the later transformations. Two immense serpent profiles ornament the entrance, deeply incised and so placed that together they present the front view of a single snake, the arched door representing its yawning mouth and the forked tongue forming a very low dais that extends nearly to the first step of the landing. On a protruding serpent head at the right of the door stands a squat defaced figure, interpreted as an eagle-clan warrior, while on the opposite side a similar one surmounts a war drum.

Upon passing through the distended jaws of the great serpent, one enters a circular chamber about 16 feet in diameter and over 11 feet high (*fig. c*).[63] A broad low bench of living rock, some 4 feet wide, extends around the inner wall of the inclosure. In the center lies a large sculptured eagle altar, the wings half-spread and the head raised off the floor, its fierce curving beak facing the entrance. The smooth line of the bench is broken by three animal figures, cut somewhat flatter than the altar. Two of these represent eagles; between them, and directly opposite the door, is the figure of a jaguar or ocelot, flattened out like a rug, with furry head and bulky paws carved in the round and the tail extending up the wall. The sculpturing shows competence, avoiding the conventionalization of elements difficult to represent. All the eyes are cut in such a manner as to suggest inlay. Small cists occur at intervals in the wall, perhaps for the personal and ritualistic objects of those who participated in the ceremonies.

On one side, the temple structure blends into the natural rock, where there are marks of a waterfall. On the right, a series of three stairways mounts beyond it to the upper levels of the hillside. Here is furrowed an elaborate system of gutters, cut in the solid stone. A deep channel also follows the outline of the circular wall from above. These may have been designed to protect the buildings from the gushing tropical rains, but the rush of life-giving water from the mountain ledge into the fertile valley may well have been used for symbolical effect.

Two other buildings on the site make use of the living rock. One is a large rectangular chamber, with three walls as well as the floor carved out of the hillside. The other, constructed of stone and mortar in an unusual semicircular form, has a rectangular antechamber, with fire pits and pillar foundations cut from the solid floor. This building boasts a fluelike vent on one side reminiscent of the air shafts of Southwestern kivas.

Near here is a wall, once buried by later construction, with a fresco of warriors. A large pyramidal base of more common type holds a predominant position on the edge of the cliff, and beside it, overlooking the gorge, is the outline of a circular masonry structure, the shape and position of which seem to indicate some sort of observatory.

Other monolithic structures are found at the site of Texcotzingo nearer the Mexican capital, where there are basins, or baths, carved in the rock of the hill, as well as an elaborate system of channels.

The pottery remains at Malinalco have been identified as Matlatzincan and Aztec, and the site is believed to date from the 14th or 15th century.[63] It would seem a pre-Aztec creation which was taken over and rebuilt—an assumption that would account for the mutilation of the carvings and the different types of construction to be found there.

There are on this site certain resemblances in idea that lead us far afield. The eagle and jaguar motifs seen in the monolithic temple occur on carved panels in Chichen Itzá devouring human hearts. (See *Pl. 63*.) The entrance into the temple through the yawning jaws of a serpent is found more than once in the ancient Maya city of Copan. And the position of the ruins, perched daringly on a rocky ledge, recalls somewhat the balcony houses of the Cliff-dwellers of the Southwest. The four carved animals in the interior do not have the complex and conventionalized expression of Aztec monumental carving, but display a greater realism, though stylized, a lighter and more simplified manner, much more closely related to the modeling and carving of the Indians north of the Mexican border. The snake to the right of the outer doorway is reminiscent of the reptiles from Tenayuca, to be discussed on the next page, and of Chichen Itzá, except that it has flint blades bristling from its body instead of undulating plumage.

There is a large round structure at the Ocmulgee National Monument near Macon, Georgia, called the Ceremonial Earth Lodge. It is 42 feet in diameter with benches and seats around the inner wall. Opposite the main entrance stands a raised effigy platform in the shape of an eagle made of stone and mortar and represented with outspread wings. It is by no means stated that identical tribes produced both of these works, but a relation or influence of idea can be felt. Many pre-Columbian peoples claim in their legends to have "come from the north." Linguistic kin of the Nahua, as we have seen, extend even today as far as Oregon and Montana, and we meet repeatedly with the tradition of eagle-warrior clans in pre-Columbian cultures of both Middle and North America. The similarity of the Earth Lodge in Georgia and the carved rock temple at Malinalco is another evidence of the distance that influence, perhaps even peoples, may have traveled in medieval America.

CALIXTLAHUACA

The infrequent round shape occurs at Malinalco in what might be called "negative" and "positive" forms—the circular chamber carved from the ledge, and the round building constructed opposite it on the small plaza. The latter realization is met also at Calixtlahuaca (*fig. d*), a Matlatzincan site in the valley of Toluca.[76] Among the numerous ruins, two deserve special mention here: the remnants of a barracks-like settlement at the base of the hill, thought to have been a "seminary" for priests or living quarters for young warriors, and the round Temple of Quetzalcoatl shown in the illustration. The different angles of the sloping wall sections visible in the photograph are the result of the second and third rebuilding of the temple-base. The latest enlargement seems to have been made during the 15th century. Each terrace was edged with projecting stone serpent heads placed at intervals. A few of these still stare out of the wall, giving an idea of the original impressive effect.[57] Here too, as in Malinalco, pottery of Matlatzincan and Aztec types was found. With its conquest by the Aztecs, however, the site seems to have been abandoned, and the Aztec town was laid on the plain.

TENAYUCA

One more ruin should be presented before we leave that high plateau, the Valley of Mexico. Six miles north of Mexico, D.F., are the remnants of an Aztec temple at San Bartolo Tenayuca. Cortés and Diaz both mention this town. It lay directly in the path of the Conquest and had strategic importance in the siege of Tenochtitlan, for the pipeline of clay culverts which furnished part of the drinking water for the Aztec capital was situated on the northern shore of Lake Texcoco, not far from Tenayuca. Fighting occurred around the place in 1520, and the Spaniards destroyed the water-supply system. Diaz speaks of it as Puebla de las Sierpes, "the town of the serpents"; and Torquemada, the Franciscan historian of the early colonial empire, complains that the destruction of this and other pagan temples after the Conquest was so superficial that they could all too easily be reconditioned.

Nevertheless, this edifice seems to have fallen into disrepair and oblivion.[146] Before 1925, when the ruins were excavated and partly reconstructed, it had been the popular belief that the mound was of natural origin, overgrown as it was with vegetation upon which the village cattle and poultry fed.

The temple-base (*Pl. 11, fig. a*) is 58 feet high and measures 162 wide and 201 long, exclusive of the great double stairway which, extending beyond the base, adds another 45 feet to the general length. It is faced with cut stone laid with mortar and then covered with plaster. Brilliantly painted designs studded with projecting serpent heads of carved stone break the rigid character of the broad surfaces. The two temples on the summit were probably of more perishable material, with wooden roofs, plastered and painted. Atop the solid proportions of the base, they must have looked like gaudy lids.

The twin stairway (*fig. b*), nearly 150 feet long, belongs to an earlier structure unearthed in excavation and rises behind the mass of masonry at the left in the picture. It has the usual very steep grade. Wide ramps at the side of the stairs and a double one in the center, which divides the imposing flight, are crowned with large masonry blocks, visible at the top center of the general view. They show clever masonry work, with keystones set between the large flat slabs and at right angles to them, firmly integrating them with the body of the structure. All the corners or edges are bonded in the same manner. It is assumed that the edifice was dedicated conjointly to the gods of war and rain. This would indicate two buildings, one beside the other, on the vast platform (117 by 140 feet). Here the hieratic conception triumphed, probably to the detriment of architectural beauty.

The most characteristic feature of the temple-base at Tenayuca is the long row of serpent bodies stretched along a low platform at the foot of this structure, as if guarding its three unbroken sides. There are one hundred fifty-six coiled snakes, their carved heads, some gigantic, projecting beyond the edge of the terrace on which they lie. Here we are confronted with evidence of mass production, for only the heads of the reptiles are carved of solid stone. The bodies are composed of smaller stones and mortar and appear rather shapeless now, although a definite outline was doubtless achieved by their original covering of painted stucco. Traces of blue, red, black, ochre, and white are still visible on some of the figures. The hues were applied according to orientation: blue predominates in those on the south and southeast, and black on the north and northeast. The bright flowing colors, applied very liquid on fresh plaster, must have once made the coiled serpents seem shimmering and alive.

Two great "fire serpents" crowned with symbolic headdresses lie apart from the others on the north and south sides of the temple, some 10 feet from the base (*fig. c*). These are connected with altars and oriented toward the sunsets of May 16 and July 26, special days in the ceremonies of the cult.[146] The characteristic rendering of the head is noteworthy, with the tongue hanging sideward as at Malinalco and Xochicalco.

The archaeological importance of Tenayuca is greatly augmented by the fact that investigations have revealed buildings of seven different epochs within the largest and last temple-base, together with intermediary changes and additions. All of these were edifices with double stairways and two temples. The first building measures 104 feet by 58 by 26 feet high and carries back to the earliest migration of the Nahua-speaking Chichimecan people into the Valley of Mexico at the end of the 12th century in our era. Thus the time-span involved is around three hundred years.

The digging at Tenayuca revealed pottery, jade beads, obsidian, stone and copper objects, indicative of at least three different stages of civilization super-imposed on each other. As it is so near the capital and, in its last phase, of such a late date, we can be sure that many of the buildings wrecked by the Spaniards were similar in type.

Other important excavations near the capital were made at Copilco and Cuicuilco at the foot of an extinct volcano, Pedregal, where at some undeterminable prehistoric time settlements were buried by lava flow. Until recently this site was believed to be extremely ancient, but the artifacts found here can be connected with other known sites. Possibly it was in existence when the first base of the Sun Temple at Teotihuacan was laid down.[151] The *metates,* or maize grinders, discovered are almost indistinguishable from those in use today.[76]

TAJIN

The Totonac people, who flourished between the 11th and 13th centuries, inhabited the semitropical regions between the coastal lands and the high plateau in what is now the state of Vera Cruz. Although characteristic figurines and other small objects fashioned by them are found widely scattered throughout the district, eloquent evidence of high civilization is concentrated in only a few places.[136] Six miles from the town of Papantla, northeast of the Valley of Mexico, lies the Totonac temple, El Tajin, "the thunderbolt" (*Pl. 12, fig. c*).

The temple-base is one of four artificial mounds grouped around a plaza; other ruins are spread over quite a distance. This striking substructure (*fig. a*) is 82 feet square, has an approximate height of 70 feet, and rises in seven receding terraces, the last of which served as the sanctuary floor. The clean-cut, accurately fitted stone slabs of the edifice show even in decay the excellent quality of workmanship, a strong contrast to the rougher masonry in the Mexican Valley.[151] In its profile, the building is actually akin to the Temple of Quetzalcoatl at Teotihuacan, as each section has a low battered base supporting a rectangular panel. At Tajin, however, each terrace is completed with a cornice, projecting obliquely, and instead of the extravagant richness of sculptured decoration, seven tiers of niches—apparently ninety on a side which would make three hundred sixty in all—are arranged with amazing rhythm and symmetry.

This number, corresponding as it does to the days in a regular calendar year, reflects knowledge of an accurate day count and its application in the religious and social life of the people. Each panel of niches is accentuated by its position between the slanting base and angled cornice, suggesting that the recesses might have been used as day-shrines. They do not lead into the edifice but serve only as stone frames, perhaps for idols, incense burners, or offerings. At the corners of the building they are open at the sides, giving greater lightness to the whole structure. There are indications that they were plastered inside and painted.

A broad stairway (*fig. b*) leads to the top on the east side, inclined toward the building like a ladder so that its base extends well beyond the substructure. This method of construction is common among the Maya also. The wide balustrade, typical of all later Mexican and Maya buildings, is present, and may have had at least two recesses built in at the foot. The center lane of the stairs is broken by several niche stations, standing in groups of three, with vertical walls and heavy oblique cornices. Although they are not so large or so complex as the others, the detail is thus kept in uniform style with the rest of the construction.

Ceremonial daises or built-in altars at the bottom of the stairway occur in the Early Maya sites. Even today at Chichicastenango, Guatemala, where the Maya-Quiché Indians still practice many of their medieval customs, we find an analogy. At the foot of the semicircular stairway leading to the door of the church, there is an open construction, like a fireplace, with two shelves and a stone slab laid on top. Here the Indians commence their ritual, lighting and swinging their *incensarios* filled with copal, which are not permitted within the building. Whoever has witnessed the tense and agitated ceremony there, with the façade of the church shrouded in clouds of copal smoke, can imagine the impressiveness of a pre-Columbian ceremony.

Scattered about the ruins of the ancient plaza were found a number of carved stones, two of which are shown in the chapter on sculpture. (See *Pl. 63, fig. a* and *Pl. 83, fig. c.*) Here, however, attention should be called to the manner in which the smooth stone surfaces are alternated with stucco, the flat sections stressing by contrast the application of stone relief where it occurs.

The ruins around Tajin are not the only typical Totonac settlements. There is another Totonac site with characteristics similar to Tajin's at Yohualichan, thirty-six miles south of Papantla, as well as later buildings in other places in the state of Vera Cruz.[136] It is interesting that part of this region now lies outside the Totonac language belt and that Nahua is spoken there.

Although the work of the Totonac builders was doubtless influenced by the greater neighboring cultures, they achieved nevertheless their own individual architectural expression. The region where this type of architecture is found formed perhaps a pocket in which the style was best preserved. The Totonac structures demonstrate best that the pre-Columbian temple-bases, aside from the accident of geometric form, have nothing in common with the pyramids of Egypt.

MONTE ALBAN

One of the most extensive ruins in the Mexican Area is a hilltop settlement in the southern part of Mexico (*Pl. 13, fig. a*), seven miles to the southwest of the thriving state capital, Oaxaca, "place covered with trees." Called by the Spaniards Monte Alban, or "white mountain," it rises 6331 feet above sea level. It is here that the discovery of a unique grave-treasure of gold, turquoise, pearl, jade, and bone was made, which awakened general interest in pre-Columbian civilization more than any other single revelation within the last century. These findings will be discussed in their respective chapters, but the site deserves consideration on its own merits.

This dead city of the Zapotec, and later the Mixtec, peoples has the most beautiful topographical situation of all the ruins in the Mexican Area. Situated on a promontory of immense size, it overlooks the convergence of three valleys, with the peaks of the Sierra Madre del Sur forming a dramatic backdrop for the scene. Hilltop sites are not uncommon in the Oaxaca region, though other peoples in Mexico and Central America seem to have preferred valleys and plains. The dominating position of the ancient city, some thousand feet higher than the fertile fields that provided it with its food supply, and the ruggedness of the steep slopes minimized the danger of attack.

The mountain has seven summits, all of them covered with grass-topped mounds, concealed temples, palaces, baths, and tombs. The settlement is said to extend over twenty square miles, and indeed, when one looks over the surrounding slopes on a clear morning, the whole region appears shaped by the hand of man. It might be said in passing that so bountiful is the Valley of Oaxaca that of all Mexico Cortés chose it for his marquisate, although politics and intrigues at home prevented him from ever enjoying his realm.

According to the opinion of Dr. Caso, who conducted the excavations, Monte Alban was rather a ceremonial center than a military fortress.[24] Its history falls into five periods, the first four covering the time when the Zapotecs or their immediate predecessors ruled here, and the fifth and last connected with the activities of the Mixtecs on the same spot. Altogether a time-span of some two thousand years of civilization elapsed before the coming of the white man.

There is a Mexican opinion that Monte Alban, as a settlement, is even older than the famous and much acclaimed sites of the Maya Area, some of the most important ruins of which are located in Chiapas, a neighboring state to Oaxaca. The beginnings of all these cultures are shrouded in obscurity. Nevertheless, the cluster of structures as it now stands shows acquaintance with the architectural accomplishments of the Maya.

In contrast to the other sites of the Mexican Area, in which one pyramidal base or a small group seems to command the spot, we find here a number of monticles, averaging about 30 feet in height, giving a very different but in no way less grand impression.

The city apparently centered about a vast plaza, 1000 by 650 feet, accurately oriented and dominated on the north and south by two immense artificial mounds, each of which supported a number of buildings. On the long sides it was flanked by a row of lesser elevations, varying in size and height, their rear walls erected on the brink of the mountain. Roughly down the center and parallel to these lies another group of monticles, and there are many more beyond the plaza, still untouched by the excavator. To have need of and maintain so many structures would indicate a flourishing civic and religious life, one that required numerous ceremonies, participants, and dignitaries.

The practice of superimposing one building upon another was prevalent also here; in one case five separate floor levels have been uncovered. The earlier periods seem to be characterized by more durable structures, erected of larger slabs and set on lower platforms, and occasionally worked slabs are found used again in later buildings. All the edifices were greatly enhanced by the bland coating of stucco, sections of which were painted in bright colors.

Judging from the architectural material now visible at the site, great stylistic differences are not apparent, but each building has, nevertheless, individuality and variety of detail. The stairway may be a massive, almost separate structure, beginning at a distance from the base of the temple mound with smooth unbroken balustrades like buttresses on either side; or it may be incorporated into the edifice, nestling, as it were, between the shoulders of the terraced podium. Or again, flanked by wide ramps, it may occupy a full side of the substructure with several abrupt vertical breaks. In one case, Monticle J (*fig. b*), a narrow vaulted passageway cuts into the structure behind the stair. Note the glyphs on the walls.

The great stairway of thirty-three steps at the north end of the plaza (*fig. a, upper right*) is believed the widest in all pre-Columbian America. It is nearly 125 feet broad and 40 high. The ramp here becomes a primary feature. It is 39 feet wide on either side, and with its static extended surface counterbalances the mounting line of the stairs.[22] The double meander that decorates the structure is an ornament characteristic of the site and is most clearly seen in *fig. c,* showing Monticle M.

Pl. 14, fig. a gives the view looking south from the top of the stairs. A number of square sections of masonry, presumably the foundations of pillars, are visible. In the foreground is a sunken court, somewhat reminiscent of the Citadel at Teotihuacan. This complex continues in a group of platform mounds, many yet not investigated, rising in an irregular mass of terraced walls and sloping steps, in itself a mountain of masonry. *Pl. 15, fig. a* shows the north end.

As in numerous other pre-Columbian sites from both the Mexican and Maya areas, a ball court was found, here in the northwest corner of the plaza (*Pl. 14, fig. b*). As a whole, it does not compare artistically with those of the Maya, but has, nevertheless, a beautifully flowing broad line of stairs and is well proportioned with daises cleverly applied. Here particularly, the complete disappearance of all embellishment prevents us from receiving an adequate impression.

But even without the ruins of religious and civic buildings, the overwhelming number of carefully built and decorated tombs would secure for Monte Alban a particular place in medieval American history. It seems that the Zapotecs especially developed the tradition of housing their dead in masonry tombs. The subterranean chambers at Mitla, also within the Zapotec realm, are more imposing in size and show greater skill in decoration, but both types testify convincingly to the importance of an after-life in the beliefs of these people.

Beyond the main cluster of buildings, where a few burials have been discovered, the sloping hillsides constitute an extensive cemetery. Jagged stones from ancient tombs lie scattered far and wide across the tilled fields of the region. The burial chambers all have a somewhat similar construction, rectangular in shape and roofed with stone slabs, laid flat from wall to wall or placed together to form an inverted V. They are not comfortable places for the living, as they are generally too low for one to stand erect in and are suffocatingly hot, but they provided ample space for several dead with their personal paraphernalia, for incense burners and funerary urns, in which the cremated bones of disinterred bodies were placed for a second burial.

Pl. 15, fig. b shows the reconstructed entrance of the fabulous Tomb 7, discovered in the relaying of the road which leads to the great plaza. Of Zapotec origin, it had been appropriated by the Mixtecs, but since their time had lain undisturbed. It can be seen that the grave chamber was covered by a building with a chapel-like room at the end. In some tombs this edifice amounts to a veritable little temple with podium and stairway of considerable size and generally a patio in the center. A narrow flight of stone steps, once concealed, leads down to the entrance, where two large stone jambs support the heavy lintel.

The entrances to the tombs of Monte Alban are frequently decorated. A serpent (*fig. c*), probably represented with a painted body, guarded the door of Tomb 125, and a pottery figure (*fig. d*) was discovered cemented firmly above the doorway of Tomb 104. The headdress here is unusually detailed and the large jade mask depicted on the breast should also be noted.

The interiors were made of stone, with one niche always built into the wall opposite the doorway and one, or sometimes two, in each of the long side walls. These are often empty, even in an unviolated tomb, but in certain cases have been found to contain pottery and jewelry. It is a matter of speculation whether these recesses indicate the degeneration of a former cruciform construction, as is held by some Mexican archaeologists. One structure in the form of a cross has been found at Monte Alban, but the type is more frequent in the Mitla region. The walls were often stuccoed and sometimes painted, an example of which, the most remarkable discovered to date—the interior of Tomb 104 mentioned above—is reproduced in *Pl. 264*. This practice of interring the dead in decorated chambers, built with impressive portals and vaulted roofs in a manner to suggest houses, brings to mind the Etruscan graves of Tuscany and Umbria, which also had their subterranean halls with frescoes and pottery sarcophagi.

The region of Monte Alban has been riddled by treasure hunters ever since the Conquest. Most of the temple-bases have been ruthlessly tunneled, doubtless with the mistaken idea that they were pyramids built over the tombs of kings, and many of the recently excavated graves show signs of age-old plundering. It is fortunate that some were spared for 20th-century archaeology.

One of the outstanding pioneer archaeologists of the Maya Area, Alfred Percival Maudslay, showed his brilliant intuition when, after finishing his repeated and thorough surveys of the Maya country, he became interested in Monte Alban. At that time he was working a small gold mine, which he had inherited, at Zavaleta near Oaxaca City, but his chief ambition was to excavate and study the near-by Zapotec site. Around the turn of the century, however, an archaeologist was still looked upon as somewhat moonstruck. The motives of research were regarded with suspicion and reluctance, despite the fact that adventurers came and went almost at will, camping for a few days on the site and moving on unchallenged. In vain Maudslay lobbied and wrote to the authorities for permission to carry on his work. Even the fact that he held an honorary title from the University of Mexico was of little avail. After his years of success and fame in the Maya jungle, he became restless and disheartened over the failure of this new project, and, unwilling to wait longer, he sold his property and sailed for England. Some of the older residents of Oaxaca still speak of this great personality with real attachment, invariably mentioning the beautiful garden on which he spent so many hours during the years he lived there.

Governments and attitudes have changed since then, and in 1931 a more enlightened administration gave authority to Dr. Caso to begin work at Monte Alban. No one can estimate the loss that occurred during that lapse of thirty or forty years before scientific methods were applied in the excavations, but the great number of so-called "Oaxaca" type specimens of jewelry, jade, and pottery that are current on the market or have found their way into museums and private collections can give us a faint idea of the riches once buried in the Zapotec and Mixtec graves.

MITLA

Our last stop on the way to the Maya Area is at Mitla. The town is situated some twenty miles southeast of Monte Alban, and in contrast to that hilltop settlement, lies in the lap of a fertile valley. It is on the route which once connected several important pre-Columbian centers and its culture profited from this. The district has retained its importance, and now the Pan-American Highway will pass this way. According to one chronicler, in 1494 the place fell into the hands of the Aztecs, interested in controlling the road by which cocoa was sent from the Isthmus of Tehuantepec to the Mexican highlands, but if there was an Aztec occupation of the town, it seems to have left little impression on the arts of the place.

The Aztec word *Mictlán* signifies "underworld" or "realm of the dead," while the Zapotec name means rather "house of beatitudes." [129] Tradition has it that here dwelt the Great High Priest of the nation, who was consulted by dignitaries from far and wide.

As Mitla had never been buried or overgrown with vegetation, it was among the first of the ruined cities to be described. Speculation ran rife as to the age of the buildings, and fantastic uses were contrived for them, which subsequent examination has failed to corroborate. In view of the devastation of the Conquest and the ruthless methods of early "explorers," it is a miracle that the ruins of Mitla exist at all. Indeed, enough stones were carried away to build haciendas and churches, one of which rises from the flank of an ancient quadrangle, and farming goes on in the midst of crumbling plazas.

Interest at this site centers in three large quadrangular groups, which show great originality in style and ornament. Happily, enough remains of these to give an idea of their architecture. Although they do not seem to have been carefully related to one another, each in itself is accurately oriented.[49]

The building called the Palace of the Six Columns (Palace II) is the best preserved (*Pl. 16, fig. a*). It stands at the north end of a complex of two quadrangular courts, each about 150 feet at the greatest width and placed obliquely, corner to corner. The courts are inclosed by nearly vertical ramparts, 6 or 7 feet high, which served as bases. In the center stood a square altar or shrine, the outlines of which are visible in this photograph. The plaza was paved with thick cement and, according to a custom prevalent in Mexico and Central America, it as well as the stuccoed surface of the podiums and the floors of the buildings was stained red.

As it stands, the façade of the palace measures 133 feet long by about 14 high. A broad steep stairway leads up to the imposing triple entrance. Its walls, sometimes 4 feet thick, are constructed on the usual core of irregular stone and adobe mortar, with an amazingly intricate facing of smooth, well-cut trachyte in various sizes, tenoned into the cement core (*Pl. 17, fig. a*). The slanting base-line is present, and above it are rectangular panels of fretwork set within the turns of a double-coursed meander, such as was used on the ramps and terraces of Monte Alban. This is topped with a course of stone slanted outward in opposition to the incline of the base. Large slabs mark the corners. The four round holes visible above the paneled sections at the entrance were doubtless for poles supporting an awning. The lintel, more clearly seen from within, consists of three immense stone blocks, each some 10 feet long, 2 to 4 feet thick, and 5 broad. On the outside it is ingeniously carved to harmonize with the composite fretwork panels on the walls.

The photographs illustrate more clearly than any text not only the great architectural imagination necessary for the conception of such a grandiose plan, but also the technical knowledge required for the execution of a design involving so many front levels and such counterpoint of decoration. Stucco and paint must be added in imagination to all the plain surfaces of the buildings as they stand.

At the end of the last century the enthusiasm for all that was classic laid much emphasis on the Greek-type frets used in the ornamental panels at Mitla. But while classical Europe used the grecque in a narrow line as edging to an undecorated surface, in Mitla the fretted panels with smooth stone bands as frame made up the wall itself.

The fretwork is composed of small pieces of stone, cut and arranged in a mosaic-like manner into not less than fourteen separate designs (*Pl. 16, fig. b*). The grecque and the simple square combine in rhythmic sequence or fantastic zigzag into patterns, including the cross, the diamond, the step-fret, interlocking T's, and many other variations which alternate upon the walls in splendid harmony. It is noteworthy that the component pieces are not uniform, as is usual with the blocks or tiles which we combine to form a varied geometric design, but that each piece was obviously cut for the spot which it occupies. The stones have tenons at the back and thus are imbedded into the mass of mortar behind the panel with the same technique, as Thompson points out, as that used in fabricating the turquoise plaques and shell mosaics, but on a larger scale.[151] Eighty thousand pieces are said to have been needed for the wall of the inner court alone.

The patterns in their strict geometric build-up seem to be derived from textile designs. The complete absence of human, animal, and plant motifs is noteworthy. As the fret, and particularly the step-fret, or "winged fret" as it might be called, is a sign of the Great Plumed Serpent, there is doubtless also symbolical significance in the decoration here.

By this time all confused comparison to Greek and Roman art should have been dismissed from the mind of the reader. The restless polyphonic decoration of the palaces at Mitla has nothing in common with the suave homogeneous structures of the classical world, however serene and balanced its effect may be at a distance.

The triple doorway opens upon the Hall of the Columns, 23 feet wide by 125 long, which runs the full width of the building and seems to have been stuccoed. The six huge tapering stone columns down the middle of the floor are 11 feet high as they stand and probably are sunken some 4 or 5 feet below the cement floor. Their diameter is over 30 inches and their weight approximates six to eight tons each. They served as supports for the roof, which was built apparently in the traditional manner with poles laid across heavier beams and sealed with mortar or plaster.

From this inner hall a small door leads through an anteroom into an open patio, 31 feet square, flanked on all sides by long narrow inclosed chambers (*Pl. 17, fig. b*). Decorations similar to the outside of the building embellish the court, while the walls of the narrow rooms carry free-flowing bands of the composite reliefs, separated from one another by only a single narrow course of smooth stone (*fig. c*). The mosaics were painted white on a red ground,[129] and the interplay of light and shadow on them even today multiplies their amazing variety. Just as the recurrence of a rich and ingenious melody in a symphony does not dull our ears, so these fretwork variations please the eye on every wall and in every position they are found, however often repeated.

It may be assumed that the other buildings facing the open plazas were similar in execution but had generally a single long narrow hall. These impressive edifices are called "palaces" because their structure was definitely different from the type known to be temples throughout Middle America. The room arrangement would have lent itself well for audiences and consultations, if not too congenial as household quarters. None of the buildings seems to have other access than by way of the great courts of the quadrangles.

In the west quadrangle of the same complex are found the two subterranean chambers that give special importance to the site. The entrances (*Pl. 18, fig. a*), constructed with stone lintels and jambs, as is the case in the buildings, lie in the plaza near the center and were probably closed with a slab or sealed. At the foot of the descending stairs an uneven passage runs in each case directly under the building, so that the great cruciform vaults may be said to lie rather within the artificial base of the edifice than actually underground. They were doubtless constructed from above, then sealed with the floor. The photograph shows part of the upper floor of the palace, as well as the construction of the passage beneath.

The impressive subterranean galleries are about 5 feet wide by 6½ to 8 feet high. The cross arms extend some 42 feet, or, in the case of the shorter ones, 12 to 15 feet. Large stone slabs, evenly cut and fitted, form the ceiling. The tomb below the north building has composite mosaic-like panels such as are used in the outside walls, while in the east vault the fretwork decorations are carved in the stone (*fig. b*). Other cruciform vaults are known within the environs of Mitla. All these underground chambers were robbed of their contents so long ago that no clue remains of what they may have contained.

The two other palace complexes at Mitla have no substructures but stand on the ground level so that the buildings inclosing the various quadrangles have continuous walls. Nevertheless they all show such uniformity of plan and decoration that they must have been erected within a time-span not too remote from the Group of the Columns just described. Remnants of murals in negative painting have been found on some of the inner lintels (see *Pl. 265, fig. a*), where figures resembling those of the codices are drawn with fine red lines on a grayish plaster and the background filled in with brilliant red.[49]

The Zapotecs are thought to have taken possession of the Mitla region about the 11th century, and how many centuries of pre-Columbian life the site witnessed prior to that is not known. The ruins shown here are placed between 1200 and 1300. We may assume that there was some antecedent architecture before this splendid and perfected style, for that which we see today must have been not only late chronologically, but the highest achievement of their talent.

The variety of buildings in the Mexican Area is manifested in the eight architectural sites here presented. Beyond the fundamental homogeneity of idea, not one can be called a copy or a reproduction of another. Relatively low podiums follow mountain-high temple-bases. Predominantly flat surfaces, smoothed over with a bland covering of stucco and paint, stand not far from terraces decorated with sculptural ornaments in barbaric pomp. In one case animal representations, in another purely geometrical bands and patterns show the divergence in imagination. Wide panels of low relief contrast with sculpture in the round, and huge blocks, with carefully fitted smaller stones. What is common is the disposition to rise above the natural level, to make the place of ceremony or worship dominate its vicinity. Another mutual feature is the gregarious character of the buildings; in every case that we know, adjacent mounds prove that numerous structures added their weight to the general effect. Ritual had a primary part in the life of the medieval Americans. Their religious ceremonies were likewise their theatrical show and required a number of settings.

These sites radiate a spirit alien to us. Some may belittle it, but none can deny that majesty lies in the structures. Whether crude in workmanship or sophisticated in execution, all their variants remain consistently within the same framework of thought.

MAYA AREA

In Mexico we saw within a comparatively short radius the diverse architectural achievement of various peoples. The Maya Area, on the other hand, we find populated by a single race throughout the Middle Ages, who, though stimulated by outside influence and later even dominated by another nation, retained its striking talents and special characteristics in art and civilization. The language map even today shows remarkable solidarity in this region extending from Tabasco throughout Yucatan and covering most of Guatemala and a section of Honduras, roughly the territory occupied by the ancient Maya.[52]

Each Maya city presents great originality of conception in its architecture and variation in detail, but a distinct continuity of character is nevertheless traceable from the first sites, which date from about the beginning of our era, to the powerful Toltec-influenced cities of Yucatan that prospered until shortly before the Conquest.

The great civilization that once flourished here was based on the development of agriculture. Life was dependent upon and religion was closely allied to the crops, and rain or drought was a vital factor in the existence of these people. The custom of burning off and replanting a succession of fields was ingenious enough, considering the primitive quality of the tools at hand and the terrific vitality of the jungle, but the method tended to exhaust the soil, which produced less and less after the first season, even if allowed for a time to lie fallow.[66] The fluctuations of population, whether sudden or gradual, which led finally to the abandonment of the great sites is attributable in part to these facts.

One of the conditioning factors of Maya building was the presence of limestone practically throughout the area. Lime was extracted and excellent stucco, cement, and lime mortar were produced at a very early date.

Out of this knowledge these people found their own ingenious solution to the roofing problem by inventing a type of corbeled arch. The Maya builders are sometimes spoken of disparagingly for not having discovered the principle of the keystone arch. Ignorance of this architectural device, however, is not considered a disgrace elsewhere in archaeology, and there is no need for the Americanist to apologize for it. The famous structures of Mesopotamia, China, Egypt, and Greece—to mention only the best known of the ancient civilizations—are not belittled because of a lack of it. Their architecture is acknowledged as great and splendid, although they all used horizontally laid stone slabs and wooden beams in roofing. With them even the corbeled vault was rare. The subsequent illustrations should convince any one that medieval America also achieved great building without the knowledge of the Roman arch.

The Maya corbeled vault made use of a series of stones firmly held at one end and so placed that each course overlapped the one below it; thus the sides gradually approached each other. Usually a slab capped the arch. The earliest vault so far discovered appears at Uaxactun in Structure A-V, tentatively dated toward the end of the 4th century.[131] The excellent cement of the limestone regions served to make the arch essentially monolithic. The use of wooden cross-beams was common, though their purpose is still a matter of discussion.

A number of variations were developed, all using the same principle, from the spectacular trefoil arch at Palenque to the bottle shapes at Tulum and other Yucatecan east-coast sites and the rounded constructions at Labná and Chichen Itzá. The great height of the vaults from the spring-line necessarily conditioned the appearance of the outside of the building, giving an extensive upper zone, or "entablature section," characteristic of the Maya and well adapted to lavish decoration.

The chronology of the Old Empire falls roughly into three periods: the Early, beginning in the first centuries after the birth of Christ and closing in the 7th century; the Middle, which lasted only about a hundred years, and the Late, which extended from the early 8th century to 889, the last date recorded on stelae. These periods make themselves apparent in the art production, and were first differentiated by Dr. Spinden on the basis of the evolution of the carving on stelae uninfluenced by the dates they bore.[137] The Late Period is sometimes called the Great, since most of the famous Old Empire cities came to their flowering within this time-span, reaching the zenith of their creative genius in mid-8th century. The date 790 marks the peak of time-recording and is found on stelae, altars, or lintels of nineteen Maya sites.[150] The term "Transition" is sometimes applied to that period between the decline of the Old Empire and the emergence of the New.

The great cities of the Old Empire are difficult of access, with many of them situated in the depths of what is today an almost impenetrable jungle. Chicle hunters, tapping the forest for raw material for chewing gum, have rendered pioneer service in locating and reporting many a ruin, and their trails are used even today by archaeologists when a site does not afford a landing for an airplane.

UAXACTUN

The earliest structure known to date was excavated at Uaxactun, which lies north of Lake Flores, Peten, Guatemala, and about ninety miles west of Belize, port of British Honduras. This site appears to have been occupied for one of the longest spans of time in the Old Empire, although not in unbroken continuity, with date sequences ranging from 327 to 889. It is large, with a number of beautifully laid-out groups of buildings. As in Mexico, there is evidence of frequent alteration and rebuilding.

In one case (Structure A-I) five antecedent substructures were uncovered beneath the ruins of the sixth and last. All, down to the earliest, revealed the characteristic fundamentals of Maya construction. They were built over a loose core of fill and rubble covered with a backing of concrete, upon which a facing of cut stone was applied. In the substructures of this complex can be traced the entire progression of the technique in applying the facing, from the tenoned-in type of stone locked into the cement behind, through a rough veneering, to a final and perfected facing only superficially bound to the hearting.[135]

The temple-bases investigated consisted of receding terraces, generally three, each with slightly battered profile and one stairway. All bore a smooth stucco surface, but there had been apparently no attempt at decoration. The temples on top seem to have been of poles and thatch, some with a low masonry foundation wall and post holes suggesting roof construction. There is no conclusive evidence here of the famous vault which was to flower in so many rich variations at a later period. The excavations of this group yielded a large number of painted pottery vessels, extraordinarily fine.

In the great plaza of the city were unearthed stone monuments, the dates of which correspond to A.D. 328. At the same time an edifice was uncovered (*Pl. 19, fig. a*) that apparently had already been buried at the time the stelae were erected. It was in remarkably fine condition, having been preserved by the building superimposed upon it.

This early structure, E-VII, is of a different style from that of the later edifices in the city, and might be called pre-Maya. It consists of a well-proportioned temple-base (*fig. b*), 85 feet square and 25 high, of rough undressed stone, covered thickly with brilliant white stucco. A series of low receding platforms with heavy projecting cornices makes up the lower portion of the base, and wide stairways with balustrades lead up all four sides. The last section consists of a considerably higher terrace block. Large grotesque masks decorate the abutments. The subtle handling of the stairways gives suavity to the whole building. Indeed, the stairway as decorative factor is as fully utilized as in the much later buildings of this and the Mexican Area. Astonishing ripeness is revealed in the sure command over contour and mass and the excellent feeling for light and shade. The dramatic sense, so often present in the architecture of the pre-Columbian cultures, is strongly evident here.

Whether or not a building once stood on top of this structure is a matter of conjecture. No evidence was found at the time of excavation. There was probably some kind of altar, even perhaps a roof, which could not have been of very solid construction.

Certain features already present in this early example forecast those that characterize Maya building. The gigantic stucco masks are the forerunners of the stone masks and the stucco reliefs that constitute the crowning glory of Maya architecture. These masks, which here might already be considered rigid and conventionalized in their idea, hold their own throughout the course of Maya building, although techniques became more mobile and the field for delineation more varied. The striving for imposing elevation, always a factor in the architecture of the Maya, was exaggerated and consciously applied with great effect, especially in the cities Tikal, Guatemala, and Palenque, Mexico. The altar sheds on the early bases grew into temples of more solid structure, with inner divisions into sanctuaries and antechambers, and the decorative motifs, first applied to the substructure, were transplanted later to the temple itself and lavished chiefly upon the upper zones.

COPAN

The earliest description of the ruins of Copan, Honduras, is to be found in a letter dated March, 1576, from Diego Garcia de Palacio, an officer of the *Audiencia de Guatemala,* to his king, Philip II of Spain. It is, however, as Maudslay writes, "not to Palacio's letter, which was only comparatively recently unearthed from Spanish archives, but to the charming pages of Stephens and the beautiful drawings of Catherwood that the world in general is indebted for a knowledge of the wonders of Copan." [81]

This intrepid gentleman, John L. Stephens, was commissioned in 1839 by Martin Van Buren, President of the United States, to make a general survey of the possibilities of a canal across Nicaragua connecting the Atlantic and Pacific, but was balked in this task by civil and guerrilla warfare then prevalent in Central America. He nevertheless succeeded in journeying nearly three thousand miles through the strife-torn interiors, visiting eight ruined cities, which he discusses with truly brilliant perception and accuracy in his famous book, *Incidents of Travel in Central America, Chiapas and Yucatan,* illustrated by the English artist, Frederick Catherwood.

So enthusiastic was Stephens about Copan that he bought the ruined city for fifty dollars in cash, with the idea of moving as much of it as possible to greater safety. Difficulties of transportation, however, prevented him from carrying out his enterprise.[58]

In this great religious center may be seen one of the finest examples in the Old Empire of the elaborate city-planning of the Maya. Many of their early cities do not appear to have been so carefully oriented as those of the Mexican Area and their position was seemingly influenced by the character of the landscape.[49] There was apparently little concern over the matter of defense; within the cities there are no remnants of fences or walled inclosures. The buildings were generally linked with one another by staircases or broad mounting terraces, with that kind of community spirit that blended all into one body of architecture.

The general view of the site as reconstructed by Maudslay will give a clearer idea of the complicated grouping than any lengthy description could (*Pl. 20, fig. b*). Ruins belonging to the city extend for many miles but the area here shown along the river bank doubtless constituted the heart of the community.

In the foreground is visible an immense mound, roughly rectangular in shape, with additions and outcroppings, upon the top of which, over one hundred feet above the natural level, several buildings of various sizes are grouped about two sunken courts. That the Great Mound is for the most part artificial has been revealed by the river, which, in the shift of its bed during the centuries, has cut deeply into one side, disclosing in the cross-section not only the hard-packed rubble of the core but also several pavement levels of concrete and a number of drains leading from the upper courts. It is noteworthy that the sides of the Great Mound and of the various courts are faced with an almost unbroken series of steps, extremely gracious in their effect and indicative of superior building.

To the north of this structure is situated a vast open plaza on the natural level (*fig. a*), surrounded on three sides by grass-grown ramparts and low platforms, the foundations for smaller buildings. Its position on the site is designated by *a* on the model. Carved altars and fragments of monuments stand in the field, stelae of rulers and priests, some set over small cruciform vaults containing caches. There are a number of mounds, apparently ruined substructures, near by, some arranged to form quadrangles. The chief evidences of human habitation lie at the left in the picture of the model.

The visitor's first great impression of Copan is of the two imposing stairways that stand at right angles to each other, forming the southeast corner of the plaza. The broader of the two extends across the entire side of the Great Mound. Giant gray ceiba trees have gained a firm foothold on the very summit of the buildings, planted there by nature after the city was abandoned, so that now the monumental weather-beaten statue at the foot of the stairs is nearly always in deep shadow.

The stairway to the east (*b* in the model) is not so broad as the first and belongs to a separate substructure which, however, is contiguous to the Great Mound. This steep narrow temple-base was greatly damaged by a recent landslide, and of the temple which once stood on top, only traces of the cement pavement remain. The stairway (*Pl. 21, fig. a*), under reconstruction at the time of our visit, ascends at a characteristically steep angle and is 26 feet broad. The risers of the steps, calculated to have numbered eighty to ninety, each about a foot high, carry carved hieroglyphic computations, the longest Maya inscription yet discovered. The glyphs are executed with beauty and precise detail and so arranged as to be read in lines across each step, not, as was usual, in columns. The many figures representing the elements of Maya time-count—human, animal, and monster heads in various positions within their shieldlike frames, and the dots and bars which stand for numbers—constitute a gigantic open scroll, a frozen page of a strange medieval book at which we gaze in fascination, even though conscious of our own mental limitations in fathoming its meaning.

About every twelve steps, in the center, a carved seated figure is placed, priest or dignitary magnificently arrayed, each with his head framed in a monster's jaws. One of these statues is missing (see *Pl. 87*); the rest are heavily damaged, yet each is arresting for its individuality. A giant stela stands at the foot of the stairs facing a carved altar, and behind it another altar-like platform is built into the body of the staircase.

The stairway is flanked on either side by a balustrade, 3½ feet wide, with curved, almost crescent-shaped masks (*fig. b*). Although only a few of these are left in place, they seem at one and the same time to bind the stair to the substructure and, with their winglike effect, to disencumber the whole mass of its weight. All the carving was apparently only roughed in before the stones were set in place and finished afterward.[39] The inscription dates the stair in 770, placing it among the latest structures at Copan; stylistically also it shows some of the most mature work.

Copan too has its Ball Court (*Pl. 20, fig. d*), which lies at right angles to the Hieroglyphic Stairway in the position indicated by *c* on the model, although reconstruction has proved it to be of very different design than Maudslay shows.

It was a comparatively narrow open court and smoothly paved. The low slanting ramps on either side present a feature different from the ball courts in the New Empire in Yucatan, where the walls are high and vertical. Apparently the game was not identical in all regions. The top of the ramp is decorated by a number of gigantic parrot heads. To the right and left behind these, rise buildings that were perhaps used by the chiefs and high priests, while the dilapidated stair at the north end may have served as the stand for the common people. In the axis the tall stela "points up" the linear composition. The whole construction forms an ideal arena in which from any point one has a feeling of proximity to the players.

In the West Court on top of the Great Mound is an unusual building (*d* in the model), reconstructed by the Carnegie Institution of Washington and named Structure 11, or the Reviewing Stand (*fig. c*). The substructure is severe, with plain walls and a series of doorlike niches. Doubtless paint on a plastered ground furnished added decoration. Six steps lead up from the level of the court, the top riser of which carries finely carved glyphs. The only other ornamentation is two kneeling figures, one at either end of the top stair. The legs, in profile, and the squared shoulders, as well as the fantastic appendage attached to the creature's back are executed in relief, while the demon head and the torch in his left hand are worked in the round. There is animation in the malevolent face, and the writhing snake held in tusklike teeth is realistically carved.

The structure on the summit is decorated with beautifully executed glyphs, and fragmentary sculpture about the entrance indicates that it represented a yawning serpent jaw.[39] Were it not for the foliage, this height would command a splendid view of the great plaza.

On the East Court of the Great Mound stands the Temple of the Sculptured Doorway, or Structure 22 (*e* in the model). The building remained in a state of partial preservation until 1934, when it was razed by an earthquake. Maudslay's careful notes and photographs were of great assistance when its excavation and restoration were undertaken shortly afterward.[159]

The edifice (*Pl. 22, fig. a*), originally about 80 by 40 feet, is built of the soft greenish tufa abundant in the region and is accurately oriented. It stands on its own E-shaped podium on top of the 20-foot terrace that frames the entire court. It is dated in mid-8th century and was not erected over an older structure. Close by runs the slash cut by the river which has now been diverted from its destructive course. A stair of seven steps (*fig. b*) laid with unusually massive stones mounts to the entrance. The top one is carved to represent the jaw and lower lip of a scaly monster, and two curving stone tusks are inset at the sides. Large composite masks were found in place at the corners, and finely carved figures in the round, of the type known as Maize-god and illustrated on *Pl. 90,* decorated the façade. It contains four rooms, vaulted apparently in the typical Maya manner and separated by what appear to us as disproportionately thick walls, some of which are nearly 9 feet through.

The north chamber may have been the inner sanctuary. It is raised over two feet above the general floor level, and its only access is by way of the superb sculptured doorway (*Pl. 23, fig. c*) that gives the structure its name.

This doorway stands unique in all the architecture of medieval America that has been preserved or reconstructed. It occupies two-thirds of the wall space of the narrow anteroom which one must enter first, but, set back and shielded by the outside walls, it is invisible from the outside. A sculptured human figure, larger than life size, sits hunched at either side (*figs. a* and *b*), crouching above an enormous death's-head carved from a single piece of stone. The men support on their backs the twisted mass of a fantastic two-headed monster, whose shoulder and bent limb are visible directly above the human head. The face of the beast rests upon the upraised hands, while the writhing body forms the lintel, held in place by a thick wooden beam. In and out of the S-shaped convolutions of the creature weave small grotesque human figures with elaborate headdresses and jewels, their arms and legs interwoven as if in struggle with the elements. The high sill is also carved with death's-heads and glyphs, so that the entire entrance to the inner room is framed with sculpture.

The carving was covered with a thin layer of plaster and once brightly painted, refurbished so often that some of the exquisite detail of feathers, incised decorations, tassels, individual hands and feet were lost in the thickening coating. From the sockets that are still visible in the walls, it appears that the doors to the adjacent rooms were closed with screens or curtains, doubtless of brilliant hues.

A ceremony witnessed here must have been immensely awe-inspiring. But whether we go to the trouble of imagining a scene from the sunken world or examine the doorway only as a piece of architectural sculpture, the highly decorative management of mass and line, the pulsing rhythm in the various motifs are arresting for every one.

The word "baroque" still carries with it a tinge of disparagement in the United States, although in Europe and Latin America the style is highly appreciated. It is intended here only as praise when we venture to describe this sculptured doorway as the best Maya "baroque." Baroque it is—in feeling, in its complication of design and ebullience of detail, in the dramatic dynamics of its whole conception, in the untrammeled freedom of its execution.

There can be no doubt that this elaborate portal had involved mythological significance for the Maya. The heavy mysterious creature has been interpreted as the sky monster and the two crushed human figures upholding the monstrous garland as two of the four "Bacabs" who support the four corners of the firmament.[153]

In it we have a document in stone, voicing the supernatural occult elements behind Maya religion. This is not one sculptor's arbitrary interpretation of some religious or mystic thought, but the articulation of a complex collective imagination expressed with such clarity that even the Christian of the 20th century is struck, not only by its physical power but by the vision of this alien and vigorous fantasy-world.

TIKAL

Tikal, "place where spirit voices are heard" (*Pl. 24*), is one of the larger sites in the Maya Area, the ruins occupying roughly one square mile. Situated on a plain in the district that includes the northeastern part of Guatemala, with the Usumacintla River and Lake Peten, it belongs to the region where Maya civilization reached its greatest height. Its dates extend from the Early Period to the 9th century.

Like other ancient Maya cities of importance, its plan is characterized by a large court or plaza, stretching in this case over 300 feet from east to west, within which a great number of stelae and altars were grouped.

Owing to its comparative isolation, Tikal has been less visited than most of the larger Maya sites. The first written report appeared in 1848, extremely late in comparison with other descriptions that were made shortly after the Conquest or during the viceregal period. Unlike Copan, Quiriguá, Chichen Itzá, where various institutions, chiefly American, held government contracts over a period of years for the thorough study and preservation of the site, Tikal has never been systematically excavated. The clearing of the dense jungle growth was always a major problem to the investigators, who had only a limited time to spend among the ruins. All existing photographs show a tangle of vegetation and felled trees, restricting a grasp of the city's grandeur. Less sculptured material has been found here so far than one would expect in a city of its cultural height, but many revelations may be expected when exhaustive excavation is undertaken. The Government of Guatemala has a road now under construction which will shortly open up this important region.

Two types of buildings are, in general, distinguishable in Maya sites: the "temples," usually single structures with an inner room or sanctuary, placed on a separate lofty pyramidal base; and the residential type or "palaces" of more rambling proportions usually built on lower, broader platforms. In the latter the high priests and leading nobility are believed to have dwelt or functioned, while the simple populace erected thatch-roofed huts of wood and withes, such as are pictured on the façades of certain buildings and in the murals of a later period (see *Pl. 32, fig. a*).

Besides five major temples, Tikal contains an unusual number and variety of palaces, no two alike in outer appearance or arrangement of apartments. There are also several truncated pyramidal bases with no trace of a building on top but with stairways leading up all four sides, in the manner, though apparently without the ornamentation, of the structure described at near-by Uaxactun. The Castillo at Chichen Itzá with its nine terraces and four stairways from four directions, erected some four hundred years later, is an interesting hark-back to this ancient type (see *Pl. 41*).

The buildings of Tikal are, relatively speaking, the best preserved of the Old Empire. This is due partly to the very thick walls and few doors, in contrast to the thinner walls and wider portals at Palenque, for instance. Besides, the palaces were frequently constructed with an upper tier of rooms, which, in collapsing, served to preserve the lower story.

The use of wood is a characteristic of the site. Beams of the extremely hard *chico-sapote* were employed at the spring-line of the narrow Maya vaults and also as lintels, where several were placed side by side to cover the span between the massive walls. The fact that it has rotted or been torn away has caused the collapse of many of the entrances and surmounting masonry. Surviving fragments, one of which will be discussed later (see *Pl. 274*), show that much of this wood was elaborately carved in low relief and painted.

Superimposed stories are unusual in Maya architecture, evidently because of the great weight of masonry involved, and whenever a two-story effect was desired, it was generally achieved by the "stepping-back" of the second tier and placing it over a solid core. In Tikal, however, two and even three stories are found, actually built one above the other.[156]

The Palace of Five Stories (Structure 10), called by Teobert Maler the

Sacerdotal Palace, is an example of this. It rises at the edge of a wide ravine with one of the terraced hills directly behind it. A retaining wall from the bottom of the gorge supports the first two stories, forming a wide esplanade in front of them, as shown in the plan (*Pl. 25, fig. b*). These actually back against the hillside, but the three upper stories, receding some 30 feet from the façade of the lower section, stand free.

Each story is marked by a projecting entablature section, beginning at the spring-line of the inner vault and extending beyond its peak, which is decorated with carving or stucco work (*fig. a*). There are no signs of stairways either within or without the palaces, and it is surmised that the upper levels were reached by wooden stairs or ladders.

Inside, the first four stories each contained two rows of rooms, one behind the other—fourteen in all, not counting the rambling wings. The width and height of the chambers were conditioned by the inverted-V-shaped vault, averaging about 5 and 13 feet respectively, while in length they varied from 8 to 25 feet. Maler calculates the height from the lowest esplanade to the topmost edge of the frieze of the fifth story as nearly 90 feet.[75]

The other residential buildings show great variety in the arrangement of chambers—some opening on courts, some on galleries—which are often connected by narrow passages. Small round or square apertures were constructed in the walls, probably for ventilation. Inside, around the sides of the rooms, are a number of low benches, built of stone or of rubble plastered over. The walls are also smoothly plastered, and several incised drawings have been found both in palaces and temples, though there are few traces of color. In a chamber of the third story of the palace just described a stone carving in relief was discovered, picturing a woman of rank presenting a high priest with a fattened turkey as sacrificial gift. Cupboard-like niches are frequent in the palaces, and there are indications that hangings may have covered them as well as the doorways.

In contrast to the diverse palace buildings, the five major temples show an unusual uniformity of plan. All stand on truncated pyramidal bases, considerably steeper than those in other Maya sites. All of them are divided into nine terraces with the exception of Temple II, which has four. The profile is slanting and the ground plan often shows inset corners and offset panels. A broad flight of stairs leads up one side. In each case there is only one entrance to the temple building. The vaulted chambers usually number three, one behind the other, connected by a series of beamed passageways or corridors that are often more spacious than the rooms themselves.

The extremely limited space of the interiors in comparison with the great thickness of the walls has frequently been pointed out in descriptions of the temples of Tikal, but this mass was evidently deemed necessary to support the enormous weight of the high decorative roof-comb, one of the most individual features of the site. This structure—a veritable headdress of masonry, weighted with ornament—seems to have no other purpose than the further embellishment of the edifice and extension of its height, an effect so sought after by the Maya builders.

Often the back of the roof-comb seems to descend in a line with the rear wall of the building and in some cases the substructure beneath it falls away at a steeper angle than in front. In Temple II, Maler, taking into consideration the fact that the top of the roof-comb had crumbled, estimated the total height of temple and roof-comb at about 73 feet, while its base measured only 68.

As imposing as it appears, this is the smallest of the five temples. Temple IV, in the western section of the city, is the tallest. The substructure here stands 147 feet high and carries on the top a temple building and roof-comb which together approximate another 80 feet. Its stairway is 58 feet broad at the base. In the photograph on *Pl. 24,* taken from across the great plaza, reading from left to right Temples III, II, and IV can be seen. The stunning effect of the staggered heights is evident.

At this site the evolution of the roof-comb can be traced from what might be considered the earliest type attempted—that of massive walls on more or less solid foundations—through a series of experiments aimed to lighten the weight and thus enlarge the interiors of the temples. The crumbling of some of these constructions reveals that hollow spaces were introduced, until, in Temple V, the roof-comb approximates two leaning walls which gradually converge. From this, it is only a step to the lattice-work and the lighter roof-combs in the buildings of Yaxchilan, Piedras Negras, and Palenque.[157]

PALENQUE

The variety and high artistry manifest in its buildings elevate Palenque to an extraordinary position among the ruined cities of pre-Columbian civilization, though it is quite small when compared with the religious centers just considered. It is situated in Chiapas, the southernmost state in Mexico, some hundred and fifty miles from Tikal, and lies at the mouth of a deep gorge, flanked on three sides by steep wooded hills and on the north by a broad sloping plain. The region is heavily forested, damp, and truly tropical. At all times can be heard the music of falling water.[49]

Although difficult of approach, this city has been the object of numerous visits and investigations in the last century and a half. In 1787, on the order of the King of Spain, Captain Antonio del Rio "explored" it under protection of several companies of Spanish soldiers. Two hundred Indians with axes and bill-hooks were set to work clearing the ruins of the jungle vegetation. The house-keeping of the 18th-century colonial soldiers here in the wilderness can be imagined. Stones were removed at convenience to make fireplaces, hooks were driven through the fragile stucco on the walls for the hanging of armament and hammocks; the horses were stabled under roofs which remained. The Indians were illiterate, suspicious, and full of superstition.

"I am convinced," writes del Rio, "that in order to form some idea of the first inhabitants and of the antiquities connected with their establishment, it would be indispensably necessary to make several excavations. . . . By dint of perseverance I affected all that was necessary to be done, so that ultimately there remained neither a window nor a doorway blocked up, a partition that was not thrown down, nor a room, corridor, court, tower, nor a subterranean passage in which excavations were not affected from two to three yards in depth." [18] It is to the true glory of the builders at Palenque that after such "investigations," anything at all remains today. Since then, the ruins have thrilled many visitors. However, like Tikal, the place was never thoroughly explored.

Of all the sites, Palenque demonstrates most clearly that the Maya had a broad and elastic architectural conception which they adapted to local conditions and topography, never allowing it to become crystallized into stereotyped patterns that limited their artistic activity.

The entire terrain is graded and terraced. The mountain stream, which runs out of the gorge and through the narrow valley where the city stands, is directed into a vaulted culvert four feet high, apparently large enough to accommodate the swollen waters of the rainy season. Farther below, masonry construction of somewhat different type serves as a bridge or viaduct. Thus in an area which must have been a much frequented part of the city, the unruly stream was brought under control. Today, however, the upper end of the channel has become clogged with débris and, unrestrained, the water pours over the ground, damaging the foundations of the buildings.

Palenque's damp and rainy climate may have influenced its distinctive type of architecture. In all the buildings the entablature section has even a more marked inward slant than at Tikal, running roughly parallel to the angle of the inner vault. The roof surface, consequently small, is also sloping, giving the general effect of a mansard.

The chief buildings here consist of a palace complex and five temples, three of which are grouped around a quadrangular court. Open courts, terraces, and stairways connect in a logical system. Doorways are many, three or five in a row, and are placed with a sense of balance—extending in some cases across the entire façade of the building, with the wall spaces between them so reduced that they seem like squarish pillars. Within, the chambers are always arranged in groups of two vaulted galleries, one behind the other.

The stone of the region is brittle and consequently difficult to work, and the buildings are covered either with stucco, modeled into life-size figures and painted, or with facings of large thin slabs carved in relief. Examples of these are shown on *Pl. 79* and *Pl. 91, fig. a.* Holmes notes the lavish use of color both inside and out. Black, white, blue, two shades of red, yellow, and green are visible, with traces of repainting. The plain surfaces of inner walls also show signs of having been tinted or decorated in colored geometric designs.

An especially involved plan can be observed in the Palace Group (*Pl. 26, fig. a*). It stands on a platform mound, measuring 30 feet at its greatest height and about 200 by 225 feet across the top.[49] The buildings inclose four sunken courts, and the whole complex seems to have been surrounded, except on the south, by a double gallery, divided into a number of chambers. Frequent doorways give access to these rooms on both the inner and outer sides, and occasional connecting doors are cut through the central partition. This is also pierced by a series of trefoil openings through the vault section, an unusual construction, best visible in the next plate. All the lintels were of wood, and their collapse has greatly damaged the façades.

Fig. b shows the west face of House A. On the relatively broad ramp, as well as on the pierlike sections of the substructure, large human figures are carved in relief. Panels of incised glyphs alternate with the carvings and appear also on the risers of a few of the steps.

More or less in the center of the group, on a base about 30 feet square, stands the remarkable three-story tower, one of the most unusual constructions in pre-Columbian architecture (*fig. a*, right center). A massive central pier contains a stone stairway only about 20 inches wide. Each story consists of a narrow gallery around this center block.

Towers, both square and round, occur, though infrequently, in other regions.

The Caracol at Chichen Itzá has an ascending ramp around a circular inner column, and, in the Andean Area, the grave towers, or *chulpas,* are somewhat similar in shape. In the Southwest, some of the Cliff-dwellers built tower-like constructions which were supported on one side by the cave wall.

The temples of the Sun, the Cross, and the Foliated Cross are all small gems of Maya architecture. They stand together but each on its own base, facing a quadrangular court across the ravine from the Palace. Their substructures are spreading and relatively low.

In *Pl. 27, fig. a,* the ruined Temple of the Cross is seen, the outer façade of which has collapsed, leaving only the stumps of stuccoed piers and revealing the inner wall and entrance to the sanctuary. Débris is piled almost to the spring-line of the vaults, and it should be remembered that the vertical lower walls rise about as high as the arch, that is, a little over 10 feet.

The model shown in *fig. b* gives a clearer idea of the structures. All three appear to have had triple doorways in the front with the remaining wall surface devoted to decorative stucco reliefs. The sloping frieze sections offered an excellent opportunity for bold flowing design, and elaborate roof-combs fittingly crowned the edifices. This feature here consists of two walls slanting toward each other, as at Tikal, but the mass was so lightened as to form only a trellis, a background for figures and other ornaments molded from stucco. Stones have been discovered projecting from the building which may have served as steps to the summit. Other jutting pieces were fixed in the masonry as support for the larger masses of stucco, much as wood or wire forms are used by a sculptor to-day. The height of temple and roof-comb is about 35 feet.

The inner corridor of each of the three temples is divided by transverse walls into three rooms. The middle one contains the "sanctuary" or tablet chamber, constructed against the back wall like a small building, with outer frieze, projecting cornices, wooden lintel, and vaulted inner space. Here were found, set into the walls, the magnificent tablets of limestone, from which the temples derived their names. Upon each is carved a different central symbol, officiating priests, and columns of glyphs. They will be discussed in greater detail under sculpture. (See *Pl. 75.*)

The thick outside walls are pierced with small T-shaped apertures, one or two to each chamber, doubtless for ventilation. The V-shaped concrete mass which forms the sides of the vaults is also cut through, above the partition walls, with large windows shaped like keyholes. All these features have great decorative value, serving not only to lighten the weight of the building but to increase and diffuse the illumination of the interior. Their function as ventilators will be appreciated especially by those who have experienced the suffocating humidity of inclosed quarters in the tropics.

Although the temples at Palenque are quite similar to one another in their construction and artistic conception, individuality and variety are apparent in each, and the effect, though homogeneous, is far from monotonous. Nowhere in Palenque has one the impression of mass production.

Louis J. Halle, Jr., explorer and naturalist, gives a just summing-up in his recent book. "The temples of Palenque . . . are exquisite rather than imposing; refined, rather than massive. They are quite content with the earth they stand on, and do not, like their predecessors, reach for the sky. Like precious jewels, they are beautiful and complete in themselves. . . . The earlier gods (if they are gods) in the sculptures of Tikal, Copan, Quiriguá seem to represent great natural forces, the forces that caused the maize to grow and the rain to fall; these gods, here at Palenque, are the members of an elegant aristocracy that rules gracefully over the destinies of man. There is a touch of courtliness about them that you do not find in their more barbaric forerunners." [42]

PIEDRAS NEGRAS

A day's ride by mule up the Usumacintla River, which separates Mexico and Guatemala, brings one deeper into the country of precipitous gorges to Piedras Negras, a site discovered much later than Palenque and one of primary importance. Some of the finest stone carving of the Old Empire, discussed under sculpture, comes from this city. The buildings are generally in a very bad state of preservation, but the excavations of the University of Pennsylvania have revealed interesting architectural details.

The site shows much rebuilding, as well as frequent minor changes in the substructures, entrances, and stairways. Sometimes as many as five separate layers were superimposed. Very heavy rear walls suggest the use of roof-combs, although the lack of débris indicates that these may have been dismantled later. One building (J-29) shows a narrow entrance hall and raised sanctuary reminiscent of Temple 22 at Copan. The vault seems not to have made its appearance here until quite late, roughly in the 7th century.

The terraced substructures at Piedras Negras are elaborate in plan with rounded and inset corners, raised panels, projecting buttresses, and coffered sections. Remnants of gigantic masks, one 4½ feet high and 9 wide, testify to the type of ornamentation.

The series of built-in platforms and carved "thrones" within the palaces indicate that these edifices served ceremonial purposes. There are no signs of fire or domesticity in them, while masonry platforms on the edge of the city suggest foundations there for the living quarters of the hierarchy.[120]

RIO BEC

In the region of the New Empire, between the 7th and 10th centuries, an architectural style very different from that of the most splendid period of the Old Empire is evident. Changed environments and contact with other nations left their imprint on the Maya; besides, any artistic activity that lasts for centuries undergoes a natural evolution. Certain organic elements which had in the beginning functional importance became purely decorative. Technical difficulties which at first limited the expansion of architecture were eliminated, and the inclination and talent of the builder turned toward new possibilities and new problems.

Until recently the southeastern section of the Yucatan Peninsula was very little known. Maps published at the beginning of the present century still defined as "Territory of Independent Indians" the region which today covers parts of Yucatan and Campeche. In 1908 Maurice de Périgny found on the border between the states of Campeche and Quintana Roo an ancient city which he named Rio Beque, after the stream that ran near by. In 1912 the Peabody Museum of Harvard University sent an expedition into the same territory under Dr. R. E. Merwin, seconded by Clarence L. Hay. Another group of ruins was found a quarter mile distant from that of Périgny and the two were distinguished from each other by calling them Rio Bec A and B in the order of their discovery.

The newer site achieved considerable importance. *Pl. 28* shows the building of Rio Bec B and a model of its theoretical reconstruction. The material is here rubble, faced with a veneer of precisely cut limestone, as is usual in Maya building, and the walls were covered with plaster, now present only in sparse fragments. But the difference in style when compared with that of the Early Period is seen at a glance. It does not stand on a monumental base. On three sides it rises directly from the ground and only in front of the entrance, which faces east, is there a terrace, in this case about 5 feet high and 35 long.

The structure is actually of the palace type, but the eye is deceived by its most outstanding feature, the two towers 55 feet high at the corners of the façade. In contrast to the tower in Palenque, these contain no rooms and their only function apparently is to serve monumentality. Huge masks of stone covered with stucco are applied on the frieze sections and above them rises a small roof-comb. A steep flight of stairs leads from the terrace straight up the face of each. The door at the top is blind, and the angle of the stairs (only eight degrees from the perpendicular) so sharp that even the Maya Indian with his wild-cat tread would have been unable to ascend them; only a bird could have hopped upon them.

Thus the imagination of the builders incorporated the old tradition of a steep substructure and a temple on top, complete with sculptured frieze and roof-comb, into their new style, transforming the former complex edifice into a purely decorative feature with little reduction of scale. Structure II at Horniguero shows a similar artistic scheme. Such a monumental presentation as here pictured is rare, though we shall later see miniature replicas of dwelling houses used to embellish the façades of larger buildings, as at Labná and Uxmal.

To the side of and a little behind the towers, stone trellises, single vertical walls, stand side by side on the roof (*fig. b*). Unlike the roof-combs at Palenque, they do not run the entire length of the building; they comprise a decorative screen rather than the heavy double-walled "headdress" of the Old Empire. The human figures, over life size, applied in stucco, are effectively brought out against the perforated background. By comparing the roof-combs on the towers, which reproduced the earlier type, it will be seen that the screenlike constructions in the center of the building are deliberate modifications for a new effect.

The difference in length between the east and west sides, which are more than 84 feet long, amounts to only an inch. This accuracy may be taken as evidence of the technical skill of the Maya builder, and when a structure shows greater asymmetry, we may assume that the divergence was intentional.

There is an entrance on each of three sides, the back being a solid wall. Rio Bec B contains six rooms. All are vaulted with the corbeled arch and are about 16 feet high, relatively spacious. The grille-work panels on either side of the doors, the high foundation incorporated as an integral part of the building, the absence of stone steps before the doorways are features which recur in other sites in Yucatan.

Since no stelae and little pottery have been found at Rio Bec B, it is difficult to assign a date to it. Nevertheless, it can be roughly dated between the 8th and 10th centuries.

The site was characterized by enough individuality to attract further investigation. The next expedition relocated Rio Bec A and added other important ruins to its survey, but the quarter mile which was given as the distance from one site to the other proved a vast one in the jungle, for Rio Bec B has never been found again. The jungle is indeed a jealous guardian of its mysteries.[45]

On the threshold of the 11th century—and here it is impossible not to recall by contrast contemporary Europe with its barren gloomy buildings and its attenuated sculptures—the Maya civilization entered its final flowering, centered at this time in the northernmost part of the Yucatan Peninsula. Towns, hitherto provincial, attained importance and grew into artistic centers. The Toltecs, pressed by invasions in the north, were moving from the high plateau of Mexico, and their influence, both good and bad, becomes increasingly evident in the culture of Yucatan.

There can be no doubt that the era, which came into being with the League of Mayapan, brought new and noteworthy elements into Maya architecture. The flamboyant spirit that dominated the architecture of the Old Empire changes and, in many cases, the stylistic effects of the New seem, in comparison, calculated. New plastic figures are introduced into the decoration and there is a change in the general proportions of the buildings. We see rambling edifices replacing the tightly woven structures of the older regions and incidental ornament instead of systematic elaboration. These new building influences are apparent throughout Yucatan, as well as on the East Coast. The fact that they are often puzzlingly diverse and do not always seem to fit the general scheme of Toltec attributes may be ascribed to the presence of scattered tribes from southern Mexico, dislocated in the general out-surge.[154]

From a constructional point of view, many technical difficulties of the Old Empire were overcome, resulting finally in thinner walls and more spacious interiors. Probably the greatest innovation for the Maya Area was the introduction of the column, and its use as functional as well as decorative element should be noted. It was a relatively late achievement in pre-Columbian architecture. In the Mexican Area we have seen the great monolithic shafts at Mitla; the Huaxtec and Totonac regions also had columns, but put together from small chipped stones imbedded in mortar. Its use in the New Empire, however, was never universal, and it did not appear in Yucatan until long after the Maya had settled there. While nearly all the seacoast sites have this feature, only about ten of the very many investigated in other regions of Yucatan boast it.[67]

Had it been known to the builders of the Early Period, Maya architecture would have produced very different manifestations. But the time from its appearance to the arrival of the Spaniards was too short for a culture to revolutionize and transform the basic principles of its architecture. Besides solving the problem of space inside the building, it made wider entrances possible and was sometimes employed to support corners. Engaged, it furnished a new decorative motif for slenderizing the massive piers and breaking the wall surfaces.

The buildings of the New Empire were often very large, with many rooms arranged on several levels. Stairs were dramatically placed; from first to last, the imposing effect of the broad stairway remained one of the most characteristic features of Maya building. Portal arches came into use, and stone lintels sometimes replaced wooden ones, especially on the outside.

On the façades, geometric patterns appear, often the result of the conventionalization of symbolic animal shapes, and monster-masks, chiefly of the Rain-god with his projecting hooked snout, rise in tiers on walls or corners or decorate the panels above the entrances. The old and the newly acquired style elements were condensed, compressed into an ornamental system. The free-flowing curve of the old Maya is occasionally seen, but in general the designs are angular in line. Human figures appear as elements of decoration in the friezes, as atlantes holding cornices or altar tables (see *Pl. 93, fig. a*).

The general custom of erecting stelae at the termination of a definite time period had been abandoned in the Old Empire after 889, giving way, perhaps, to records in the form of manuscripts and codices. For this reason, the dating of the sites in the New Empire is at present often more precarious than in the older regions.

TULUM

Tulum, the principal settlement on the East Coast of Yucatan, was first described by Stephens, who tells in his lively yet exact manner how he and his companions battled there with impossible conditions, not the least of which was a plague of mosquitoes. The Temple of the Frescoes, discussed later, was stumbled upon by Mr. Catherwood and Dr. Cabot just as the party was packed and ready to turn its back on the infected spot. Unwilling to leave the new find unrecorded, they prolonged their stay until good drawings and a precise description could be made.

The first striking feature of the city is its situation. It lies at the edge of the sea on a precipitous cliff about 40 feet high that forms a natural wall 1300 feet long on one side (*Pl. 29, fig. a*). From the water, the site is imposing, and we may well suppose that Tulum was that "city as big as Seville" mentioned in the first reports of the *conquistadores*. Many important cities in Yucatan were fortified—an innovation in Maya city-planning, the result of the general conflict of the times.[67] Here we find not only the natural bulwark utilized for defense but a long stone wall about 20 feet thick and from 15 to 20 high built to inclose the city on the other three sides. (See also *Pl. 301, fig. b.*)

Archaeological evidence points to the colonization of the coast of Yucatan between the 5th and 7th centuries, and it would appear that by 560 Tulum was settled. Then comes a hiatus with no identifiable remains. The greatest period of Tulum seems to fall during the 13th and 14th centuries, and the great wall is dated early in that epoch.

The largest edifice, called the Castillo, is illustrated in *fig. b*. Including the two wings, it measures 100 feet across the base. Originally it appears to have been a rectangular structure of the palace type built on a low platform, the ends of which now form the two side wings. The ceiling is flat, laid on cross-beams in the manner used at Mitla, and composite round stone columns, capped with square abacuses, support the entrance. Later the center of this building was filled in to carry the weight of the upper edifice, and a grand stairway, 30 feet wide, was superimposed up the center of the still broader original steps. The heavy buttress at the back of the structure is also impressive.

The upper section is interesting for its bottle-shaped inner vaulting, common in Tulum and in some other East Coast sites, and for the entrance columns that represent a rattlesnake, with head recumbent and tail supporting the lintel and cornice. This is a new feature in Maya architecture, but as Chichen Itzá has the finest of the type, it will be illustrated there. (See *Pl. 40, fig. a* and *Pl. 42, fig. b.*) In the recesses above the doorway separate ornaments were placed. Two corridors, each 26 feet long, make up the interior of the building.

The other structure of special importance at Tulum is the Temple of the Frescoes that was discovered by Stephens's party. *Pl. 30, fig. a* shows the west, or main, façade, and *fig. b,* a model of the same, a little more from the side so as to include the hypothetical wooden stairway arrangement. This temple also went through several architectural transformations. The original contained one chamber only, about 7 feet by 11, three sides of which were later inclosed by a colonnaded passage so that now the façade measures 27 feet. Between the columns can be seen the remnants of frescoes on the main wall (once the outside), better preserved than most because of their protected position (see *Pl. 265, fig. b*). The upper room was a later addition.

Study of the profile, beginning with the low step on which the whole sturdy structure rests, reveals a remarkable difference in verticalities. This outline is governed in part by the bottle-shaped inner vault, the spring-line of which comes much lower than that of the usual corbeled arch of the earlier period. The outward slope of the exterior wall is actually an element of strength as it tends to balance the interior projection.

The sunken stucco panel over the doorway, with its figure of the Diving-god executed on a framework of stone, is a frequent feature in Tulum and other East Coast sites. Abundant mural painting also seems to have been common. Dr. Lothrop finds general similarities in the frescoes to the rendition of certain Maya codices. Another point of affiliation might be found in the recessed panels with broken or modified cornices, such as those at Monte Alban in which pottery figurines were set (see *Pl. 15, fig. d*). The plastic human features of the huge faces on the corners are as yet unrecorded elsewhere. Neatness of finish and the lavish use of color add up to a picturesque impression, in spite of the somewhat peripheral character of the decoration.

Fifty-four ruins have been counted within the walled inclosure of Tulum, as well as two small buildings, like watchtowers, on the walls. Beyond the barrier lie many more which have as yet never been approached or described.

These walls have been the scene of many battles. After the unrecorded fights of pre-Columbian days, the site was occupied three times by the troops of the Mexican Government in an attempt to subdue the independent Indians of the region. In this case the wall kept the invaders in, beleaguered from the side of the jungle by their intended quarry. Peace was made in 1913 and the rights of the natives were acknowledged. Since 1920 several chicle concessions have been granted in the district, one of which has established headquarters near the site of Tulum.

SAYIL

Approximately in the same geographical latitude as Tulum but across the peninsula in the western part of Yucatan lie the ruins of the great Palace of Sayil. According to tradition, the city was already a powerful center at the time of the founding of the League of Mayapan.

The edifice (*Pl. 31, fig. a*), one of the most spreading in Yucatan, measures 275 feet across the front and about 130 deep. It is made up of three tiers, each in turn set back and resting on a solid core well within the outer shell of vaulted chambers. A broad stairway at the front of the building leads to the top of the third story, and at the rear is another, a later addition. More than eighty rooms were counted in the one building, some over 30 feet in length and nearly 16 wide —an unusual span for the Maya corbeled arch.

The ground floor, now completely in ruins, may have been elaborately decorated (Stephens says so), while the top story apparently was left quite plain. This, however, serves to throw the finely proportioned second story into even sharper relief. Here the column, as decorative as well as functional element, is repeated and modulated, bringing to the essentially massive façade of Maya architecture an open, almost airy touch. The single shafts in the unusually wide openings are 6½ feet high, bulging at the center, and crowned with a square abacus. Compact rows of slender engaged columns make up what wall space there is. We have just seen the use of columns as entrance supports in smaller buildings at Tulum. Rather a technical solution there, here this architectural element is applied with greater freedom and subtlety and becomes the striking feature of the building.

Composite stone masks and other carvings are applied on the frieze in the center and over the two doorways. A lively serpent with gaping jaws and diminutive body can be identified, as well as a diving figure in the same posture as that at Tulum, here terminating in a square grotesque mask. The column motif is repeated between the carvings and separates the horizontal lines in the moldings.

It is possible that this suave motif, used here so effectively, was derived from the wood construction of the primitive houses of the common folk. These houses were usually built with a thatched roof and rounded ends and had only two doors, one on each long side, which furnished good ventilation.

Fig. b shows a present-day house, the wall of which, formed of small logs, harks back to ancient tradition. A number of suggestions for the graceful façade of the Palace of Sayil might have been derived from the forerunner of this type.

LABNÁ

Not far from Sayil are situated the ruins of Labná, a contemporary city. The Great Palace, the west section of which is illustrated in *Pl. 32, fig. b,* shows a certain similarity to Sayil, with its columnettes and masks, but even more to

Uxmal that will follow. It consisted of several stories and stands on a podium almost 20 feet high, about 400 long, and 250 deep, facing a vast plaza.

Groups of neatly tied columns in relief set off the doorways and are put to effective use at the corners. The serpent motif appears in a new interpretation in the vertical panels on the left. At the angle of the frieze (right center of picture) projects a serpent's head with gaping jaws from which a human head emerges. This is another favorite motif in northern Yucatan, notably in the much photographed fragment from Uxmal.

The stones of the composite frieze section are combined with much surface decoration, such as incised rosettes and frets in relief, which makes the work still more elaborate. At the base of the building appear short cylindrical elements, an endless spindle row.

The Labná Gateway (*fig. a*) furnishes an excellent example of the independent portal arch as used by the Maya in northern Yucatan. This photograph presents the side that faces the Palace court. The spring-line of the vault, on a level with the lower edge of the frieze, can be readily seen, and the eye follows the curving line of the rising stones to the top, where a broad but relatively thin slab bridges the gap. The span is about 13 feet. The lattice-work, scalloped zigzag motif, and stepped elements in the upper molding will be met frequently at other sites.

Above the two doorways, each of which leads to a small chamber, are replicas of the huts in which the populace lived. Shaped stones represent the peaked thatched roofs, even showing the ridgepole and the tuft above it. These niches, together with the doors and the tall arch, assist in producing a vertical effect rare in Maya building.

On the back, the Gateway is plainer and has no doorways. Two great composite frets decorate each side of the frieze with a pattern that is also used impressively on the Governor's Palace at Uxmal. (See *Pl. 36, fig. a.*)

Another view of Labná (*Pl. 33, fig. a*) shows the west façade of Structure XI of the Portal Group in the foreground, with a wall decoration of columnettes related to that shown on the preceding plate. The panels that appear on first glance to be masks are purely geometrical and are characterized by delicate tracery.

Beyond and above this structure, the sharp profile of another building demonstrates more clearly than any description the meaning of "flying façade." Here this highly decorative, unsupported construction rises on a line with the front wall to a height of 30 feet, and, according to Stephens, was covered with colossal figures and designs in stucco. At the neighboring site of Sabacche, a small temple (*fig. b*) has as its only ornament a flying façade with graceful lattice-work.

Fig. c takes us to Chichen Itzá, where the Red House (Casa Colorada) shows a more sturdy example, with mask panels flanked by frets as decoration. As in the preceding structure, the entire building is otherwise plain. A model (*fig. d*) offers a cross-section of the same edifice. It can be seen that in this case besides a flying façade there was a roof-comb, which was placed over the massive inner wall. The structure of the corbeled vaults is also well illustrated.

On cathedrals of the Late Romanesque in Europe a purely decorative screen-like wall serves similarly to enrich the building with sculptural and architectural embellishments.

KABAH

Kabah is a neighboring site which flourished at the same time as Labná and Sayil. The place is interesting, not so much for any structural differences it may present but on account of the splendid application of the mask as decorative feature.

Palace I at Kabah, a most unusual building, even among the great variety in Yucatan, stands on a low platform measuring over 150 feet across the front (*Pl. 34, fig. a*). It is in very bad condition and at one end has entirely collapsed, revealing a section of the inner structure, with smoothly dressed stone surfaces and a second narrower row of chambers behind the first. Remnants of a roof-comb, which Stephens describes as 15 feet high and 4 thick, are still visible, composed of well polished and evenly laid stone blocks that form an openwork step-fret.

A portion of the north wall about 25 feet long is in the best state of preservation (*fig. b*). Here we are confronted with an original idea. Six tiers of masks —one in the foundation, three in the middle wall, and two in the frieze—cover the surface of the building.

As a result of their serialization, the uniformity of the masks is more than usually apparent. Each shares ears and earplugs with its neighbor except in the bottom row, where each figure with its own two ears forms a broader unit than above, giving the illusion of greater weight at the base of the building and, incidentally, preventing a too rigid effect in the repetition.

Monotony is also avoided by the plastic contours of the individual masks. The curling snouts jut far beyond the façade. Each half of the face is composed on a semicylindrical unit, while the earplugs and lateral ornaments provide a flat vertical surface. The mouths are hollow, as are the eye sockets, and outlined by jagged teeth sharpened by the shadows behind them. The conical stones set into the cavities for eyeballs give the faces animation.

As there are no lines of demarcation between the rows of masks, the moldings produce the only horizontal trend in the façade. The medial molding especially is bold and elaborate, its scalloped and zigzag band ingeniously put together of smaller pieces of stone with space enough between to allow for the added play of light and shade on the pattern. This design impressed Stephens and Catherwood to such an extent that they used it on the binding of their *Incidents of Travel in Yucatan,* and in homage to these pioneer explorers it was also chosen to border the book jacket of this survey. As Stephens writes: "The cornice running over the doorways . . . , tried by the severest rules of art recognized among us, would embellish the architecture of any known era, and, amid a mass of barbarism, of rude and uncouth conceptions, it stands as an offering by American builders worthy of the acceptance of a polished people." [140]

MAYAPAN

Mayapan, which was the religious and administrative center of the League of Mayapan, shows evidence of lengthy occupation, but most of its architecture seems to date from the early 13th century. An uncommon feature for Maya cities is the great wall, five and a half miles in length, which surrounded it.[150] Practically destroyed in the course of the devastating wars that ended its period of domination in 1461, the city fell into such complete ruin that even Stephens found little to be recorded. One circular building is reported to have stood until the early part of the 19th century, when it was struck by lightning and demolished.[109]

UXMAL

Certain legends place the beginnings of Uxmal in the 5th or 6th centuries and make it a center of the first Toltec immigrants to the region.

Pl. 35, fig. a pictures the highest structure on the site, called the House of the Dwarf, or Adivino, meaning "the soothsayer." The name is legendary and the same edifice is also known as the Temple of Kukulcan, the Maya name for the Great Feathered Serpent. The substructure measures some 240 feet long by 160 wide and rises at a very sharp angle to over 80 feet. Besides its height, the unusual elliptical form is immediately striking. Some of the even slabs are still in place, attesting to the skill with which the rounded corners were faced.

Two splendid stairways ascend on opposite sides. The broader one, said to have more than two hundred steps (see *Pl. 305, fig. a*), leads up the east face to the topmost platform, upon which stands a rectangular building with three chambers. It is interesting that the central room does not face the stair, as one might expect, but opens on the opposite side toward the west. From this vantage point the panorama of the Uxmal region opens up, a vast level expanse of jungle bush. The rounded contours of artificial mounds, overgrown and bristling with green, roughly mark the extent of the city. Depressions toward the northwest indicate the sites of former wells, now clogged with vegetation and dangerously infested with malaria.

Just in front of the doorway, another building, about 22 feet square, juts from the side, as if grafted onto the temple-base, its roof on a level with the upper esplanade. A narrower and perhaps even more precipitous stairway leads about two-thirds up the substructure to its entrance. In the interior, two chambers are set one behind the other, in the manner of Tikal. The façade of this temple, as well as the supporting walls, is a mass of elaborate composite stone ornamentation, showing an enormous mask above the doorway, flanked by tiers of smaller ones.[49] The broken surfaces of the decoration must have formed a stunning contrast to the smooth facing of the base and the austerity of the building above it.

The loftiness of the structure has led to the opinion that it was a sacrificial temple. Intact, in the full brilliance of its barbaric colors, with the splendid figures of its high priests moving on the stairways and along the narrow platform, it doubtless presented an impressive spectacle for the people gathered below.

Across a small court from this great pile lie four separate buildings of the palace type, grouped to form a square (left in *fig. a*). These were called by the Spaniards the House of the Nuns, a name derived, according to one version, from the cell-like chambers of the complex—ninety in all—and, to another, from the elaborate stone lattices of the friezes and the delicate carvings which reminded the conquerors of the lace work of their nuns. The entire complex stands on a large artificial platform, about 15 feet high, and the irregular inner court measures about 258 feet long by 214 wide.

After the visit of Fray Antonio de Ciudad Real to the "very renowned edifices of Uxmal" in 1588, he wrote the following description of the Nunnery.

"The jambs were of stone carved with great delicacy. On the façades of the building, both on those which face the plaza or courtyard, as well as on those which face outward, there are many figures of serpents, idols and shields, many screens or latticework and many other carvings which are beautiful and fine, especially if one look at them from a distance like a painting of Flanders, and they are all carved from the same kind of stone. In the middle of this building a great arch is made so that it takes in all the depth of this building and therefore it is the entrance to the courtyard or the above-mentioned plaza. It would appear that this entrance had been plastered and that on the plaster painting had been made in blue, red and yellow color, since even now some of them remain and can be seen." [124]

Each of the four buildings is quite different in ornamentation. Notable are the small models of houses set into the friezes of the north and south structures and, on the west building, the great serpents carved in the round that wind in and out of the pattern for the entire length of the façade, bringing animation to the geometric design of the frieze (*Pl. 36, fig. c*). The east building (*Pl. 37, fig. b*) is unusual in that the stone lattice-work runs around all four sides. The large V-shaped motifs, representing double-headed serpents, are subtly spaced in relation to the doors. A tier of Rain-god masks crowns the center entrance, and the corners bear superb masks of the same deity, so placed that the profile with the great hooked nose projects at the angle (*Pl. 36, fig. b*).

Each building is raised on its own podium, so that the towering flying façade of the north structure seems at a distance to merge with the comparatively low building opposite and to form a single colossal and magnificent façade (*Pl. 37, fig. a*).

South of the House of the Nuns, two crumbling parallel mounds indicate the site of a ball court. Beyond this lies an immense rectangular platform, about 600 feet long and 5 high. A second and smaller terrace with practically the same contours rises from this, like a gigantic tray, upon which is set, on the third and smallest podium, the House of the Governor (left, *Pl. 35, fig. b*). The name, like all the others at Uxmal, is a creation of the Spaniards, based rather on imagination than fact and inspired no doubt by its grandeur.

The plan of the structure falls into three parts: a central section and two wings, separated by two transverse arches, 20 feet high by 25 deep, now walled up (*Pl. 36, fig. a*). Eleven doorways break the façade. All the lintels were of *sapote* beams, 8 feet long, 18 to 20 inches wide, and 12 to 14 inches thick.

Stephens writes that at the time of his visit in 1839 nearly all the wood was in place, successfully supporting the great weight of stone above it,[140] but when we saw the site nearly a century later, many of the beams had fallen to decay, carrying part of the composite sculptured frieze with them and giving the building a dilapidated appearance. Since then, the Mexican Government has undertaken extensive conservation. In the opinion of many, the House of the Governor was the best preserved structure in the region even before the recent work began.

The lower part of the walls is faced with masterly cut stones, uniform in size and so skillfully shaped and joined that no mortar can be seen between them. The elaborate composite frieze, 10 feet high, runs all the way around the building, a distance of 720 feet.[49] Here the sculptured motifs are arranged into a gigantic counterpoint. Coffered frets on a lattice ground follow one pattern, and a line of masks in an immense meander crosses and recrosses them. The serpent bars appear, supporting rows of glyphs—rare in Uxmal—and small human figures crown the doorways.

At the right and somewhat behind the Governor's Palace, on a sort of spur of the second terrace, stands a very dilapidated building called the House of the Turtles, from the realistic carvings of this reptile worked into the upper cornice (center foreground, *Pl. 35, fig. b*). The sole decoration of the frieze consists of a row of engaged columns in corduroy effect, also seen at Sayil and Labná.

Roughly west of this group an impressive serrated roof-comb with nine gables looms over the thick vegetation (right background). This belongs to the north building of another quadrangle group, now practically demolished. The edifice bears the name of the House of the Doves, as the perforations suggest a dovecote. The manner of construction, however, and the stones projecting at various points indicate that it was a backing for an elaborate stucco relief, remnants of which were noted by Stephens. A transverse arch divides the structure, forming an entrance to the inner court, as in the Nunnery. The entire north wall has collapsed, revealing an interesting cross-section of Maya vault construction.

This patrician city, Uxmal, is characterized by its homogeneity. Although not ranged in streets, the buildings are well placed in relation to each other. The whole city was set on artificial platforms, and the courts and connecting ways were paved with finely polished cement. A native limestone of soft yellow or pinkish-gray tone was used throughout. The masonry is of uniformly fine finish, and excellent craftsmanship is also shown in the careful treatment of the foundations and in the delicate fillet-moldings. Although familiar elements are used in the composite carved decorations, the effect is varied and individual. The broad entablature sections generally cover almost half the wall space and, with their boldly projecting cornices, dominate the façade like splendid feather head-dresses.

CHICHEN ITZÁ

The name, Chichen Itzá, meaning "the mouth of the wells of the Itzá," has reference to the two natural pools, or *cenotes,* within the confines of the settlement, a factor which made the site invaluable in a region where there is no surface water.

The buildings of Chichen are the most understandable for the European-trained eye. They have about them a certain lightness that has not been met before. The architectural line is less complicated; the ornament, considerably simplified and more sparingly used. It would be difficult to define how much of this was due to outside influence and how much to the natural evolutionary development through the thousand or more years which are covered by Maya architecture. The divergence and variety of ornamental detail are proof of the constantly moving spirit which urged the Maya builders onward during the centuries.

Chichen Itzá shows great diversity in building types. Some features, familiar from the Old Empire, reappear here used with assurance, while other early characteristics are found diluted in concept. On the other hand, vigorous new elements make their appearance to take their place beside the old. The Nunnery (*Pl. 38*), the Red House (*Pl. 33*), and the House of the Three Lintels (*Pl. 39*) are identified as belonging to that early era when the great cities of the Old Empire were still thriving. From the late 10th to the 13th centuries many new edifices were erected. By then new technical achievements had greatly reduced the time necessary to complete a single building.

During and after this period, Chichen Itzá was a great pilgrim center. One of its *cenotes* was deemed sacred to the Rain-god, and on certain days of the year, particularly in a time of drought, tribes from far and near came to petition favor for their crops. As a part of the ceremony, young girls and boys, festively attired and adorned with jewels, were sacrificed as messengers to the deity. Diving activities instituted by the late E. H. Thompson brought up jade, turquoise mosaics, gold and copper bells, copal incense, and fragments of unidentified objects which had been flung into the pool as offerings.[149]

As Chichen Itzá has been the most thoroughly investigated of all Maya sites within recent years, we shall confine ourselves, because of limited space, to the main features of architecture interesting from our point of view—that of the art-historian. For further information, we direct the reader to the various publications on the excavations.

Among the structures to be discussed here, the Nunnery (*Pl. 38, fig. a*) is generally classified as the oldest. It is, perhaps, the most massive of them all, not only in the actual stone involved but in its compact appearance. The substructure consists of a huge solid block, 228 feet across the front, 115 deep, and 32 high. Its chief grandeur is the monumental stairway, 56 feet wide, which, at the time of subsequent alteration, was continued across the face of the original structure to a new edifice on top. Maudslay shows that the balustrades were once embellished by a line of projecting sculptured shapes, like conventionalized tongues, curling at the lower ends.[81] The original building, which is of the palace type, has a slanting entablature section, reminiscent of Palenque, but here left unornamented, while the walls below it carry the decoration. The enlargement was effected by filling in the central hall of this building so as to support the weight of the second smaller structure above it.

On the ground level, to the east of the substructure (left in the illustration), are a wing and two separate annexes, which, from their decoration, are judged to be from about the same period as the main block. *Fig. b* shows the façade of this L-shaped wing, some 35 feet wide and covered with elaborate masks. The ornate moldings, the upper quite different from the lower, are so heavy that the entablature section seems to overhang the lower walls. Even the flaring coping stones are carved.

The treatment of the doorway, which suggests a serpent's head, is strikingly original. In the center of the frieze and within a sort of aureole is a seated statue with flowing feather headdress. Two serpents form a frame about him. Colors originally enhanced the effect. In this entrance with all its details, we feel a liveliness akin to that of Romanesque stone work in Europe.

Of the two unattached annexes which complete the complex, the one visible at the right in *fig. b,* called the *Iglesia,* or "church," is the smaller but by far the more lavishly decorated. It is about 38 feet by 14 and 20 feet high. With its walls leaning slightly outward and the lower surface a band of plain masonry, the structure seems top-heavy with carving.

About three miles from the Nunnery, in Chichen Viejo, or Old Chichen, stands the House of the Three Lintels, surrounded now by jungle bush (*Pl. 39, fig. b*). This serene little palace is built without platform on a low foundation ornamented with lattice-work. As the level of the floor is about three feet from the ground, it has been suggested that wooden steps or a short ladder was used for the ascent to the doors. The three entrances, two of which have stone lintels inscribed with carving, lead into separate vaulted chambers. The middle wall section is plain, as is usual in the later period, and an engaged column is set at each corner. A snake motif, the same zigzag that delighted Stephens at Kabah, runs all the way around the house, bringing a welcome contrast in the otherwise restrained ornamentation.

The structure has variety in its horizontal and vertical lines and must be visualized as strongly colored. The Maya architect took the effects of *plein-air* into full consideration, reckoning with the brilliant lighting of the tropics to show off his building to advantage.

The Caracol (*Pl. 39, fig. a*), one of the rare round buildings of the Maya Area, dates from the Mexican period of the city. It was probably connected with the rites of the Wind-god, Kukulcan, just as the round structures of Mexico are associated with his Mexican counterpart, Quetzalcoatl.[109] At the same time, it is possible that the building may have served as an observatory. Inside, two vaulted circular galleries inclose a masonry core, within which lies the spiral ascent that gives the building its name—"snail shell" or "winding stairway." There is a small chamber on top, now almost in shambles, with a stone-lined passage facing due west. Carefully checked investigations have shown that a diagonal drawn from the right jamb of the inner door to the left one of an outside aperture marks the line along which the sun sets on March 21st and September 23rd, or the vernal and autumnal equinoxes.[117]

The tower itself measures 36 feet in diameter and about 43 in height. Skillfully posed on its two irregular platforms, it reveals an architectural maturity that recalls the famous round structures of Rome and Ravenna. Visually its most arresting feature aside from its form is a five-part molding, the double flaring bands of which seem to be tied in by the fillet, as if by a ribbon. A fringe of serpents and figures in panels constituted other ornamentation on the walls. Around the edge of the upper terrace, incense burners in the form of human heads with hollow eyes and mouths were set along the coping. We can visualize the tower as it stood intact in the velvety tropical night, its curving walls illumined by the glow of burning copal.

The sacred ball game played an important part in the life of this religious center. Chosen from among the physically outstanding youths, the ball players were accorded special privileges, and, when victorious, were overwhelmed with gifts from the ruler and nobility. The great Ball Court (*Pl. 40, fig. b*), 120 feet wide and flanked by two massive walls, 274 feet long by 28 high, formed an impressive stadium. Compare the different types of ball-court construction at Monte Alban (*Pl. 14*), Copan (*Pl. 20*), and Chichen Itzá to see how the game varied.

On one end of the east wall, which forms a narrow esplanade in front of it, and overlooking the Court, stands the Temple of the Tigers (*fig. a*)—the only one of this complex to be reconstructed. A corner is visible at the extreme right of the lower illustration. The name derives from the confused Spanish term *tigre;* the "Temple of the Jaguars" would be more exact, as there were no tigers in America. The only opening of the temple is toward the arena, and the approach is by way of an insignificant stair at one side. In front there is very little space, and we may surmise that the building was used only in ceremonies connected with the game—perhaps a box for the hierarchy.

The profile of the building is quite different from that which we have grown accustomed to regard as typically Maya. Carved serpent bodies cling to the edge of the podium and their gaping heads project from the balustrade. The large stone blocks that strengthen the corners and the high battered base of the temple building extending almost halfway up the sides of the doorway are rather suggestive of Mitla. Two massive serpent columns divide the entrance, their heads resting on the floor, while the bodies rise vertically beneath the lintel and the tails curve first forward and then upward across the façade, terminating in a fantasy design of conventionalized rattles and plumes. They were once brightly painted and their deep-set eyes inlaid with obsidian or some colored substance. The plumes of the tail hide part of the carved frieze, which was, nevertheless, completely worked out.

The entablature section is not so sharply differentiated here as in most Maya buildings. A fine carved frieze of jaguars, approaching a circular shield in groups of two, extends clear around the building. Although the same motif is continuously repeated, the movement of the beasts is not stereotyped but fluent and differentiated enough to give a realistic impression. A similar motif, but executed with less distinction, was unearthed among the débris at Monte Alban.[24]

The jaguar frieze is framed by bands, upon which plumed serpent bodies intertwine about a row of symbolic disks. Above this, the entire upper portion is set back, a crest adorned with conventional snake designs, panels of disks, and small "spindle" columnettes. Maudslay speaks of an open fretwork, no longer extant, around the top of the building and a central ornament of three crossed arrows bound with a ribbon—a Mexican symbol.

Within there is a vaulted antechamber and an inner room, the stuccoed walls of which were covered with frescoes in lively yellow, red, brown, and blue, today almost obliterated (see *Pl. 263*). The jambs of the doorways consist of square engaged pillars, intricately carved in relief with figures in ceremonial dress.

The Temple of the Tigers is a shining example of the deliberation and assurance with which the Maya builders even of a late period used the decorative motifs handed down to them.

El Castillo (*Pl. 41*), sometimes called the Temple of Kukulcan, faces the straight lane that leads to the Sacred Well. The nine receding terraces that make up the substructure, some 75 feet high, successively diminish in height and the coffered design on each—suggestive of Monte Alban—is reduced proportionately. This subtle method of handling the terraces gives the whole structure an effect of lightness as well as exaggerated height. The stairways, extending beyond the base in typical Maya fashion, serve to emphasize the remarkable feeling that the building is rooted in the ground and stands poised like a tree. Two feet wider at the top than at the bottom, they appear even steeper than they are. (See *Pl. 304, fig. a.*)

A system of numbers is involved in the architecture. On each side of the temple-base, using the stairway as a dividing line, are two sets of nine terraces; this adds to eighteen, the number of months in the Maya calendar. There are four flights of ninety steps each, or three hundred and sixty in all, the number of days in the Maya year, as the short "month" of five days, used to balance the time-count, was considered unlucky and not "recognized."

The temple building itself is constructed with a heavy battered base. The entablature section no longer receives major attention and is adorned only by masks above each door. There are four entrances, oriented approximately to the four directions, with the broadest on the north divided by two gigantic serpent columns such as were seen in the Temple of the Tigers. Here, as well as in a number of other buildings at Chichen, a sort of fretwork rises out of the edge of the coping. The lintels were of *sapote* wood, all visible parts decorated with a delicate tracery of figures.

The pre-Maya temple-base at Uaxactun and the Toltec-Maya El Castillo both apply four stairways mounting the sides of a pyramidal construction. They are among the first and last creations of a continuously developing style which fed nevertheless from the same deep roots.

The interior arrangement of the temple of El Castillo offers a departure from the old. It is obvious that new conditions demanded greater interior space; the ritual was expanding, the cast becoming more numerous. The inner sanctuary, flanked by narrow galleries, is made more spacious by the use of three vaults supported on heavy *sapote* beams, which in turn were held by two massive carved pillars on a line with the door jambs.

Within the substructure of the Castillo were found almost intact a smaller base with only one stairway and a temple which had been filled in with rubble and covered when the new building was erected over it. The floor of the present structure is only three feet above the roof of the old. At the heart of the buried building, the jaguar throne illustrated on *Pl. 92* was discovered.

With its four similar sides the Castillo is the most dramatic building in Chichen Itzá. Its effect, however, is far beyond the theatrical; it was erected not for a passing night's entertainment, but for the eternal stage of Nature.

East of the Castillo lies a vast irregular quadrangle called the Court of the Thousand Columns. It was encompassed by a covered colonnade, roofed, like the inner sanctuary of the Castillo, by a series of vaults resting on beams. The square pillars which supported these were carved and brightly painted with life-size figures of armed warriors. The single profiles are individual, the movements varied, the costumes diverse, showing that even in a period of heightened activity no stencil was used for the designs. Enough color remains to give not only an idea of the dress and weapons of those days but also of the magnificence of this great open hall.

Standing on a spur of the colonnade, the Temple of the Warriors (*Pl. 42, fig. a*) represents the last high architectural period in Chichen Itzá. The resources of the Carnegie Institution of Washington and the ingenuity of its staff have made it possible to reconstruct this building out of a heap of débris.

Its stairway leads in an unbroken line through a cleverly constructed well in the colonnade vaulting to the top, where again, before a wide entrance, colossal serpent columns rise. Snake bodies are suggested on the ramps and terminate in fierce projecting heads. On each side of the stair at the top, small warrior statues stand with outstretched hands, the standard-bearers of ancient times, and before the portal reclines a sculptured figure of the type called Chacmool (see *Pl. 93, fig. b*).

As a result of the transformation in building technique, the temple, which has been reconstructed without the entablature zone and roof, is larger and more nearly square than earlier ones. Its walls are less massive than those of older buildings. Rain-god masks figure in the façade (*fig. b*), and serpents' heads in the round project from the plain wall surfaces with their spreading feather collars carved in relief.

The two chambers of the interior are about the same size, 61 feet by 29. In the first, the roof was supported by three transverse vaults; in the inner one, by five, placed at right angles to the others. Both rooms seem to have been painted with bright dadoes or impressive scenes (see *Pl. 263, fig. a*). Built-in masonry benches were revealed and altar slabs supported by small atlantean sculptured figures. During reconstruction, an earlier smaller temple was discovered, which had been filled in when the Temple of the Warriors was built.[94]

Chichen Itzá presents many changes in traditional Maya construction. Although the buildings became less massive, and therefore less durable, the interior space was greatly enlarged. The general outline acquires a plainer, more austere character. Decoration becomes diluted and more incidental. The style reminds one now of the Old Empire, now of the Mexican high plateau, now of the Zapotec region.

All this is an indication rather of transition than of degeneration. Although at the time of the Conquest such imposing cities as Uxmal and Chichen seem to have been deserted and Maya genius appears to have been at a low point, this does not necessarily mean a complete extinguishing of their creative and artistic capabilities. Just as in the Old World long periods of artistic stagnation were relieved by upward trends, in the land of the Maya their glorious tradition might have recovered enough to produce somewhere a third empire, had it not been torn asunder by impact with European civilization.

INTERLYING AREA

The present political boundaries of the Central American countries do not coincide with the prehistoric confines of their native peoples. East and south of the Guatemala border are the republics of Honduras and El Salvador. There the influence of the Maya and of the later migrants from southern Mexico, generally called the Pipils, is strongly visible, not so much in their scant architectural remains as in pottery and jade. Farther down, in Nicaragua, Costa Rica, and Panama, this gives way. The proximity of these lands to the South American continent made them more susceptible to tendencies from the south.

Architectural remnants of high artistic quality have not been found in these Isthmian regions up to the present day. It is possible that ruins of considerable importance may be discovered after further excavation. However, the *conquistadores* make no mention of any monumental architecture here comparable to that in the other areas.

In the applied arts, these people achieved much of consequence. A very positive artistic trend is prevalent in the pottery of all these countries and in the excellent metal-work wherever it appears.

ANDEAN AREA

The ruins of the Andean Area are concentrated chiefly in what is today Peru. In the coastal regions where there was much sand and clay, great edifices were constructed of adobe brick and clay blocks. In the mountains, stone, dressed and laid with amazing precision, was generally used.

While terraced substructures are the rule on the coast, in the highlands the temples and palaces rise from the ground. Nor do the remnants indicate exclusively buildings of religious or hieratic character. There are, in addition, fortified community dwellings of a type more advanced than found in the Southwest, and outspoken citadels appear both in the highlands and the coastal regions. Defense walls, infrequently met in any of the other areas, are a familiar feature here. The architectural differences between the ruins of the coastal regions from Ecuador to Chile and those in the mountain valleys and promontories of the Andes show how many tribes were working their way simultaneously toward a higher civilization when the coördinating skill of the Incas finally brought the whole territory under one head.

Most of the illustrations for this section will show structures built of perfectly shaped stone blocks, fitted with inexplicable skill without the use of mortar. Adobe and clay were also used, as well as rough stone laid in clay.

Bonded and locked joints are the rule here. Even in early phases of Tiahuanaco, copper cramps were employed. In some places, a sort of interior lock was fashioned, by means of which a groove in one block fitted over a corresponding protuberance in the other. All of these methods are especially efficacious in an earthquake region—as is the lack of mortar—and may account for the astonishing state of preservation of many of the ruins today.

The Andean Area brings a perfected line in the construction of rounded walls and corners, producing in many cases semicircular inclosures and even complete circles, as in the burial towers. The window, virtually non-existent in the Mexican and Maya areas although used in the Southwest, is also rare here, but niches of many types are frequent.

The less pretentious buildings, the huts of the common people, were put together of wood, reed, or adobe in the coastal regions, and of adobe, chipped stone, or stone blocks with and without mortar in the mountains. The roofs seem generally to have been thatched. The simple one-family dwelling remained throughout pre-Columbian times a modest abode. The great achievements of architecture in the Andean Area are the temples, palaces, and fortresses, which were at the same time the quarters of the priesthood, the nobility, civil and military officials, and their attendants.

After having seen the masterpieces of architecture in the Mexican and Maya areas, with their sometimes graceful, sometimes grandiose, always eloquent structures, one cannot escape the impression that Andean architecture is comparatively uncommunicative. In construction of their buildings, the talent of these intensely organized people was earthbound; nor did they often aspire to lavish and flamboyant decoration.

CHAN-CHAN

The northernmost section of the coastal region formed in pre-Inca times a kingdom, very rich and far advanced in the arts. Spanish historians tell us that the sovereign of these people was called the Grand Chimu, and that they were subdued by the Incas about four generations before the Conquest.

The first illustration on *Pl. 43* shows the ruins of the Chimu city, Chan-Chan, probably settled during the period between 800 and 1000, where the rivers Chicama and Moche form a very arable plain. It adjoins the present city of Trujillo, founded by Francisco Pizarro and named for his own birthplace in Spain.

The great extent of the ruins is evidence of the importance of Chan-Chan, which authorities accept as the capital of the wealthy Chimu people. The city covers about eleven square miles with four clearly defined "suburbs," or outlying districts, all encompassed by a high wall (see also *Pl. 302, fig. b*). It is constructed of adobe, which in the arid climate attained an almost concrete-like hardness. Districts of low rectangular houses alternate with vast terraced temple mounds, several hundred feet long and sometimes as much as 150 high.[139]

Irrigation for the cultivation of the land was highly developed. High in the mountains, an aqueduct led off the water of the Moche River and carried it along the valley on a lofty embankment, some sixty feet high, whence it was distributed into reservoirs and through smaller stone-lined channels across the plains. There were extensive gardens within the city itself, each with its irrigating canal.[77]

It is lamentable that time and treasure hunters have so devastated the city that it is difficult now to form an adequate picture of it. The enormous terraces upon which the temples stood are crumbling away, haphazardly tunneled through by reckless despoilers. The stuccoed and painted walls are in ruins. The roofs are gone, the verandas, once supported by the twisted trunks of trees, have vanished.

Fig. b shows a detail of the ornamentation applied on an adobe wall here. It is noteworthy that the patterns were always of small format and similar to the decorative motifs of the pottery, weaving, and metal-work. A Chimu design has always so much individuality that seldom can it be mistaken for one of another culture. The arabesques are made up chiefly of geometric elements, often conventionalized forms of birds and fish. The continuous flowing quality of the decoration shows perfection of technique, and by a change of pattern and composition in the more involved schemes, a monotonous effect is avoided.

PARAMONGA

The ruins of Paramonga (*Pl. 44*) lie at the southern end of the Chimu Kingdom, a few miles in from the ocean, occupying strategically a key position. For this reason, the name La Fortaleza, "the fortress," is most fitting. The adobe complex crowns the summit of a hill, rising in terraces, each of which is surrounded by a wall of clay. Four bastions that take advantage of the natural contours of the hill guard the corners. The greatest exterior length is 900 feet, while the innermost wall measures 600. Within the fort there are the remains of rectangular houses separated by narrow passageways.[139] An outer wall—which would today be called the first line of defense—encircles the entire structure. Remnants of this are most clearly seen in the foreground and in the upper right of the photograph.

The renowned scholar of Andean cultures, Philip Ainsworth Means, caught the spirit of the place when he wrote: "Dead and abandoned though it is now, it fills the beholder with the realization of the defiant pride of its builders; bristling . . . with a well-armed garrison provided with spears and spear-throwers, with bows and arrows, with stones and slings, with maces, clubs, and knives of copper, bronze, silver and gold, arrogant with banners, a-shout with battle-cries, it must indeed have presented itself as a redoubtable obstacle to further progress northwards. . . ." [84]

The fortress was taken by the Inca, Pachacutec, under whose leadership the Empire attained its greatest extent, power, and wealth in the early 15th century. With the fall of Paramonga, the Chimu people came under the sway of the Incas.

Yet, when we look at La Fortaleza, we can well forget the details of its past. Its commanding position, its thick walls, and jutting bastions speak an intercontinental language. It is the romantic fortress without locality, race, or age. From its protruding angles a valiant fight could have been waged against superior numbers of medieval warriors anywhere.

LA CENTINELA

The territory of the Chimu Kingdom terminated on the south around the fortress of Paramonga. Beyond lie a number of fertile valleys watered by rivers that empty into the Pacific. There is evidence that these regions also were inhabited from a very remote period. Proof of the dense population lies in the remains of extensive irrigation works that in some cases exhausted the river water before it reached the sea.[84]

In the Central Coast regions, interesting cultures are found in the valleys of Ancon, Chancay, and Rimac, where there are numerous architectural remains. Especially noteworthy is the site Pachacamac, the ruined walls of which once carried splendid polychrome fresco designs.[160]

On the South Coast the chiefs banded together in what is known today as the Chincha Confederacy, but the organization was not so closely knit as that of the Chimu. Their pottery and other applied arts prove that commercial intercourse existed not only with their immediate neighbors but also with the north and the highlands.

Means believes the Chincha Valley to have been an urban center comparable to Chan-Chan in the north, and, together with the Ica Valley, to have been the seat of the culture known as Ica, or Late Nazca, between 900 and 1400. As the territory of the Chincha Confederacy lay nearer the original realm of the Incas, it was subjugated earlier than the Chimu Kingdom, and the remains at

La Centinela, the largest and most prominent of the adobe ruins here, are representative of both pre-Inca and Inca periods.

This ruin measures some 1060 feet by 500, and in places attains a height of 50 feet. In its midst rises an irregular terraced temple-base (center, *Pl. 45, fig. a*), entirely surrounded by spreading palaces on platforms of varying heights. The general outline of the original construction is difficult to ascertain because of the havoc wrought by rain, earthquakes, and treasure hunters. Besides, as the ancient adobe bricks are far harder than new ones, they bring a price ten times as high in the market. Another destructive factor lies in the large crosses hung with the votive offerings of pilgrims, which have been erected on commanding points among the ruins. As some are nearly thirty feet high, they require a solid foundation, for which the material close at hand has been utilized. Walls were destroyed and levels disturbed so that it is now often impossible to trace the original lines of a building.[161]

Although the adjoining palace (*fig. b*) is of adobe, it shows the influence of Inca architecture. The most interesting characteristic of the structure is the niches, which, used in a building identified as late, probably date from a time when Inca domination had penetrated to this point. The hole to the right is recent and fortunately superficial, the work of treasure-seeking excavators who apparently gave up on reaching the sand at the heart of the adobe construction.

Niches have been found elsewhere in medieval America, fashioned of chipped stone in the kivas of the Southwest and hewn from the solid rock at Malinalco. We have mentioned niche-like constructions at Tajin, Labná, Uxmal, Mitla, and shall see many in Inca buildings in the highlands constructed of stone blocks. The niches at La Centinela are found in interior as well as exterior walls and consist of several types: large ones rising immediately from the floor; medium ones, resembling windows; small ones, either vertical or horizontal. The sides and back walls were whitewashed and some are double-framed with painted decorations. Objects which may have served religious purposes were found in a few.

Inside, the palace is divided into systems of galleries and chambers, with open courts and broad stairs that point to ceremonious living. Traces of wall-paintings show geometric patterns in red, black, and green, producing a decorative effect similar to that of our many-colored papers or stenciled walls. The indications of canals and reservoirs inside the palaces help one to imagine the pompous scale of life as it was lived here before the Conquest, with plants and flowers embellishing the buildings.

Although powerful cultures flourished farther south on the coast, whatever ruins remain are buried under shifting sands and give no noteworthy impressions. The Nazca Valley was an ancient focal point of culture because of its unfailing water supply. But early Nazca architecture is virtually unknown; the name is most often mentioned in reference to its pottery and textiles. The artistic characteristics of the district extend to neighboring valleys.[84]

The Paracas Peninsula, situated about a hundred miles north of the Nazca region, should also be mentioned here, although it owes its greatest fame to its excavated textiles, which reveal great variety and technical superiority.

Southward along the shores of the Pacific is found a strip of coast extending as far as present-day Chile that apparently did not support a dense population even in pre-Columbian times. Its aboriginal inhabitants were fisher folk, who used *balsas,* or floats, of inflated sealskin.[77] Neither legendary history nor minor arts of greater interest are evident.

It would appear then that below the Nazca and Paracas centers, the wave of civilization slowed down, and for further significant Andean cultures we must turn inland to the mountains. Here, especially around the shores and islands of Lake Titicaca, which today marks the border of Peru and Bolivia, there are early architectural remains of great importance.

TIAHUANACO

Lake Titicaca is a large body of water, 120 miles long and 40 wide, lying high in the Andes at an altitude of over 12,500 feet. The ruins of Tiahuanaco, situated near its shores, are considered among the earliest in the highland region and constitute another important center of pre-Columbian culture which developed at an exceptional altitude. The name is apparently of no great antiquity. The story goes that an Inca visiting the site, ancient even in his day, received a message there brought by a runner. Pleased with the young man's speed, he called him to rest, saying, *Tia, huanaco,* "Be seated, guanaco," giving to him in compliment the name of the fleetest of the llama group.[77]

The site of Tiahuanaco reveals several periods besides the final Inca. Classic Tiahuanaco is associated with the use of lava pillars and blocks and copper cramps for bolting the masonry together. This was followed by the Decadent Tiahuanaco period, in which stones from earlier buildings were reused in a cruder style.[8]

The most conspicuous and artistically important of the ruins at Tiahuanaco is the great monolithic gateway, generally called the Gateway of the Sun (*Pl. 46, fig. a*). Cut from a single piece of extremely hard trachyte, rather dark in color, it stands 7 feet 2 inches high, 13 feet 2 inches wide, and 18 inches thick. The stone is dressed with precision, its lines are perfectly drawn, and the right angles turned with absolute geometric accuracy. An elaborate carving decorates the upper part, while the wall space below is plain, except for two carefully cut niches. How the prehistoric workmen of the site were able to quarry, transport, and carve a stone of such mass in such a finished manner is an unanswered question.

Applied like an ornate headband, the sculptured section shows one principal figure as center of the composition (*fig. b*). He is presented in an elaborate tunic with a girdle embellished with puma heads. Means identifies him as Viracocha, the Creator-god, supreme deity of the highland folk.[84] The large square face framed by a radiating headdress is the most sharply defined element. A number of symbols, which may be part of a mask, are incised on the face, and round tears course down the carved cheeks, apparently typifying rain. The two highly conventionalized objects held in the hands are balanced in composition, though different in detail. One seems to represent a spear-thrower, the other, in the left hand, a quiver containing two darts. Standing on a terraced platform, with snake heads curling at the foot, he is attended by forty-eight personages of smaller size. The low relief in which they are carved stresses their subordination. These minor figures consist, in the first and third rows, of winged men, bearing staffs or spears and wearing tufted headdresses; in the middle row, they are personified birds, wearing cloaks, with their crested heads held high, in a similar arrangement. The deep carving of the eyes, like those of Viracocha, suggests inlay. Below the group runs a horizontal band composed of sun medallions set in an interesting version of the fret.

The little figures are either running toward or kneeling before the Creator-god—their posture, with ambiguously spread feet, might be explained either way. In contrast to their active pose, Viracocha stands on his pedestal in static immobility. The objects which the attendants hold divide the flowing horizontal rows into squares, forming vertical divisions throughout the design—like vigorous beats in a musical composition. The rhythm, even if strange, must impress us with its virility.

We understand this carving better if we look at it as a symbolic expression of cosmic order. The fact must not be lost sight of that this art was created and kept within prescribed limits, spiritually and technically, by the formalism of a hierarchic and religious culture that apparently became crystallized at a very early period. From this time on, the iconography of these figures is so fixed that they are easily recognizable in the pottery, fabrics, and metal-work of a number of Andean cultures.

The west side of the Gateway has no sculptural embellishment, but a number of deep carved niches were chiseled into the walls, some of which seem to have been fitted with doors. The inset doorway with its suggestion of a lintel is interesting.

The Gateway of the Sun stands in the northeast corner of a large inclosure, called the Calasasaya, which measures 440 feet on its longest side and is constructed of upright pillars with smaller blocks set in between. On the opposite side of the same complex is a fine stairway of six monumental steps hewn from massive blocks of lava. An enormous natural mound lies to the south, nearly 700 feet on a side, and faced with cut stone. Other doorways, also carved from single pieces of stone, have been found in the vicinity.[84]

The Gateway is identified as Classic Tiahuanaco, which falls between A.D. 600 and 900. As stone is the chief medium of architecture in the highlands, the locations and influences of Tiahuanaco can be traced over a widespread area. After 900 this fountain of culture began to lose its vitality, and new trends emanating from the Incas later become noticeable.

TITICACA REGION

Before leaving this section, however, we must view another type of building, the *chulpa,* or burial tower, usually rectangular but occasionally round in shape. The material of some of these is adobe, of others, uncut stone laid in clay, or large stone blocks set without mortar. These structures occur in a wide range, extending from the region of La Paz to the outskirts of Lima.[84]

Figs. a and *b* on *Pl. 47* show *chulpas* situated near Lake Titicaca. The first are Inca in style, the second, Classic Tiahuanaco. The round tower on the left (*fig. b*) is 39 feet high and 16 in diameter, widening as it rises so that at the spring of the dome, the diameter is nearly 5 feet greater than at the base. The cornice, 3 feet wide and somewhat protruding, seems to bind in the flaring line. The material is hard compact basalt, admirably cut, laid in almost even courses, and beautifully fitted. The largest of the stones, near the ground, is 5 feet high. To lift blocks of such dimensions to position without pulleys somewhat the same method may have been used that is still seen in some Latin American countries—

a rampart of earth is piled up beside the building and the heavy stones are pushed to the desired place upon it.

The low narrow entrance opens upon a vaulted chamber, 12 feet high and 10 in diameter. The ceiling of corbeled construction was once stuccoed, and in the center of it is an opening which leads to a smaller upper room, also with circular vault. Here human remains and pottery sherds were found at the time of exploration in 1877. All the *chulpas,* however, had been ransacked for centuries, the floors dug up, and the walls pried into, so that there is no record of the type of burial they contained.[139] The building on the right in *fig. b* shows where stones have been carried away since the Conquest.

Besides the technical skill displayed in the construction of these towers, we feel a radiation of considerable dignity. Where the dead were so honored, their spiritual bequest must also have been venerated. The *chulpas* of Sillustani are said to have come down from pre-Inca times, perpetuated legends. At the same time, they might be called the forerunners of Inca architecture, which in later centuries rose to grandeur.

CUZCO

We now reach the confines of the domain of the Incas, later so powerful. These people seem to have descended from one of the mountain tribes in the region near Cuzco or Ollantaytambo, some thirty miles to the northwest. They cultivated maize and potatoes as their staple foods and tended herds of llamas. After the decline of the Tiahuanaco culture, they rose to power, gradually gaining new strength and experience for their future expansion.[84]

Historically and geographically, the region around Cuzco and the valley of the Urubamba River with its tributaries remained the heart of the Inca Empire even at its height. Geographical conditions made this country with its perennial water supply a cultural center—one of the most important from an architectural point of view in medieval America.

Cuzco itself, the capital of the Inca Empire at the time of the Conquest, lies a few miles west of the river, at an altitude of 11,380 feet, surrounded by gardens, orchards, and cultivated fields and hemmed in by mountain peaks. Although it is only fourteen degrees south of the equator, its climate is rather chilly. A living city today, it boasts numerous remnants of Inca times. *Pl. 48, fig. a* shows an ancient wall later used as foundation for Spanish colonial dwellings. Stones of similar texture and size were trimmed to fit closely together without mortar, a sharp contrast to the *mélange* of masonry from post-Columbian days.

In this picture characteristics of Inca building are evident which will appear on a much grander scale in following sites. The fitting of irregular blocks is amazingly perfect, as can be seen in *fig. b*, the ruins at Tampumachay, near Cuzco. Sometimes the stones are rather rounded, and sometimes, as in the foundation of the Monastery of St. Dominic in Cuzco, so smoothly dressed that the joint is scarcely felt with the hand.

The ancient capital, laid out on a geometric plan, would seem rather forbidding to us, with its narrow paved streets and solid dark walls. Probably few of the houses were, however, more than one story high. Running water coursed through certain sections.

The puritanically sober stone blocks of the palaces and temples were sometimes embellished by decorations of fine textiles and sheets of gold. It is said that a golden frieze ran all the way around the outside of the Temple of the Sun and the interior walls and ceiling were plated with the same precious metal. An enormous sun disk, also of gold and incrusted with emeralds, covered the west wall, so placed as to reflect the rays of the rising sun at the time of the equinoxes. Five fountains played from pipes of gold within the temple, and outside was a garden with birds, trees, flowers, and little animals, all of gold and silver.[30] Other temples, dedicated to the moon, the stars, thunder and lightning, and the rainbow must have been as ingeniously adorned.

At Kenko, in the environs of Cuzco, is a ruin with an admirably precise semicircular wall, which according to authorities was an amphitheater in Inca times. In the center stands a solitary animal-shaped rock, about which the rites may have centered.[164]

SACSAHUAMAN

On the hill which dominates the city of Cuzco from the north are the impressive ruins of the fortress, Sacsahuaman (*Pl. 49, fig. a*). The name is said to denote "the highland whose attack meant human corpses for the hawks." [139] Sacsahuaman rises in three jagged terraces to a total height of almost 60 feet. The fortress is constructed of heavy stone blocks of irregular size, joined without mortar. The first wall is 1200 feet long and averages 27 feet high. One of the giant boulders used in the construction measures 38 feet long by 18 high and 6 thick.[84] The second terrace steps back 35 feet and is 18 feet high, while the third recedes about 18 feet and is 14 high. The stones were quarried at a distance, sometimes of several miles, and had to be transported over rivers and across ravines. Contemporary Europe, which had the advantage of iron tools, pulleys, and wheeled vehicles—all unknown to the pre-Columbian native—could not have fitted these great blocks with more masterly precision. The walls today remind one somewhat of the ruins of Moorish fortresses in Spain and Africa.

Beyond the ramparts there are signs of living quarters. Water was supplied the garrison by means of canals, in part subterranean. On the very summit of the hill are broad "steps," hewn from the living rock and cut with matchless skill (*fig. b*). This dais is called the Throne of the Inca, but its purpose is unknown.

There are certain differences in construction which may indicate that the fortress was started by a pre-Inca people and only strengthened and enlarged by the same dynasty that in the end fought the Spaniards here. The outstanding position that Sacsahuaman holds as a masterpiece of construction, however, remains unquestioned.

It continued as a stronghold until shortly after the Conquest. Juan Pizarro, half-brother of the *conquistador,* was mortally wounded here in one of the battles between Spaniards and Incas, and here was dealt one of the last blows to independent Inca power. When the Indians lost the battle, the commander of the fortress hurled himself to the ground from a high promontory.

OLLANTAYTAMBO

Ollantaytambo, "the plain of the spider," [139] lies about thirty miles northwest of Cuzco in the valley of the Yucay, a tributary of the Urubamba. One of the several key fortresses that protected the "Sacred Valley" from the incursions of wild tribes from the north, it is among the most interesting ruins of the Andean Area, either from a historical or legendary point of view. Constructed in pre-Inca times and used throughout the regime of the Incas, it witnessed a Spanish defeat when its walls repulsed the attack of the troops of Hernando Pizarro. Here also is laid the scene of a famous drama of Inca tradition—the tale of a young warrior, an obdurate ruler, and the youth's tribulations in winning the lovely maiden—which could not have been staged against a more romantic and picturesque background.

High mountains rise precipitously all around the site, and a river flows through the valley at the foot of the cliffs. From here a steep path leads upward to a small artificially broadened plateau, and on this level space six immense stone slabs, averaging over 12 feet high and 6 broad, stand upright against the mountain side. According to early sources, here rose the Great Hall of the fortified palace of Ollantaytambo.[77] If used as inside walls, the smooth stone slabs must have produced much the same effect as the wood panels in European medieval halls.

The slope of the mountain below the palace was later cut into deep terraces, the walls of which were faced with stone and used as the inner walls of buildings. The Hall of the Niches (*Pl. 50, fig. b*) shows one of these. The protrusions visible on a number of the stones are thought by some to have been left for convenience in handling. Each of the nine niches, which may have held household goods or equipment, is 26 inches high by 16 deep with sides made up of single blocks. At the far end of the narrow structure is a handsome doorway, characteristically wider at the base, with a lintel that is dressed on all four sides. E. George Squier notes sockets carved on several blocks for T-shaped copper cramps, such as were found also at the ruins of Tiahuanaco.[139]

Another narrow gallery of tall niches above a series of terraces is seen in *fig. a*. Here the wall surfaces show the great differences that existed there in stone work. The lower terraces are composed of polygonal masonry, built of small stones, crude and rough in appearance. The center section, which may be of earlier date, is also put together like a jigsaw puzzle, but here much larger stones are used, dressed with care though lacking uniformity in size and shape. The wall with the niches is laid in even courses with well-spaced joints. Each lintel is a large smooth slab, and the task of lifting such pieces in this restricted passageway can be imagined.

The fountain is the only sign of life remaining. A steady stream of water splashes from the stone mouth into a small basin, to issue again from the double opening a few feet below. Running through the time of the pre-Incas, the Incas, the Spanish rule, and into the present day, it is the only living link with the generations that once teemed here.

The ground around and above Ollantaytambo is graded for agriculture. Ruins of dwellings have been found on the hillsides. Following the line upon line of walls, still unshaken, on these sites, one is awestruck with the consummate skill of these early builders. The structures seem an embodiment of the cyclopean power which was able to build an empire spreading 380,000 square miles, as intricate in its coördination as is this admirable masonry.

PISAC

Agricultural terraces with their undulating outline, cut from the sloping hillsides, form a significant and dramatic setting for the citadel of Pisac, some fifteen miles northeast of Cuzco in the Urubamba Valley. Situated on a mountain plateau and overlooking the river and three converging valleys, a position comparable to that of Monte Alban, it had great tactical advantages.

The major part of the citadel lies 1000 feet above the river bed. Double- and triple-walled forts were worked into the defense system, with the walls and towers so placed that the fortress was practically impregnable to attack with such weapons as slings, darts, stone axes, and clubs. The scattered buildings and minor fortifications which crowd the terraced slopes would indicate that Pisac was almost a province, supporting not only a large number of warriors in the garrison but a considerable general population.

Back of the settlement lies a vast system of terraced fields, which here, as at Ollantaytambo, reached perfection. Hundreds of miles of them, carefully constructed and irrigated, produced crops which could provide for a widespread population. It is probable that Pisac was one of the hill garrisons that not only guarded the passes but provided depots where the garnered food supply was stored for the Empire as a reserve in case of war or a failure in the harvest. Ruined granaries and remnants of other separate buildings about the site bear out this theory.[48]

A section of smaller rooms worked into a semicircular unit is seen in *Pl. 51, fig. a,* connected and separate inclosures without their roofs. The thatch has long since fallen in and moldered away, but there is every reason to believe that the covering of these buildings was as neatly and skillfully constructed as their walls. The structure stands on the brow of the hill, and far below can be seen the contours of the meandering river valley.

The so-called Temple Group (*fig. b*) represents the climax in stone cutting and fitting. Nowhere in the Inca domain, or even in the world, can a higher grade of megalithic architecture be found. In addition to the expert finishing, the stones are cut in uniform sizes and laid in absolutely even courses. Vertical joints are avoided and even today the walls are still remarkably plumb. The thick rounded blocks for the corners had to be prepared with special care. The three window sills in the center are perfectly level and their lintels could not have been more evenly laid with modern tools.

The building with the curving wall (*Pl. 52, fig. a*) was the Sundial, or *Inti-huatana,* "the place where the sun is tied up." For this the top of a ledge was leveled, except for a truncated cone carved from it projecting from the floor (*fig. b*). It was inclosed within walls but open to the sky. The projection, in tracing with its shadow the course of sun or moon, is believed to have served as a pointer on the flat table of living rock.

When Squier visited the place, before 1877, he was told by the governor of the province that a flat bronze ring had once encircled the projection. Perhaps this was marked for astronomical observations, for the early Spanish chroniclers mention devices by which the Incas were able to determine the solstices and compute eclipses.

The elliptical wall which incloses the sundial rock reaches 20 feet in height. Here again is a remarkable piece of construction, with every unit executed, one might say sculptured, for its own particular position. It has an amazingly finished aspect in comparison with the irregular cyclopean blocks of Sacsahuaman. Crumpling walls of various types attest to the long occupation of the site.

There are a number of sundials within such temple courts in Inca settlements. All records of the *intihuatanas* show them to be carved from living rock. Their immobility seems to have been a major consideration. Perhaps a device which was part of the earth itself, living and natural—not to be tampered with arbitrarily by the hand of man—was held desirable for the observation of nature's greatest wonder.

The beauty of Pisac is enhanced by the soft pinkish gray of the granite used throughout. The irregular height of the remaining walls, the huge finished stones scattered here and there do not give it the appearance of dilapidation but rather the charm of a child's unfinished game with blocks, colored always by its monumental scale.

MACHU PICCHU

Last in our sequence, although among the first in importance, are the ruins of Machu Picchu, situated less than fifty miles northwest of Cuzco on one of the numerous mountain "knees" carved out by the Urubamba. This mountain fortress lies on a long ridge between two lofty peaks, the higher of which (10,300 feet) bears the name, Machu Picchu, or "old peak," while the lower (9000 feet) is called Huayna Picchu, or "young peak" (*Pl. 53*). Machu Picchu, as a name, became familiar to the public with the discovery and exploration of the site by Dr. Hiram Bingham in 1911.

Until this date there were only rumors of ruins in this general region. Wiener in his "picturesque but unreliable" book, *Pérou et Bolivie,* mentions hearing of them while he was in Ollantaytambo around 1875, and friends of Dr. Bingham reported local tales of their existence. The Urubamba River, here 6400 feet above sea level, is unnavigable at this point even for canoes. It flows between such sheer walls that all passage along the shore line was impossible, and the produce brought from the region into Cuzco had, until recently, to be carried a roundabout way over snow-filled passes.[12] Late in the last century the Peruvian Government constructed—rather, blasted out—a mule trail following the gorge of the river, and this new means of communication opened a new sector also to the explorer. It fell to the lot of the American expedition to find the site, which, to their good fortune, had been little disturbed by treasure hunters and was damaged only by the overgrowing mountain vegetation.

Here in the saddle between the two peaks, 2000 feet higher than the river bed, stands the ruined citadel, laid out with constant regard for the terrain. While toward the west was located the ceremonial and religious center (*Pl. 54, fig. a*), the greater part of the inhabitants apparently lived in the eastern section (*fig. b* and *Pl. 305, fig. b*). Water channels, bath-houses, smoothly rounded walls, all of fine white granite, furnish typical details of Inca architecture. With the growth of the population, dwelling houses and artificial terraces for agriculture were laid out in all directions wherever the precipitous rocks left space for them. Inclined ramps, narrow streets, and long stairways connected the parts of the fortress. Buildings were wedged in among boulders and under overhanging ledges, so ingeniously fitted that they stand today as firm as the living rock (*Pl. 55, fig. a*).

In the different edifices of Machu Picchu, the full variety of stone construction in the Andean Area can be observed. Superlative craftsmanship is displayed in the sloping wall that continues the line of the steep ledge used as a foundation (*fig. c*). In contrast, the terrace walls in the background, more clearly visible in *Pl. 56, fig. b,* show such rough fabrication that one wonders if they could be the work of the same people. Both flat and gabled roofs were used (*Pl. 56, fig. a*). The characteristic niches and well-cut windows of mature Inca style can be seen everywhere (*Pl. 55, fig. b*). Some of the protuberances on the stones are now believed to have been used in lashing on the roofing.

The history of Machu Picchu is still a matter of dispute. Some authorities are led by the variations in the masonry to conjecture a long life and numerous changes. Dr. Bingham holds the site to have been the capital of the first Inca ruler, around the 9th century, and to have been abandoned in the 14th for Cuzco.[13] According to Dr. Luís E. Valcárcel, the two-story houses, the considerable number of greatly expanded stairways, the three-sided, walled-in temple, and the plug-projections on the great stone blocks present pre-Inca features.[6] It is true that at the beginning of an empire, such a citadel would have been of great importance; and later when the Inca power had expanded and become stabilized, the population could have afforded to move to a less intrenched position. All pottery and tools found here, however, clearly show Inca style, and excavations so far have failed to produce traces of separate or considerably earlier cultures. For this reason, Means dates its construction in the first years of the 15th century, during the reign of Pachacutec. There is also a tradition that Machu Picchu was the last refuge of the Incas after the Conquest. Thus legendary tradition and historical evidence vacillate between placing it among the first or the final strongholds.

In this book where the extant remains of medieval American art are under discussion, Machu Picchu needs no proof of venerability to insure its prestige. In the daring and majesty of its isolation, it is a perfect expression of the austere and orderly mountain folk who created and maintained it.

In viewing the architecture of medieval America from the cliff-dwellings of the Southwest down into the Andes with its *grand finale* of Machu Picchu, one is overwhelmed to see such diversity in the methods used by these peoples in solving their building problems. Houses built on the earth and temples rising from impressive substructures, sober granite walls and flamboyant sculptured façades existed on this continent as it lived its own life and went its own way of development.

"All European architecture," as John Ruskin wrote, "good and bad, old and new is derived from Greece through Rome, and colored and perfected from the East. The history of architecture is nothing but the tracing of the various modes and directions of this derivation. Understand this once and for all: if you hold fast to this great connecting clue, you may string all the types of successive architectural invention upon it like so many beads. . . . Those old Greeks gave the shaft; Rome gave the arch; the Arabs pointed and foliated the arch." [118]

But pre-Columbian America knew nothing of this development in the Eastern Hemisphere, connected and cross-fertilized from many sources during the last five thousand years. For this reason, medieval American architecture would be of unique importance even had its achievements been less great than they are.

IV

Sculpture

THE nature of sculpture and the inherent possibilities in the material for the imitation of natural form make it perhaps the most immediately comprehensible of all the arts. Architecture has somewhat the same universal appeal, yet to grasp the full majesty of a great building requires some familiarity with the culture of the region. Painting, limited to the flat surface, has developed stylistic mannerisms of its own; and its forms of expression are so idiomatic that one does not feel the beauty in a fresco or canvas unless he is acquainted with the civilization which produced it. A cloud in a Chinese painting looks very different from one on a canvas by Titian. We are able to recognize and enjoy both because we have learned to understand the pictorial expressions of both Chinese and Venetian schools; but for a person absolutely ignorant in the field, these pictures would have little to tell. A case in point is that of the Oriental with his tradition of placid even lighting. He is irritated and confused by our chiaroscuro; to him the shaded half of the face in a portrait simply looks dirty. Thus, the limitation imposed by two dimensions has enforced artificiality on painting and circumscribed its appeal. Sculpture, on the other hand, less restricted, stands free, awakening a more catholic response. It transcends both time and continents.

In the Eastern Hemisphere, sculptural expression and techniques were interchanged by Asia, Africa, and Europe—witness the Greek influence in some of the Buddhistic statuary—but medieval America had to develop its own principles, drawing on its experience in clay modeling and the carving of wood and bone. The small toylike figurines of the archaic period might be viewed as the predecessors of the superb stucco wall reliefs of Palenque and Comalcalco; the carved bone tools, the precursors of the Maya Maize-god of Copan, sculptured in stone.

One might go so far as to say that the high quality of pre-Columbian art is most apparent in its sculpture. The charm of the crystal frog (*Pl. 256, fig. a*) can be sensed immediately; the figure of the seated Aztec leaning on his arms (*Pl. 61, fig. a*) or of the rattlesnake (*Pl. 60, fig. a*), indolently coiled, requires no explanation. Even a tyro in the arts can see and understand these subjects and will, most probably, even derive some emotional reaction from them.

The pre-Columbian sculptor shows great feeling for his material. Egyptian carving was "conditioned" by the native granite employed; Assyria used limestone; Tanagra, clay; Donatello chose bronze; Rodin, marble as well, while the African primitive carved in wood. The Maya artist worked out his technique and his style of expression in the material locally at his disposal. Limestone was common, which also furnished stucco for his wall reliefs. The Aztec carver frequently used trachyte, serpentine, and other rugged stones. The plastic talent of these peoples found expression also in jade, bone, and wood, which will be presented later.

It is impossible for us to take the full measure of pre-Columbian sculpture, for much of it that we know functioned as ornament, either built in or applied to a building, and what we see today is only a fragment of the original, stripped from its setting. Furthermore, as in many early civilizations, color was applied lavishly to both sculpture and architecture and must be kept in mind in any attempt to visualize the living art.

Our civilization tends to evaluate an art by the way it depicts the human figure. Even according to this standard, some of the pre-Columbian sculpture would rank high. But one factor must be taken into consideration: various cultures have very different ideals of beauty. The flattening of the forehead generally practiced by the Maya appears to us unnatural, but in 15th-century Florence, the beauty ideal of the ladies, as immortalized by Piero di Cosimo and his contemporaries, shows that the hair was shaved off for two to three inches above the brow. In medieval America, besides the sloping forehead, artificially elongated in childhood, crossed eyes, also promoted early, and a receding chin were deemed marks of beauty. Moreover, the grotesque and the horrifying, often repulsive to us but nevertheless strikingly effective, played a much larger part in their art than in ours. Realism is frequently almost submerged in esoteric symbolism, but in many cases truly sculptural talent shines through, making immediate contact with us. Ease and subtlety of pose and balance of movement are often so humanly expressed that alien elements can be disregarded and the sculpture enjoyed without a discordant note.

One type of sculpture did not exist here: that is portrait statuary. Although certain stelae and other smaller pieces, such as the Totonac *palmas,* show individual characteristics, or even features of portraiture, they cannot be accepted as actual likenesses of a particular person; rather they are condensations of racial and traditional trends. In other early civilizations also, a so-called portrait of a person—frequently made after his death—was strongly idealized. Our humanistic and individual approach to the subject was absent in pre-Columbian America. The arts there never went beyond serving a hieratic purpose, and did not reach the level of "art for art's sake."

Not all of our five areas in medieval America were equally articulate in sculpture. The most impressive work in stone is restricted to the Mexican and Maya areas. Parts of the Southwest and Southeast modeled animal and human subjects into their ceremonial and utilitarian vessels. A number of scattered regions offer stone bowls with plastic animal decoration, and the ingeniously carved pipes of the Southeast and Central United States (shown in "Facets of Daily Life") prove command of the medium there. The Andean Area also produced sculpture in stone, but these people never reached the full use of the three dimensional in carving on a large scale, and their work is angular and strongly conventionalized.

Two lines of sculptural development can be observed: carving in relief and in the full round. In the following illustrations, examples of different degrees of both of these will be shown. Some of the earliest statuettes found are already conceived with consciousness of the three dimensional. Elsewhere the subject is depicted by scratching its outline across a stone slab—drawing with a chisel rather than sculpturing. The carving out of different levels to emphasize the contours produced relief. The background, already lowered, had then only to be carved completely away to show realistic outlines in the round, and the subject conceived in such a position that all unnecessary stone could be chiseled off. The statue that resulted, however, was often still flat, more of a cut-out than a plastic body. It will be noted that some regions seem to have found the relief completely expressive and satisfying, without reaching for the three dimensional. In certain instances, such as the Maya stelae, plastic and incised details appear on one and the same stone.

In order to bring out contrasting artistic qualities, a chronological presentation was avoided in this survey, as it would have necessitated showing much from the Maya before the Mexican. The chapter starts with the less articulate specimens of carving. We must not forget that all civilizations developed slowly. The inventions of a prehistoric people advanced at an adagio tempo. More time was needed in that age for the ripening of ideas than in our own, when the pace has been accelerated by the accumulated experience of centuries.

MEXICAN AREA

On the Zapotec-Mixtec site at Monte Alban, Oaxaca, carved stones from the earliest period were found with human and glyphic content.[20] *Pl. 57, fig. a* shows a slab that once decorated the base of a structure. A human figure is the main theme, and a pictograph presenting a bird and other signs is drawn in the upper left corner. In this carving the smoothed and polished surface of the stone was used to high-light the principal features of the subject. In between and around them the lines are deepened, probably by pecking with a primitive stone chisel, and the background worked up into a dull finish. The contour lines are deepest around the head and body; more shallow incision is used for details, such as the fingers. The half-open mouth, strongly emphasized lips, and low forehead are well brought out. An ornament hangs over the stubby nose, and the round ear-plug is sharply carved. Had the ear been merely suggested by a lightly incised line, it would have looked more natural, but chipped out as deeply as it is, the emphasis has disturbed the realism. The struggle to define the three-quarters pose with crossed arms and legs is obvious. Yet there is a feeling of human flesh in the carving. It is not a serialized portrayal, such as occurs, row on row, in Egyptian and Assyrian reliefs, but has rather the terse quality of a cartoon.

The second slab (*fig. b*), presented as a companion piece, has an orderly column of glyphs. In contrast to the first, where the entire surface of an irregular stone was utilized, the subject is neatly framed within a well-defined oblong depression, and instead of a single direct portrayal, the representation, which consists of a serpent head in the upper half and a human figure in the lower, is rigid and condensed. Thus motifs from life became conventionalized into glyphs which had associated meanings. The bar and four dots at the bottom are numerals.

These stones have been classified as belonging to Monte Alban Epoch I. The breadth of the artistic talent of the Zapotecs is documented in the clarity with which, even at that time, both figural and glyphic subjects were executed.

The relief work in *Pl. 58* has advanced considerably beyond mere incision and makes use of several planes. The first illustration (*fig. a*) is of a limestone fragment found at Tilantongo, Oaxaca, where it had been used as building material in a Spanish church. The Mixtec god, Five Death, is represented, identified by the skull with ear-flaps and the five dots carved before his face.[24] He wears an elaborate headdress of sweeping quetzal feathers, with three stiff eagle quills pointing upward, and a patterned kilt edged with bells. On his right arm he carries a shield and in his hand three darts. A pouch is hung over his left arm and in that hand he holds a decorated spear-thrower. His jewelry consists of bracelets and anklets, a great rectangular ear ornament, and a necklace with a carved mask and three large pendants, probably of jade. The deity seems to have faced another figure at the left where the stone is broken off.

Little realistic impression is conveyed in the carving. The most plastic element is the half-veiled eye, so effectively executed in the jades of the region. From an incised spiral (noted in the preceding plate), the ear has reached a characteristic conventionalization. Head and feet are out of proportion; most of the accessories, such as the shield and the three pendants of the necklace, are exaggerated. The headdress is rigid, with little feeling of feathers in it. The composition seems primarily concerned in outfitting the subject with all the trappings prescribed by tribal iconography. In its linear conduct we do not yet find a truly sculptural language.

Warriors in full regalia are depicted on a fragment of Aztec stone carving (*fig. b*). Although nearly every object pointed out in the Mixtec relief appears here, differences in the manner of execution are immediately noticeable. Figures are better proportioned, heads and feet more naturalistically represented, and faces and especially thighs show certain rounded contours. Not only is the technique more advanced and the outfitting dissimilar, but, in contrast to the airless static Mixtec figure, the gestures here are those of human beings, even if orthodox; their involvement in an action can be sensed by everyone. The undulating serpents above them, besides being of symbolic importance, serve as an effective and decorative border.

Pl. 59, fig. a shows a sculpture of a woman which comes from the Huaxtec region, Vera Cruz, the inhabitants of which, though ethnically related to the Maya, show little similarity in their art. The piece is 26 inches high. Liberated from the stone which surrounded it, this carving more nearly approaches a statue in the round than any of those yet presented. Completely three-dimensional delineation is still lacking to a great degree, and, in spite of the cut-outs at the neck and waist, the impression of a stone slab prevails. While the arms and hands are flat, the face is quite plastically executed. The half-closed eyes and parted lips give it the expression of speaking or communicating, a characteristic that is more or less widespread and will be noticed in the best sculptures of the Maya also.

The so-called pulque vessel of the Aztecs (*fig. b*) is carved of green quartz phyllite and is about 14 inches high. The sharply projecting head seems to wear a mouth mask, the edge of which is visible toward the ear, and inlay must have once embellished the eyes. Flowing plumes and dart-shaped streamers make the transition to the cylindrical body of the vessel, the surface of which is covered with a design of human figures, monsters, and glyphs, a decoration full of movement.

Although certain features about the piece point to the Aztecs, it is not certain whether it is a product of those people. The type recalls clay *incensarios,* or incense burners, which have heads protruding in a similar manner from the sides of large jars. (See *Pl. 121, fig. c.*)

The statue of the Goddess of Agriculture (*fig. c*), 21 inches high, embodies many characteristics of Aztec stone carving, with its compactness, its feeling for the material, the angular sculptural lines, and the presence of realistic features among others highly conventionalized. Almost a third of the statue is taken up by her heavy complicated headdress, which has cockades on the sides and a protrusion like a bowknot in the center, typical Aztec decorations. Her face, strongly sculptured, holds its own against the massive plain surfaces that frame it. She carries what are probably two maize ears. About her waist dangles a snake, his rattles shaped like hearts. The feet are carved with naturalism in sharp contrast to the conventionalized hands with their symbolic objects. A proof that the statue has not fully graduated into the three dimensional lies in the superfluous stone connecting the headdress and the shoulders.

How able the Aztec carver was, however, to convey a realistic effect in three-dimensional sculpture is demonstrated in the three animals on *Pl. 60.* All are executed with striking power and are so well composed that they are equally effective from all sides.

A rattlesnake, approximately 2 feet high, is shown in *fig. a,* woven into the knot typical of the reptile. Teeth and tongue are conventionalized in best Aztec tradition, and the scaly rattles, conscientiously portrayed, have been used with good decorative sense against the smooth coils. The various planes of the soft folds in the body are cleanly worked out and, with the light and shadow effects, produce an unusual, yet realistic impression.

The toad (*fig. b*), almost 6 inches long, has the same good qualities. The

pose of the body, alert expression, and clean sculptural finish, all contribute to
our unhesitating acceptance of the piece.

The animal in *fig. c,* 17 inches high, is generally called a dog, although the
claws and stubby fleshy tail are not in the least canine. It is possible that the figure, despite its convincing appearance, is not intended to represent a real animal
but a mythical creature, supplely modeled and natural though it appears, as it
lazily grins at the sky. If so, the statue documents all the more the genuine artistic ability of the Aztecs, for to carve a figure from their fantasy-world so well
that it appears alive even to us is a veritable achievement.

Aztec sculpture at its best is presented in the figure of a seated man (*Pl. 61,
fig. a*), more than 2 feet high. His relaxed but attentive pose, showing the same
passive awareness that characterizes his present-day kin, is the first thing that
strikes us. Headdress and massive ear ornaments are executed in detail, otherwise a general plainness is adhered to throughout the carving. It is this very
plainness that clinches the forceful effect of the piece. The human in the figure
predominates; in regarding him, we are not overwhelmed with symbols from an
alien civilization. The body has the elasticity and vigor of a big cat, and the
eyes, though nothing but wedge-shaped slits, seem to be peering into the distance.
How much deliberation went into the statue is manifest in the fingertips of the
left hand, which, though partly concealed, are still clearly delineated. There is
life even in this small detail, for the fingers seem really to grasp the knee.

The next statuette (*fig. b*) obviously comes from a different, though not inferior culture. It shows a recumbent anthropomorphic figure, 16½ inches long.
As a whole, it gives the impression of a human, but the ears and pawlike termination of the arms bring animal elements into it. Such adaptations—the Sphinx
for one and Mercury for another—occur in many mythologies. The provenience
of the carving is not known, nor is it clear just what it represents. According to
one opinion, it is classified as belonging to the Huaxtec culture in northern Vera
Cruz, to another, as coming rather from the central or southern part of that
state. All these regions produced excellent sculpture.

Detached from any culture, however, it can be enjoyed as pure sculpture.
Good observation and articulate talent are combined to convey the alert expression in the face and the animation of the body in repose. The back has a smooth,
finely curving line, very plastic, and the softness of the body is beautifully
brought out. Note the similar attitude in the pottery whistle (see *Pl. 118, fig. c*).
There are traces of red on the piece. Holes are bored in the earlobes for the

‹ 111 ›

addition of separate ornaments, and the deep-set eyes may have been inlaid, although in their present state they still give a full impression. If the seated Aztec above can be said to be executed in a major key, this statuette might represent a minor.

In the next plate, another non-Aztec carving is coupled with an Aztec to bring out further differences. The first statue (*Pl. 62, fig. a*) is thought to have come from the state of Vera Cruz. A springiness of the legs, an easy position of the arms and hands are immediately perceptible. The head sits firmly on the shoulders and is in perfect proportion to the body. Headdress, earrings, and garment are the only decorations. The teeth are visible, as in *Pl. 59, fig. a,* and again the far-away look is noticeable in the face. Opinions are divided as to whether it represents a man or a woman. The pose is feminine but the slender body and the loincloth could be that of a youth. None of the higher pre-Columbian cultures tended to exaggerate the differences in the sexes.

Compared with the seated man in the preceding plate, the Aztec carving shown in *fig. b* is somewhat inferior. In the former, a more concentrated sculptural mass was produced, yet it has more life. The expression of the face here is dulled somewhat by the blank eyes, which, without the color that once must have completed them, make it rather forlorn. This statue is the least vital of the four, but if considered alone, it has a certain positive interest.

The concentrated quality of much of the best Aztec sculpture may have been due partly to the material used—trachyte or a hard basalt, often dark in tone, in contrast to the softer, lighter-colored limestone that is common in the lowland regions. Straighter lines are employed in the execution, the edges and corners are sharper, the mass is more geometrical. A greater smoothness and fluidity of line characterize the statues of non-Aztec cultures, and more ease can be observed in the pose, although from a sculptural point of view they frequently present more difficult problems.

The Totonac relief (*Pl. 63, fig. a*) shows a section of panel from the northeast corner of the Greater Ball Court at Tajin. The scene depicts a human sacrifice. The victim is laid on a high curving stone, while one priest holds his arm and supports his head and the other wields the stone knife with the point at his breast. A fourth figure is seated at the extreme right, bearing a standard. The Death-god with outspread arms and legs descends from above, between the two officiants, and on the left stands another skeletal figure, with a scroll before his jaws denoting speech. A simpler speech scroll emerges from the lips of the sacrificing priest. The unfriendly content of the relief must not prevent us from noticing the good spacing in the scene and the fine clear outlining of its many details. The fretlike scroll motifs in the border appear frequently in the Mexican and Maya areas, reaching in their application as far south as the Ulua Valley in Honduras.

In *figs. b* and *c* we have an instance of the same symbolic theme worked up by different cultures into individual stylistic patterns. The plaque of fired clay (*fig. b*), about 27 by 29 inches, is said to have come from southern Mexico. Every detail of the eagle is utilized to a highly decorative effect. The spreading feathers show great variation; the attacking gesture of head and beak is brought out with force and realism, and each talon has its distinct and logical place—one grasping the object which the bird is devouring, while its more stable counterpart clutches the perch. The technical difficulties to be surmounted in modeling such a piece were not small; yet it is executed with vigor and freshness. The background is unusually deep and all contours sharply defined. Fret-scroll elements, similar to those on the preceding relief, fill in the empty spaces above the bird.

In *fig. c,* a section from a wall at Chichen, the same subject appears, here transposed into stone and expressed in the idiom of another culture. The technical and stylistic differences in the two works are immediately apparent. In the flatness of this relief and the changes effected in certain details, much of the power of the terra-cotta piece has been lost. True, the same attacking quality is evident in the head and beak, and the tail feathers are in exactly the same position. But the flowing line of the back is broken, and the whole figure is straighter, so that the gesture of the over-size claw becomes exaggerated. The scroll motif appears again above the bird, but in a somewhat different version.

The Totonacs who erected the superb structure of El Tajin (see *Pl. 12*) produced also one of the most sharply minted sculptural styles of medieval America. Their culture, centered in the region of central Vera Cruz, appears to have reached its artistic peak about the 13th century, when parts of the Mexican and Maya areas were feeling the spread of Toltec art. The art of the Totonacs has a special flavor, whether they make use of general themes or those of their own invention.

There are three types of stone sculpture characteristic of the region, two of which are more or less unique. One of these, the strange horseshoe-shaped carvings known as yokes, is presented on the two following plates. They average about 1½ feet in length and are made of polished diorite.[151] Their purpose is still a matter of conjecture. According to some sources, they were found in graves accompanying objects of burial; others would have them used in penitential ceremonies or placed around the neck of a sacrificial victim, although numerous representations of sacrificial scenes, preserved in stone and paint, show no such shape in connection with the bloody rites.

Realistic and abstract elements are combined in the yoke on *Pl. 64,* one of the most ornate extant. The stone is of unusually fine quality, light and even in color. Above the sharply delineated human head, the muzzle and eyes of a monster-mask are visible. The design is smoothly carried over from the curving side to the flat surface on top, and the hand clasping the upper rim is especially noteworthy. One end of the yoke is reproduced in *fig. b,* showing a somewhat different face and mask. However, a homogeneous style is well preserved throughout.

Although it is the artistic content of the pieces that interests us, the symbolic importance for their makers can be sensed by a glance at the three photographs on *Pl. 65. Fig. a* shows a yoke with closed ends, carved in front and on the sides to represent an owl, while the inside is blank. The second one (*fig. b*) is open, with a human face cut in low relief. The third (*fig. c*) bears an all-over pattern, both inside and out, featuring another head, this time in profile, in the curve. Excellent carving characterizes all three, although in each case the prescribed shape of the stone limited the plastic expression.

In the manner of execution, however, they do not fall into a single group. In the first, the subject is carved on the rounded sides in somewhat high relief, with bold thick lines and straight elements predominating in the design. The cameo face in the second is expressed in robust terms, with admirable economy of line. The third shows great refinement, not only in the interweaving decorative stream of the familiar fret-scroll that covers the entire surface but also in the profile, physically little different from the one beside it but carved with a finesse comparable to the jades. The crossing of one branch of the restless pattern over the hair of the figure is a virtuoso touch.

The second distinctive Totonac type, the use of which is unsettled, is found in the axe-shaped heads. They are believed to have been of ceremonial importance or used as architectural decoration.

The one on *Pl. 66, fig. a* is about 8½ inches high and less than 2 inches thick, tapering toward the face. This extreme flatness, a characteristic of all such pieces, makes their purpose still more problematical. The features are clean-cut, with all curved sections emphasized. The protuberance on the forehead indicates, perhaps, an ornament, and the glyphic decoration painted or tattooed on the cheek is said to be Zapotecoid.

The second specimen (*fig. b*), over 9 inches high, not only presents a different physical type but is differently carved. Both pieces, nevertheless, show a certain uniformity in general shape and a relationship in their sculptural build-up. Despite their strangeness and thinness, both have about them something of a portrait; the individuality of their features is clearly seen when one is compared with the other.

Similar wedge-shaped carvings have been found also in the highlands of Guatemala (see *Pl. 97, figs. a* and *b*).

After viewing the so-called yokes and axes of the Totonacs, we come to another type of sculpture peculiar to these people, generally designated as *palmas*. These are usually made of volcanic rock, unpolished, and range from 9 to 24 inches in height. Although only single figures are presented on *Pl. 67,* couples, group scenes, and sometimes even animal shapes occur amidst stylized designs.

Fig. a shows a standing man wearing a large headdress which resolves into a decorative pattern with fret-scrolls. The figure, like the others here reproduced, is kept in perfect proportion—a great advance over numerous other pre-Columbian cultures. Expression and pose are animated, and not a single element is portrayed in that exaggerated manner which not only often disturbs us but prevents the work from being generally accepted as one of high standard. Note the tattooed scrolls at the sides of the mouth which recall those of the preceding plate.

The head in *fig. b* is sharply modeled within a bird's beak. The simplicity with which the flaring plumes of the headdress are treated is a contrast to the involved decoration on the other examples shown.

Perhaps the finest details of all are presented in *fig. c.* The hair, tied with a large bow, is clearly defined and, besides the usual costume accessories, there is a bag held in the man's left hand. Much of the stone, the top part of which is missing, is devoted to scrolls in beautiful permutations.

Neither stiffness nor heaviness is felt in these carvings with their interesting blend of relief and three-dimensional sculpture, and, in spite of the use of common motifs, each shows individuality in its ornamentation. The patterns on the garments, carefully delineated, add their decorative value to the compositions.

Totonac *palmas* always have a flaring top and a definitely concave base—features that indicate a particular use for all of them. It has been suggested that they were applied architecturally; they are, however, completely finished in appearance, with no raw sides or ends. Since some were allegedly found in graves, the idea that they were fashioned as memorials might be considered, a theory further supported by the fact that each has a distinctly different theme. The number of them that have recently come to light with unknown provenience might also point to burials. They give the impression of miniature individual stelae, larger examples of which will be seen in the Maya Area, each also with its distinctive details.

Sculptured heads from four different regions, all within the Mexican Area, are presented on *Pl. 68*. The first (*fig. a*) was, according to information, removed from a grave near Oaxaca in the last decade of the 19th century. Including the neck, it is 10½ inches high. The carving is remarkable for its terseness of expression. Its plastic language is quite alien to the region where it was discovered. The headdress is simplified, and the ears, pierced both at the top and bottom, show a stylization not met heretofore. Tattoo may be denoted by the five beads at the corners of the mouth.

The head in *fig. b* was part of the legacy of Maximilian of Habsburg. Of dark green stone and about 7 inches high, it might easily be classed among the jades. The unrealistic narrowness of the piece, suggestive of the axe-shapes, is counterbalanced by the virtuose carving of the features. In accordance with the beauty ideal of a number of pre-Columbian areas, the forehead is elongated. The "flame" medallion between the eyes and the broad outlined "eyebrows" are reminiscent of the jade masks in *Pl. 248,* while the conical form of the sculpture and the extended tongue, together with the sly yet benign expression, recall the puzzling creature in the Tuxtla statuette (see *Pl. 235, fig. d*) and the pottery head from Kaminaljuyú (see *Pl. 132, fig. b*).

Xipe-Totec, the God of the Flayed, is apparently the subject of *fig. c.* Doubtless the bloodiest ceremony of the Mexican religion was that which paid homage to this deity. After sacrificing a prisoner of war, the priest put on the skin of the victim, covering his face and most of his body with the gory trophy. The rite involves imitative magic in its attempt to invoke in nature the rebirth of vegetation, which is looked upon as a new skin for the earth.[25]

SCULPTURE

The head here is 10 inches high, carved of extremely hard stone, pale in color. Little opportunity for plastic detail is offered by the face covered with the skin of the flayed, but the sagging eyelids are tellingly depicted. The headdress with its cross ridge is ornate, incised with decorations of uncertain glyphic character. Traces of red can be discerned.

A different type of stone, less hard than the one just described, was used for the carving in *fig. d*. It appears to represent a masked head, perhaps an aspect of death, with its emaciated cheeks and startling eyes. The deep corrugations are most effective, carried through to define not only the forehead, brows, and the cheek bones, but even the angular jaw. The mouth has Olmec analogies, discussed in the chapter on jade. A heavy rounded ridge cutting across the top of the headdress in a line similar to that in the preceding picture gives a bold accent. The origin of the piece is not known, but one somewhat like it, found in the corner of the state of Guerrero at a crossroads of several distinct cultures, may furnish a clue to its provenience.

These four heads represent something more than strange or sinister portrayals, for they testify to the spiritual latitudes of these peoples and demonstrate impressively not only the scope of their imagination but their ability to express it in three-dimensional form.

In making the transition to the Maya Area, we present on *Pl. 69* Totonac and Maya reliefs side by side to demonstrate some of the differences in the sculptural languages of these two neighboring cultures. The two Totonac pieces come from central Vera Cruz, the Maya from central Chiapas. Although the first carving represents the best in Totonac, we shall see far finer sculpture from the Maya Area in later plates than that from Tenam.

On the stone slab (*fig. a*), nearly 6 feet high, is carved a chief—evidently a ball player—and his attendant, who seems to be helping him dress. His headgear is complicated, with the sausage-like ridge seen in some of the axes and a cascade of five feathers behind. A double string of beads is around his neck and two sets of bracelets on his left arm. His right arm and hand are bound, as if for a contest of some kind. Knees and feet are heavily ornamented, the right more than the left. His kilt clings to the lines of the body as if of a soft woven material. Dignity and condescension are embodied in the figure. His beard is sharply defined (compare with *fig. b*), and where it meets his upraised arm and the headdress of the attendant, the problem of placement is well solved.

The curving lines of the second figure serve as a good foil to the upright pos-

‹ 117 ›

ture of the superior. Although this part of the stone is damaged, enough remains to give a satisfactory impression. He seems to be fastening the belt of the chief, and his hands convey well the action of pulling and adjusting. Note that the fingers of the right hand are bent outward unrealistically, as are also those of the chief's left.

The friezes that frame the top and bottom each carry a different motif, not one line of which is loosely or uncertainly carved. Many of the details in the composition could have been simplified if desired; the double tie of the chieftain's girdle, the natural uneven fall of the drapery both show virtuosity in carving.

The carved back of a marcasite mirror (*fig. b*) comes from the same cultural circle, and one can discover a similarity not only in its etching-like clarity but even in the features of the face. The head here also is shown in profile, turned to the left, and the beard, mentioned before, is sharply defined. Hair, cap, and earrings are made up of ingeniously contrasted lines. The face has life and strong characterization. In the frame, particularly on the left, a fret-scroll pattern, reminiscent of the type of decoration which is used with such fine effect on the Totonac yokes and *palmas* (see *Pl. 65, fig. c* and *Pl. 67*), gives a further indication of relationship.

With the second stone slab (*fig. c*), excavated at Tenam, Chiapas, we enter the Maya Area. In its linear conduct and clarity this low relief is inferior to the Totonac piece. In comparison there is a loss of life and living proportions; the air in the piece stiffens, and the human body becomes a mannequin for the recording of the paraphernalia of Maya full dress. As detailed as it is, the elaborate costume in the Totonac stela is wholly subordinated to the personality of the wearer.

The carving has, however, highly characteristic features of Maya representations. The pomp so typical of Maya ceremonies is very evident; the headdress is spread out to decorate the entire upper portion of the stone; the lavish ear, neck, and breast ornaments are meticulously depicted, together with belt, breechcloth, and footgear. Note the folds in the drapery behind the legs. The left hand holds a spear-thrower or staff, and the right, a pouch, much larger and more elaborate than anything seen hitherto. This profile also is turned to the left, but the body is posed facing full front, with the feet turned outward. The experience and ability of the carver can be judged from the fact that he did not feel himself restricted by the vertical frame of the stela but let some of the decoration overflow into the border.

SCULPTURE

MAYA AREA

The sculpture of the Maya at its best ranks without question among the highest artistic achievements of medieval America. From the earliest times that we are able to reconstruct, these people carved stone and modeled stucco to combine with their architecture. As the preceding chapter has shown, sculptured lintels decorated chambers as well as doorways; busts, masks, whole entrances were executed with a flood of plastic elements. Tablets and panels with fine and sophisticated incised compositions had a place both on the outside and inside walls.

Independent of the structures, though an integral part of the city picture, was the stone monument called a stela, a large slab or shaft that sometimes reached a height of 35 feet and a weight of more than fifty tons. Stelae were erected in the great plaza and before the temples at certain intervals of time—during the Great Period generally every twenty years—and are believed to have commemorated not only the passing of time but also historical events. This Maya custom covered the years between A.D. 328 and 889. The idea behind it is somewhat analogous to that of the obelisks of Mediterranean civilizations, but the sculptural execution is different. They bear the figures of priests or chiefs, always in ceremonial regalia, and hieroglyphs fill the remaining space. Much of the text is still unsolved, but the dates recorded serve as invaluable contributions to our knowledge. While certain dates will be given here, it is not our purpose to provide a chronological sequence but rather to point out the great variety of stylistic and sculptural solutions that this people found for a circumscribed subject.

A comparison of the three Maya stelae (*Pl. 69, fig. c* and *Pl. 70, figs. a* and *b*) will show how sculptural details can differentiate a concept which at the core is identical. In all three monuments a figure arrayed in full Maya splendor is carved in relief and placed within a frame. They all stand in uniform pose, bodies front, feet spread and pointing outward, heads turned in left profile. The left shoulder is higher, and the chin is superimposed on the right. All wear elaborate ceremonial dress, the details of which will soon be familiar to the reader. On the great headdress the casque just above the forehead represents the head of a monster. A mass of plumes, doubtless the shimmering gold-green feathers of the quetzal, tops the headgear. Elaborate bead necklaces with carved pendants deck the chest and shoulders; the wrists and legs are also bejeweled. The clothing consists of a short kilt with heavy ornamented belt and an apron-like "sash" extending down the front. Ornate high sandals cover the feet. Glyphs appear on each stela, but are differently placed in every case.

‹ 119 ›

On Stela 16 from Tikal, dated 711, is carved a dignitary holding a ceremonial bar (*fig. a*). The evolution in the depiction of this ritualistic object has been extensively studied by Dr. Spinden in his *Maya Art* and others after him. The heavy headdress overlaps the frame and feathered ornaments reach out even behind the body.

Stela 10 from Xultun (*fig. b*), a site not more than twenty-seven miles northeast of Tikal, is one of those bearing the latest date deciphered. Its figural decoration is still more involved. While in the Tikal stone, elaboration was lavished on a single person, here we discover several minor figures. A priest carries a miniature jaguar seated on his right hand and holds in the curve of his left a demon with a swinging leg. In the lower left corner an attendant can be discerned. At least seven masks are incorporated into the priest's attire. His broad collar with its carved medallion is especially effective. The upper part of the sandals, as in the preceding piece, are fashioned into masks, here facing toward the heel instead of the instep.

The Tenam stela is characterized by a compositional restraint infrequent in the Maya Area. The sculpture, both here and in the Tikal slab, is executed with a preference for straight lines and simple curves, while the third shows a predilection for rounded pearlish elements and curling loops much more difficult to carve. The larger component parts, more clearly separated units, and greater variety of line give it a more plastic effect.

All these variations of gesture, ritual objects, and garb signify changes in style from one site or period to another. The elasticity of expression within the limits of a strict iconography is one mark of the high artistry of the Maya.

If Stela H at Copan (*Pl. 71, fig. a*), believed to be from the late 8th century, is compared with those just described, a decided sculptural difference can be noted. The dignitary is *en face* and has stepped out of the frame. The outlines of the monument follow somewhat the contours of the figure, so that it more nearly approaches a statue. A beautifully woven and ornamented skirt is discernible, with even the pendants on the edge carefully expressed in carving.

It is characteristic that the Maya never worked out their stelae into figures in the round; although the figural elements experienced considerable change—in attitude, facial expression, and execution—and even the glyphs were modified as their style developed, the monuments never entirely lost their slablike form.

Quiriguá is justly famous for its sculpture. Although the site lies only about twenty-five miles from Copan as the bird flies, the traveler has a much longer journey, for the direct road that existed in pre-Columbian times is overgrown with jungle vegetation. Stela D, like a number of monuments here, has two figural sides, the better preserved of which, that on the north, is shown in *fig. c.* The material is the reddish-brown sandstone native to the site, which adds a somber dignity to its carvings. The height of the sculptured slab is about 20 feet, the width 5, and the thickness 34 inches.

The figure does not stand out so free as at Copan, but the Maya's love of changing plastic surfaces is even more manifest. The only undecorated section is the face; the rest of the stone is an exposition of the sculptor's tremendous skill and arduous labor. From headdress to ankle ornaments a studied elaboration is evident. The glyphs (the east panel visible in *fig. b*) are gems of medallion carving; indeed, according to Dr. Morley, glyphic execution reached its peak in the panels of stelae D and F at Quiriguá.[91] Its date is 766.

Here should be mentioned the strange and inexplicable monuments, like boulders in shape and covered with involved carving, that are frequently found near the stelae at Quiriguá. Called "turtles," these altars are believed to symbolize the earth-monster. Their symbolism is so involved, however, that an intense familiarity with them is necessary for their appreciation. The sculptural talent which executed them is manifest in other types of carving easier for us to grasp.

Monuments with seated figures—a feature rare in Maya stelae—are presented on *Pl. 72.* The type occurs several times at Piedras Negras. In a somewhat damaged state, but with content still clear enough to be enjoyed, is Stela 6 (*fig. a*), which bears the date 687. A dignitary sits cross-legged within a shallow niche. The figure proper is almost 4 feet high. His monster headdress and breast ornament are quite massive, but this stocky muscular personage does not seem weighed down by them. Note the virtuose touch in the carving of the loose knot just below the collar. Vertical columns of glyphs adorn the frame and smaller glyphs are incised on the drapery above and even in the arch formed by the curving feathers. The figure holds a pouch decorated with a brilliantly executed little monkey-head medallion, which dangles across the lower section, connecting the main subject with its frame.

Stela 14 from the same site is presented in *fig. b.* The much deeper niche, with the looped material above the head, is still more suggestive of a canopied throne. The seated dignitary has much in common with the preceding one—the details of the headdress and the pouch in his hand are more clearly discernible in this case—but here he is a character in a scene. Before him stands a full-length figure with upturned face, an offering in his hand. The pose of the chief, noble and self-assured, is in good contrast to that of the subordinate, who seems to do him homage. A third person, almost obliterated, is suggested in the lower right. The unprecedented blend of different plastic depths not only serves to bring out the central subject but even gives a sense of perspective. Despite the sections that have suffered from exposure, the stela illustrates fully the dignity in Maya art.

The execution of all details is done with the hair-fine finesse of a copper engraving. Great care was given to the dress of the standing figure. Note the decorated band and the knotted fringe on the edge of the lower garment and the openwork band with frets just above it. A single feather of the headdress is swept up with great artistic courage, as if blown by the wind or tossed up by the gesture, making a smooth transition from the upper section of the carving. Another feather, from among those he holds, turns downward, making contact with the headdress below. A series of footprints is just discernible coming from the right and mounting the ladder-like construction that seems to lead up to the throne.

The glyphs, placed unobtrusively and with great decorative effect on the throne, hanging drapery, and the plain section beside it, refer most probably to the ceremony involved. The date is interpreted as 800.

Fig. c shows Stela I at Quiriguá. The shaft is about 13½ feet high and has on the front (not shown here) a chief standing in conventional pose. Our picture reproduces the back of the stela, where amid a welter of plumes a small seated figure is carved. Although he occupies relatively little space considering the mass of the stone, he radiates concentrated power. The flowing headdress is well arranged, breaking out of the niche and guiding the eye to the Serpent Bird hovering above him. The body of a double-headed monster serves as frame, carved with the symbols of various constellations, its heads distinguishable on either side near the dignitary's knees. Below the figure is a grotesque mask as throne, from which hang two outflaring frets.[91] The date is 800.

A lively inner movement connects one section of the carving with the other, and the upward sweep of the feathers at the base close the design effectively, preventing it from running into the ground. Although the composition may have little meaning for us, it has an artistic maturity which holds together concisely the whole world of pattern it contains.

‹ 122 ›

SCULPTURE

In the monuments from Piedras Negras shown on *Pls. 73* and *74,* the subject matter has achieved real freedom and the technique, great refinement. A full view of Stela 40, which is more than 13 feet high, is presented in *fig. a* of *Pl. 73.* It is dated 746. The central figure is shown kneeling upon a podium that divides the sculpture in two sections. The bust on the lower half offers, in the main, familiar elements and is quite rigid in its inflexible gaze. The great revelation of the piece is conveyed by the figure above with its symbolic action, a representation of the Maize-god scattering corn. We are at once struck by the fact that he has neither the stiffness of pose nor the static weight of body so characteristic of the stela figures already seen; much breathing space is allowed him. This differentiation between the two figures may have been deliberate; facing in opposite directions and so contrastingly conceived, they effect a crescendo through their very independence.

The kneeling pose of the Maize-god (*fig. b*) has the softness and complete linear freedom of some of the Palenque stucco reliefs or the best painted vases, even though the hardness of the medium here made the execution of such a graceful line considerably more difficult. The headgear, with its lacy ornament shaped like a bishop's mitre, rounds out the dignity of this extraordinary figure, and the mask or head attached to the back of the god is executed with fastidious care. Such careful delineation of the hair is unusual in Maya art. The hands are exquisitely expressive in their separate gestures, the left holding a decorated bag containing the seed which the right is dropping. Falling kernels of maize are discernible just before the open palm, and leaves of the mature plant, curling like fleur-de-lys, decorate the border. Dexterity, intelligence, and devotion created this figure—emotionally the most immediate among all Maya sculpture.

Stela 12 from Piedras Negras (*Pl. 74, fig. a*) is perhaps the finest expression in stone relief left by the Maya. The monument is 10⅓ feet high, about 3½ wide, and 1½ thick, and weighs about four tons. Its material is native yellowish limestone, which, when freshly quarried, is soft and easily worked. It was broken into four pieces but is now restored to such an extent that its original appearance can be easily imagined. This and the one just described are uncarved on the back.

The narrow sides of this stela are inscribed with hieroglyphs in accordance with Maya custom. The deciphered date is 795. It should be remembered, however, that in some cases dates may have had commemorative significance and would not necessarily coincide with the time the monument was erected.

‹ 123 ›

On the face of the rounded slab, at the top, is sculptured a person of authority, seated on a dais and looking down upon the scene at his feet. He is probably the one-time ruler of the site now called Piedras Negras. In his hand he carries a long befeathered staff. Two attendants, also richly dressed, stand on either side a little below, and between them crouches in suppliant pose a figure who is perhaps the chief of a conquered people. He is unbound and still wears his necklace and other ornaments, an indication that he has been accorded the honors of war. Eight smaller figures crowd the lower space, possibly captives destined for sacrifice. All are bound with rope and have been despoiled of their necklaces and ear ornaments.

The scene as here presented makes the best possible use of relief. The lack of perspective is compensated for by grouping the units of the story-telling composition on different levels, one above the other; those in the foreground are carved in very shallow relief, while the background behind the main figure is considerably deepened, in the manner already seen in *Pl. 72, fig. b.*

To our modern eye, the group of prisoners is perhaps the most rewarding. Here, on a relatively narrow surface, is recorded a character study of eight human beings with a *triste* future. Their arrangement is completely devoid of any schematic representation—so often encountered when a mass has to be pictured—and in pose and facial expression each one has individuality. The huddling together of their bodies and the jumble of upturned faces alone would convey the desperation of their plight. Especially clear for closer study are the three in the lower right corner (*fig. b*), where the stone is still intact. While the rest look more or less toward the ruler, on whose decision their fate depends, the man on the extreme right lets his head hang. Apparently the oldest among the prisoners, he has lowered his gaze, bitter and without hope. Small details such as the hair, the expressive postures of the hands, and the knots and folds of the breechcloths, excellently drawn (note the third from the right), prove that each figure in the composition, whether ruler or captive, received the same careful attention.

Some of the minute jewel-like glyphs incised on the dais and elsewhere may refer to the occasion here commemorated, while those on the bodies of the prisoners probably give the names of the captives or the town or tribe which each represented.

Our admiration of this piece grows when we consider that it was carved without metal tools, with only the use of flint, obsidian, or other hard-stone implements and abrasives, such as sand. The effect is of an etching in stone.

Palenque, whose great artistic refinement was displayed in its architecture, reveals the same high achievement in sculpture, both stone and stucco. The stone tablet in *Pl. 75, fig. b,* consisting of three large slabs and dated 642, stood against the back wall of the inner sanctuary of the Temple of the Sun. It is carved in very low relief and records a scene from an offertory ceremony. On the right, standing upon the back of a prostrate figure, is a priest—a little under 5 feet tall —holding in his hands a statuette with a demon mask. His body, pulsed through with life, can be picked out from the mass of confusing detail. He is drawn with amazing surety and the gesture of offering is realistically conveyed.

A smaller priest on the left is also occupied in making an offering of a statue. He too stands on a figure, which in this case is kneeling, bracing itself on its outstretched arms. A shield with a mask and two crossed ceremonial darts or lances fill the space in the center, while below is an altar-like construction, supported by two seated figures. All the subordinate persons in the piece are masked. They are posed to bring out a certain symbolic meaning for the Maya and demonstrate for us admirable skill.

Among the glyphs is a date interpreted as 2359 B.C., so remote that it is thought to be some legendary or astronomical reference. It is noteworthy that the framework of dates on all three sanctuary inscriptions of the group (the temples of the Sun, the Cross, and the Foliated Cross) are closely interrelated. The same principals also appear—the tall, somewhat obese priest with his scant garments and mitre-like headdress, and the smaller figure, wrapped in intricately knotted scarves, with a flower waving above his head—but placed in varied settings.

Originally the panels reproduced in *figs. a* and *c* flanked the doorway to the same sanctuary, as shown in *fig. d,* Catherwood's sketch made in 1841. They were removed and are at present set into the outside wall of the village church of Santo Domingo Palenque. The relief at the left shows a young person in resplendent regalia, his headdress branching in several directions, his chest covered with elaborate decoration, and his heavy ornamented belt featuring a jaguar head. His right hand curves downward and his left, upward in a precious manner, which is reminiscent of the symbolic gesture of the Maya Maize-god of Copan. (See *Pl. 90.*)

In the other panel (*fig. c*) appears a stooped old man with a shrewd sly expression. He is dressed in a jaguar skin, over which hangs an unusually long string of beads. Both hands clasp an object held to his mouth, from which smoke seems to emerge. Familiar symbolical decorations, many of them not interpreted as yet, are inserted where space permits. The same sure and animated linear conduct that characterizes the great tablet above is manifest here.

The ruins of Yaxchilan, sometimes known as Menché, lie in Chiapas also, on the shores of the Usumacintla River. This site has become famous chiefly for its masterly sculptured lintels.

On Lintel 53 from Structure 55 (*Pl. 76, fig. a*) we witness for the first time here a scene pictured frequently in Maya art, in which two figures are facing each other. The smaller of the two is represented in full profile. His pompous attire is worthy of notice. The large package that he carries weighs down his right hand, while the left rests on top nearly on a line with his chin in a natural well-observed position.

The individual who receives this offering is undoubtedly the more important personage. He stands in a stela pose, feet spread apart and face in left profile. This three-quarters position is indicated, as is general in Maya art, with one shoulder somewhat raised. All the majesty of his office is apparent in his dress. Many details, usually obscure, are here remarkably clear through the variation of pattern. A broad jade bar hangs across his breast, and medallions and pendants with human faces, both frontal and in profile, are applied liberally throughout the costume. In his right hand he holds a manikin scepter, extraordinary in its clean carving and well-preserved state. As the great headdress demands more space than is available, its top feathers vanish beyond the frame and return to it, a rare feature. Feather ornamentation appears also from behind the figure on each side, and single feathers, curving upward, counterbalance the downward-trending lines. This little-known but very remarkable carving presents Maya iconography at its best, both in spirit and execution.

Lintel 15 from House F, to use Maudslay's nomenclature (*fig. b*), has become well known since his publication. At the right, a worshiper kneels before a huge serpent, from the jaws of which a divine figure issues. It should be noted that kneeling is a posture of reverence which we take for granted but which was practiced in very few Asiatic and Polynesian religions. The hands of the supplicant, holding what is probably an offering in a basket container, are well carved, with the right remarkable for its foreshortening. Although his face is turned in profile, his body is presented nearly full front, enveloped in a heavy robe that is beautifully patterned and edged with a different design. The details of the hairdress are used to a highly decorative effect.

The second participant in this scene is one of the most important of the fantastic symbolic creatures in Maya mythology. Rising from a vessel that contains cone shapes similar to those in the hands of the kneeling figure, it has the body of a serpent but ends in a human head, with a human right hand extended in a communicating gesture. The windings, scrolls, and smaller incised motifs are all taken from a settled artistic vocabulary.

In a comparison of the two reliefs, it will be noted that while *fig. a,* from the year 766, conveys a greater sense of realism in pose and gesture, *fig. b,* with the date 702 ?, surpasses it in decorative quality. In the first, differentiations are made by varying the pattern on the more or less uniform plane of a blocked-out relief; Lintel 15, on the other hand, uses also variations in the depth of the carving, giving a more plastic impression. The diagonal division of the field is unusually subtle. There is another striking distinction between the two tablets: in the first piece the priestly figure dominates the scene; in the second, the dignitary is subordinated to the supernatural.

The contrast between a blocked-out relief on the one hand, producing angular detail, and free-flowing, almost three-dimensional plasticity on the other can also be observed in the carvings on *Pl. 77,* once called lintels but now believed to have served as ornamental wall panels. On Lintel 1 from Piedras Negras (*fig. a*) is carved a chief with an attendant, receiving the homage of six kneeling warriors. He stands in the conventional pose, wearing a rich headdress and feather display, breast ornament, shield, and woven materials finely conveyed. His companion is a pace or two behind him, smaller and of less importance but nevertheless lavishly attired. The great rings around his eyes denote paint or a mask.

In excellent contrast to these two who stand in dignity, anchored by their staffs and theatrical in pose, is the closely knit composition of the kneeling warriors. Their heads and headdresses are distinctly separated, but below the shoulders they blend into one mass. While there is some differentiation in detail, especially in height, we feel that all six of them express a uniform action. The glyphs that frame the scene on three sides are neutral in effect, so dynamic is the figural portion.

Lintel 3 (*fig. b*), also from Piedras Negras, was found in a temple which stood near some of the most beautiful stelae in the Maya Area, including those shown on *Pl. 72, fig. b,* and *Pl. 74.* It is a tragedy that this sculpture should be so seriously damaged; however, like a magnificent fragmentary torso, it still speaks with the eloquence of true art.

The lintel measures roughly 4 feet by 2 and is 5½ inches thick. Almost the entire surface of the stone is carved in relief to a maximum depth of 1½ inches. A ceremony is probably pictured—a less warlike gathering than that just discussed, as no weapons are visible. In the center of the composition, on a rectangular altar or throne, a chief is seated, perhaps the personification of a deity. A number of such built-in thrones have been excavated at this site. On this one the boldly carved back is shown draped with a spotted jaguar skin, and the covering with its tasseled fringe is carefully executed. While the chief's face is mutilated and the right arm, probably raised, is missing, the one detail of his left hand, as it grasps the edge of the dais, is enough to prove the high quality of sculptural talent involved.

The group at the right, judging from the space used and the size of the bodies, seems to have consisted of four figures, two adults and two children. The extended arm of the one on the end is undercut and made fully plastic, a rare occurrence in Maya sculpture. At the left stand three persons cut in very deep relief. Their postures are varied and realistic, their arms crossed over the breast in the Maya gesture of reverence.[79]

In the foreground below the altar, seven others are seated, with a tall tripod vessel placed on the ground in the center of the group. There is rhythmic flow of line and movement in the whole scene; the masterly execution is particularly clear in the harmonious blending of the many different poses. Even in the fragmentary state of the piece, their attentive attitude is evident. Sculptured details, such as hands, feet, fingers, and even nails are portrayed with perfect clarity, and the delicate fabric of their garments is meticulously conveyed. All probably wore ornamental headdresses; the one immediately in front of the chief still shows the outline of a long-billed bird, distinguishable against the dais.

Judging from the existing background, at least four of the heads in the group must have been carved in the full round. The end figure at the right gives an idea of the lightness of the whole composition in the freedom of his pose, as he sits turned expectantly toward the center, leaning on his hand. At the opposite end, enough remains of the first figure to convey not only his gracious carriage but also the refinement of technique in cutting out the section behind the neck.

Delicately carved hieroglyphs are executed in both cameo and intaglio. One hundred fifty-eight characters are inscribed in fourteen different groups, the greatest number known on any lintel.

Upon comparing the two pieces reproduced on this plate, we are astonished to notice such divergence, not so much in ideology as in the plasticity of execution, in carvings from the same site, both dated 761. It would seem that within the autarchic art of one city much individual talent came to expression.

After having seen these lintels, we can more easily imagine the fragment from the same site (*Pl. 78, fig. a*) before it was demolished. In the center, which was probably part of the frame of the composition, stands a human figure, feet apart and back to us. We notice again the sculptural trick of lowering one shoulder to express a more plausible pose. The headdress, although not very elaborate, contains some new features.

The second figure must have been the last person of the scene within the frame. His arms are folded; some details of a headdress and breechcloth are all that is discernible. In its present condition it has an impressionistic softness and, as a fragment, it perhaps comes nearer to us than it would have when intact. Remarkable command of the medium is shown in the juxtaposition of very shallow relief and deep plastic carving.

In a much better state of preservation is a very thin stone slab from Jonuta, Campeche, on the border of Tabasco, Mexico (*fig. b*). It is 38 inches high. This bearded Maya with his sloping forehead, almond eyes, and protruding under lip, executed with the sharpness of a copper engraving, could be a character study. The fact that the farther leg and arm are shown lends a certain plasticity to the shallow relief and more life to the figure. He is draped with a jaguar skin and bears a vessel heaped with objects reminiscent of those on some painted Maya vases. A parrot behind his head is exquisitely drawn—note the ruffled wings, open beak, and the realistic depiction of the two claws. Judging from the size of the scroll with the glyph panel at the upper left, the piece may have been a part of a larger composition, one which these details make us long to see.

Relief work in stucco came to its supreme expression in the perfection and flamboyance seen at Palenque. Piers of the buildings are covered to their full height with figures that approximate life size. Within, walls are incrusted with medallions. Each structure carries out a separate theme, yet in style all are homogeneous. Stucco work throughout Palenque, whether figural or abstract, speaks one idiom, not only highly articulate and technically preëminent but one which also approaches those principles by which we judge art.

To produce these reliefs in delicate stucco under tropical conditions was certainly a technical achievement, for the preparation of the background, preliminary and final modeling, and the drying must have been threatened by the general dampness of climate and often imperiled by torrential rains. How well they were executed is proved by the remnants that have survived—all too few, but in relatively good condition, considering the fact that Palenque's latest known date falls in mid-8th century.

It was the custom to refurbish stucco surfaces from time to time with a thin coating of plaster that was then colored, and there are places in Palenque where the face of the original is covered with several layers.[81]

The stucco relief in *Pl. 79, fig. a* occupies a full pier on the west front of the Palace, House D. A figure in dancing pose looks down upon another, kneeling, whose face and body are, regrettably, worn away. Although so much movement is rare in Maya art, it is beautifully and rhythmically portrayed here; weightless, the figure seems to float on its feet. The gesture of the left hand directed toward the kneeling companion is completely independent of that of the right, which carries an ornate ceremonial object.

Fig. b shows a pier on the eastern façade of the Palace, House H. Compare the elaborate bead network on the costume at the left with that in *fig. a* and on the Copan stela (see *Pl. 71, fig. a*). The personage who is standing, undoubtedly the most important of the three, is lavishly garbed. Though the face is destroyed, we detect in his body and carriage a clue to his youth and *noblesse*. His headdress, fantastically flamboyant, is balanced, though not by paired elements. A jaguar skin girds his hips, its tail hanging down the back. The undamaged human head attached to his waist in the back, which may represent a trophy or a mask, is in itself a demonstration of complete command of the medium.

A certain restraint can be sensed in both of these compositions; neither the flamboyant feathers nor the streaming hair is allowed to burst out of bounds. Breathing space is ample in both scenes. The rich frames are proof of great compositional ability, the possession only of a people mature in art.

Of a technical excellence on a par with Palenque's, even if not so ebullient, is the stucco work found in a tomb at Comalcalco in Tabasco, Mexico, only about ninety-six miles distant. This Maya site suffered a dearth of stone and built its structures of baked brick. Even in ruins the extensive area of the settlement can be perceived. Some of its edifices reach a height of 115 feet and a length of 575, but for our survey, the greatest contribution comes from the small burial chamber hidden in the undergrowth of the western part of the dead city. It was discovered on the last day of a Tulane University expedition in 1925.[15]

The reconstruction of the tomb (*Pl. 80, fig. d*), which includes even the skeleton that was lying on a low platform, produces something of the impression that the archaeologists received when they broke through the blocked doorway. In the original, both figures and walls show traces of a deep red color, with which the finely smoothed cement floor was also stained. The tomb is believed to date from the end of the 7th century.

Fig. a presents an original detail from the south wall, and *fig. c,* one from the north. Even in their dilapidated condition, both attest to great ability in characterization, for while the pose has more stolidity than in most of the Palenque stucco figures, the two faces are much nearer portraiture. The lean man on the right especially, with his bowed head, deep wrinkles, and penetrating look, is one of the most human documents salvaged from Maya art.

In *fig. b* the entire east wall is shown, more clearly seen in the reconstruction below. This group of three, the best preserved, gives a good idea of the loose, yet decoratively connected sequence of all nine figures that ornament the chamber. Each man is individual in face, figure, and action. The one on the left, in profile, stands inactive, with his arms crossed over his hanging belly. Especially spontaneous is the pose of the left arm and hand of the figure in the center, whose head is shown turned to the right but whose body faces front. The man on the right points, as if in conversation, into the space where a vertical column of hieroglyphs is inserted.

Compared with the figureheads so frequently depicted, these are people. According to tradition, the Maya had actors and jesters.[158] Whom these nine figures represent, whether chiefs, priests, warriors, courtiers, or clowns, we may never know; but it is evident that they are indicative of a grand scale of living.

The next four plates present comparative material. Two different types of stone sculpture from the state of Chiapas, a region preëminent in Maya art, are shown on the first (*Pl. 81*).

The stone tablet from Palenque (*fig. a*) was probably brought out by Captain Dupaix in the last years of the 18th century and is now in the Museo Arqueológico Nacional, Madrid. It was first reproduced by Leon de Rosny, who saw it there and published it as Yucatecan.[116] The late Marshall H. Saville, great American pioneer archaeologist, adjudged its provenience, after seeing it in Madrid, as Palenque.[127] The relief deserves more attention than it has received. It is to be regretted that such a classic example is little known, largely because of its isolation, while many more accessible pieces of weaker quality are reproduced again and again. It is believed to have been connected with an altar in the Palace Group and is judged earlier in date than the stucco figures there.[68]

The carving is executed in the best style of the Great Period at Palenque. The priest or chief admirably fills the space allotted within the plain frame. He is seated with one foot under him, leaning forward. His right arm presses against the frame, while the left, as he holds high a trailing water-lily, reaches into the opposite corner. In the palm of his hand, two of the fingers gracefully curved, he carries, according to de Rosny, a symbol of the sacred serpent. The weight in the composition lies in the left half of the sculpture, as the body leans in that direction, but this is ingeniously counterbalanced by the movement expressed in the exquisitely flowing lines on the right. The carving of all details is precise and varied; especially interesting are the headdress, earplugs with pendants, and the finely woven and decorated belt and cloth, lying in natural folds. His full profile, in characteristic pose, brings out very clearly the sloping line of the flattened forehead.

The whole composition has the same plastic air admired in the stucco-relief fragments and bears a similarity in spirit to the figures in certain jade pendants. The same delicacy of linear conduct and the same masterly use of deep- and shallow-cut detail will appear in some of the jades in a coming chapter.

Through the courtesy of Dr. Spinden, we are able to reproduce the stone statuette in *fig. b,* showing a Maya astronomer seated on a hieroglyph. It is 9 inches high and 5½ wide. According to the renowned Maya scholar, it comes from the Intermediate Period, which would place it at least two or three hundred years later than the stone tablet above. It is noteworthy that individuals seated on glyphs also appear on carved series at Copan.

While relief and full-round sculpture of the same culture and period in medieval American art usually speak the same plastic language, we observe here a strong stylistic deviation. Besides the differences inherent in a three-dimensional piece and the more limited relief, we note in *fig. b* a complete departure from the stylized manner that we observed in preceding examples and saw illustrated in *fig. a.* A robust and dynamic rhythm permeates the carving, and, instead of an aristocratically cool and remote representation, a human of flesh and blood—with even a dose of humor—sits before us. A new plastic idiom is injected into the piece that here is only the expression of power and life, but which in the following centuries changed into hardness and even coarseness. Besides the display of talent in the easy carriage of the turned head, which again faces left, the sculpturally difficult gesture of the arms and hands should be observed. In a statue carved perhaps five hundred years later (see *Pl. 62, fig. b*) they are no longer kept separate but held close to the leg, even though the greater mass of stone would have made it safe to cut them in the round had the artistic stimulus still been alive.

The great virtuosity of the Maya sculptor in composing figures within the limits of a circle recalls the distant *tondos* of early Italian painting. Just as in the case of those great Quattrocento panels, the subject matter never seemed crammed into its circumscribed space, so, in the three examples shown on *Pl. 82,* the content of each relief, no matter how intricate, is artistically balanced and fits into the frame.

A ball-court marker from Copan, 25 inches in diameter, is shown in *fig. a.* As was noted in the chapter on architecture, ball games were played throughout the southern Mexican and the Maya areas, and it is not surprising that the people of these regions set the mark of their genius on the paraphernalia required for this ceremonial sport. Two personages are carved on this piece, facing each other across an inscribed plaque. The one on the left seems to be attired in the protective armor necessary for the game, while the other, judging from his elaborate garb and the masks attached at both front and rear, might be an officiating priest or chief.

The density of composition transmits even to us something of the tension that must have preceded such an occasion, upon which at times even lives were forfeit. The creation of a ground line gives to the two individuals firm footing. Although available space is limited, they do not have to stoop to fit within the circular border, and even the headdresses have freedom of movement. Unobtrusive and subtle are the four points on the inside rim of the frame, forming in effect a quatrefoil for the relief. With its unbelievable variety of sculptural lines and shapes, this marker can be considered at present the most superb example of its type. It is dated about 600.

On a small round altar from Tonina, also known as Ocosingo, central Chiapas (*fig. b*), a priest making an offering is the sole subject. He is placed in the circular field with complete command of composition, without a ground line or other plastic element to stabilize or bind him on this difficult shape. The outer frame of hieroglyphs and the deep undecorated background set off the figure in the center admirably. His face is clean-cut, his gesture easily understood, and his pose has lightness and grace. There is in the carving dignity, maturity, and general appeal.

A second ball-court marker, one from Chinkultic, Chiapas, is shown in *fig. c*. It is 18½ inches in diameter and also bears a disk with a glyphic inscription. Here there is no ground line for the figure to rest upon. A quite unrealistic pose is depicted, and there is less subtlety in composing for a circular frame. Many straight lines cut across the field, and although they furnish interesting contrast (as in the case of the rectangle formed by the legs), they also introduce considerable restlessness. The two blocks of glyphs seem awkwardly placed, but those in the rim are spaced with remarkable facility. The date is 591.

The recording of the dress and certain technical details in its delineation do not seem purely Maya. (See *Pl. 69, fig. a*.) In fact, in the plastic language of the whole piece influence from another culture is evident. There is a flatness about the whole, a rigidity of line and a certain lack of geniality.

In their build-up the three pieces manifest somewhat a common ideology; in all of them the chief figure in the scene turns toward the left and similar details of costume can be detected. But the longer we compare each with the other, the more pronounced become their differences and the more clearly we sense a diversity of background. In the first, besides the human element, a composite mythology had to be served; in the second, the calmness of maturity and a virtuosity in expression simplified whatever had to be recorded; in the third, the idea is not crystal clear, but tinged with an elusive alienness.

Three stone fragments, each portraying a human head, are brought together on *Pl. 83* to show those considerable stylistic differences that appeared in localities relatively not too distant from one another and all connected by trade and ethnic threads. Copan lies about two hundred twenty miles from Piedras Negras, and Piedras Negras some four hundred fifty from Tajin. All three examples present the left profile, which, as may already have been observed, is the position of an overwhelming majority of high dignitaries in carvings and must have had iconographical significance.

The spirit, however, of each is characteristic. The first two are highly Maya. The Piedras Negras work (*fig. a*) dates perhaps from a later period than the Copan piece (*fig. b*), which shows a much greater simplicity in approach. Aside from this, Piedras Negras was master of relief and remained within the bounds of that technique, perfecting it to a decidedly individual degree. Copan, on the other hand, produced some of the most liberated sculpture in the round, and even this fragment shows a tendency in that direction. In *fig. c* a section of a column from El Tajin is seen. Its plastic units and the spreading of design, outspokenly Totonac in type, are utterly different from the other two.

A comparison of the eyes in the three pieces will show in the first a circular deepening, in the second a lidded half-moon shape, and in the third, a deeper hole with convulsive overhanging eyebrows. In addition, the decorative background and other accompanying features, such as ear and earplug, document how distinctive was the recording of a similar theme in a similar medium.

Pl. 84 also offers comparative material, for it is by placing examples from two cultures beside each other that we are best able to mark the differences, sometimes subtle, sometimes obvious, that characterize individual styles.

Fig. a presents a lintel from El Chicozapote, a lesser-known site in the valley of the Usumacintla River that lies between Yaxchilan and Piedras Negras. As we have already seen, this region produced superb carvings. The scene here features two people, a stooped older man and a youthful figure that might be a woman. Each is gesticulating with one hand, in both cases that on the inside, which may be a concession to compositional and decorative considerations. Both faces have portrait-like features. Here it might be remarked that the majority of early portraiture is executed in profile. Seemingly there were technical reasons for this, for individual features are more tellingly brought out in outline than in full-face representation. Even the Italians—far later than Piero della Francesca—show this predilection.

This lintel, dated about 690, is one of the few that still retain their original colors. The skin of both figures is a burning red; necklaces, earplugs, feathers, and the empty inscription field are emerald-green, while the body of the headdresses is a flame-red. Loincloths are green and blue, and the background is dark red with a blue border above and below.[74]

The Zapotec stone relief (*fig. b*), about 15 by 24 inches, presents an obvious contrast in style that requires little further comment. Here also persons are seated facing each other, on the ground or low cushions in the upper half and, in the lower, on daises.

The two figures on the right are men, judging from their cross-legged pose and flowing feathers, the other two, women, seated in Indian fashion. Note the feet under the fringe of the skirt. Both wear a headdress very similar to that found even today in Oaxaca (where it is called *tlacoyal*) and in certain parts of the Guatemalan highlands. It is made of heavy strands twisted around the head in the manner of a turban, with the loose ends left to hang down the back of the head like a tassel.[89] Woven fabrics are designated on all four figures, with the shawls around the shoulders of the women and the breechcloths of the men especially clear.

The top section of the carving is devoted to the open jaw of a monster with six large teeth. From it emerges a figure, a garland in its hand and a bubble coming out of its mouth signifying speech, probably an emanation. In the lower panel, this part is occupied by a small monkey.

In contrast to the blank background of the preceding lintel, the remaining space is filled with signs and symbols, like a page of Zapotec manuscript. Glyphs are inscribed even over part of the margin. The content is said to be calendrical, with an unusual number of day signs.[20] The two carvings, with so much similarity in theme and so little in iconography, come from sites about three hundred seventy miles from each other.

Beginning with *Pl. 85* a series of three-dimensional Maya carvings comes to discussion. The fragment from Copan (*fig. a*) was undoubtedly built into a structure, judging from the tenon at the back, and appears to be the reared head of a reptile. Even in its damaged state the piece is fresh and alive, with something of the primeval power of a Romanesque gargoyle. The surety of execution in all details attests to an iconography so established that the carver knew exactly how to give shape to an image of the Maya fantasy-world.

The human head (*fig. b*), also from Copan, was likewise probably applied as decoration to a building. The almond cut of the eyes, the somewhat aquiline nose, and half-open mouth are all details which will be found in the sculpture of Copan and regions influenced by it. In this head the upper teeth are clearly visible, while in those that follow they seem to have been conventionalized until they appear to be the end of the tongue. The rings around the eyes, denoting a mask or paint, were met in Lintel 1, Piedras Negras (see *Pl. 77, fig. a*). The wooden brace below the chin was fashioned to keep it in balance on the museum shelf.

Heads made of stucco (*Pl. 86*) were also frequently used as a decorative element on Maya buildings. Although because of their friable material most of them today are in poor condition, their importance warrants their inclusion here.

Real modeling in the features and a good feeling for the natural curves of the face are revealed in the head salvaged from Palenque by Maudslay (*fig. a*). Of the four, this quietly human piece stands nearest to our esthetic principles.

With its open mouth, teeth, and hanging under lip, the head from Piedras Negras (*fig. b*) approaches a mask in idea. This is the only one of the four in which enough of the headdress remained to make a restoration of this part possible. In the execution of all these heads certain similar plastic tricks are noticeable, but this specimen has, nevertheless, its own style. It is larger than life size and is said to have been part of a heroic figure.

Even more individuality is apparent in *fig. c,* from Uxmal, Yucatan. A fortunate preservation of some of its coloring gives us a clearer idea of the original appearance. Here we have an example of one way in which eyes were painted in pre-Columbian America: it was done by giving a light color to the eyeball, a strongly contrasting dark to the iris, and even adding a dot in the center to suggest the gleam of the pupil. The slight cast, plainly depicted, was to the Maya a mark of beauty. The painted rings recall the Copan head of the preceding plate. The face may have emerged from a monster jaw—the fragmentary remnants around it, especially under the chin, would suggest some such frame. Drawn with proportioned clean-cut lines, the aristocratically closed lips give a severe and uncommunicative expression. Baffling plastic details are visible above the nose and upper lip. But the longer we gaze at this face, the more we glimpse of the life which lies today shattered and in chips.

Fig. d comes from Louisville, British Honduras, and is about 9 inches high. Closer in expression to what might be called the Copan type, it shows a fine sense for light and shade. A tendency toward remoteness is noticeable in the veiled eyes and the abstract expression.

Among the larger examples of Maya sculpture that were incorporated into their architecture, a special place is due the imposing trachyte figure, larger than life size (*Pl. 87*), which once occupied the second place on the Hieroglyphic Stairway at Copan. The low dais upon which he sits is embellished with symbolic decoration in keeping with Maya ceremony. On the left, tassels can be discerned, with lattice-work below them similar to that noted on the Piedras Negras stone stelae (see *Pl. 72*).

There is dignity in the statue even in its mutilated state. His massive headdress is fashioned in the shape of a monster's upper jaw. The cape, meticulously carved, shows intricate textile patterns and tassels, and an elaborate belt can still be distinguished. A heavy jade necklace and bar with mask rest on his chest, and earrings almost hide his ears. The legs, too, are decorated with well-defined ornaments and the ceremonial apron hanging between them is enriched with a large bold design.

As already mentioned, every step of this great structure is covered with glyphs, and most of it, if not all, was painted. (See *Pl. 21, fig. a.*) Five statues, each different, punctuated the majestic sweep of the stairway. They must have been a splendid sight against the plastic background, vibrant with color. In no other civilization is there anything quite like it. This statue, even as it stands, uprooted from its original setting and forlorn, is still a worthy match for many a Hindu or Chinese figure in our museums, whether a 6th-century Buddha or a Judge of Hell of the later Ming Dynasty.

A number of related stone heads exist which also were not independent statues but ornaments for the entablature sections of buildings. The type was found at several sites but most are known to have come from Copan. On the three plates that follow a series of them is presented.

A head from Copan (*Pl. 88, fig. a*) shows the typical features, executed according to a well-established sculptural language. Eyes are almond shape, drawn out at the corners; the slender nose is long and straight, and a somewhat curling upper lip discloses part of the teeth or tongue. The head is pleasantly elongated, and locks of hair are represented by groups of two or three chiseled lines leading away from the face.

Another stone head from this site, nearly life size, is pictured in *fig. d*. Although the sculptural build-up is at first glance strikingly similar, there is less softness in the expression. Its shape is not so elongated, and the cheek bones are emphasized a little more. The hair is more rigid and is drawn with different strokes. The earring, here undamaged, shows the style associated with the type. In this piece the tenon at the back is visible that served to fix the sculpture into the wall of the building.

The provenience of the carving in *fig. c* is unknown, but it has positive Maya characteristics. The ear ornament, though smaller, is similar to the one just mentioned, and the open mouth also suggests the other heads. But there is no indication of hair, and the large protruding ornament applied on the forehead is a new element. The eyes have a slit line and not an almond shape; the nose is shorter, and the cheeks are more oval.

Fig. b comes from Quiriguá. Despite outspoken plastic differences, the kinship is obvious. However, it no longer has the radiation of the others. Slight changes in each feature bring about a coarsening of the expression: the eye line is drawn more toward the temples, with deeper carving in the corners; the chiseled line of the hair is much more conventionalized and less artistic; the nose is stumpy, and the mouth smaller and not so finely drawn; also, the aristocratic elongation of the head is gone, and the chopped-off lower half of the face gives to it a sullen unfriendliness. Throughout the piece the expression has narrowed down and darkened; this is the head of an idol.

In the two examples on *Pl. 89,* the carefully arranged hair that frames the youthful face is topped with the curling leaves of the corn. It is partly because of this feature that these sculptures are usually called Maize-gods. They were all created to be viewed from below, and the dramatic effect of the powerful tropic sunlight from above was carefully calculated.

The limestone bust pictured in *fig. a* is about life size for an Indian. The treatment of the hair and headdress is the same as that seen in the Copan heads of the preceding plate, and the face has the same oval shape. But here for the first time the upper part of the body is represented. The shoulder line seems somewhat abrupt and rectilinear. From the large necklace placed over the chest is suspended a grotesque mask, on the snout of which is carved another face. Pendants suggesting snake heads hang down from the jewel. Both hands were extended, the left now broken off, the right turned downward—a gesture associated with the Maize-god, as will be seen in the next plate. The face has an inward-turned expression, giving the whole piece the atmosphere of an incantation.

Fig. b presents another young Maize-god, also from Copan. Its height is 18 inches. In this side view is seen most clearly the characteristics that mark the type. A crest of softly curling maize leaves surmounts the oval face. Strands of hair, brushed back from the forehead and temples, fall in front and behind the great earplugs, creating a soft and pleasing frame for the face.[43] The head has a stronger, more impassive expression than its companion on the plate.

After observing these several examples, we are inclined to conclude that whether the sculptor worked as an individual or whether he merely conformed with the demands and restrictions of a hierarchic tradition, he gave to his work a living rhythm that was his own.

Maudslay's great contribution to pre-Columbian archaeology is not found in his books alone. During the long months that he passed in the cities of Maya splendor, he made casts—and under what difficult circumstances—of important inscriptions on stone monuments, thus enabling scholars of later generations to work on the problems of many glyphs, generally inaccessible or now even obliterated. For the cause of art, perhaps one of his greatest contributions was the transportation to England of sculptured fragments from Copan, through hundreds of miles of jungle. In London these have served as inspiration for scores who never could have seen them in the forsaken valley in Honduras.

In this collection is the crown jewel of medieval American sculpture, the bust of the Maize-god shown on *Pl. 90*. Life size, it is said to have been one of a series that decorated the exterior wall of the Temple of the Sculptured Doorway (Structure 22).

The date of the temple appears to fall in mid-8th century. Here a comparison with the Europe of that time is recommended. After the migratory waves of Asiatic nomads had swept over that continent, monumental art there was in eclipse, and we must turn to the large Buddhistic statues of Asia to find great sculpture contemporary with this period of Maya art.

This bust of the Maya Maize-god has suffered many misfortunes, but luckily the general sculptural lines are not too damaged for our enjoyment. Even though the top section of the headdress is broken, it still tends to enhance and elevate the figure. The smooth forehead, somewhat flattened in accordance with the beauty ideal of the Maya, is emphasized by the upward sweep of the hair. The eyes look down in a baffling and fascinating way. Note that they have no realistic outline; the upper eyelid protrudes slightly, showing no actual rim, a great and crucial difference when compared to the others, naturalistically finished. The carved half-circle of the eye sockets helps bring out the desired expression, which changes with the variations of light. The upper lip is drawn up a little, giving a definite impression of speaking or chanting.

It is the mouth and eyes that decide the success of a sculptured face, whether the subject be an actual portrait or an idealization. And probably the softness of the eyes and the enigmatic character of the mouth in this carving are responsible for the title, "The Singing Girl," which clung to the statue until the early 20's. One is apt to interpret the ingratiating gesture of the figure, its supple rounded proportions—deceptively un-Caucasian—as feminine, while actually they are evidence of the feline grace that is a characteristic of the Maya even today. The soft merging of the shoulders into the upper arms is not only a good piece of realistic sculpture but gives to the figure the sensuous radiation of a young body.

All the ornaments represented were probably of jade, for metal was rare in the Great Period. The large protruding beads that form a necklace and frame the monster-mask set off the smooth surface of the body with their light and shadow effect. They also furnish us with unquestionable evidence of a genuine Maya style of stringing jade beads. A wide cuff adorns each wrist, and a belt and loincloth are suggested at the waist. A comparison with the bust on the preceding plate, the plastic principles of which are identical, will prove the superlative quality of this carving.

Consideration and clarity are manifest in the execution of the arms and hands. The palms show even the life line. The right hand curves downward in a condescending and inviting gesture, while the pose of the left conveys at one and the same time divine blessing and admonition. A similar position, implying both invocation and restraint, is met in Asiatic art, but there the right hand points upward and the left, down. In Buddhism this is interpreted as signifying "without fear" and "charity."

The spell of the Copan Maize-god is strengthened by the spiritual message conveyed through it. The longer we look at this serene figure out of an alien world, the more we are loosed from the beauty ideals of our own civilization. The radiation of a spirit expressed in so overwhelming a manner takes hold on us. We are aware of a communication being delivered and feel the poorer because of our inability to understand it. He seems to be a link between mankind, transitory and restless, and the celestial Creator.

After this chapter was already written, an appreciation of this statue appeared in the posthumous volume of essays by the great English art-historian and critic, Roger Fry, among lectures on Egyptian, Mesopotamian, Aegean, Negro, Chinese, Indian, and Greek art. We quote:

"In the finest works of the Maya culture which preceded the Aztec, we find a much more surprising freedom from the rectilinear geometric bias . . . , a plastic sensibility of the rarest kind. I do not know whether even in the greatest sculpture of Europe one could find anything exactly like this in its equilibrium between system and sensibility, in its power at once to suggest all the complexity of nature and to keep every form within a common unifying principle, i.e. each form taking up and modifying the same theme. The oval is of extraordinary beauty in its subtle variations upon the main idea—you will note how a too exact symmetry is avoided by bringing the lock of hair on one side further over the cheek than on the other. Here then we find the expression of a sensibility of a very high order. There is also I think undoubtedly vitality, a powerful suggestion of the inner life—of a strange tension of spirit—of an almost tragic cast."

In an attempt to avoid an anticlimax after the Maize-god bust, we turn to some aspects of architectural relief that offer a contrast. A few relief carvings used to embellish the bases of buildings were shown under architecture. *Pl. 91* presents other examples, included here under sculpture because of their hybrid character and the fact that they are considered independent of the structure.

Fig. a pictures a detail from the base of the Palace at Palenque. Artistically these figures in stone fall far below the gracious stucco reliefs that appear exactly above them, and they are dated earlier, in the beginning of the 6th century. They are well worth study with their modeling, sometimes grotesque but always expressive, reminding one in their linear conduct somewhat of the Comalcalco stucco work. (See *Pl. 80.*)

An interesting parallel takes us out of the Maya Area to the Zapotec-Mixtec site of Monte Alban, about three hundred miles from Palenque. Here among the ruins of an early temple, stone slabs were found bearing incised figures referred to as "Los Danzantes." The first illustration in this chapter (see *Pl. 57, fig. a*) presented a close view of one of these; *fig. b* shows several others. These figures are not recorded in the plastic style of Palenque, but rather are crude and petroglyph-like. Yet, power of observation, surety of line, and humor are noticeable in them. What a veritable cycle of cartoons they must have formed, ranged one beside the other in their architectural setting.

In Yucatan, the type of decoration on the base of buildings changed. The human figure was forced into the background, and, as a result of a more barbarous ideology, animals and monsters took over the field. A section of a stuccoed wall from the Maya site Acanceh, in northern Yucatan (*fig. c*), shows this trend. It is dated in the early 8th century. Projecting cornices covered with patterns of the same iconography leave a broad zone in the center for the main decoration. This space is further divided by double stepped bands into panels, and a figure, a fantastic blend of the human and animal, is placed in each. Prominent are the bat, serpent, and squirrel in human pose and gesture. The speech scroll occurs several times. As grotesque and strange as they are, they bear the unmistakable mark of good craftsmanship and are highly decorative. When first uncovered, the whole was brightly painted.

Artistically the most uncouth carving on this plate is *fig. d,* a section from the base of the Temple of the Warriors at Chichen Itzá. The panel here is also framed but the protruding bands are this time undecorated. Again the subject is animals in somewhat humanized poses, but the brilliant individuality of earlier Maya art, its free and spontaneous character are no longer in evidence. The eagles and jaguars that alternate in flat relief, with glyphic signs strewn among them, follow a stereotyped pattern, identified with the Mexican occupation of this town.

Because so often the exact purpose of an excavated stone object can only be guessed at, it is a special occasion when an original painting can be produced to document its use. *Pl. 92, fig. a* presents a restored mural found on the north bench of the filled-in Temple of the Chacmool at Chichen Itzá, showing a warrior chief seated on a throne that is carved in the likeness of a jaguar. The head of the beast is depicted looking toward the spectator, and the two forelegs are clearly drawn; his curling tail hangs down at the other end.

This very type of seat was found in a chamber of an early structure that was encased within the temple-base of the well-known Castillo, where it may be seen in its original position today (*fig. b*). It is 33 inches long, 27 high, and carved from one block of stone. The animal was painted a brilliant red, and apple-green jade disks of remarkably fine quality were inlaid for spots and eyes. A large turquoise mosaic was inserted in the middle of its back. Its white teeth, remarkable in their ferocity, are all intact. A comparison of the two photographs will show how well the mural complements the statue, giving us an authentic glimpse of an episode in a Late Maya ceremony. Waldeck publishes another jaguar throne in the so-called "beau relief" stucco at Palenque.[166] Attention should also be called to the puma seats of the Inca Empire. (See *Pl. 277, fig. a.*)

Before closing this review of figural sculpture in the Maya Area, it seems appropriate to bring examples of carving in the round, in which the human shape was frozen into a highly unrealistic pose. It is interesting to note that this deterioration is coincident with the non-Maya period of Yucatan. Both of the following specimens come from Chichen Itzá.

Pl. 93, fig. a shows two atlantes which served, as the photograph clearly indicates, as entrance pillars for a small building. Certain parts are blocked out of the mass to suggest the human figure, its hands upraised, as if holding up the lintel of the door and, ultimately, the roof. Despite the clumsiness of the general impression, the columns appear less heavy in effect than they would have uncarved. Smaller figures in atlantean pose are found at this site supporting the slab of an altar or dais.

The monolithic statue illustrated in *fig. b,* nearly 5 feet long, is designated as

Chacmool, or the Red Tiger. Such semireclining figures, with knees drawn up and upper body raised on the elbows, are quite common in northern Yucatan and are also found from the Totonac region in the Mexican Area as far south as El Salvador. They seem to have served as a sort of altar and are believed to date from the 11th or 12th century. The round concavity clasped by both hands was apparently used for offerings or incense. The breast is decorated with a conventionalized bird, a motif seen on other sculptures at Chichen Itzá. In comparison with the other ornaments, the headdress and earplugs are executed with more detail, showing serpent heads in low relief among other patterns.

The statuary presented on this plate is the uninspired ending of a long and rich artistic vein and represents one of the several low points that every civilization doubtless experiences. The power and monumentality we have seen have here become, for the time being, stereotyped mass production, static and earthbound.

As the main consideration of this survey is to display artistic highlights of the various cultures, selecting subjects that would appeal to the general reader's esthetic sense, certain material of specialized interest and occasionally even carvings well known among archaeologists have been omitted as delaying factors. The line of artistic development often does not follow along anthropological and ethnic borders, and therefore a survey from the esthetic point of view has sometimes to work from a different angle.

There are, however, certain types of sculpture in the Mexican and Maya areas which should be mentioned, although they are not illustrated here. Among these are the mammoth heads and reliefs, problematic but articulate, found at Tres Zapotes, Vera Cruz, and at La Venta, just across the border in Tabasco. From the scant material available at present, this region, fertilized by several first-class cultures, seems to have produced an interesting art of its own, not only in stone but in pottery and jade. A fuller knowledge of this territory will doubtless throw light on several problems of pre-Columbian archaeology.[141]

Mention should also be made of the colossal heads and crude human and animal figures, reaching a height of 5 feet in certain cases, found in the department of Escuintla in Guatemala and still farther down the Isthmus in El Salvador. Although rarely of great artistic merit, they display good carving ability and are significant as cultural milestones. The recent excavations in the region of Cotzumalhuapa in southwestern Guatemala—in the same district as well-known El Baul—have brought to light sculpture of an amazingly fine quality.[155]

The next illustrations take us into the southern periphery of Maya influence to the Ulua Valley in the northern part of Honduras. Here the arts that developed in Yucatan and Guatemala blended with those of the highlands of Honduras and were tinged with Chorotega influences from the south.

Among the most interesting manifestations of this district are the calcite vases, executed so perfectly and with such artistry that only some of the alabasters from the Mexican Area (see *Pl. 257*) may be said to rival them. The material, indigenous to this region and generally classified as a marble, is milky in tone with a delicate bluish-gray vein. Although the cylindrical shape occurs in early Maya pottery and, in smaller size, even occasionally among the early Mexican cultures, there can be little doubt that the pieces of this type originated in a single cultural circle.

Pl. 94, fig. a shows a low tripod bowl, about 4 inches high, with grinning heads, probably monkeys, as handles. Two scaly bands inclose the decorative panel, the top one running to the right, the bottom, in the opposite direction. Between them, in the center, is carved a conventionalized mask or head. An oval mouth with teeth is the first feature to be noticed; just above it are almond eyes and a headdress of scrolls, perhaps stereotyped puma ears. The additional eyes, one on each side, are discussed under *fig. b*. The rest of the panel is filled in with two rows of fret-scrolls, generally interpreted as serpent tails, which occur in a more loosely knit pattern in various Maya carvings and can also be traced in decorative designs from even farther north. (See especially *Pls. 76, fig. b,* and *274* for Maya and *Pl. 63, fig. a,* for Totonac examples.)

Lately this single itinerant motif has been torn from its indigenous *milieu* and presented as proof of direct Chinese influence in pre-Columbian art. A closer comparison of it with patterns that appear in Asiatic art is undertaken at some length in the chapter, "Evolution or Influence"; here we are concerned only with its development as an organic decorative element of a Middle American culture.

Fig. d presents another low tripod of ingratiating form. It is about 5 inches high. The legs of this piece are carved into puma heads, and the handles project from the sides of the vase like gargoyles. The double row of scrolls appears again, the pattern forming two gaping serpent profiles, the curling snouts of which meet above a mask similar to that in *fig. a*. In these we find an explanation of the separate eyes that were carved at the right and left of the face in the other piece. The general effect is less concentrated than in the first example, because of the change in the framing bands. Carved frets interrupt the sequence of scaly motifs in the upper border and occupy the lower one exclusively.

The vase in *fig. c* is about 6¼ inches high, without legs but with a raised base embellished with openwork. The whole decorative outlay resembles in principle the two pieces already discussed. A larger and more angular scaly band runs again without interruption to the right at the top and to the left at the bottom. Bats' heads form the handles and below them bodies are suggested. The mask in the center of the scroll pattern is omitted, but one eye is carved just below the top border, a detached and floating motif, and a foot appears beneath it among the scrolls. The larger surface may account for the use of three instead of two rows of scrolls to fill the panel, or this addition may be due to some technical limitation or a disinclination to carve bigger elements. This larger surface, which could take more plastic decoration, may also have inspired the button-like centers in which the scrolls end. It should not be forgotten that all these marble vases were fashioned with simple stone tools.

The vase in *fig. b* is 7⅜ inches tall and has a diameter of 6½ inches. It also stands on a raised base. Two jaguar heads, one looking up and the other down, make up each handle; conventionalized feet grasp a ball between them. A second pair of feet for each head is carved in relief on the surface of the vase at the side and may serve as a clue to the floating foot just mentioned. This piece carries more decoration than the others; even the base is ornamented with relief, and the openwork is more complicated, suggesting a fret. The scaly band flows away from the inserted rectilinear motif that interrupts it at the top and toward it at the bottom. Three rows of serpent-tail scrolls encircle the main body, among which, on the photograph here shown, four eyes are visible. Doris Stone points out that these are connected with heads in profile, two on each side.[142]

One of the most beautiful specimens of the Ulua vases is reproduced on *Pl. 95, fig. a*. It is 9⅝ inches high and also has a bottom rim with openwork. The handle represents a puma clasping another animal. Five rows of scrolls ranged about a mask in the center cover the main body of the vase. In none of the others is the fanciful play with the spiral carried through with such logic. Faces in profile are easily recognized beside and below the mask, and even feet are inserted here and there. The scales of the top band move to the left and those at the bottom to the right.

Fig. b is a very shallow basin, less than 2 inches high, without a base and with only one handle. Here a single band of rectangular scales is present in the upper border and one row of spirals in the main panel. The manner in which the spirals are combined into a ∽ shape is suggestive of the undulation of a serpent body, an impression that is carried out in the plastic serpent head as handle. Single scrolls form the blunt end of the reptile's snout and the hinge of the jaw, while a smaller spiral emphasizes the protuberance above the eye. This scroll motif, which is an outstanding feature of all Ulua vases, belonged to the inner core of the artistic imagination of these people, and wherever there was an opportunity to apply it, they have done so. (Compare the composition of the serpent profiles in *fig. a.*)

That these elaborate marbles were highly prized—their use was probably restricted to the ruling class—is proved by the fact that pottery imitations have been found over a wide area, with, in certain instances, even the handles fashioned into animal form. (See *Pl. 143.*) These shapes from clay, however, have nothing of the arresting beauty of their prototypes. Crude marble vases were unearthed at Kaminaljuyú in the Guatemala highlands and in quite late stratifications in Peten and British Honduras.[152]

INTERLYING AREA

Of the two seated figures on *Pl. 96,* one is from Guatemala, the other, from Costa Rica. The first (*fig. a*) is 11 inches high and shows a kneeling man, without ornament, both hands at his chin. Whether it is a prayerful gesture or only a contemplative pose we do not know, but we cannot escape its human appeal.

The second piece (*fig. b*) belongs to the Guetar culture, which occupied the Costa Rican part of the Isthmus and carved its statues from lava of varying fineness.[167] Note that the pose here is the same as that in the Aztec statue (see *Pl. 61, fig. a*) with even the fingers suggested clasping the knees. The curve of the back and the distribution of weight in the figure make him come alive. The headdress composed of three small lizards in relief is unusual; customary headgear for such stone statues is a conical cap, probably representing the pointed, wadded-cotton helmet of the warrior, which will be seen on the next plate. A comparison of the sculptural details of the two carvings will show that the eye in the Guatemalan piece is egg-shaped and encircled by chiseled-out surfaces, while in the Costa Rican both eyelids are separately indicated.

It would be easy to say that these two statues are "primitive" carvings, but closer inspection will reveal an innate subtlety in them. There is a human softness and sincerity about them which makes them sympathetic at first glance.

The shape called ceremonial axe-heads for lack of a better designation has already been met in the Totonac culture of Mexico (see *Pl. 66*). Now, far to the south in Guatemala, this form appears again in the first two pieces illustrated on *Pl. 97*. The theme of the carving here, however, is not the human head; it has become a more condensed and considerably more mystic subject.

In *fig. b,* 11 inches high, a man is shown leaning backwards in a decidedly forced position against a flight of steps. He may be a sacrificial victim, whose breast is to be torn open to cut out his heart; the steps then would represent the stairway before the temple where this bloody rite is performed. The carving, even in its strongly angular lines, is executed with power and expression. A vulture tearing at a skull is the subject in *fig. a,* an axe 12 inches high and extremely thin. A similar theme was used in a pottery vessel from the Andean Area (see *Pl. 163, fig. a*). In contrast to the Totonac axe-heads, the stone in both of these is pierced. Little elaboration is spent on either, but every line is tellingly placed.

The man with arms akimbo (*fig. c*) presents another example of an independent statue from Costa Rica, boldly executed, with good plastic feeling especially in the legs. He is a little over 4 feet high. The style of headdress is interesting, with its coiled snake and amphibian figure. In this connection it may be noted that the alligator or crocodile is a primary motif in the art of the entire Interlying Area. The combination of the two reptiles, the simple tattoo marking over the body, and the changed features in the face are evidence that we are out of the region where Maya influence made itself felt directly.

Still more novel in sculptural expression is the piece in *fig. d,* about 14 inches high. The two figures, connected by their linked arms, represent "the dual officiants" at a human sacrifice. The one at the right holds a human head, while the other carries an unidentified object in his uplifted hand. Neither shows much individuality in expression. This statue is unique in that two persons are carved from one block of stone. The piece is said to have come from the region of the Guetar culture. From the artistic affiliations found here, the district seems to have been a meeting ground for influences from the south rather than the north.[65] (Compare with *Pl. 225*.)

Although household objects doubtless received artistic attention, few of them remain for our consideration. Fortunately some stone implements have survived to add to the incomplete mosaic of pre-Columbian life. In *Pl. 98* three *metates,* or mealing stones, are illustrated, upon which maize or cocoa beans were ground with a stone roller.

The first (*fig. a*) is Chorotegan in type, although it comes from Santa Lucia Cotzumalhuapa in Guatemala. Its length is 47 inches and its height 21. The serpent head is finely stylized, and the smooth transition of the head into the body of the piece is effected with much suavity. Note the roller shaped to fit the grinding surface.

In the second *metate* (*fig. b*), from Costa Rica, the animal is more realistically brought out, with a puma head, four legs, and a curling tail. The diamond pattern here is reminiscent of the carved figures just discussed from this region, and the ᔆ motif on the edge recalls the Ulua vases.

Openwork introduces variety into the execution of *fig. c*. This *metate,* 29 inches long and 12 high, comes from Nicaragua and seems to represent a puma or jaguar. Quite expressionistic in manner, it conveys a remarkable sense of life, even potential movement. The arabesque on the back of the head, the dissimilar bands that ornament the grinding surface, and the elaborate openwork feet are all highly decorative. So much was undertaken here in stone that the piece was too fragile to withstand the centuries and was discovered in fragments.

All three of these objects served an identical purpose but what individual approach and execution are manifest in each.

In this same area and on somewhat the same artistic level were the low chairs, almost like footstools, upon which it was the privilege of the ruling few to sit. An example of the type in pottery is shown on *Pl. 149*. Ecuador had larger U-shaped stone seats supported by a crouching human figure.

ANDEAN AREA

On our route to the Andean Area, those pre-Columbian sculptures deserve mention that are found around the town of San Augustín, Colombia. This district, some three hundred miles south of Bogotá, is now far-sightedly being converted by the government into a national park. The statues represent human and animal figures in static, often cubistic shapes and in some cases are 14 feet in height. They are crude when compared with the material illustrated. It is noteworthy, however, that they possess certain ideological expressions characteristic of the carving of other areas, though distorted through lower mental and technical abilities.

The sculptor's art in the Andean Area should not be measured by the same standard applied in the Mexican or Maya. Pottery, weaving, and metal-work here were so highly developed that even had this region used stone only in its phenomenal architecture, its place in medieval American art would be secure. There are, however, certain examples that should be presented, not only because they offer new styles but because they broaden the horizon of artistic achievement within the Andean Area itself.

The stone slab in *Pl. 99, fig. a* is about 8 feet high and comes from Cerro Sechin in the Casma Valley (northern coast of Peru). Upon it is drawn a figure with head turned to the right and feet pointing in the same direction; the torso is in more of a frontal pose, further clarified by the position of the two arms. The left hand, grasping a ceremonial bar, is notably unnatural in drawing. As in the Maya stelae, the left shoulder is lower than the right, seemingly a sculptural trick, applied also here to foster an optical illusion.

The carving as such is rather in the nature of incision, without any pretense to plastic effect; nowhere is the superfluous stone cut away. The purpose of the whole composition seems to be simply the recording of a powerful and ferocious personage, although our eyes see mostly the grotesque in it. The style shows affinities to the Chavin culture.

In the high mountains of central Peru lies a small village called Chavin de Huántar. This is the site of extensive ruins consisting of high platforms faced with dressed stone and containing an intricate series of galleries on three distinct levels. A considerable amount of stone carving has been found about the site, and while it may not actually be the center of distribution of the style, all pieces of this flamboyant type are designated as Chavin. Thus, as in the case of Tiahuanaco, the term "Chavin" refers both to a site and to a culture or style.[8] The granite monolith from Chavin shown in *fig. b* is considered to date before the 6th century. This stone, also known as the Stela Raimondi after its discoverer, is 6½ feet high with a greenish cast. A short standing figure is represented wearing a lofty headdress, a veritable tower of masks. Certain motifs of this carving—the branching snake heads, jaguar masks, and claws—appear also in the works from this region in other media (see *Pl. 195*). The ceremonial staffs in both hands and the feet, turned outward, remind one of the god in the center of the Gateway of the Sun at Tiahuanaco, except for the fact that the two scepters here are identical. The stylized detail work is finer, and, since the head is not protruding as in the Tiahuanaco carving, the plastic effect is different. An abundance of masks and conventionalized decorative elements make the monolith a rich ground for students of Andean iconography.

Somewhat clearer for the untrained eye to grasp is the massive statue illustrated in *fig. c*. It was found at Tiahuanaco, and the boy at its head gives an excellent idea of its colossal size—nearly 24 feet in length, including the base. The mass of the stone was carved down into a rectangular block with little allowance made for the arms and hands. Familiar Classic Tiahuanaco patterns are strewn all over the piece, and some of the figures in profile, especially those on and below the arms, resemble closely motifs on the side of the Gateway. One is struck with the condensed and complicated artistic ideology, though its full meaning is problematical to us. A certain organization and refinement can be observed in the decoration, which with its sometimes abstract designs is reminiscent of the textiles of this area.

Smaller objects from these cultures bridge more easily the way to our imagination. The stone animal bowl (*Pl. 100, fig. a*), 13 inches long and 6½ high, is classified as belonging to the Chavin style. It has the shape of a puma. The head is quite realistically portrayed with bared fangs and eyes that were originally inlaid, though its body is made somewhat overweight by the demands of the receptacle placed in its back. The several motifs applied all over the creature may point toward a sacrificial or ceremonial use; besides straight, "clover," and ∽ elements, the Greek cross appears several times, another argument that motifs can be and are invented independently in localities isolated from one another.

The second stone bowl (*fig. b*), about 5 inches high and 26 long, including the handles, is of later manufacture. The piece came from the highlands of Peru and is of Inca style. As will be seen in the chapters on pottery and weaving, the Inca rule established a high level in conventionalized patterns and forms. In this stone bowl the ornament, although originating in nature, is distilled into an agreeable but unindividual decoration. Its appeal is in its suavity and meticulous finish rather than in its design.

It is an enigma why a people so able as those in the Andean Area in modeling clay or casting metal or in shaping intractable stone at will for their building did not easily achieve the higher manifestations of sculpture.

In reviewing the sculpture of the Mexican and Maya areas, we recognize details of orthodoxy surprisingly similar, such as the animal-mask and feathered serpent; yet stylistically, that is, in the matter of sculptural language, these peoples show great temperamental differences. As the Mexicans tended toward mass in their architecture, so they revealed the same feeling for mass in their sculpture. The Maya, on the other hand, perfected the relief in its many aspects, displaying a love of elaboration, of broken surfaces and curving lines that is characteristic of all their art. Dealing less with planes and solid masses than with balance of detail, their work shows greater refinement though less pungency than the Mexican, and reaches its greatest height in its rare three-dimensional statuary.

Like most of the earlier non-European civilizations, the pre-Columbian peoples in their artistic expression seem to have appreciated the beauty of youth without worshiping it, to have respected age without sentimentalizing it. The more terrifying aspects of nature, which they must have had to face in their precariously balanced life, are not shunned in their art.

V

Pottery

MEDIEVAL America fashioned its pottery vessels by building them up of coils of clay, smoothed with the hand or a small implement—a bit of gourd or a sherd. In books on the subject, the absence of the potter's wheel is usually remarked upon apologetically. However, we venture to say that in some ways it worked to an advantage. In those ancient civilizations that employed the wheel from early times, pottery shapes were soon standardized to a few highly refined and universal types; the disappearance of the human figure in utilitarian ware can be ascribed to this factor. The pre-Columbian potter, on the other hand, unhampered by a mechanical device, was proficient in a wider range and variety. His rounded shapes show the life of the hand which fashioned them, and his talent for modeling had free rein to create some of his most original and artistic work. It is this manifestation of genius which will be given the most space here, for a stratigraphic and strictly chronological presentation is not our purpose.

Mention should be made, however, of the inestimable value to archaeology of the amassed material of pre-Columbian pottery. The making of pottery was universal in all our areas, and most excavations reveal at least sherds. Fragments found about a settlement or in its refuse heap frequently lie in layers representative of different periods of time. Thus, the potsherds can be tabulated into a general comparative scheme by their stylistic distinctions, and objects found in close proximity to them correlated. One of the important results of this has been to modify some of the dating derived from stelae, for the pottery has given a much broader view. Laboratory investigations have advanced so far that now, through the analysis of the basic material, the sand or pottery bits used to temper it, the type of slip, and manner of decoration, local and traded ware can be identified, an important factor in tracing cultural interrelations.

In certain regions of the Southwest, household utensils were first made of baskets, sometimes daubed with clay to make them water-tight. Later clay alone was used for bowls and pots, but with the traditional conservatism of primitive man, features of the basket persisted for centuries; not only the shapes were retained, but even the texture was imitated in the design. We find the same tendency to cling to tradition in our own lives. Although columns are no longer necessary to support the roofs of our public buildings they nevertheless adorn many façades, and although the necktie has been reduced from a protective scarf to a mere band without any practical purpose, it is still considered essential to our costume.

The range of pottery production in medieval America is broader than that of most early civilizations in the rest of the world. Here, within the span of a relatively few centuries, an amazing variety was produced, from the basket imitation to the inimitable fresco vase. This chapter, therefore, has the most illustrations in this survey, because each of the five areas offers beautiful and distinctive examples of the art. Besides an overwhelming display of bowls, jars, pitchers, and plates, with countless styles of rims, necks, legs, and lugs, we shall see earthenware painted, carved, stamped with molds, modeled, and sculptured into rare inventions, and, as a crowning achievement, even emerging as individual portraiture of a sort. The choice would be still greater had it not been for the practice of "killing" pottery to release its spirit before it was interred in a grave, or, among the Aztecs, at the lapse of the 52-year cycle. As we review the great variety of these vessels, it is interesting to contemplate the large share that women had in the craft.

The ceramic production of the New World was highly praised by the Spaniards. At this time, because of the tradition of the Moors who had brought the full flowering of Persian art with them to Europe, Spain led in this field. Indeed, the Italian word *majolica* is derived from the Spanish island of Majorca, whose inhabitants had much to teach the Italians in glazing and coloring. Sahagun writes, after seeing the markets of the Aztec Empire, that all the techniques and shapes of the motherland were to be found here. Glazing was unknown, but a high durable polish was obtained by applying a wax preparation, which still keeps its sheen after centuries in the ground.

THE SOUTHWEST

The tradition of basket-work, already mentioned, is corroborated by a large pot (*Pl. 101, fig. a*), 13 inches high, found in Apache County, Arizona. The piece is built up in coiled bands from the bottom and the basket imitation goes so far as to suggest the sustaining frame.

The smaller and more shallow bowl in *fig. b* is constructed on the same principle, but incised frets suggestive of an interwoven pattern were added. In comparing the two, a certain smoothness and refinement in the later one is noticeable, though the first has power and directness.

In the group of bowls from Arizona (*fig. c*), all bright in effect, linear motifs appear as decoration. Except for the one in the center, they are said to date from the 9th or 10th centuries. In form they show less skill than the first two; there is about them an air of groping and uncertainty, as if their makers even in the act of fashioning them had not known how they would turn out. These simplest of shapes are far from perfect, and the same lack of assurance is evident also in the patterns, which show unremitting struggle with the decorative impulse. It is not surprising to find the center bowl dated 13th century; it offers the most complicated design in an execution most nearly approaching good standards, although even here the pattern elements are still far from orderly and the circle in the center shows an unskilled and irresolute hand.

In *fig. d* the human figure appears as decorative element. The human and animals strewn on the inside of the bowl are executed with a really primitive hand, which even had difficulty in spacing them to advantage. The general impression, both in design and shape, is of hesitancy and unevenness.

Another type of pottery is presented in *fig. e*. This round heavy-walled piece is thought to have been an incense burner. It comes from the Hohokam district, which also produced the fine bone carving illustrated in *Pl. 285, fig. a*. Hohokam means in the language of the Pima Indians, "the people who have gone," and is used today to denote one of the most powerful early cultures in the Southwest. The successful working of both clay and bone, together with a manifest ability to represent animal life, is proof of advancing civilization. Round, well-shaped medallions on the jar bring the repetition of a young bird in a gay mood. The hopping, leaping, little figure has the naïve charm of a Walt Disney cartoon and forms a rhythmically moving pattern around the piece. The color is dull red on a buff ground.

Pl. 102 presents jars, or *ollas,* running as large as 16 inches high, from the 12th and 13th centuries. The shapes vary from the round to the elongated, but all five are settled in form. The decorations make use of the most involved permutations and variations—generally of the zigzag used as a fret or in checkerboard, triangular, saw-tooth, and rectangular patterns, with the always grateful contrast of solid white against solid black, sometimes lightened by hatching. Particular skill was required to adapt the meandering designs to the bulging shape. Each jar has attraction, vigor, and an amazing amount of individuality. It will be observed how refined the same shape and same pattern elements have become in the time-span of a few centuries. Such ancient Pueblo *ollas* are known to have been kept long as heirlooms.

Here (notably in the center jar of *fig. a* and in *fig. b*) we first meet a "negative" design, in which the pattern appears in the natural light color of the body of the piece, while the background is painted. Startling and ingenious effects are sometimes achieved by using this "reverse" method in interlocking patterns.

Pl. 103 shows widely diversified types of various periods from pueblos in New Mexico, Arizona, and Colorado. The rather shallow bowl from Apache County, Arizona (*fig. a*), is 9½ inches in diameter and dated between the 10th and 12th centuries. It carries a conventionalized body of a reptile, with two heads only suggested. The diamond design is flat and very much simplified so that its effect is predominantly decorative. Note the same idea in the brocade on *Pl. 175, fig. b*.

Fig. b, from Sikyatki, Arizona, shows a more advanced talent and bears a later date—14th century. The hand in the center is introduced here not as realistic representation but as a symbol, perhaps of magic. It shows observation and skill in the spacing of the fingers and the exact drawing of the cuff section with its ornament. The more or less abstract design, suggestive of a bird, that starts at the lower left of the arm and circles around the bowl, terminating on the right at the wrist, is deliberately placed and heightens the feeling of esoteric meaning. The outside of the bowl is also decorated. Here we meet the same elements of stylized drawing that have survived in the sand paintings of the Southwest and furnished the primary inspiration to modern Hopi ceramics.[73] The colors are brownish black and red on a yellow ground.

The deeper bowl in *fig. c* is tentatively dated in the 14th or early 15th century. The outside has a long fret design in black, outlined in white, on a slip of clear red; the inside shows a light-colored negative scroll bedded in shaded sections. In spite of the countermovement of the elements, the whole pattern gives a revolving impression. This piece is also from central Arizona.

Fig. d, from near Deming, New Mexico, is more advanced in its pattern development—the most sophisticated of the group. A curving fishtail can be discerned attached to a semicircular figure with four dark feet or fins. Bands in the natural light clay of the bowl are used to outline all the elements of the design. Fine parallel and crisscross lines give variation. Its appeal is apparent, independent of its symbolism.

The water container from the ruins of Mesa Verde, Colorado (*fig. e*), demonstrates how skillful the Cliff-dwellers had become to fashion successfully such a vessel of friable clay. Carried to work in the distant fields on a band, it kept the water fresh for a long time; even our age utilizes the cooling property of unglazed pottery. The decoration has two main motifs: the interlocking step design in the middle and the linear embellishment in the zones at either end. Good feeling for balance is shown by the placement of the heavy, more involved panel in the center.

Whether intentionally or not, *fig. f,* an early gray-ware piece from Arizona, has the drollness of a toy for grown-ups. It is 8 inches high and also a water carrier. The body is constructed on the same principle as that in the preceding jug, but the addition of four stocky legs, an animal head, and handle proves greater originality. It reminds one of the *aquamanile* (bronze water carrier) of medieval Europe from about the same time. The long zigzags in black and white give life to the static shape, and its spontaneity makes sure contact with us.

The mug shape must have been quite common in the Southwest, as many such pieces exist in various collections and museums, although no two have ever been found identical in design.

The three illustrated on *Pl. 104, fig. a* come from the heart of the Cliff-dweller region, and date from about the beginning of the 11th century. The tallest is nearly 5½ inches. There is enough difference in decoration to demonstrate the extent of individual artistry among these people. Considered from left to right, the first has a combined design of three different elements in a large zigzag; the second skillfully varies one motif, the oblique fret; the third is the most complicated, with its central panel of repeated rectangles (in itself a clever management of the negative white and positive black), as well as an upper and lower border and decorated handle. The similarity of the form to the European tankard is evident.

The double jar (*fig. b*) from Mesa Verde is smaller and dates from about the middle of the 13th century. The coupling of two pieces into one is an advance, and the pattern has become routined. It should be noted that the oblique lines in the panels of each side run from the handle toward the outside edge, producing a centripetal effect pleasing to our eye. The flaring rim is also interesting and unusual.

The pottery dipper in *fig. c* is intricately decorated with motifs now more or less familiar. On the handle, the progression of the design from a simple double-outlined meander to a series of interlocking step-frets in black and white is accomplished with delightful ingenuity. The fret appears again in the bottom of the bowl combined with spirals that harmonize with the curve of the utensil.

The cream of Southwestern pottery is displayed on *Pl. 105*. The earliest piece among them is on the left in *fig. a*. This jug, with the curious animal head as handle, dates from the 9th century and comes from the San José River in western New Mexico. What intricate motifs are here applied and how well they are harmonized. The sweeping composite elements of the main body are counterbalanced by the more rigid and controlled checkered band around the neck.

The bowl beside it repeats a single pattern in the three bands. It is a finely executed design, one difficult to space. There is subtle counterpoint in the shifting of the pattern that emphasizes the saw-tooth white line running obliquely across the vessel.

In the piece at the right a completely new decorative approach is introduced. The upper half is bare except for the lacelike star around the mouth; the lower varies two motifs that cross each other on a dark ground. Two stubby handles indicate that the jug was made to be suspended on a cord or band. Both of these pieces are from the upper Gila River, New Mexico, and date from the 13th century.

The three kiva jars from Mesa Verde (*fig. b*) are all Pueblo III, a period of high attainment. In each case the shape is perfected without being cold or impersonal. The patterns show the routined application of motifs developed throughout the centuries, and the jars still retain their glazelike polish after all these years, a contrast to the chalky surfaces of older pieces.

Attention should be called to the analogy in the designs in this row to those directly above them. The one on the left shows the spiral in combination with single hatching; the jar in the center uses parallel bands of step-frets, this time with a more horizontal effect; the light pattern on the dark upper half of the vessel on the right outlines the same star that encircles the rim of the earlier one above it. All three have precisely wrought rims, set back a little from the openings and decorated.

In *fig. c* a jar of a very different character is presented, another Sikyatki piece from the 15th century. (See *Pl. 103, fig. b.*) Although the shape is one of the most difficult to form, it is the design which makes the piece outstanding. The butterflies or moths alternate with geometric elements, placed with mature artistic sense. Burnt tones of tan and red brown on buff, outlined in dark brown or black, make up the color scheme.

Although from across the Mexican border, the polychrome jar in *fig. d* belongs organically to the Southwest through its language of shape and pattern. It comes from Chihuahua and is dated in the 15th century. It is of a creamy highly polished ware and about 8 inches high. The band with its pennant-shaped detail running obliquely across the bulging body of the piece probably denotes a textile. The two beady-eyed parrots, one upright, the other upside down, in the triangle at the left are completely stylized, yet drawn with very good feeling for the subject.

Even more striking is the head, fashioned with a minimum of modeling and emphasized by color. Although the face is not all-important, the simple trick of leaving it white above the variegated surface of the rest of the jar draws our attention to it. The hair-fine line of the eyebrows contrasts with the heavy strokes on the cheeks, which probably denote paint or tattoo. Note that the eyes are cut in such a way that they seem to look at one from any angle, a characteristic that is brought out in the photograph. This little vessel combines the humor of a toby jug with considerable native dignity.

In the pottery of the Southwest a special place must be reserved for the bowls from the valley of the Mimbres River in southern New Mexico (*Pls. 106* and *107*). The population here did not live in cliff-dwellings or in community apartment buildings—at least, no remnants of these exist—but in pit houses. Their humble architecture would not lead to the expectation of any special artistic manifestation. They made the usual corrugated pottery and other common types, the shapes of which were also conventional. But on the matt inner surface of their food bowls they developed a style of silhouette, human and animal, that is unique in pre-Columbian ceramics. Only at Coclé, Panama, 2800 miles to the southeast, do we find a somewhat related approach. Naturalistic representation was apparently not intended; the figures serve as decorative motifs and a story-telling quality of rare charm emerges from these bowls.

Besides the human figure, birds, deer, antelope, dogs, rabbits, fish, insects, and reptiles are used, as well as fabulous creatures who step out of the fantasy-world of these potter artists. The bowls have a fragile appearance, and with their chalky surface recall to mind the naïve but expressive Rhages bowls of 13th-century Persia. Mimbres pottery is not colored; the ground is without exception a whitish slip and the figures are applied in black.

The basket-weave piece (*Pl. 106, fig. a*) shows a well-spaced pattern, covering the inside without margins. The unevenness of the hand-drawn lines lends vibration to the design.

In *fig. b,* the composition fills the entire space, regardless of the large amount of "air" left about the figures. The two men are primitively drawn, but their placement, whether intentionally or not, gives a sense of perspective. The fish-monster, much larger, dominates the scene. A human arm and leg emerging from the body may denote a masked figure. In contrast to the solid black of the two men, the fish is decorated with an S design and other patterns. Of the three fine black threads issuing from its ferocious jaws, the lower ends in the hands of the first and smaller figure, while the two others continue on to the second. These lines are all that connect the three characters in the scene, and one feels that the artist who put them there knew how to bind loose elements into a whole. This piece is dated about 1100.

The swallow (*fig. c*) is completely stylized, his bill unrealistically drawn in profile. The saw-tooth edges of the wings and the cloudlike swirls give a sense of poise and airy ever-changing distances.

Humor is apparent in the mosquito bowl (*fig. d*). The eleven pests buzzing around are really to be sensed. They are depicted with little variation, although some of the legs are pulled in more than others to avoid overcrowding. From whatever side the design is viewed, it shows a swarming movement around a center.

A ring of fine square meanders edges the turtle's shell (*fig. e*), and wavy lines are used to suggest its accordion-like neck. It seems to swim across the plain surface. The mouth is depicted in profile, as was the swallow's, and, as there, the scalloped margin is eased in with a series of fine lines and wider stripes.

The bowl with four grasshoppers (*fig. f*) is divided into lozenge-shaped fields and a squared center. The insects are well caught, although not strictly naturalistic. Their delicate transparent wings are crisscrossed vertically in two cases and obliquely in the other two.

It is regrettable that most of these bowls were "killed," thus impairing their appearance.

The "rabbit wheel" (*Pl. 107, fig. a*) presents an involved use of the zigzag, with the animal heads fitted neatly into each irregular field. The ears are stylized, one above the other, and the whole pattern gives a feeling of rotation.

In the grasshopper bowl beside it (*fig. b*), the zigzag and square coil are combined in an effective border. Although quite differently portrayed than the insects in the preceding plate, details are marvelously well observed, notably his jagged hind feet and cutting jaws.

In contrast to the first piece on this plate, the bowl with the four turkeys (*fig. c*) is quite static. Its squared center and rounded white fields are similar to the divisions seen before. The birds are recognizable, although composed largely of rectangles and diamonds with a few contrasting curves. Their fan tails are especially striking.

In *fig. d,* another of the unusual geometric-patterned bowls, the familiar saw-tooth design is featured within a wide margin. A heavy black band outlines the edge of the vessel, while the decorated area is confined within three narrower circles. The fine square coil in the center is characteristic of Mimbres drawing; it has already been seen in the grasshopper and turkey dishes above.

Fig. e shows a less stylized turkey, penned in with two heavy margin lines. It is drawn with linear economy and an observant eye, and is perhaps the most pictorial of all.

A few pottery specimens from Arkansas and the Southeast (Gulf States) are incorporated here (*Pl. 108*) to show what was produced in a neighboring region and to illustrate the great diversity in concept and approach. If we compare this pottery with that on the preceding plates, we are astonished by the profound differences in the people whom we group under the one general term "Indian."

Fig. a, from Arkansas, some seven hundred miles from the heart of the Southwest, presents a completely distinctive shape, a long-necked bottle on a vertical base. The straight neck carries a static step design, the convex body a swirling pattern, both blended in the one piece with good feeling.

Fig. b, also from Arkansas, noteworthy for its fine ovoid form and slender shapely neck, is definitely related to the other, yet brings enough divergence in form and decoration to be illustrated here. It is 10¼ inches high and done in ochre-red and cream.

The small bowl from Louisiana (*fig. c*), only 2¾ inches high, offers another original shape, even after the many variations in the Southwest. Considerable technical skill is revealed in the execution of the design, characteristically Mound Builder. The crisscross background, against which the smooth double bands are laid in S-shaped patterns, produces a lacelike effect, and the rim is decorated with separated, well-proportioned motifs.

Fig. d, a burial urn, 17 inches high, comes from Georgia. It is of dark brown color and has a spiral pattern stamped all over the outside. The ingenious application of the stamping block lends a continuous wavy movement to the repeated pattern, not only avoiding monotony but giving strength to the whole. The vigor of the ornament, as well as the shape of the vessel, reminds us of the capacious bronze *gulyás* kettles (more easily recognized when spelled "goulash"), which were commonly used by Asiatic migrants as they moved on Europe.

A precipitation jar is shown in *Pl. 109, fig. a,* probably used in salt making for removing impurities from the mineral springs near the place where it was found in Missouri. Although there is nothing remarkable in the material or its surfacing, considerable skill was necessary to make such a long piece with its relatively narrow opening. There is suavity in the form of the cap and the way it fits the top.

The two incised water bottles (*fig. b*), 7 and 6⅛ inches tall respectively, come from Arkansas. Original shapes and a beautiful black polished finish make these pieces outstanding. The novel technique of incision made after firing and the fine adaptation of the decorative patterns deserve mention. In the shallow channels traces of red paint can be detected.

The brown effigy bowl (*fig. c*), also from Arkansas, is a little over 8 inches high and has a burnished finish. The head and tail of a horned snake are worked out at the sides for handles. One could not expect these additional elements to be too realistic, limited as the potter was by the undistinguished cooking-pot shape of the bowl, but a certain attractive naïveté must be admitted, which elevates the piece above the purely utilitarian.

As a shape, the incised bottle (*fig. d*), 7 inches high, from the Mound Builder culture in Louisiana is again distinctive, and in its incision it too demonstrates a slightly different approach. There is a virtuosity in keeping the lines always equidistant while covering the whole surface with its swirling motifs; where they are interrupted, the modulation of the motif occurs without any trace of hesitancy, guided by a sure talent.

POTTERY

MEXICAN AREA

The Mexican Area, as well as the Maya which follows it, presents an amazing versatility in handling the humble clay. Here can be seen simple shapes taking on sophisticated proportions or lavish decoration; toylike figurines, primitively conceived, grow into life-size images. Certain representations of human subjects were made with the use of baked clay molds, but, as a result of this technique, were seldom highly artistic.

Pl. 110, fig. a, a jar 15 inches high, comes from the Zapotec-Mixtec site of Monte Alban. Although the shape is not complicated, it is anything but "primitive." It is somewhat similar to the one in *fig. b,* but the neck is longer and hobnail protuberances add plastic effect. The dignified line of the two "handles," actually spouts, betokens real civilization. Burnished but apparently unpainted, the vessel has something of the primeval strength of an early Chinese bronze.

Fig. b shows a jar of baked clay with polychrome design on a stucco ground. Again, the apparent simplicity of the piece should not mislead us to underrate the artistry embodied in it. There are centuries of development behind the deliberate contours, the bulky body, and flaring neck. The decoration, applied with much skill, shows a monster-mask and other fantastic elements belonging to the iconography of Teotihuacan. It reminds one of an early cloisonné of the Eastern Hemisphere.

The funerary urn in *fig. c,* about 9½ inches high, also comes from the Teotihuacan region. In comparison with the other two, it shows a number of advanced features. With its three legs and lid, it is a composition of several elements. The broad rim of the cover, extending well beyond the wall of the vessel, creates a roof effect that gives it finish and individuality. The cylindrical knob on top, in harmony with the sturdy legs, is a new idea. Both urn and lid are decorated with motifs cut out and engraved. A mask with a broad feather headdress can be discerned in the center, and other designs of glyphic content are strewn over the sides. This piece too could find its counterparts in earlier Asiatic civilizations.

The three pitchers illustrated on *Pl. 111* come from three different Mexican states. *Fig. a,* about 11 inches high, was found in the Toluca Valley, west of Mexico, D.F. With its geometric decoration on a henna ground it is rather somber in aspect. Because of its size and the convex band below the rim, it was the

< 163 >

most difficult of the three to shape. *Fig. b,* over 8 inches, is a Mixtec product from the Oaxaca region. Its polychrome motifs show a healthy enjoyment in the play of color and line and great surety in applying geometric units to a spherical surface. The third (*fig. c*), although not so finely proportioned as the first, has the most charm for our eyes because of the colorful butterfly frieze on the shiny chocolate-brown of the body. It is smaller than the others and comes from Puebla, the center of the renowned Cholula ware.

Of the three tripod vases in the lower row, the first (*fig. d*) is Zapotec and 7½ inches high. The negative-painted step-fret in the central band recalls the composite stone panels at Mitla. The body is yellow, the upper section cream, and the "background" lines and markings are dark brown; inside it is painted red and chocolate. The other two (*figs. e* and *f*) both come from the Mixtec region. Note the use of serpents to represent the legs on the smaller. They are hollow and contain clay balls or pebbles to make them rattle. The last of the three shows a mature hand in the unhampered application of the glyphic decoration. The ground is red; the figures are white and applied with fine fluency and spacing. The tripod form was a favorite in these parts of the Mexican Area, and the numerous finds show much variation.

Pl. 112 presents two single figures and a group from the country of the Tarascans—a people who, even at the time of the most powerful Aztec expansion in the 15th century, were successful in maintaining their artistic independence. How long they inhabited the region northwest of Tenochtitlan, in what is today the state of Michoacan, is not known. An outspoken and characteristic flavor can be observed in every piece which has come down from them. In their long-headed, flat-bodied figurines, they succeeded in catching a remarkable variety of expressions and attitudes, unusually striking even when compared with the talented work of the rest of the Mexican high plateau.

Fig. a represents a woman in miniature, only 4½ inches high, leaning over her *metate,* grinding corn or making dough. The face with its absorbed smile is very expressive. The bend of the youthful body, the caplike headdress, and the necklace are all more suggested than realistically depicted, but, as always in Tarascan modeling, the whole figure is transfused with a communicative spirit. It could be enlarged considerably without losing any of its vigor.

The seated man (*fig. b*), 28 inches high, is said to have come from Jalisco and dates from about the 12th century. The head has received the most attention and carries through the weary pose suggested in the body. Although the figure is rather shapeless and the arms and legs are out of proportion, the piece makes immediate contact with us through its genuinely human content. Even in their utter strangeness, these pottery representations show us people as human as we are, with the same universal appeal as the more famous Tanagra statuettes.

The group of dancing women (*fig. c*) demonstrates even more forcefully the talents seen above. On a disk about 9 inches in diameter, nine figures dance about three others seated in their midst, yet the piece does not appear crowded. The arms of the nine are interlaced, creating a long rhythmic line. There is tension in the circle as the women lean forward looking with animation toward the center. Again, it is not realism that arrests us, but the peculiar story-telling quality that knows no boundaries in art.

Miniature figures are grouped on *Pl. 113*. The first one (*fig. a*), a mother with an infant at her breast, has certain characteristics seen in the Tarascan work, especially the grotesquely sharp nose, but there are differences in the manner of modeling. The eyes and mouth are represented by deep concavities instead of rolls of clay, and the general outline is more broken. Not only does the baby give the impression of a doll, but the whole piece seems toylike.

Fig. c is even more reminiscent of the examples on the preceding plate. It shows a figure lying on a litter or bed, bound by bands around his chest and ankles. The facial expression is stereotyped, but the aliveness of the extended legs and imprisoned arms is well communicated.

Although among the oldest in pottery types, with their roots in the archaic period, the "pretty ladies" of *figs. d* and *e* show an amazing number of individual details. Certain plastic features place them close to the Tarascan region. The tallest is 5 inches high. The arching eyebrows and large slanting eyes are applied rolls of clay, while the mouths, sometimes protruding, sometimes concave, are formed by incision. Hairdress, ornaments, and pose of the hands demonstrate the enjoyment of their makers in equipping each figurine with the whims of momentary inspiration. Traces of color—which must have added considerably to the effect—may be seen on some of them.

The little man in full regalia (*fig. b*), slightly enlarged as shown, is different in type, probably nearer the center of the Aztec Empire. From his posture, he seems to be dancing. The modeling introduces several new touches to our group, with the free handling of the swinging arms and flowing headdress especially noteworthy.

In the Colima region, which lies beyond the Tarascan, on the west coast of Mexico, dogs were frequently modeled (*Pl. 114*). Some breeds of this animal were raised in Mexico for meat. They are frequently found in graves, perhaps intended as guides to the after-world.

The dog in *fig. c* is about 11 inches high and 15½ long. The deep tomato-red color of the piece is highly burnished. Softness of line and liveliness are apparent from the first moment of observation. The intent eyes, alert tail, and hanging belly of such an animal are familiar to all of us.

The naïve humor of this ware is emphasized by the arrangement of the seated dog and baby, two liquid containers (*fig. b*). The saucer-like rims around the openings on the heads make them still more amusing. Remnants of paint are visible in the eyes of the boy.

The recumbent dog, 7½ inches long (*fig. a*), is made of a brownish clay. Here the characteristic high polish is considerably damaged, but its condition cannot detract from the interest of the vase. The difficult pose chosen for the animal is executed with simplicity and shows the ease with which these potters handled such a problem—as if modeling were a favorite pastime.

The tripod jar (*fig. d*) comes from this same locality and has the same squat plumpness that characterizes the sagging body of the dog beside it. A vegetable is probably represented, with feet in the form of parrots. The neatly turned rim is noteworthy. All of these Colima pieces are unusually three dimensional in quality and bear looking at from any angle.

With *Pl. 115* we come to examples of clay modeling on a larger scale. *Figs. a* and *b* show two Tarascan warriors handling some sort of weapon—clubs or spear-throwers. The first is 2 feet high, the second even taller. They are similar in general posture, and both wear helmets and protective armor with high collars, but there is considerable difference in details. *Fig. b* has perhaps more facial expression, and parts of his armor (which may have been painted in *fig. a*) are worked out plastically. Some of the clumsiness of both statues may be due to the difficulty of shaping such large and asymmetrical pieces out of clay. Nevertheless, definite action is conveyed by the expectancy reflected in their faces as well as the swinging pose of hands and bodies.

The two lower figures take us into other regions, where we find quite another approach to the subject matter and very different techniques of modeling.

Fig. c is only about 6 inches high, but commanding none the less. This little warrior comes from Chiapas, near Palenque, where, as we have seen, there was abundant tradition for working in soft plastic materials. In contrast to the Ta-rascan type, suggestive but never really elaborated, there is rich and effective detail work here. Considerable skill was necessary to build up the statuette out of many little elements, added one by one. Small as it is, the face is a character study, and the exaggerated stance and defiant gesture are admirably caught. The resplendence of the attire is augmented by the mask with its spreading head-dress, suspended upside down on the breast like a war trophy. From the stand-point of design, the incised lines that flare from the pectoral and are repeated in the figure's cropped hair and on the fringe of his sash contribute much toward holding together this ebullient portrayal.

The large seated figure, 13½ inches high, comes from Vera Cruz (*fig. d*), a region also where clay modeling and stone sculpture were equally well ad-vanced. It has neither the naïvely conceived gestures of the first two nor the salty individualism of the warrior, but rather the composure and restraint that inevitably appear as a people become bound by the conventions of a hierarchy. The shoulders and arms have agreeable plasticity and the hands and feet are carefully detailed (compare with those above). It was once painted, as were most of these statues.

As an intermission in the rich succession of ceramic statuary, we offer four pieces that are primarily shapes. *Pl. 116, figs. a* and *b* show the infrequent shape of large plates. They come from Cholula, not far from the city of Puebla. The talent of the potters in this district is manifest again in the varied decoration of this relatively late form. The plates are dated mid-14th century.

The round jar over 8 inches high (*fig. c*) represents the body of a coiled snake. The convexities, difficult to shape, are emphasized by the narrow brown-and-white band that denotes the belly. We have no information on its proveni-ence, but the row of glyphs on the collar-like rim of the jar, which show a strong similarity to those on *Pl. 111, fig. f,* and the painting of the serpent head indicate late Zapotec or even Zapotec-Mixtec style. A remarkably similar example, with the addition of tripod legs, is to be found in the Museo Nacional of Mexico, where it is identified as Mixtec.[100]

The cylindrical vase (*fig. d*), about 15 inches high, comes from the state of Vera Cruz, supposedly the Huaxtec region, which bordered on the Totonac. The material is baked brown clay. There are four panels on the sides, each pic-turing two human figures with headdress, one above the other, holding ceremo-nial objects. The design was first cut out and then orange, brown, and cream paste inserted in somewhat the manner of cloisonné. The work was done with such masterly craftsmanship that even with the vessel in sherds the coloring remained intact. Artistic deliberation is evident in the alternation of the shades.

The five heads on *Pl. 117,* all from the Mexican Area, demonstrate the amazing variety that found expression there in clay. *Fig. a,* about 1¾ inches high, was part of a figurine belonging to the early period of culture at Zacatenco, a site near Mexico, D.F.[162] The body to such a head usually had round tapering legs and short arms, somewhat similar to the figures shown on *Pl. 113.* Despite the fact that modeling is restricted here because of size, a pleasing aspect has been achieved. Outstanding is the Y-shaped ridge serving as nose and eyebrows. In the eyes, the hollows representing pupils in a suggested iris are conscious sculptural additions, their effect calculated. The deft coiling of the hair or headdress finishes the piece successfully. It does not yet have intellectual content, but is very close to it.

The female bust opposite it, with arms only indicated (*fig. c*), comes from Guadalajara in Jalisco. It is about 5 inches in height and has a slip of color. The elongated head, augmented by the tall headdress, and the aquiline nose place it in the group of Tarascan types. The ragged line of the ears is unusual. This piece also lacks real spiritual quality.

Different, artistically mature peoples exchanged inspiration in that sector of Mexico where the styles of Yucatan, Oaxaca, and the lowlands of Vera Cruz meet. The head in *fig. e,* about 8 inches high, would seem to come from this region. The slit eyes with their painted button-like centers are a rare feature, as are the protuberances on the headdress. It is probable that the color around the mouth denotes actual painting of the face.

Similar plastic characteristics appear in the much more realistically modeled head of *fig. b,* about 11 inches high. The same type of eye is present, though it looks more natural here. The face emerges from a monster's jaws, the upper teeth of which are clearly discernible, although the protruding snout is broken off. Involved decoration is applied with virtuosity—almost daring—in this brittle material. The lozenge-shaped spirals above the ears are decorative elements found also in Maya and Toltec art. The youthfulness of the face and the maturity of its execution lead us to accept the piece without hesitation.

The pottery head from Vera Cruz (*fig. d*), 6½ inches high, is one of the type commonly known as "Totonac laughing faces." All are rather square, with large caplike headdresses that extend to the ears, and many bear frets. The monkey in relief is an unusual addition. The achievement of a definite facial expression is a sign of a high artistic level, and the obvious smile spread over this piece gives it real spiritual content.

Aside from the differences that are apparent at first glance, it is worth while to observe the different plastic treatment of the eyes on this plate, from those formed by the archaic fillet technique (*fig. a*) to the realistic (*fig. b*) and the sculpturally mature (*fig. d*).

The little figure from Tempoal (*Pl. 118, fig. a*) belongs to the Huaxtec region. The face is stolid; what slight emphasis it has is given it by the modeling of the nose, mouth, and high cheek bones. Its decorative effect is due to its painting, which lends real meaning to the somewhat clumsy clay body.

Fig. c is a pottery whistle, about 9 inches long, from central Vera Cruz. The droll toylike little figure lies in an unusual attitude. (Compare with *Pl. 61, fig. b.*) Despite a rather heavy execution in the hands and feet, it is done with a good shot of realism. With the rounded modeling of the features and the tight-fitting headdress, reminding one of a medieval jester's cap, the head bears some resemblance to the Totonac laughing head of the preceding plate.

The terra-cotta masquette (*fig. b*), 6 inches high, comes from the Tuxtla district in Vera Cruz. It represents the moan bird, the Yucatecan screech owl, popularly associated with death. Its glyph is used in the Dresden Codex, generally with evil import.[137] This piece, though relatively small, makes a positive impression, strengthened by its rocket-like build-up.

Another terra-cotta masquette of the same provenience (*fig. d*), only 3½ inches long by 2 high, depicts the leaf-nosed bat as the Death-god. If it is compared with the figure above it, a similar sculptural language will be noted. The holes for the eyes, nostrils, mouth, and ears are executed with calculated effect, and the succession of rounded surfaces is subtlely varied by plastic and incised detail. The precision in the piece gives the impression of lapidary work rather than modeled clay.

In the last centuries before the Conquest, the potter grappled with larger subjects, also with ease. *Pl. 119* presents two life-size figures of baked clay, both from the high plateau of Mexico in Aztec times, made in several pieces, then put together. According to the accepted interpretation, *fig. a* represents a priest wearing the flayed skin of a sacrificial victim. There is little beauty for us in this piece, with its dull eyes and gaping mouth. Yet it embodies a high degree of technical ability in both the modeling and firing, so expertly done that it has withstood the vicissitudes of the centuries.

Although the face in *fig. b* has not much more expression, in idea it approaches more closely our comprehension. The figure stands nearly 5½ feet high. The rounded turban-like headdress is an unusual feature, as are also the very long ear pendants. The costume is typically Aztec, especially the armlets, which were made of gold decorated with feathers, and the sunburst at the groin. This was fashioned of a thin plaited material and originally had a cone in the center, since broken off; a similar ornament was often worn on the head. The whole chest is hung with necklaces, and the sandals are faithfully represented. While certain details may recall the terra-cotta statues of the Etruscans, a closer observation of the piece moves it back into the almost impenetrable realm of pre-Columbian ideology.

Equal virtuosity in modeling clay is revealed when the high plateau is left behind and we move south into the Oaxaca region, from which the material for the next four plates is selected. Especially typical of this district are the effigy funerary urns and incense burners that feature human and animal figures. In most cases the base is broad, and behind the main figure is a large empty pocket or jar in which incense was placed or, as the case might be, the bones of the deceased for secondary burial. These vessels were usually covered with a red wash, and sometimes as many as four colors are found painted on a single piece.[151]

On *Pl. 120* the two jaguar cave gods, 19¾ and 16½ inches high respectively, are presented, said to have been found in a cave temple near Guila, Oaxaca, facing each other on opposite sides of a funerary urn. The Indians called them "messenger dogs of the gods," and indeed they have certain doglike characteristics. They are, however, fantasy creatures, existing only in the imagination of the Zapotecs, but executed and transmitted with an expression startling in its clarity of conception and richness of detail. The faces with their glaring eyes and open mouths, the heavy necklace cords, pendants, and bells, as well as the fantastic claws, are all worked out with care. The watchful attitude is well conveyed and the animals are formidable enough to frighten away any intruder who might venture to disturb the peace of the deceased.

The feet of the next figure (*Pl. 121, fig. a*) are much like those of the "dogs," though the upright posture, the torso, and arms are distinctly human. The head is animal, but it wears the earplugs and headdress of a dignitary. Pierced eyes and mouth lend ferocity to the statue, and the rich necklace of bells and the loin-cloth add to the baffling representation.

The second illustration (*fig. b*) shows an older man in full regalia, holding a glyph or symbol in one hand and a small shield in the other. His expression is as pointed as any cartoon's: smiling to himself, he seems to know much that we can only guess at. There is a certain top-heaviness in the piece, an exaggeration of the head and headdress, characteristic of most pre-Columbian figural repre-sentations. Composed and static when compared with the ready-to-spring pose of the two jaguar gods, this statue seems to typify the power and shrewdness of a priestly caste.

A blending of realistic features and fantasy elements is excellently demon-strated in *fig. c*. The piece is 32 inches high and comes from Tomb 77, Monte Alban, dated in Epoch II. A well-defined head is the center of the composition, crowned by a monster-mask, the nose and eyes of which are clearly visible. This is one of the few human faces which one feels might be portraiture. The some-what cross-eyed look, the arrogant half-open mouth, and high bald forehead pre-sent in quintessence a high priest who stands well toward the top of a powerful hierarchy. Unfortunately the photograph cannot show the subtle build-up of the various planes in the modeling, all serving to emphasize the head. The plain semicircular collar and the wide undecorated "wings" of clay, like a screen in the background, stress the sharp characterization through contrast. The flaring rim at the top, skillfully incorporated as part of the headdress, is the mouth of the incense burner or urn.

A number of subjects were used in the decoration of incense burners. The human figure generally constituted the main motif, but variations in pose and embellishment exhibit a rich and modulating fantasy-world.

The seated human wearing a strange mouth mask (*Pl. 122, fig. a*), 33½ inches high, was excavated at Atzompa and is placed in Monte Alban I. It is a representation of the Rain-god, who is characterized in Maya iconography also by a long hooked nose. Primary attention is centered on the head, although the upper part of the body, arms, and hands are worked out well. The lower part is only suggested and the feet, in their stiff horizontal position, have only four toes. Incised lines on the headdress—unusual with its flaps—reduce the preponder-ance of blank surface.

Fig. b, also an incense burner, comes from a later epoch, Monte Alban III. It is 16½ inches high. Here the main body of the piece is frankly utilitarian.

The lower section with its painted decoration may represent a temple platform, upon which three human figures are performing a ceremony. The main person, with shield, is seated on a block or altar, while two elaborately dressed attendants, carrying ritual objects, stand on either side. In its idea, the piece has a certain analogy to the story-telling pottery jars of the Andean Area.

Figs. c and *d* present seated personages. While the second dignitary is executed on the whole with more decorative skill, the representation shows greater conventionalization—note again the four toes. He wears a fine carved mask on his breast and his cape is edged with braid—a serpent symbol in Zapotec-Mixtec grave finds—very effective in pottery. The whole obligatory paraphernalia of his costume is so much more lavish that, compared with the first, he appears a rich man beside a poor one. In the characterization of the faces, both pieces are equally strong. The flaring "wings" of the two headdresses serve as excellent frames. *Fig. c* is a peripheral example of the type above it. He wears a monster-mask and wide collar, suggestive of the last head on the preceding plate. There are traces of blue paint on his beads and red on the tongue and nose.

The utilitarian purpose of the first three pieces on *Pl. 123* is so subordinated in the design that the urn proper cannot be seen in any of the photographs. All the subjects are human figures in natural three-dimensional representation.

It is doubtful if another piece showing such a delightful buffoon as that in *fig. a* could be found among all the effigy funerary urns and incense burners in the Oaxaca district. He is a little over 16 inches high. His cross-eyes, snub nose, and open mouth, and the lines of his carefully combed hair all draw attention to the face, but shoulder cape, hands, legs, and the ornamentation are executed with rare consideration and skill. As he sits there, so well behaved with his hands on his knees, he confirms the description of some of the early chroniclers who reported these people as jolly and credulous before the maltreatment of their conquerors changed them.

The war chief in full regalia (*fig. b*) carries a thick staff in his right hand and a shield with mask and pendant feathers in his left, both interesting features. His head is placed within the beak of a bird-mask and his costume shows an unusual detail in the birds' heads on the breast, probably of metal.

The same bird-mask headdress reduced to a mere shape appears in *fig. c*. The statuette is 20 inches high. Although the position of the hands adds to the stiffness of the pose, the wavy outlines of the circular skirt and ruffled anklets counterbalance any rigidity. The spirals on the garment and the ornament above the nose are new details to us. As a composition, this figure has more line and vibration than the preceding one.

In *fig. d* (not an urn) we have a nude figure, 13½ inches high, of tannish color, without any decoration except a tall headdress that bears glyphs, the lower one of which is the Zapotec sign for 13. In contrast to the preceding pieces, laden with ornament and symbolic appendages, it presents simply a young human body, treated with a good sense of realism and proportion. The cross-eyed expression and open mouth of *fig. a* have here lost their grotesque character, and the position of the legs, with hands resting on knees, familiar in various manners of execution on other plates, is here graceful and natural. The arms and shoulders are beautifully modeled; fingers and toes, carefully detailed. Signs similar to those on the headdress are incised on the breast. He appears to be watching intently, perhaps as an onlooker or waiting to take part in an initiation ceremony. Here we have the first case in which decorative elements were omitted which might detract from the subject—a live youthful human creature.

The clay representation of a warrior (*Pl. 124, fig. a*), 23½ inches high, is dated in Monte Alban II. Both posture and gesture here are new. The pushing movement in the whole figure—perhaps a dance pose—is in contrast to the static pieces that have preceded it. There is ease in the modeling, not only in the general attitude but in the small additional decorations. The eyes are somewhat similar to those on the Atzompa vessel (see *Pl. 122, fig. a*), also of an early period. Plain surfaces behind the headdress and in the loincloth serve as contrast for the embellished sections.

In the various examples presented, the free treatment of the subject will be noted: figures are met both standing and seated in widely varying poses.

Fig. b is a small cylindrical vase, 5½ inches high, from the excavations at Atzompa. A vessel of this type must have been used as a container for small offerings, perhaps jade, turquoise, or pearls. Important for us is the cameo-like sharpness of the relief, showing a human head surmounted by a bird-mask. The most difficult lines and planes are achieved without a sign of hesitation.

The uniqueness of the large pottery statue (*fig. c*), nearly 3 feet high, begins with its pose, some details of which can be reconstructed only by guesswork. The flexed legs are most infrequent in pre-Columbian modeling, as is also the position of the arms, the left resting on the knee, its hand grasping the broken right, the direction of which may have been forward or upward. Besides the posture, another unusual feature is the number of small decorative ornaments, applied with the greatest skill yet observed. Particularly impressive in their exactness are the armlets with mask and beaded frame. The proudly held head is masterly, not only in execution but in expression, and crowns a mature and dignified body. The sharply demarcated line in front of the ear suggests that the figure is wearing a mask. Such a grotesque "harlequin" nose as his appears on the small jade in *Pl. 251, fig. c,* which comes from El Salvador, as well as a jade mask from the Guatemala highlands, now in the University Museum at Philadelphia. The headdress seems to be a band with long ribbons hanging down the back.

This piece represents a peak in the pre-Columbian artist's modeling in clay. Few strange details are present to disturb our enjoyment. His dash gives him universal appeal; his litheness is comparable to that of a gladiator. However, where the figure belongs stylistically is a puzzle; it has few characteristics of the region where it was found.

MAYA AREA

In the pottery of the Mexican Area the human figure is frequently seen in combination with vessels of utilitarian purpose, a practice which also carries into the other areas to the south. The ingenious blending of the abstract and realistic noted here is found among all pre-Columbian peoples.

The first two examples in *Pl. 125,* one from the Mexican and one from the Maya Area, show an incense jar worked into each piece as an integral part of the composition. *Fig. a,* from Puebla, Mexico, and 7 inches high, is a tripod fashioned to represent a crouching man with a large round jar strapped to his back. Its conception is true to life; even today the traveler may encounter such a figure bearing a burden held by a cord across the chest. The disproportionate belly and uneven length of the legs serve primarily to stabilize the vessel. (Compare with *Pl. 297, fig. a.*)

In *fig. b* the *incensario* is in the form of a large bowl or kettle, held on the lap of a man whose legs have been simplified into two crescents, drawn one over the other, to constitute a base. This piece, our first from the Maya Area, is of dark red fired clay and about 9 inches high. It comes from Lake Amatitlán in Guatemala. The head seems uncomfortably pressed between the heavy headdress and its vertical "wings." (See *Pl. 122, fig. c.*) Large earplugs, a very long breast bar, and beadwork directly under the chin are added. The incense bowl and the figure are blended with a freedom that reconciles us to the alien artistic impulse that created it.

In the shaping of the large jar from Guatemala (*fig. c*), 16 inches high, its utilitarian purpose predominated. However, the addition of the animal snout and suggested ears convert it at once into a living subject. The two low handles take on the semblance of arms akimbo, and the brown and black design painted over the white slip gives the impression of a textile blanket.

The two lower vessels of *Pl. 126, fig. b* from Chiapas and *fig. c* from Isla de los Sacrificios, Vera Cruz, are used as connectives between the Mexican and Maya areas, coming, as they do, from sectors where characteristic artistic influences mingled with one another.

The rounded contour of the jar just discussed is met again in *fig. b,* although this piece has no zoömorphic elements; the three handles and painted motif leave no place for an association or suggestion of human or animal form. It is simply a utilitarian vessel, which, when found, contained remains of cremated bones and cloth. It is nearly 12 inches high and has a flat base. Besides the decoration, which is quite conventionalized, hasty but fluent, the most artistic feature is perhaps the finely finished curving lip.

The painted beaker (*fig. c*) ranks higher from all points of view. The more involved form, complicated as it is by the pedestal, shows a development. A deliberate continuation of the dark stripes, which run parallel on the vessel but are splayed on the base, accenting its line, proves that the craftsman well understood the modulation of pattern. The vertical lines are good contrast for the outspokenly horizontal frieze at the top, where a serpent-like monster is represented with elongated gaping jaws.

Three ochre-red pottery pieces are presented in *fig. a.* The beaker at the left has complete stability and perfect proportions, enhanced by its rounded rim and the flange just above the base. (Compare it with the crystal cup from Monte Alban, *Pl. 255, fig. a.*) The plate, the largest of them all, measures 13½ inches across. Its shape is remarkably symmetrical, and the even rim and clean precision of the depressed center, olive-green in color, are noteworthy. Especially unusual is the conical bottle (right), with its body flaring from the vertical base only to narrow sharply again at a completely different angle—one which must have been difficult to fashion with the hand. There is a suggestion of a painted band at the neck, above which the piece seems to have been finished in a darker tone. In this group there are only plain surfaces, no decorative patterns, yet what refinement is apparent in the shapes—all made without the use of the potter's wheel.

The effigy vessels on *Pl. 127* are constructed in such a way that the upper part with the head forms a cover for the lower hollow section, used as a container. Those in *figs. a* and *b,* together with the covered tripod vase (*fig. c*), come from Kaminaljuyú, an early Maya or even pre-Maya settlement in the highlands of Guatemala.

Fig. a, 8 inches high, represents a hunchback, generally an omen of evil. The shape of the body may have been influenced by the desire to create as much hollow space as possible. However, other parts of the figure, particularly the detail work in the face, counterbalance any distortion and make of the piece a striking characterization. Headdress, ear ornaments, necklace, belt, and loincloth are green, the body is crimson, and the mouth, scarlet. Ingenious perforations in the headdress, one of which is visible just above the ear, were arranged to light up the eyes and mouth.

The seated woman (*fig. b*) is not handsome but certainly an excellent bit of caricature. She is 11 inches high. Finer incision work than that on the boy below her adds to the interest of the jar. Her garment is a burnished olive-green, very effective against the dull rippled gray of the rest of the piece. A playful enjoyment in decorating, whether with applied strips of clay or incision, is evident in the exquisitely executed bowknot of the skirt. The belt also is tied in front with another carefully depicted bow.

The covered tripod jar (*fig. c*) is 18 inches high and dark brown in color, with a single incised panel on the front that shows traces of red paint. The bird on the lid is a novelty. A duplicate in design, although about 5 inches shorter, is owned by the Museum of the American Indian, New York. In an art where some individual touches are nearly always present, the existence of such a striking counterpart is worth mentioning. Another similar vessel is in the museum at Teotihuacan.

At the site of Uaxactun, already discussed in the chapter on architecture, the Carnegie Institution of Washington, under the leadership of A. Ledyard Smith, made important discoveries in the field of pottery as well as in other arts. Through the great generosity of the Institution, we are permitted to reproduce here some of their unpublished material, which adds new aspects to the unfolding panorama of Maya art. A publication of the Institution is in preparation that will treat the archaeological finds in detail.

The first of these objects to be presented here is the effigy jar in *fig. d,* about 8 inches high. It shows a cross-eyed boy whose eyes are lighted from behind in the manner described under *fig. a.* The material is blackish in tone and highly

polished, with the incised decorations brought out in white paint. It is noteworthy that the pose of the legs and hands in each figure on this plate is different
though equally well defined.

One of the greatest artistic achievements of the Maya was their painted pottery. Vessels of fired clay, not particularly distinguished in shape, were covered
with a thin coat of stucco and the smooth inviting surface then decorated with
painted figures and glyphs, frequently of story-telling character. Although the
scenes represented were composed for the limited circumference of a pottery
piece, they have the space-filling quality of a fresco.

The same iconographical concept prevails in them as in all the other products
of the Maya, whether of stucco, metal, wood, or jade, in flat or in the round.
This use of an identifiable language is found in all high civilizations before
the Renaissance. Chinese, Babylonian, Egyptian, and Cretan art each had its
distinctive manner of delineation, which enables us to assign a single piece, according to its characteristics, to the civilization which produced it.

In the Maya and Andean areas particularly, as in Greek vases, painted scenes
of story-telling content give us revealing glimpses of the life. Because of
their pictorial decoration, these pieces might be discussed under painting, but
since they are primarily vessels, they will be considered here, as one of the crowning achievements of pre-Columbian pottery. Neither the porcelains of China
nor the majolica of the Mediterranean would be placed in any other category
than that of pottery, regardless of their painted themes.

Here it should be pointed out that although each artistic product of the Maya
bears the distinctive Maya stamp, it is nevertheless treated with a clear realization of the qualities of the medium in which it is created. The Maya were the
only people of medieval America who developed a distinct artistic idiom for
each material. In their best works they made full use of the monumental possibilities in stone, the modulation inherent in clay, the shapes slumbering in a raw
piece of cloudy jade, and the potentialities for flowing decoration in the fresco,
whether on a wall or a clay vessel.

One pottery piece from the Teotihuacan culture has already appeared with
a mythological subject painted on a stucco ground (see *Pl. 110, fig. b*), but the
technique will be more readily discerned in those on *Pl. 128.* In *fig. b,* from
Kaminaljuyú, the form is not simple. The sides of the jar are slightly concave
and it stands on three slab legs; it has a lid, the knob of which is strikingly like
that on a Mexican vessel found nearly seven hundred miles away (see *Pl. 110,*

fig. c). Such resemblance provides renewed stimulus to consider the connections between the early cultures of the Mexican and Guatemalan high plateaus. Remnants of a monster with flamboyantly drawn feather decoration are clear on the painted surface, even though somewhat battered. The subject flows freely over the cylindrical body of the vessel, and an equally artistic pattern appears on the lid.

Among pre-Columbian pottery of this type, none ranks higher artistically than the fresco vase in *fig. a*. This vessel, 7 inches high, is one of those found at Uaxactun. The bottom of the piece flares out with a sharp edge counterbalancing the overhang of the cover. Its tripod legs are a little shorter than those of the Kaminaljuyú piece and are better digested into the body. The lid is smoothly rounded, without a knob, and its solid black surface, together with that of the legs, sets off the delicately colored composition.

The unrolled design of this vase is shown in *fig. c*. It consists of two panels of unequal size, each of which shows two personages seated on jaguar skins, facing each other. The man on the extreme left is the figure seen on the jar above. Their gestures are of iconographic significance, and the columns of hieroglyphs, if deciphered, would probably shed light upon the subject.

The amazingly refined designs must have been executed by artists of calligraphy. The whole decoration recalls the finest technique of manuscript illumination (see *Pl. 266*). There is ease and lightness in the depiction of the dignitaries, and all glyphs, inside and outside the frames, are placed with an outspoken feeling for their decorative effect. Delicate tones of yellow, red, jade-green are used with black outlines. When in perfect condition, with its colors alive, the piece must have been the equal of any ceramic product of the Old World.

Other cylindrical vessels with painted story-events were found in early Maya sites. The pieces pictured here, however, differ from the Uaxactun fresco vase in that the background is usually colored and the design is built up in a less delicate way—more like a wall-painting than a page of manuscript. One may presuppose formative stages for this type of pottery, despite its apparently early date, for modeling would seem to have preceded painting, and simplification of the vase form for the purpose of receiving picture records must be regarded as a later development.

Pl. 129, fig. a presents another Uaxactun vase, cylindrical in shape and 9 inches high. The ground is a rich red and below the rim a cream-colored band bears hieroglyphics outlined in black and painted, some in red, some in pale orange. Five human figures and a jaguar constitute the main characters in the scene (*fig. c*). A chief wearing a wide collar of feathers, or perhaps of jade, and a large headdress is seated cross-legged on a dais. Behind him stands a smaller person in a fringed cloak, bearing an object in his hands, while the next in line carries a ceremonial standard of splendid feather-work. Two imposing figures face him, both arrayed in colorful textiles and rich headdresses, with feathered insignia at their backs. Faces and bodies are painted. The first carries a baglike object; the second, a long staff. Between them sits a jaguar, who holds a neat package bound with a ribbon, similar to cache vessels with votive offerings found in excavations. The two rows of glyphs inserted in front of the seated chieftain give a date equivalent to A.D. 140, as deciphered by Dr. Morley, and must refer to an event that took place centuries before the vase was made, which perhaps commemorates the occasion when the two ambassadors appeared before the ruler here depicted. Other glyphs scattered about the piece may identify the individuals.[132]

The scene is strange, but we cannot escape the drama in it. A meeting between two different peoples is evident from the detail of their dress and ornaments; the figures are far from standardized and gestures and colors also serve to differentiate the characters. The whole painting has splendor, dignity, and movement.

Fig. b presents the painting on a tripod dish from Holmul, a site not far from Uaxactun. Its decorative composition reminds one strongly of that on the preceding vase, not only from an iconographical point of view but also through its facile and flamboyant spirit. The center of the bowl contains a definitely framed tableau, in which stands a high priest in full regalia, his profile turned to the left and his right arm outstretched in a ritual gesture. A small figure faces him in the left corner, and at his back is a stylized feathered serpent, in which are submerged a human figure and, just below it, a jaguar swinging a censer. The inside rim of the dish has a row of precisely painted hieroglyphs around the edge, with eight "snake-birds" spread out below them. Despite the delicacy in the construction of the central figure, it has static weight, in contrast to the circular motion of the design in the border. This effect is enhanced by the bold use of solid black in the square that frames it.

The cylindrical painted vase in *Pl. 130, fig. a* is 9 inches high and comes from Chamá in the Alta Verapaz district of Guatemala. A decorative band of chevrons replaces the glyph border of the preceding vessels and is repeated at the bottom. The meeting of seven persons is pictured, two of them apparently leaders, judging from their darker painted bodies and the concentration of action in and around them (*fig. c*). The bald-headed chief at the right, whose forehead is markedly flattened, is draped in a large jaguar skin and carries a decorated lance. Several of the protagonists show sparse moustaches. Their dress is quite different from that seen in the vases just described, and attention should be called to the fan shape some of them carry. The scene radiates tension and displays more action than is usually depicted. There is restlessness in the curling lines of the drawing and the many cross angles. The vivid portrayal of grotesque features is as powerful and sure-handed as in Chinese art.

A vase 8 inches high from Ratinlixul, also in the Alta Verapaz district of Guatemala, is shown in *fig. b*. Between the chevron border at top and bottom is pictured a dignitary borne on a journey in a litter carried by two men (*fig. d*); five more individuals make up his entourage. His necklace and turban-like headdress stand out from the others and the jaguar, or dog, below the litter may be further indication of his rank. He also carries the woven fan insignia seen above. The bearers and the porter, who follows with a large pack held by a tump line, are depicted as smaller persons with humble attitudes. The four officials beyond are painted with enough detailed decoration to differentiate them from the others. Three of them carry paddle-shaped clubs, while the last in line bears a small round package in his left hand and rests his right on his left shoulder. The cylinder shape of the vessel makes the procession endless. Only three glyphs occur. The curved lines used in the preceding vase are recognizable here, but the expressive vigor is lacking. Poses are repetitious and there is no sense of action. However, the longer we look at the unrolled design, the more we catch of the atmosphere of pomp and ceremony. The ruler in the litter has the sensual and autocratic appearance of a maharajah.

Pl. 131, fig. a shows a vase about 6½ inches high from Nebaj in the Guatemala highlands. On it is painted a chief sitting cross-legged, his right hand holding a ceremonial object and his left bent in an amazingly deliberate and free gesture. His costume, which resembles those on the vase just described, is worked out in detail, even including the fringe on the cloth. The attendant behind him could have stepped out of an Oriental fable illustration, as he stands with arms crossed looking toward the low altar with its basket-like object. Glyphs appear above the kneeling figure, others are framed in columns, and a panel behind the attendant contains a longer inscription. The colors are quiet in tone, with the designs in red and orange against a yellow-buff ground and outlines and details in black. The drawing has real dash. Executed in a manner that was practiced also in the Near and Far East, its assurance of line could not be improved upon even there.

In the other three illustrations, the story-telling theme is diluted into decorative and finally degenerate patterns. *Fig. b* is another Chamá vase, but not a simple cylindrical shape. The form with its fluted lower half, suggestive of a vegetable, is an early Maya type.[40] The neck of the vessel above the chevron band—which runs, as may have been noticed, nearly always from left to right—presents a cylindrical surface upon which a seated figure is painted. The headdress, flowing in two directions, is so arranged that despite the "low ceiling" its decorative effect is fully realized. A particularly brilliant detail is the left hand as it rests on the hip, the fingers curling most preciously.

On *fig. c,* which is about 7 inches high, a quetzal is featured below the band of glyphs and between the framework of two light ribbons, with plumage so spread as to fill, in a highly artistic manner, half the main field. The depiction is not realistic, but is satisfying none the less because of the virtuosity of its transformation into a stunning decorative scheme.

Fig. d is a peripheral example of this art. From its style it may be surmised that it comes from El Salvador, the southernmost region of direct Maya influence. First it will be noted that instead of the cylindrical form a keg shape is produced, which is much more difficult to decorate. The depiction of the face and dress is different from those just considered; the presentation is less calligraphic and more "painted." The staring eye, the angular features, the lack of abundant facility in the drawing, and the large surface of undecorated background are characteristic of the pre-Columbian pottery of this section.

In *Pl. 132* we have the utilitarian cylindrical shape fashioned into human heads. *Fig. b,* from Kaminaljuyú, is 11 inches high and pinkish buff in color. Two elongated ears serve as handles, and the lower end of the piece, superfluous for the representation, resolves smoothly into decoration. A turban-like headdress marks the rim, going all the way around; otherwise, the back is plain. The eyes are wise and living, and the nose has a fine narrow bridge. The problematical lines that characterize the mouth have already been met in sculpture (see *Pl. 68, fig. b*) and will be seen again among the first of our jades in the Tuxtla statuette (see *Pl. 235, fig. d*).

Fig. a, 7 inches high, comes from the early Maya site of Quiriguá, best known for its excellent stone sculpture. It was found in a dark corner of a ruined structure, broken into twenty-three pieces, but as only one small fragment was missing, a perfect repair job was possible. The elongated line of the other head is here modulated into jovial roundness, and the shape is further removed from the cylindrical form, following instead a curving line that flares slightly toward the base. The face is clearly outlined at the sides and finished with a short beard. A smooth inset rim suggests that there was once a cover. In color, the eyes, earrings, fillet, and mouth are a dull bluish white, the beard and fillet decorations, red, and the body is a rich cream. The jar reminds us of Mochica portrait vases (see *Pl. 160*).

The whistle fashioned in the likeness of a Maya standing with arms crossed (*Pl. 133, fig. a*), 6¼ inches high, is allegedly from Yucatan. One runs across this passive yet alert pose even today in the Maya Area. The piece bears traces of yellow paint. Behind the arm is the mouthpiece of the instrument.

The fragment 4¼ inches high (*fig. c*) is another whistle, also said to come from Yucatan. When intact, the figure must have had a pose similar to the one above it, but with the left arm crossed over the right, showing the hand and fingers. There are also differences in the headdress and breast ornaments. But the facial build-up is the same, even from the point of view of modeling, although intricate tattooing makes the expression here bewildering.

Fig. b, 7 inches high, was found at Palenque by William H. Holmes in a tomb in the base of the Temple of the Cross. The flowing headdress with its loop is done with especial virtuosity. Executed in the best tradition of the site, the figurine is the finest of this group.[49]

Another whistle (*fig. d*), 4½ inches high, comes from Tabasco, a state that borders on Yucatan. This piece is chunky and less plastic than the others, and the pose and headdress are different; nevertheless, all four possess a strong inner relationship. Each is individual, yet all are held together by the framework of Maya characteristics.

The theme of mother and child, perpetuated in many arts and universally understood, also engaged the talent of the pre-Columbian potter. Four cultures are represented on *Pl. 134.* Two examples (*figs. a* and *d*) from the Mexican Area are included to show the technical and stylistic differences in various regions not too widely separated to be influenced, at least indirectly, by one another.

‹ 182 ›

The toylike piece (*fig. a*), from the state of Morelos, not far from Mexico, D.F., is without doubt the least advanced of them all; at first glance it appears little more than a monkey that clings to the shoulders of the mother. The long slanting eyes, the heavy legs, tapering to a point at the feet, are archaic characteristics. Gesture and movement are limited in the struggle for articulation. Yet the theme is clear enough to have appeal.

The figurine (*fig. d*), 6½ inches high, speaks a very different language in its modeling. The contours are no longer uncertain, and a definite mood is transmitted through the clarity of its plastic execution, typically Tarascan. It is a contented scene; the protective curve of the mother's arms is very expressive.

A still different pose is seen in *fig. b*, from Solcajá, Guatemala. Here the mother clasps her child about the waist, and the baby holds both hands to its mouth in good international fashion. The crude modeling gives her a somewhat anxious expression. This statuette is only 5 inches high and is fashioned from coarse brown clay without a trace of other coloring. The ears of both mother and infant are pierced for the addition of ornaments.

The mother with a child and dog (*fig. e*), a little more than 6 inches high, was found near Palenque. She has a broad stance and complacent expression. The child, his hand held firmly in hers, seems to be seated at her side. An unusual feature is the hair that hangs about his shoulders. The puppy clasped at her hip is amusingly realistic and brings to us a new glimpse of Maya life.

While Maya talent created the large and magnificent stucco reliefs of Palenque and Comalcalco, we have no clay statuary of large size from this region, such as was seen in the Mexican Area. The figure of a goddess and warrior (*fig. c*), only 12 inches high, is one of the largest pieces yet found. It comes from the state of Campeche in Mexico, within the realm of the Old Empire, and is said to date from between the 7th and 10th centuries. It is a masterpiece of modeling and carries within it deep spiritual content. No longer the simple mother and child theme, it shows a female deity with a warrior nestling at her knee. Even with the disturbing effect of the broken arms and cracked face, we can realize the young body, beautifully proportioned and enticing. She must have worn originally an elaborate headdress, only the center of which now remains. The curving lines of her shoulder, breasts, and lap radiate great sensuality, an impression that is enhanced by the ecstatic expression on the warrior's face and the gesture of his hand as if he would lose himself in her sheltering presence. The heroic proportions of the goddess in comparison with the warrior's figure are an indication of the transcendental import of the piece. The pair are inclosed in a magic circle permitting no intrusion. In the slight protective bend of her head and the upward turn of his, there is evidence that the Maya, too, realized the existence of that mystic borderland where the mother and lover in woman merge, inseparable.

The artistic dash that we enjoyed in the painted pottery appears also in lightly incised figural compositions on similar shapes (*Pl. 135*).

In the 5-inch vase said to come from Yucatan (*fig. a*), a single figure dominates the jar. His upturned right hand is making a significant gesture, pointing perhaps to a column of conventionalized glyphs on the opposite side of the piece, shown in the photograph on the left. Flesh and bone are suggested throughout the slender body, which has life and elasticity, nobility and grace.

The cylindrical chalkware jar, 4¾ inches high (*fig. b*), is said to have been found in a tomb at Zacualpa in the Guatemala highlands. On the inside, it was painted black, with red pigment rubbed into the incised lines; on the outside, there is no trace of color, except for the creamy tone of the clay. Again a single figure is depicted—interpreted as the young Maize-god.[69] His elaborate headdress of flowing feathers and flowers seems almost to mark off a margin below the rim of the vase. He too looks toward a column of glyphs incised beyond the lines of the waving headdress. The foreshortening of the right hand is perfectly indicated. The figure has a hurried wind-blown rhythm, and shows a talent which knew how to produce lines at once vigorous and expressive in a limited space. (Compare the gesture with that on the gourd-shaped Chamá vase, *Pl. 131, fig. b*.)

Fig. c, a slightly flaring cylindrical vase, comes from Asunción Mita in southern Guatemala, near the border of El Salvador. It is yellowish buff in tone, 8 inches high, and its entire surface is covered with incised decoration. The figure here is standing and his headdress fills the space at either side. The same impetuous gesture of the hands occurs again. His left arm, raised to shoulder level, reaches beyond the flowing feathers as if pointing, and his right moves downward, the outstretched fingers turned toward his body. This vase shows a condensed etching-like design, while in the other two a higher degree of fluency and a more virtuose touch are apparent.

After seeing these revelations of the sound and versatile ability of the Maya potter, it is not surprising to find him master of still another type, the vase with relief decoration (*Pl. 136*).

It required technical perfection and stylistic maturity to produce the gracious egg-shaped vessel from Uaxactun (*fig. a*), excavated in a burial. It is 8 inches high. The surface is divided into two decorated parts, representing in both instances two seated persons gesticulating to each other. The upper part of the relief is once again framed by a band of glyphs, a characteristic of certain fresco vases already noted. A well-proportioned base adds suavity to the composition. Coming from one of the oldest settlements, this piece testifies to early mastery in this field also.

Fig. b shows a brownish jar, 6 inches high, from Zacualpa. Its chief decoration consists of three human figures, depicted from the waist up, with large headdresses that are expanded to ornament all the free space. As the figural content is by now familiar, we are free to consider how the relief was produced. There are vases which seem to have been made in two halves with the help of a mold or stamp and then fitted together. In such a case, a rough uneven line shows clearly the imperfectly welded edge, particularly on the bottom. But even then the blending of the relief decoration in the two halves is admirably done and only very close study reveals the slightest break in the continuity of the design. In other examples of this type, no joint can be discovered. Even though the reliefs may have been executed by another method, as yet unsolved, the term "carved ware," which is often applied to this type of pottery, is not completely satisfactory, for it implies a deeper background and more sharply cut detail.

The technique of incision on the tripod vase in *fig. c*, as well as its shape, reminds us of the funerary urn from Teotihuacan (see *Pl. 110, fig. c*). It comes from Kaminaljuyú and shows three mask sections, each different, surrounded by affluent decorative elements. The material is a fine black ware with a high polish. Red coloring matter was painted on or rubbed into the sunken background to make an effective contrast. The slits in the feet are noteworthy. A much stronger stylization in the design can be noted than in the other pieces on this plate. While in all cases there is a tendency to cover the available space, two different plastic effects are evident. Here the relief is blocked out, with extensive flat surfaces, and plasticity is indicated by incision.

The bowl in *Pl. 137, fig. a* is rounded in shape and rimless. It bears two medallions in relief, each with a human figure as central subject. Columns of glyphs, lightly incised on the pale buff surface, flank the panels. The side here illustrated shows the marks of restoration, but even so we can delight our eye on the facility of line. A figure, half lying, rests his elbows and right knee on what appears to be a couch, his left leg extended and raised almost as if in flying. His hands support a small vertical tablet inscribed with glyphs. Above him, on the right, is poised a bird, apparently a pelican, executed in a decorative though unrealistic pose. The two lozenge shapes coming out of the open beak—or going in—connect it with the human. The medallion on the other side, composed in as masterly a fashion although somewhat simpler, shows a man in profile seated on a low stool before another panel of glyphs. In each case the frame is rigidly observed, with not a single detail breaking over the double line of the border.

For this piece we have no provenience, but surmise that it came from Yucatan. We have seen a similar bowl in a private collection in Merida. The fact that an object was found in a certain locality, however, does not necessarily mean that it originated there; many articles were traded for their beauty and rarity, both in pre- and post-Columbian times, traveling far and passing through many hands.

Fig. b, an interestingly shaped bowl presenting a jaguar seated within a medallion, comes from Yucatan. It is of pale yellow material with traces of red sizing and black spots painted on the animal. The creature wears a cape tied around its shoulders, a loincloth, and a headdress with the familiar image of the Long-nosed God, as well as wrist and ankle ornaments and a noseplug.[137] The head is modeled plastically to a certain degree, while details on the animal body are emphasized by incision. The feet and part of the headdress trespass upon the compositional frame. Such liberties, far from impairing the artistic unity of the medallion, actually enhance it, showing talent and experience. The relief here is worked out more deeply and decisively than in any case seen hitherto. With its sharp outlines and compact composition, it bears a telling resemblance to a jade carving.

The medallion frame probably represents a water-lily stem coiled and knotted, with two blossoms branching out at opposite sides.[137] These framing lines are more deeply incised than the jaguar. In this connection, it might be mentioned that the water-lily is associated with the style of Palenque, appearing, among other carvings, in the panel from the Temple of the Sun (see *Pl. 75, fig. b*) and the relief at Madrid (see *Pl. 81, fig. a*).

The Guatemala lowlands, not far from the border of Honduras and El Salvador, is given as the provenience of the heavily decorated jar in *Pl. 138, fig. a,* long famous as one of the most outstanding pieces of Maya ceramics. It is 7¼ inches high and presents an intricate pattern composed of deities in human and animal form, with ritualistic paraphernalia and symbols so coagulated that it is difficult to separate the individual decorative elements. In the illustration, we see two heads turned toward each other, typically Maya in feature, surrounded by a baffling maze of detail. The plastic variety in the piece, emphasized by the shadow effects of the unusually deep relief, make it alive, and the smooth band of the rim does much to "tame" it and hold it together. This vessel must have been really sculptured, since only this technique could have produced the different levels. It was found in a vaulted tomb not far from Quiriguá, and its sculptural compactness and ideological impenetrability place it certainly very near to the enigmatic stone altars of this early Maya site.

The tall cylindrical vase in *fig. b,* 11¾ inches high, came to the National Museum at Washington from a private collection in El Salvador. It is said to have been found at Ataco in northwest Salvador and is one more example of the intermingling of styles in that part of Central America where Guatemala, Honduras, and El Salvador meet. In this corner lies the ancient shrine of Esquipulas, a pilgrim center even today that draws Indians with offerings from all directions, the Catholic prayers adapted to their own rites. There is no doubt that pilgrims traveled this same road in pre-Columbian times and that an exchange of artistic influences resulted.

The vessel is of a shiny brown ware. Two plain zones at the top and bottom set off the plastic center, where two double rows of human heads, elaborately framed, encircle the vase. The same hatching was seen on the sunken background of the jaguar bowl in the preceding plate. Above, below, and dividing the composition are series of delicately incised glyphs, non-Maya in character. All these decorative elements are knit together with endlessly winding and interlacing bands. The heads, all facing right, show little individuality. Admirable is the unobtrusive virtuosity which created this spectacular piece.

As to its technical build-up, we may only conjecture. But whether it was put together by applying clay rolls or sculptured out of half-dried material, whether it was stamped with variously applied clichés or, as is most probable, produced by a combination of techniques, it is unique.

The foregoing illustrations have demonstrated amply that there were periods when Maya pottery approached in quality real sculptural art. If bowls, jars, and vessels of such exquisite workmanship have survived, how rich and amazing must have been the realm from which they were drawn.

Pl. 139, fig. a displays a sculpturally stunning relief executed on a somewhat concave cylinder. Its two panels, bound together by a band of Mayoid glyphs, present almost identical subjects—the only known instance of a full standing figure appearing on a relief vase. A chief in full regalia is shown against a relatively deep background, which enhances the plasticity of the figure. Many details are recorded that are generally indistinct. In his upraised hand he holds a ceremonial baton; in the other, a shield. Tightly woven cords with tassels hang from his waist in the front and rear. Another feature that has not appeared so sharply defined before is the tall fanlike ornament, which seems to be affixed at the back of the waist and extends above the head, its feathers distinguished from those of the headdress by different treatment. This is probably the same ornament used to such decorative effect in *Pl. 129.* Suspended below it is a human head, a trophy, with upturned face and hanging hair. A very rare feature in Maya art, it is here extremely realistically portrayed. The mottled coils of an immense serpent body are suggested near the lower frame, affiliating the work even more closly with stone and wood sculptures. The piece was bought in El Salvador.

Fig. b, said to have come from the Salvadoranean border in Guatemala, also makes use of a horizontal band of plastic glyphs, Mayoid in type but heavy-footed symbols when compared with the precision of those just seen. On the main panel of the vessel is an incised design representing a fantasy animal with a long curved neck and a head that hangs almost vertically from the upper frame.

In the examples shown in *figs. c* and *d* the formerly strong artistic trend is petering out and changing into new forms and patterns. The first, a jar from El Salvador, 9 inches high, has a fine matt finish. Its glyph band, better carved than that of *fig. b,* is quite plastic and well spaced, and the alluring tactile quality of the surface below it compensates for the lack of other decoration. The piece has a solid line and is by no means degenerate.

The shape in *fig. d,* from Honduras and 9 inches high, shows a divergence from the cylindrical type. The band of Mayoid glyphs is still a feature, but here they lack plasticity and appear incised rather than carved. Painted patterns in red and black, somewhat faded now, make up the main decoration against the orange color of the ware. The two handles with small animal heads protruding from them are a non-Maya addition, an element that we shall meet frequently in the next area on our way southward.

The diminutive flacons, or flasks, shown on *Pl. 140,* some no higher than 2½ inches, come from the southern Maya border. They are comparatively rare and belong to a type distinctive enough to indicate some specific purpose, as yet not definitely known. Traces of mercury and cinnabar, materials highly prized in pre-Columbian America, were found in some of them.[14] Cinnabar was used in paint; mercury, for magic and perhaps in metallurgy. The flasks also might have carried medicines. From the carefully modeled rims, stoppers may be assumed.

Fig. a, 3 inches high, from Honduras, is not only beautifully executed from a technical standpoint but has the most story to tell. Two seated figures, identified as Fire-gods, face each other, separated by a column of glyphs. Other glyphs appear as decoration on the narrow side panels. The two deities show strong similarities to mythical figures from Maya codices, and some of the symbols appear to have come from such a source also. However, the characters on the convex sides are classified as pseudo-glyphs.

It is not necessary to analyze each decorative element to appreciate the admirable skill displayed in this small flask. The even finish of the contours and the perfection of the bottle form show it to be the product of an expert and routined hand. A stamp was probably used for molding the ornamented surface. The workshop must have been in southern Maya territory, from where the type spread as far as Yucatan in the north and El Salvador in the south. Because of its small size and the valuable liquid it must have contained, it would have been likely to travel far. George B. Gordon found several examples, one especially elaborate, in the Ulua Valley.[41]

The influence of this shape and decorative scheme manifests itself in an unexpected variety. Obvious imitations of coarser material and cruder execution have been found in various parts of the region. The other three flasks pictured in the first row (*figs. b, c,* and *d*), all from El Salvador, show such derivation and are of interest because of their provincial craftsmanship and peripheral design.

In *fig. b,* an oblong form with one figure on the side, the outline is less graceful and the framing band heavier. The face and body have little expression, recalling the small heads of the tall vase in *Pl. 138, fig. b.* On top there is a peculiar recumbent skeleton figure which seems characteristic of this brick-shaped type and is found also on the next example (*fig. c*), in which a higher artistry is evident. This flacon, 2½ inches high and without a trace of paint, is made of fine-textured, putty-colored clay. Not only is the shape well proportioned but glyphs appear—apparently conventionalized glyphs that are purely decorative. In the next flask (*fig. d*), a crude local pattern of animal elements makes up the panel. This piece is noteworthy for its covering of brilliant turquoise paint.

In the second row, the orange-ware bottle in *fig. e* comes from Yucatan and bears an impressed design of a figure with flowing headdress. The edge is interestingly corrugated and the decoration is unusual, but the imprint is shallow and degenerate when compared with the precise work in the piece above it. *Fig. f*, 5½ inches high, is deep red and presents a departure in shape. A human head is modeled in high relief—an unusual feature—and there are lightly incised pseudo-glyphs on the narrow sides. A very distant cousin of the first flask is shown in *fig. g*, 7 inches high. The neck is fashioned into a human head and the two handles are shaped to represent arms and hands, bringing a completely different concept into this series. The doughnut form is very unusual—we have to go to the Central Coast of Peru to find a similar shape. *Fig. h*, 3 inches high, is a likeness of a tomato or a squash, plants indigenous to this country. With its rich red color and its neat naturalistic modeling, it runs a close second in workmanship to the flacons with the best figural relief.

All of these specimens demonstrate once more how versatile was the creative genius of the pre-Columbian potter, even within the confines of one area, and how widely local tastes or artistic limitations changed and varied one utilitarian shape. The flask form is an ancient one. Chinese pottery has known it from prehistoric times, and from there pastoral peoples have carried it into Europe.

When utilitarian vessels were fashioned in the shape of animals or humans, a kind of grotesqueness resulted (*Pl. 141*). The right half of the buff, 8-inch double jar (*fig. a*) is modeled to resemble a *pisote* (a member of the raccoon family), holding its snout with its paw. The legs, both front and back, are slightly plastic, with paint added to emphasize them and decorate the body. The jar is so constructed that it makes a whistling sound when a liquid is poured from the spout at the extreme left. This peculiarity, its double form, the connecting tube, and the bridge handle are characteristic of the Andean Area (see *Pl. 158, fig. b*). The fact that the piece here was unearthed in Kaminaljuyú and is made of a local clay gives a further clue to possible influences between distant areas of pre-Columbian civilization.

The bowl with tripod legs representing human heads (*fig. b*) is a large piece and comes from the Quiché region of the Guatemala highlands. The broad somewhat humorous features of the faces recall the Tarascan figures of the Mexican Area.

In *fig. c,* 6 inches high and from Zacualpa, Guatemala, a turkey forms the body of the rounded jar. The blackish ware has a high polish, and remnants of dark red paint are still visible, portraying very well the puffed-up creature with its spread wings dragging on the ground. This effigy jar is unique in the region where it was found. It has been classified as Chorotega ware indigenous to Nicaragua [69]—again evidence of the movement of styles and shapes from distant cultures.

The clay sarcophagus (*fig. d*) is 3 feet long and comes from Nebaj in Guatemala. It represents a fantasy animal with wide-open mouth. Four feet, resembling bear paws, are suggested on the cover, and the whole piece rests on four animal legs. Despite the clumsiness of the shape, a sense of proportion was maintained. The piece is very rare. It would seem to be influenced by strong non-Maya traits, although it comes from the heart of the Guatemala highlands where many interesting Maya customs still prevail. With its bulbous snout, thick coffee-bean eyes, and the little ball decorations applied near the mouth, it has at least an ideological relationship to the first incense-burner cover illustrated on *Pl. 144.*

On the southern border of the Maya region, where peoples with very different cultural concepts lived, the meeting of two strongly characterized creative streams produced amazing results. Patterns once spiritually significant were conventionalized to mere ornament. Pseudo-glyphs applied as decoration on flasks have already been seen, and such symptoms will be more frequently observed as we enter regions where the Maya influence thins out. On the other hand, new decorative schemes make their appearance and new subjects rise to dominance, so that the work still remains vital—showing divided influences, but not degenerate.

In *Pl. 142, fig. a* we have a jar from El Salvador, 6½ inches high, with a bird as central design, probably a pelican, holding some multiple-armed water creature in its beak. It is not naturalistically represented: the wings are divided symmetrically on either side of the body, as if viewed from above, and the legs are thick and of the same color as the feathers. Dots are effectively used to set off the head and breast. The ability here displayed in spreading the subject so skillfully that it fills the surface without demanding additional decoration is a non-Maya trait.

Also from El Salvador comes the tripod jar (*fig. b*), 5½ inches high. The protruding handle is modeled into a monkey head, and black and red paint are used to represent the other parts of the animal against the buff surface of the vessel. The abstract design below the rim is interesting, as well as the checkered pattern on the legs.

In *fig. c* another monkey jar is presented for comparison, this time from distant Coclé in Panama. The head is a small button, defined by paint, and the monkey claws have been ingeniously abridged in black on white. The form of the vessel is more complicated and is divided with good decorative sense into two main sectors. Circles, not squares, are the outstanding ornament.

On the cylindrical shape of *fig. d* a bat with outspread wings is drawn on a dark ground in each of four square medallions. Here, as in the bird above, the use of the primary theme to its best decorative advantage is apparent. Symbolical elements and aberrations of glyphs encircle the vase as minor motifs, and dark spots are used as accent throughout the design.

Fig. e shows a vase, about 9 inches high, from the Ulua Valley. A loose representation of two figures clasping each other is the main theme. The dot outline, noted also in the first jar, appears, extending from the headdress down the back. All the other elements, repeated constantly in "running bands," are here mere line and color, their one-time symbolical import now hazy. The rhythmic whirl of the design is refreshing and delightful.

All the vases on *Pl. 143* come from Honduras and show different versions of the style which reached perfection in the more permanent marble.

The transformation of symbols, so diluted as to be practically unintelligible, into a lively decorative pattern is illustrated in the first (*fig. a*). Plastic detail enters in the shape of two reptilian heads as handles, their painted bodies spread below them. The other decorative units are so drawn out and interwoven that little of their meaning can be disentangled. This piece, 10¼ inches high, comes from Lake Yojoa, only about twelve miles from the Ulua River where the exquisite marble vases (see *Pls. 94* and *95*) were found.

In *fig. b* incision with no coloring furnishes the decoration for the same cylindrical form. A loose mask with a plastic nose occupies the center of the piece. The scrolls, wavy lines, and the slanting-S motif show kinship with the more condensed patterns on the marble vases, and the two bird heads, projecting like handles, also suggest a common ancestor. A flaring base and rim give the jar a certain finish.

In *fig. c* we have a vessel of the same type, 9½ inches high. Here the details of the central mask are not so much incised as indicated by perforations. How

---

strictly certain features were retained, in spite of the break-up of the primary idea, can be observed in the horizontal slit eyes of the two masks, as well as the swirls of the headdress. An animal that might be a monkey is applied at the sides. Although less artistic and more poorly executed than the other two, this vessel, with its simplified form and the step-design band around the rim, makes a still better connection with the Ulua marble vases.

INTERLYING AREA

Trade influences as well as the general versatility of the potter make it difficult to lay down stylistic borders along the bounds of ethnic groups. *Pl. 144* presents three pottery covers of incense burners (the first, from a Maya region), which, though all serving the same purpose, vary greatly in expression and manner of execution.

The most massive in body and sinister in composition (*fig. a*) comes from the Alta Verapaz region of Guatemala. We have already seen examples of the excellent ceramic art of this district and this piece likewise shows good workmanship in modeling. The open mouth, the stumpy nose, and other details in the face recall the animal sarcophagus on *Pl. 141, fig. d;* even the finger-pinched border is similar.

A crocodile is modeled on the cover of the *incensario* from Nicaragua (*fig. b*), his curving tail forming a handle. There is something amusingly human to us in his attitude. His features, though caricatured, are well conveyed.

In the crocodile from Costa Rica (*fig. c*), the ornamental indentation seen on the last piece is transformed into openwork. Despite the stylization, the impression conveyed is realistic, and the same living creeping quality is expressed as in the one from Nicaragua.

It is interesting to compare the eyes of the three specimens on this plate. Those in the Guatemalan piece are elongated "coffee beans." In the Nicaraguan, they bulge from the cheek, while in the Costa Rican crocodile they are cut around, with a sharply indented pupil.

The first two vessels on *Pl. 145* are both from Costa Rica. In the tripod effigy jar (*fig. a*), 12½ inches high, the two heavy legs and the tail, which serve as feet, are rattles. Plastic additions of an animal head and two shorter "arms" are tied into the piece by the skillfully applied designs in batik-like negative painting. In this process the pattern is covered with a protective layer, and the rest of the surface painted, so that on removal of the covering the design stands out in the natural color of the jar. The expanse of undecorated surface on the body of the animal produces good contrast. This form is a favorite in the region, but the minor details of embellishment are always varied. The colors, as in all four examples given here, are tones of orange, orange-red, and dark brown on buff.

In shape, *fig. b,* more than 9 inches in diameter and 13¼ inches high, is built on the same principle, but with the elimination of the zoömorphic. Instead of the tripod feature, this large egg-shaped vessel has a hollow base, which contains the rattle. The protruding edge just above it is modeled with great subtlety. Motifs in negative painting are spread over the entire surface, with even the blank medallions used with decorative interest in the brown ribbon that encircles the jar. Bird and animal designs, some of them similar to those in *fig. a,* can be detected in the ornamental bands, which, in a clever variation of width and content, are deftly applied to bring out the complicated form.

The shallow tripod dish from Nicaragua, not far from the Costa Rican border (*fig. c*), shows relationship to the other two both in concept and decoration. The shape again manifests skill and ease in modeling, and the plastic monster heads are particularly expressive. Clay balls that rattle are visible in their mouths. The painted elements are less concentrated, and a sort of dilution of the former warm and pulsing talent is apparent.

Fig. d, 8 inches high, was found in the Zacualpa region. The shape was undoubtedly inspired by the type from Costa Rica (*fig. a*), though it is clumsy and less in proportion. Its somewhat spreading design recalls pieces from Honduras and El Salvador (see *Pl. 143, fig. a*). Nothing could show more clearly the infiltration and exchange of artistic ideas. The Zacualpa region produced highly individual pottery of its own as well as specimens that show very strong Maya influence. What powerful fountains of non-Maya style there must have been in the south to assert themselves here.

The site of Coclé, named after a river in Panama, was put on the archaeological map by the expeditions of Peabody Museum of Harvard University, joined later by Brooklyn Museum and the University of Pennsylvania. The narrow isthmus that connects two vast continents served as a bottle neck for many stylistic movements. Individual development, however, was not crowded out in this funnel; on the contrary, the region produced an outspoken style of its own, although certain influences from the north and south are evident. On *Pl. 146* we see a variety in both shape and decoration which, even if not completely un-precedented elsewhere in medieval America, nevertheless documents the high degree of individuality in the art of Panama.

The bottle (*fig. a*), 8 inches tall, belongs among the élite of pre-Columbian pottery. Form and decoration are harmonized with rare artistic judgment. To shape the body of the vessel, with its rounded lower section slanting off toward the neck at a sharp angle, was in itself not an easy task (compare *Pl. 142, fig. c*), and to add the funnel-like neck required as clever a hand. Still another sign of thorough artistry is the variety and spacing of the vertical panels. We find the familiar spiral motif, a favorite of the Coclé region, executed in white and out-lined with black on a red-brown ground. The heart-shaped design in white on the neck appears on other Coclé ware and may be a conventionalized mask, up-side down to us as seen here. The balanced yet lively impression of the piece is the result of the fortunate union of a highly satisfactory shape with decorative patterns attractive in their geometric build-up. In some of its details it reminds us of Near Eastern ware. So universal is its esthetic appeal that it could be smuggled in among pottery of distant civilizations without its identity being detected for a time.

The bowl of the pedestal vase in *fig. b,* with its deep symmetrical grooves, seems to have been inspired by a plant shape. In its lines it has such proportion and ease that, despite its monotone brownish color and the absence of applied decoration, it appears a finished product. Even in the company of the super-lative piece at the left it holds its own.

In *fig. c* a vague little animal head protrudes from one side. Legs are painted on the body of the piece on a larger scale and the ringed tail forms the handle-like spout. The spiral used in *fig. a* appears again, painted on the neck.

The low open bowl in buff color (*fig. d*) is decorated with a winged motif in red that might even have been inspired by a hand print. While the vessels described above show distant affiliations with the north, this one could be con-nected by certain characteristic motifs to the Andean Area (compare *Pl. 164, fig. c*).

The small bird effigy (*fig. e*), decorated with the spiral pattern, is in its humorous effect also closer to the south. Spirals, absolutely unrealistic as feath-ers, enhance the naïve charm of the little figure.

The presence of a variety of shapes in Coclé, particularly of the relatively infrequent plate, gives additional importance to the site from our point of view.

Pl. 147 shows five round specimens and one oblong, adorned with widely varied patterns.

The first (*fig. a*), about 12½ inches in diameter, is divided into four rectangular fields by two broad intersecting bands that contain the drawn-out spiral motif on different-colored backgrounds. Stylized "rampant" birds are placed within the fields. The combination of negative and positive painting in the design is noteworthy.

What appear to us to be purely geometric elements on the oblong shape (*fig. b*) doubtless held certain symbolical meaning for the maker, for the same mask idea seen on the neck of the bottle in the preceding plate may be discerned here also.

A wheel pattern is used as structural division for four fields in *fig. c*. Within them are painted stylized monkeys with outspread arms and legs, looking from the position of their faces as if they were hanging upside down. As in the first plate, the lively decorative effect absorbs us, leaving us without any desire to search too closely for realism in the animal representation.

In the stag plate (*fig. d*) a singularly poetical feeling for design is manifest; the head is spaced with such radiation that it fills the whole piece. Its contours outlined with black give a new artistic expression when compared with the other Coclé work. The amazingly good job of restoration should not be left unmentioned.

A zigzag design in three colors covers the entire surface within the narrow border on *fig. e,* and the lack of exact repetition makes the pattern more striking. After a moment's observation, one can feel in it the climbing crawling movement of a row of reptiles.

Fig. f is the most refined. The eight medallions are disposed on the brownish-colored plate with an interesting lack of symmetry. In five of them, crabs are depicted on a light ground; in the remaining three, a pattern resembling a four-leaf clover is placed on a dark. The various positions and angles in which the motifs are arranged give a rhythmic connection to them all. How easy it is to enjoy the production and to try to appreciate its art, but how difficult even to approach the concept which inspired it.

The talent of these people is curiously parallel to that seen in the Southwest, particularly Mimbres, not only in the artistic language of their imagination and the evident enjoyment of the potters in their work, but in the adaptation of plant and animal forms to geometric fields. There are, however, positive differences when the two regions are compared—notably in the limited breathing space and more luscious curves of Coclé.

In this Interlying Area, impulses of an artistic nature from local, neighboring, and distant cultures produced fantasy shapes that are not found in either the adjoining Maya or Andean areas. These impulses may not be expressed in so articulate a manner as in the greater cultures, but the pottery has importance, as it embodies the swirling cumulative ideas of the region and documents for us a quite different approach from that of the more powerful northern and southern neighbors.

Fig. a on *Pl. 148,* from Nicaragua, is a vase with polychrome surface and slightly modeled face. There is still much Mayoid in the manner of painting, but the use of scalloped lines from the corners of the eyes and the nostrils is outspokenly local.

The piece with four human figures, male and female (*fig. b*), probably served as a pedestal for a large bowl. It is classified as coming from Colombia, but it should be remembered that this state until 1903 also embraced what is now the Republic of Panama. The figures are elongated, like early Romanesque statuary, and arranged in couples, each holding hands as if for a dance, with the unengaged hands on their hips. The long garment of the woman in the foreground suggests an intricate textile art in this region, not one example of which has survived.

The tripod vessel in the shape of a jaguar (*fig c.*) is slightly more than 14 inches long and comes from Chiriqui, Panama. No doubt influences from Costa Rica played a part here, but while in Costa Rican ware conventionalized animal elements are woven together into one pattern, in this piece the decoration is composed of small sharply defined geometric fields connected by a red network. The expression is playful and toylike, especially when compared with the mature formidable jars of the other region. It should be noticed that realism was sacrificed to produce a three-legged vessel.

The squatting human in *fig. d* comes from Costa Rica and introduces an entirely different manner, both in modeling and painting.

Fig. e, from Venezuela, Colombia's eastern neighbor, shows a figurine with a disproportionately large canoe-shaped head, which it supports by tiny arms. It is about 18 inches high, hollow, though not a vase, and in spite of its size and top-heavy appearance, stands without support. The coffee-bean cut of the eyes is similar to that in the Colombian piece above it, but otherwise it speaks its own language. The perforations at the sides were probably for additional ornament. (Compare with the nude figure on the gold helmet, *Pl. 220, fig. b.*)

With *fig. f* we return to the Chiriqui province of Panama. This strangely shaped pottery vessel is 14¾ inches long and shows a female figure at either end, the head of each forming a wide spout. It is far from realistic and conveys a complex idea. The decorations on the neck and side of the jar are the typical animal representation of the region, in red outlined with black. Some similarity to the more brilliant work from Coclé may be seen in their rampant poses, the decorative spreading of the different elements to gain balance, the use of dots, and the comb-tooth feet. Four-footed jars such as this are rare in pre-Columbian America.

Peoples not sophisticated but artistically sound sometimes produce as striking objects as their more civilized neighbors who are bound in taste and expression by hieratic rules of orthodoxy. All pieces on *Pl. 149* show the enjoyment of the potters in modeling and embellishing their ceramic ware.

The open bowl from Chiriqui province (*fig. a*) is 5 inches high, and the light color of the clay, like a fine bisque ware, is left natural with no painted decoration anywhere. It makes a delightful impression with its miniature "atlantes."

In *fig. b* the clay stool, 10¼ inches high, must have been produced not far from this same district. Three creatures, a blend of human and animal, support the platelike top. Little animal heads are applied as edging to the seat, and a rough hatching breaks the monotony of otherwise plain surfaces.

Fig. c presents a tripod from Costa Rica, 6½ inches high. The urn shape is very fine, and the perforated legs are unusually long. We have seen tripods from other regions where the form alone, with painted decoration on the legs, seems to have been found satisfactory, but here the playful talent of the potter added the little monkey figures in a "thinker's" pose.

A similar inclination to decorate with grotesque elements can be found in the example from the Santarem region of Brazil (*fig. d*). We know little of these people on the middle Amazon River, whose artifacts, mostly ceramic, are just now beginning to be studied. Although they were apparently on a rather low cultural plane, their pottery is ornate and highly plastic. It is believed to have been made for mortuary purposes only, as it is too fragile for general use. The work shows analogies to that of the West Indies, Marajo Island, and other parts of the Amazon district.[80]

The bottle pictured here is 7 inches high and nearly submerged in exuberant detail. Two lateral branches representing slightly opened crocodile mouths extend from the body of the vessel. Each bears a veritable procession of human and animal figurines—on the end is a human with his hand to his forehead, behind him clings a jaguar, and following him is a bird. Other animal representations are modeled on the base. Every creature is shown in action, which gives the whole piece a particularly lively appearance. The mouth of the bottle is well turned and ornately decorated with various incised designs.

Below Panama, certain pottery shapes begin to reflect influence from the south. The larger mortuary urn from the Ocaña district of Colombia (*Pl. 150, fig. a*) stands over 2 feet high, including the lid. Besides the human figure seated on the cover, the decoration consists of reptilian heads and forefeet applied on the urn proper like handles—although there are also rounded grips (see center). The modeling of certain elements shows a close relationship to metal objects produced in the same country. Whether cast or clay representations, the same imagination and expression come to the fore; the lumpiness, the use of globular forms on ears, breasts, even fingers and toes are unlike anything presented so far and are suggestive of work with wax. The face of the figure shows traces of paint; otherwise the natural light color of the clay is left.

Fig. b, about 8 inches high, comes from the Quimbaya region of Colombia, famous for its metal-work. The design on the vessel proper was done in negative painting. The three quaint figures sitting on the three stumps are as hazy in expression as the face in the piece just discussed. Here there is a hint of coastal Peru.

In *figs. c* and *d* we again step over the frontier of our five areas into Brazil, but the pieces warrant it. The first is a large burial jar, 2 feet high, from the Amazon Delta. Its beautifully rounded shape is covered with a small fretlike pattern—the conventionalization of a reptile—that has given the name "alligator ware" to pottery with this type of surface decoration. There is also a creeping alligator depicted in relief on the side, the rakelike feet of which recall those of Coclé. This jar speaks a more powerful language than many of the specimens of the Interlying Area, and the lack of data concerning the region of its provenience shows how much there is to learn about these primitive but fascinating cultures.

The second alligator-ware jar (*fig. d*), 18 inches high, shows a cylindrical form rounded toward the bottom. The flaring rim with its low plastic decorations relates it definitely to the other, but the conventionalization of the pattern here is far advanced. The angular outline of the "alligator" is recognizable in the center, and the pronglike feet, as well as the dots used to represent scales, are also present, but detached and employed only as decorative elements. Its finely turned lip provides an adequate finish to the urn.

The region around the Esmeraldas River in northwestern Ecuador has revealed pottery that cannot be overlooked. On *Pl. 151* we offer for study eight small heads of clay, ranging from 3 to 5½ inches high. Except for the first, which is from Venezuela, all were excavated in this district.

The first two (*figs. a* and *b*) show so-called archaic traits. In their modeling, they are somewhat reminiscent of the figurines of the early cultures on the high plateau of Mexico, and in expression some features even bring to mind those of Egypt and China. *Figs. c, d,* and *e* have more spiritual content. These could have been fashioned in some peripheral region of Middle America. The last three (*figs. f, g,* and *h*) move toward a local style that is growing stronger and more bizarre. The faces are losing their realistic features, and a grotesque and stylized air makes itself manifest. The feeling for decoration becomes articulate, producing masks which can hold their own with those of the Greek theater.

The pottery of the Interlying Area does not bear the impress of completely civilized living and a broad established hierarchy, but rather of awakening, powerful, artistic energies and untapped resources of imagery.

ANDEAN AREA

In the Andean Area we are confronted with such new types of pottery that it would seem as if we had stepped into another world. Not only is the technique of decoration distinctive but, what is more important to us, the artistic formulation of the idea is new. Here a separate fantasy-world found expression during the centuries, creating its own pictorial language. The whistle jar, a peripheral example of which was seen on *Pl. 141,* is common in this area and also the vessel with a stirrup spout. One of the most unusual manifestations is the portrait jar from the Mochica culture, and nowhere else does story-telling pottery reach such novelistic proportions. Finally, when one tribe, the Incas, organized all this region into one vast empire, there was a tendency for their style to permeate the individual and diverse arts of the various subjugated nations.

Pl. 152, fig. a shows a stirrup-spout vessel of the Mochica, or Early Chimu, culture, which flourished along the northern coast of Peru from about A.D. 500 to

800. The piece is 8½ inches high. A man blowing on a shell trumpet, his head thrown back, forms the neck. Conchs were much valued as trade goods throughout medieval America, and such instruments were common among the peoples along the coast. The headdress is plastic and the textile pattern of the clothing clearly defined in paint. There is a sense of sound in the general attitude of the trumpet blower with his upstretched arms.

Fig. b, slightly over 10 inches high and also Mochica, is built up in a similar fashion, but the figure on the neck is a warrior in full regalia—a very different costume from the Maya and Mexican. He is shown sitting on a raft, propelled by four swimmers wearing floats at the waist. These, as well as the ropes by which they tow the raft, are plastically represented. The static pose of the grim chieftain is contrasted by the buoyant figures in the water, and the fish, only painted, retreat into the depths on a different plane.

All four pieces on *Pl. 153* also belong to the Mochica culture. *Fig. a,* nearly 10 inches high, presents a quite different shape. The warrior on top is modeled with realism, and the painted figures below him serve to carry out the martial scene. Interesting are the fernlike plants scattered about the design.

A graphic presentation of a group of soldiers driving bound and humiliated captives before them is given in *fig. b,* a vase with a flaring mouth. The suggestion of landscape—hills and desert vegetation—in the background is unusual. Such an aptitude for recording could have been successfully applied to the illumination of manuscripts had the culture reached for it.

An open pavilion is modeled on the top of *fig. c,* with people seated inside. Others climbing upward on the body of the vessel are depicted in paint, and a small figure near the stirrup, posed as if making his entrance into the pavilion, connects the flat scene with the plastic.

In *fig. d* there is no plastic decoration and the stirrup is placed not at the side but on the top as an integral part of the composition. It is nearly 12 inches high and has a design painted in brick-red on the white body. The fantastic headdress of the seated figure represents some spotted animal and has a feather "fan" behind, similar in shape to the plastic headgear of the others. His waist is bound by a snake. The step design across the shoulders of his shirt will be seen in textiles later (see *Pl. 191*). In his left hand he holds an axe, and with his right is strangling a monster pictured with a fierce human head and arms raised in conflict. On the other side the same scene is repeated. The design is clear and well divided, but angular, and in concept unsubjective. The fine outlines of this drawing, which uses much of the natural background as body of the subject, reminds us of the pottery of archaic Mediterranean cultures. Mochica pottery is painted generally in red on white, with the rare use of black. The effects are gained by modeling and careful drawing rather than by shading and color contrasts.

The plastic vessels in *Pl. 154,* all Mochica, show a lively talent for observation in the depiction of characteristically human gestures and attitudes. In each of the four figures a different pose of the body and a different modeling of the eyes are used for each moment portrayed.

In the smoothly finished vessel of *fig. a,* we see a seated figure, his hands resting on his knees. The main concentration is given to the face, which has an attentive, somewhat questioning expression. Incised marks designating tattoo are visible, and other lines across the head give a glimpse of the haircut of those days. A loincloth is suggested in paint. The details of the profile—low forehead, overhanging brows, aquiline nose, protruding lips, and receding chin—make *in toto* a powerful portrayal.

Fig. b, 9¾ inches high, shows another seated man, in this case apparently asleep. In the tilted head and relaxed features his unconscious state is definitely expressed. The crossed arms and clasping hands are taken from life.

The fragment (*fig. c*) is 12½ inches high. Despite the missing parts, the head and the intact hand testify to the modeler's ability. Here again the emphasis is on the gesture. He sits alert, his arm in action, his eyes wide open, and his expression tense. Compare him with the figure above him, whose narrowed eyes are focused in attention yet whose pose is inert. Paint, now in a bad state of preservation, must have added considerably to the effect; note the white eyeballs with their round staring pupils and the whitened finger nails. A brown shirt with light stripes is faintly visible.

In the last jar (*fig. d*), not quite 8 inches high, a man is shown offering a prayer or incantation over a lifeless form. The position of the hands is a natural one to us. The absorbed expression of the face, in spite of the closed eyes, contrasts interestingly with that of the sleeper in the piece above, as well as with the wasted body in front of him. Here the color is an important part of the composition.

The pieces on the next two plates come from the same region, but the majority of them are later in date, stylistically referred to as Chimu, or, frequently, Late Chimu. Here scenes from everyday life—documents of a people about whom we know far too little to accord them the appreciation they deserve—are modeled with an arresting display of talent.

The first (*Pl. 155, fig. a*), a double whistle jar in polished black ware, about 8 inches long and 10 high, shows two persons carrying a third in a hammock suspended from a pole, while a smaller figure, perhaps a child, walks beside it. The faces, all very much alike, are not expressive, but the plodding movement in the whole group is well conveyed. We feel that here the stress was not on the individual but the event. In other very similar vessels, the object carried is clearly a mummy.

In *fig. b* the action spreads over both flattened jars of the double vessel. On the right one stands a man with a jug bound to his back in typical Indian manner, his hands grasping a thick twisted rope by which he drags at an animal—a llama or alpaca—on the other jar. This rope is disproportionately heavy, for it also serves as handle.

Somewhat more individual expression is found in *fig. c,* a Mochica piece, on which a flat surface again offers a stage but this time with a hint of setting. The spout of the vessel is shaped to form steps that end in an animal head, and the characters are grouped at the rear as if facing an audience. The tallest is playing on a vertical flute, while a child on either side holds on to him with one hand. The boy is carrying a package strapped to his back, and over the girl's shoulder a doll is looking out from a knapsack. One can still make out the painted pattern of the man's shirt in places.. As in some of the other scenes, the staring eyes bring in a pathetic touch, doubtless not intended.

Fig. d shows a single jar about 12 inches high. The figure modeled on its rounding top wears oversize earplugs and a tall headdress with drooping feathers. He holds an instrument before his mouth with one hand and leads a doglike animal on a leash with the other. The maturely balanced shape of the vessel augments the effect of the figural decoration.

In all four of these vignettes of Mochica and Chimu life, an unquestioned ability in modeling is displayed. Always the *genre* seems to have been the aim, and it is communicated in this new language with the charm and immediacy of marionettes. Without doubt these pottery pieces were for these people a means of articulation and communication; they had no written language and often expressed through form and color much that we convey in words.

Water jars from the Mochica and Chimu cultures with animal subjects as the principal decoration are displayed on *Pl. 156.* In *fig. a,* slightly over 7 inches high, a little monkey sits on a fruit-shaped vessel in a droll position that shows what keen observers of nature these modelers in clay were. Beside it (*fig. b*), an apelike couple is engaged in lively gesticulation. A small animal perched behind the spout, a frequent addition to this type of pottery, attests to the ever-present urge and talent for decoration. The rounded jar in *fig. c,* nearly 9 inches high, is made of shiny black ware and carries low relief as well as ornament in the round. An appealing little monkey clings to the stirrup, and two bird heads look up from its base. The central band with bird shapes was probably applied by the use of a stamp. All three vessels are Chimu. It is noteworthy that similar shapes have been found executed in silver, showing the broad application of the talent of these people.

The llama jar (*fig. d*) belongs to the Mochica culture and makes use of color, some of which has peeled off. Here the vessel itself has the shape of the animal, an idea spectacularly developed in the portrait heads that will follow. On it, riding backward, lies a human figure, apparently asleep, with his head on the llama's rump and the guide rope coiled about his hand. Again the story is more in evidence than the portrayal of an individual. Although the llama is a highland animal, it makes trips to the coast today and doubtless did also in the past.

In *fig. e,* a Mochica double jar, the larger section is fashioned into the body of a parrot. Its staring eyes and brilliant variegated coloring are well conveyed by the lines on face and wings.

On *Pl. 157* are pictured some of the most naturalistic animal shapes from various regions. The kitten-like creature (*fig. a*) is Mochica. Its open mouth and glaring eyes, the feline posture, and tail curled tightly to the body are all features that are familiar. The naturalistic is not in the least disturbed by the stirrup spout in its head and back.

Fig. b comes from Ecuador. This northern neighbor of the Inca, so excellent in metal-work as we shall see, had also its masters in pottery. The vessel pictured here represents a dog in playful pose. The opening is in the head. As has been mentioned before, this animal was fattened for food in many regions of medieval America, and the fleshy body of this little creature would indicate for him such an end. The cumbersome form, with the short legs and slit eyes of a pig, is well conveyed.

The Chimu fish (*fig. c*) has corduroy sections as decoration in the center and on the tail and fins; the ubiquitous monkey appears on the handle. In its modeling the piece has the substantial character of a bronze.

Fig. d is a fragment representing the head of a puma. The combination of the plastic with painting, a characteristic of the Mochica, is masterly. Mouth, teeth, nose, eyes, and ears are modeled with realism, and a bold application of paint brings out the whiskers, dilated pupil, and muzzle. But the most telling detail is the broadening stroke down the cheek that accents the eye and jaw and makes the face powerful and ferocious.

The Mochica vessel (*Pl. 158, fig. a*), a little over 10 inches high, is a representation of the "potato mother." An autochthonous South American plant, the potato played a major rôle in the nourishment of the people of the Andean Area. Here it is personified, the vegetable form complicated with a woman's face emerging from one end; a second face in profile, visible on the side, symbolizes a new sprout. The dull earth-brown paint on the plant is a good foil for the highly polished dark red of the faces.

Fig. b is a Chimu black-ware double jar with pressed relief design. Animal figures are composed against a spotted matt background with a good sense of placement and proportion. Both parts of the vessel have the roundness of a gourd or vegetable shape, and the neck of one is ingeniously fashioned into a plastic bird's head.

Fig. c, 6½ inches high, may be a gourd. Strikingly fine execution is evident in the shapely form and in the incision work denoting the rind, its only decoration. No paint was needed to convey the subject.

The black-ware piece (*fig. d*) has the meticulous detail work of a still life. It represents a section of maizelike stalk with fruit. The balance in the piece and the reticence in decoration show superior artistry. These last two specimens come from northern coastal districts and belong to a late period, probably Chimu.

The Mochica culture, which was one of the earliest and richest in all pre-Columbian America, achieved an excellence in the modeling of human heads unsurpassed elsewhere. Hundreds of portrait jars have been excavated during the centuries and many museums possess fine examples. In spite of the number, however, each has some detail which makes its study worth while. This genius for portrayal, developed so eloquently, is a manifestation peculiar to this region, and despite the ceramic skill displayed in other parts of the Andean Area, the palm must be awarded to the Mochica potter. His all-roundness, always sensitive approach to the subject, his touch of humor, and complete control of techniques required, not only in the construction of the jar but in bringing out facial expression, are unique. It is possible that some of the portrait jars were made by means of molds, as various other types of pottery were quite commonly produced by this method on the North Coast.

The portrait vessel in *Pl. 159, fig. a,* about 12 inches high, is modeled with strong and characteristic features. The desire of the potter to make a utilitarian shape of the head complicated his task, but even so no hesitancy is noticeable in the execution. Every detail is sharp, and he seemingly had no difficulty in keeping within the given contours. The use of paint on the head covering, as frame and contrast to the face, is a studied artistic addition.

Fig. b presents a tattooed head with still more forceful details, if that is possible. This piece is only 5 inches high and was attached to the neck of a large vase. Eyes, cheeks, nose, and mouth—even the ears—are done with great facility and complete realism, which, however, is far from being boiled down to a stereotyped representation. The incised tattoo marks alienate us somewhat, but, like the wrinkles designated by deeply cut lines, have decorative as well as realistic value.

Pl. 160 presents two more heads from the same cultural circle. The modeling in *fig. a* is on the customary high level, though not as unusual as in those just seen. The detailed headdress lends special interest to the piece, as a recording on pottery of the geometric pattern-world that appears also in weaving, carving, and embossing.

For *fig. b,* the head has been photographed at an angle to make it most understandable to our *l'art pour l'art* perception. In this romantic position, it could be taken for a troubadour of the 13th century or a Florentine prince of the 14th —proof of its supercontinental appeal. The noble profile, the melancholy and intellectual expression speak a universal language.

These faces have nothing either cruel or exaggerated about them. In their physical build-up as well as in their artistic expression, they document great differences between the South American and Middle American cultures.

The Mochica also applied their skill to the depiction of the grotesque and the ill. On *Pl. 161, fig. d,* the two seated individuals with disfigured faces are gruesome reminders of the bodily shortcomings that existed among these people. Some of the examples of this type seem to show mutilation, some congenital defects, and others the inroads of disease. The depiction here of the wasted nose and lips and other repulsive details are strong marks of a general talent, both for

POTTERY

observation and realistic delineation, whether of beauty or ugliness. The pieces are about 7 inches high.

The stunning art of portrayal naturally had an influence on the neighboring districts. In *fig. a* modeling ability is still apparent although somewhat stereotyped. The face has a certain dignity. Eyes, nose, and mouth are plastically executed, and the body of the jar carries incised decoration and a painted band. In this section a kind of freezing of the expression can be noticed. Mention should be made of the false drawing of the right hand with its backward-turned fingers.

Fig. b, about 8 inches high, introduces the work of a more southern region, where the culture known as Nazca expressed itself in a characteristically different style. When compared to the great Mochica portraits and the black-ware *genre* scenes, both of which achieved their effect by sheer form and with only two colors, the completely different approach of the Nazcas is at once apparent. They use commonly five or six colors on a single piece. The vessel illustrated shows a minimum of modeling; both face and body of the woman depend chiefly on paint for their expression and decoration. The body is stiff and toylike, the face a painted mask. The figure has charm for us through its fantasy element, not through its realism. The domination of textile patterns in the art of this folk is noticeable in the way the hands are forced into the vertical and in the monster design on the skirt, a familiar one in their embroideries (see *Pl. 177, fig. b*).

The laughing old man in *fig. c,* also Nazca, is an example of what these people could do in the way of characterization if they wished. However, the talent lies again primarily in the painting, not in the plastic. The body retains the rounded outline of the jug and the four-fingered hand shows again textile influence. Much of the attraction is derived from the painted clownlike exaggeration of the features and the bold stripes on the garment.

The Mochica and Nazca cultures, so dissimilar in the style of their art, flourished at the same time, separated by about three hundred fifty miles.

Pottery from the South Coast, imposing in both shape and patterns, is shown on the four plates that follow. *Pl. 162, fig. b,* a mug from the Atacameña culture in Chile, is an exception, which, with its form and the spiral decoration similar to Southwestern pottery, furnishes an interesting example of parallel development. Remote from the direct influence of the great Andean cultures, its makers apparently followed their own artistic impulses.

Figs. d, e, and *f* are identified as Nazca [8] and show characteristic use of hu-

‹ 207 ›

man, plant, and animal motifs. Attention should be drawn to the mask on the center band in *fig. d,* reminiscent of the doll-like face of the Nazca woman. In *fig. f* small mouselike creatures run in delightful countermovement to the large feline animals in the center.

Fig. a comes from the Chincha Valley and *fig. c* from the Ica. Their diminutive patterns are closely related, featuring the characteristic textile motifs of the Ica, or Late Nazca, period.

Absolutely flat decoration appears on the two Nazca plates with fish patterns (*Pl. 163, fig. b*). The skillful hand that placed the motif on the first pulled the tail around so boldly that the figure fills the circle with highly decorative effect. In the second, the fish are rather suspended, floating stomach to stomach and facing in opposite directions. A wide dark margin furnishes good contrast. Here, as is so often the case, simplicity is the reason for the universal appeal of the pattern.

In *fig. d* a highly stylized drawing covers the surface of a typical Nazca shape, a spherical jug with two spouts. The design is executed with genuine feeling for space and suggestion of movement. The eyes of the fish are out of proportion and out of place, but aid with their rhythmic repetition the fluent and attractive pattern. There is something about the piece that suggests a neo-primitive drawing of a goldfish bowl.

With the 9th century the influence of the Tiahuanaco culture from the highlands becomes apparent on the coast. Its pattern language mingles with local traits to produce a style called Coast Tiahuanaco. Examples with modeled details from the Nazca region are pictured in *figs. a* and *c.* The former presents an unusual scene, masterly executed: a condor plucking at the head of a dead man. The piece is only 4 inches high, and its small size may be responsible for the restraint in painting. Every brush stroke is in place. Painted details on the bird are inventively stylized; a single row of eyelashes succinctly expresses the dead eyes. The gesture of picking is realistic, and the claws extending over the eyebrows is a cruel but effective touch. (Compare *Pl. 97, fig. a.*)

In *fig. c* painting predominates. The many colors used can be distinguished in the illustration. The vessel, about 7 inches high, modeled in two bulky sections, represents a double-headed serpent swallowing frogs. On the neck we find the frequently recurring animal-mask of Tiahuanaco style, in this case also double-headed. For a different presentation of a similar subject in the same medium, see *Pl. 116, fig. c.*

Figs. b, c, and *d* on *Pl. 164* show the favorite beaker shape of the Nazca, on which Tiahuanaco designs rarely occur. The figure in the first (*fig. b*) has lost certain iconographical elements which might make it more distinct; in comparison with other examples with figural representation, it is vague and inexpressive. The decoration of the piece below it (*fig. d*) consists of conventionalized heads that suggest different kinds of fish, painted within encircling bands. The lowest section also pictures heads, this time human and so designed as to form a cover of overspreading masks. In contrast, *fig. c* has only one motif, a painted stylized bird. A much more dashing hand arranged this single element and it fills the surface with incomparably more vigor than the lifeless motifs in the vase beside it. The pattern is strongly suggestive of the one on the Coclé bowl (see *Pl. 146, fig. d*).

The cold, flat, and diagrammatic style which had a certain lucidity in the highlands loses it on the tropical Pacific shores and becomes a crammed condensation of an ideological world not too completely digested. The jar with handles (*fig. a*), nearly 12½ inches high, shows its kinship to the Tiahuanaco in its rigid decorative motifs as well as in its shape. With the exception of the plastic head, the design is purely two dimensional, and it is clear that strong local artistic traditions are preserved in it.

Fig. a on *Pl. 165,* a ceremonial urn from Pacheco in the Nazca region, is about 24 inches high. Its style is distinctly Coast Tiahuanaco, sometimes called Epigonal. The main figure is identified as Viracocha by the weeping eyes that look like semaphores (symbolizing the rain-tears of the god), by the radiating aureole of animal heads and plant forms, and the belt with condor beaks. The personification of the idea is still more involved than on the Gateway at Tiahuanaco (see *Pl. 46*). The maker seems to have been so intent upon including all the symbolic and traditional trappings that little time was given to the elaboration of pattern.

The pottery urn (*fig. b*), about 18 inches high, shows the same stylistic characteristics, but somewhat loosened. The winged figure here is doubtless the same as is sculptured in relief on the Gateway of the Sun.

This is not a particularly ingratiating art to our eyes, but we must admit a powerful primeval concept behind these expressions. The certainty of the design and the fastness of color are admirable; the excellent quality of the pottery —it rings like crystal when tapped—and the fine polish make it striking. Even though the idea behind the representation is largely obscure to us, it is clear that those who fashioned such pieces knew what they wanted and were without question able to express it with good decorative feeling.

At the site of Tiahuanaco itself, we find greater ease in dealing with highly conventionalized figures. Although strongly stylized, the design seems to bear more relation to the shape of the vessel upon which it is placed, and more breeziness is apparent in its placement. Here animal and human representations are sometimes simplified to a design easily repeated, sometimes combined or blended, producing an involved scheme difficult to disentangle. The shapes themselves have more grace than those of the preceding plate.

The bowl in the upper right of *Pl. 166, fig. a* shows a four-footed animal, comparatively naturalistic—probably a llama—while the one in the upper center presents a kind of griffin, with wings, a beak, and mighty paws. The complete break-up of the subject into an all-over pattern, very decorative, is seen in the upper left, where eyes, nose, and mouth are separated and treated as single units in the design, in much the same manner as was frequently used in the textiles of the region (compare *Pl. 178, fig. a*).

In *fig. b* the center and left-hand vessels both illustrate the adaptation of geometrical motifs to a rounded surface, a talent in which the Southwest also excelled. The vase at the right features a condor as it repeatedly appears, either blocked or painted, on woven fabrics. These three, with the central bowl above, represent the Classic Tiahuanaco style, while the other two are classified as Decadent. It is noteworthy that virtually all Tiahuanaco pottery has a red slip as base, with the designs usually outlined in black or white or both. Black and white on red is one of the basic diagnostics of Tiahuanaco pottery; yellow, brown, or gray may be used to fill in the design.[8]

Although in each region of the Andean Area certain original trends were preserved, outside influences and modifications of pattern produced an overwhelming variety in pottery. On this account, and also because of the vast amount of highly artistic material on hand with scant data, there is still much left to be worked out in the stylistic classification. Certain strains, nevertheless, can be traced. The metamorphosis of one basic shape from a primitive utilitarian vessel to a most civilized and distilled form is presented in our last two plates of this chapter. The jars shown on *Pl. 167* have much in common. All have handles, three of them well down the sides, and all have flaring necks and a sharp demarcation around the middle below the main design.

POTTERY

Fig. a, a simple shape with a simple decoration, comes from the site of Tia-huanaco, but it is so universal in character that it could belong to other early cultures, either medieval American or even Near Eastern or Chinese. *Fig. b,* 10½ inches high, is from Pachacamac, a site of the Central Coast near Lima. It carries conventionalized frogs, painted in red with black outline, which have evolved into pure ornament without any consideration for realism. Its style is Late Coast Tiahuanaco. *Fig. c,* from Chincha, is rounder and more regular in shape, and its neck is utilized to depict a human head. The widely spaced painted design suggests a textile motif and is characteristic of Ica.

Fig. d, of the same provenience and period, seems more closely related to the first two than the one beside it, but actually it is moving away from all three toward the type seen in its perfected form on the following plate. The shape is elongated and a positive refinement is evident. The lines of the piece have become more graceful, and its proportions demonstrate a more mature artistic taste. The painted decoration, with its alternating color scheme, is more varied in interest and tends toward a design composed of smaller elements. This tendency becomes still more marked in the Inca period, when patterns that originated as fish, birds, and other figures are reduced to the smallest scale, far removed from the ideas which they once expressed.

The last centuries before the Conquest in the Andean Area fall under the sign of Inca domination. Smaller political units, which had already evolved an art of their own, were exposed to the centralizing force of a well-organized government, and the administrative changes that followed naturally had their effect on the mental and artistic life of the people. The carefully integrated, protected, even luxurious regime of the Empire disseminated an art, which, although utilizing traditions of the past, carried in itself a certain preciosity in shape and design and standardized its output on a high artistic level.

Nothing could better illustrate this development than the aryballos, 44 inches high, on *Pl. 168.* In comparison with any other pre-Columbian ceramic form, its refinement is outspoken. The Greek term, with its connotation of the beautifully shaped and delicately ornamented vessels of Hellas, is fittingly applied to this type of Inca pottery.

A diminutive animal head, little more than a protuberance at the base of the neck, is the only survivor of naturalism in the decoration. The shape is difficult to fashion, fragile to handle. In the design the three elements are subtly arranged and applied, separated by stripes of varying widths and spacing that give the whole a vertical character. The little unevenness that can be observed in the pattern is just enough to keep the piece lively and to avoid coldness.

Marking the end of a long road of evolution, the jar is in no way decadent; it is rather the balanced expression of a civilized people. Although their mental life and artistic temperament may have been considerably different from that of their distant relatives to the north, in quality of workmanship and richness of expression their pottery attained a level unsurpassed by any other culture of medieval America.

VI

Weaving

IN THE 16th century three great civilizations of the Eastern Hemisphere simultaneously reached a high point in the textile art.[1] The silks of China were an item greatly prized in that commerce for which Columbus braved the unknown western sea. The rugs and fabrics of Persia, with metal threads frequently interwoven in their patterns, were goods eagerly sought in European trade. Europe saw the perfection of Venetian velvets and the rise of the great tapestry-weaving centers in the Low Countries and France.

Upon recognizing the skill of the native American weavers, the Spaniards made haste to employ it for their own ends, introducing new raw materials, looms of different construction, and patterns to imitate the fabrics popular in the market of their day. Thus, the textiles of medieval America were neglected and nothing was done toward their preservation at the time of the Conquest. What we know today of pre-Columbian weaving is gained largely from excavated material.

In many cases the soil has been unwilling to give back what was interred in it. A few beautiful fragments have been unearthed in the Southwest, preserved by the dry climate, but in the Mexican and Maya areas nearly nothing remains. The famous cities of these regions lay either in the subtropical belt, where there is heavy rainfall for many months each year, or in moist tropical lowlands. In either case the delicate fabrics generally disintegrated. Some bits of material were brought up in the diving activities at the Sacred Well at Chichen Itzá, but our clearest idea of the mature textile art in these areas is derived from the elaborate costume details faithfully recorded on stelae, stone and stucco reliefs, and vase paintings. In the Andean Area, however, where both an arid climate and peculiar burial customs—to be described later—were particularly favorable for the preservation of textiles, we find our greatest field for study.

The beginning of the art of weaving in general cannot be traced, for by the time recording had progressed far enough to picture details of the crafts, textiles were well advanced. In the Eastern Hemisphere it is possible to observe the development of various techniques to a certain extent. Babylon and Egypt produced a smooth plain cloth or linen weave, which was frequently decorated with embroidery. The early Greeks made a sort of bobbin weave, enlivening the web with a spatter of flowers of a different color. About the same time, tapestry in varicolored designs appeared in Egypt.[1]

In pre-Columbian America, however, where research in the higher cultures does not carry back more than two thousand years, this is not the case. Basketry was the forerunner of textile weaving in certain parts of the Southwest and will be discussed as such under *Pls. 169* and *170,* where examples of it are shown. Elsewhere there is no evidence of the beginnings, as the earliest pieces of woven fabric known, discovered in the Andean Area and coinciding in date with the beginning of the Christian era, show the same perfection and variety of techniques as the later ones; the only development that can be traced is in style and pattern preferences.[105] This is all the more remarkable because all the techniques known to the rest of the world plus several peculiar to the Peruvian weavers were employed in this region.

As was pointed out, the regions that used the true loom coincide in general with our five areas. This implement was the hand loom, one end of which— usually a half-polished stick—was hooked to a tree, fixed between two poles, or adjusted on a wall. The other end, with a belt attached, was placed around the waist of the weaver so that a movement of the body would slacken or tighten the warp. The width of the woven stuff could not be much broader than the convenient reach of the weaver, that is, about 30 inches. Such hand looms, called "girdle-back looms," can be seen in use today, especially in the more remote parts of Middle and South America (see *Pl. 173, fig. a*). It would appear that the women did a great part of the weaving, just as they made much of the pottery, another primarily "domestic" art.

Recently more intensive investigation into the techniques of pre-Columbian weaving has brought forward the opinion that these looms were not the only type in existence. Peruvian weavers sometimes produced a cloth over 5 feet wide, which must either have been set up on a larger loom or so arranged as to allow several persons to weave simultaneously on the same warp.[104]

The raw material for these textiles was primarily cotton, but human and animal hair and the feathers of birds were also woven into the fabric. In some regions the fiber of the maguey plant was utilized. The Andean Area was particularly fortunate in having the wool of several members of the camel family, peculiar to the Andes—the llama, guanaco, alpaca, and vicuña. The finest in quality is that of the vicuña, which in suppleness and sheen bears a resemblance to silk.[133] This animal was protected by royal edict and only those of royal blood could use its fleece.[139]

The numerous spindle whorls of clay, stone, and other materials found indicate that the thread was spun everywhere by the same general method: the strand was twisted by hand and kept even by the revolving weight at the end of the thread. Two- to seven-ply yarns have been found, far surpassing in fineness those that a modern machine produces with the same materials. While Gobelins seldom contain more than twenty warps to an inch, one Peruvian tapestry is said to have had forty-two.[7]

The dyes used have been analyzed by modern research methods and found to be of mineral, vegetable, and animal origin, depending on the shade desired and the locality. They are always color fast. A rich carmine was obtained from the cochineal, an insect which feeds upon a cactus common in Mexico and Peru. Vast quantities of them had to be collected because of their minute size. Their dried and pulverized bodies were highly valued as trade goods and provided one of the most brilliant hues on the shining palette of medieval America.

Most of the textiles were probably used for apparel, but belts and carrying straps were needed, as well as bags of various sizes and durability. In addition, provision was made in the buildings for curtains and awnings, which may have consisted of straw matting or strips of fabric. Doubtless the same taste and skill that characterize their other applied arts were lavished upon their fiber hammocks, an ingenious invention of pre-Columbian America. While most civilizations used from early times a sort of bedstead that rested on the ground, the Indian of many regions slung his sleeping outfit between two uprights of his hut. Even today in tropical and subtropical districts there is great variety to be found in this survival from medieval times.

Besides varied patterns and brilliant colors, embroidery and the addition of fringe, tassels, and medallions embellished the textiles. Feathers were often incorporated into the stuff of shirts and mantles. Metal spangles, little bells, and bits of colored stone, as well as mother-of-pearl and other shell where available, were applied as trimming.

The costume of the pre-Columbian peoples appears not to have been tailored. Rectangular pieces were woven to fit the individual requirement and the patterns adapted to each. Besides the breechcloth, a man wore a loose tunic to cover the upper part of the body. Sometimes it had no sleeves, but more often short ones made of simple rectangles were sewed to the sides at the shoulder and stitched together beneath the arm. The women wore a long tunic and mantle.

In the designs, both geometric and stylized nature motifs are used. The puma, fish, birds, and anthropomorphic figures occur the most frequently in the Andean Area, often in such strongly conventionalized forms that they are scarcely recognizable. Flower and plant motifs are exceptional.

Our European ancestors learned during the centuries of contact to enjoy the textiles of the Chinese and Persian civilizations, although these carried nothing of the Greek beauty ideal in their make-up. The mythical significance of their strange-looking human and animal forms or abstract patterns was disregarded, and the bit of silk, the rug, or embroidery prized for its exotic charm.

As yet, we have not had time enough to become so familiar with the figures in pre-Columbian textiles, and their stiffness still adds to our confusion in appraising them. Probably most of the patterns had religious and tribal significance that was traditional. Of all the arts, however, weaving tends to the most rapid conventionalization of pattern, and without a doubt designs were frequently chosen for their eye appeal without regard to any inner meaning.

As several erudite works specializing in the subject of medieval American textiles have been published here and abroad in the last decades, neither the presentation nor discussion of all the known techniques is undertaken here. A glossary, however, is included for convenient reference, defining the terms met with in this chapter.[168]

GLOSSARY

Bobbin, or *weft-pattern, weave* employs wefts of various colors upon the concealed warp, the pattern being carried only by the wefts. It may be single- or double-faced.

Brocade. A single-faced fabric in which the design is built up by alternating a pick of basic weft with a pick of decorative yarn, the greater diameter and softer twist of which allow the weft to be beaten up and buried under it. The decorative element appears in a raised pattern.

Crêpe. A fabric of crinkled texture, produced by using threads of exceedingly tight twist, often combined with other threads of reversed hard twist.

Damask weave has certain wefts floated upon the face of the fabric, their smooth unbroken surfaces forming a pattern against the background of the picked warps.

Double cloth. A fabric woven on two sets of warps of contrasting colors, usually natural light and dark wool or cotton, each with its own weft of self-color. In the process of weaving, pairs of wefts alternate to form the design so that it appears on both faces but in reverse coloring, the finished webs being separate except at the edges of the design.

Gauze. A lacelike web, not necessarily sheer, in which pairs of warp threads are twisted together and the crosses made permanent by the insertion of a pick of weft.

Loom, or *warp-pattern, weave.* The counterpart of bobbin, or weft-pattern, weave. It employs the more numerous warp threads to conceal the wefts and carry the design.

Meshed netting is fashioned without a loom, since one end must be free to make the knots and turns through the loops. There are many types.

Pile-knot fabric, or *simile velours,* was formed by enmeshing bunches of fiber or wool in a loosely knitted web. The knots, caught in the loops of the single thread as the fabric grows, are usually of different color to create a design, giving the effect of velvet or plush. *Pile-knot cord* was made by binding doubled tufts of wool of various colors mixed with hair to a core of three-ply cotton yarn twisted together.

Plain weave. A fabric made by picking warps singly with a single weft. Variations are achieved by the passing of a single weft under and over pairs of warps, or of two wefts under and over single warps. When two weft threads are interlaced with two warps, it is known as *basket weave.*

Rep. A corded fabric produced by wefts of smaller diameter beaten up upon less numerous rigid warps. Similar to unpatterned tapestry weave. A *warp rep* was made in Peru by employing a greater number of warps which, in close weave, concealed the wefts. This was sometimes striped or patterned, making a kind of false tapestry.

Tapestry. A close woven fabric, in which the wefts, always of lesser diameter and softer twist than the warps, are inserted slackly under and over equal units of the warp and are beaten up so as to cover them completely, each color going only so far as the design requires.

Kelim tapestry is distinguished by vertical slits where two colors meet and the component wefts turn back upon their respective warps.

Interlocking tapestry uses a manipulation of the wefts to avoid slits, either by looping the weft of one color into that of another or by slanting the design to engage successively the same warps by wefts of adjacent colors.

Limning, called also *eccentric weft,* is effected by leaving a bare warp between adjacent colors and introducing a weft, usually black, which wraps it and, following the design, loops into both colored wefts.

Eccentric weave results from a manipulation of the wefts so that they cross the hidden warps at various angles to produce curved designs.

Figure-8 stitch results from the passing of the yarn under and over the same two warps or groups of warps.

Three-dimensional, or *needle, knitting.* A type of embroidery used for covering seams, finishing edges, and creating three-dimensional figures that are built up on a self-foundation by a chainlike adaptation of buttonhole stitch.

Tie-and-dye. A form of resist dye, in which parts of the cloth, usually a loosely woven voile or crêpe, are bound round with a cord, which is waxed or otherwise treated to resist the penetration of dye. The cloth is then dipped. When unwrapped, the parts which had been covered appear as rings, squares, or stripes in natural color on a colored ground. Successive tying and dyeing in different colors produces a multicolored patterned cloth.

Twill. A weave in which wefts are carried over one and under two or more warp threads, producing a diagonal ribbed effect. The direction of the shift may be reversed to form chevrons, diamonds, etc., in the cloth, either self-colored or patterned.

Twined technique. A system of looping fibers in basketry.

Voile. A loosely woven cloth of hard-twisted threads in plain weave with either or both elements paired.

Weft-loop, or *looped, weave* is a plain cloth of which one pick is inserted very loosely at a given interval and the slack pulled out in loops after every ninth warp or so.

Besides three-dimensional knitting and pile-knot cord, already described, the following weaves are believed to be peculiar to ancient Peru: *discontinuous,* or *interlocking, weft weave,* a method probably taken over from tapestry, in which the weft is turned back on its own warp and looped into a weft of another color; *discontinuous,* or *interlocking, warp weave,* in which the warps do not extend the length of the fabric but are looped into those of another color; *warp-weft technique,* which contrived to fill an open space with warp and weft composed of the same thread, and *skeleton weft technique,* a related weave, called by Lila O'Neale "multicolored patchwork" and believed to have been built on a temporary scaffolding of wefts, later withdrawn.[105]

THE SOUTHWEST

While weaving in the Andean Area appears before us already perfected, in the Southwest, an area known to have developed considerably later, we find interesting stages of the craft. The Basket Maker, the first figure to emerge from the archaic mists of this region, produced no textiles but was extraordinarily dexterous in fashioning baskets. That a satisfactory life can be made without either pottery or loom weaving is demonstrated by certain tribes living today in British Columbia.[103] Conceivably both pottery and weaving might branch from the skill of basketry, the former craft utilizing the shapes, the latter, the methods. Even after these other techniques were in practice, the Pueblo peoples, who followed the Basket Makers, retained a certain skill in basket-work.

There is a definite relationship between basketry and textile weaving. Before man raised the materials himself, reeds, vines, twigs, cane, rushes, leaves, and fiber offered themselves to be made into baskets, mats, and covers. Pre-Columbian baskets were usually made in one of two ways. Most were coiled; the second technique involved the intertwining of material about a set of radiating ribs. The twilled weave also occurs, but apparently not until the establishment of the Pueblo culture.[73]

The carrying or burden basket (*Pl. 169, fig. b*), 15 inches high and 32 in diameter, comes from Canyon del Muerto, Arizona, and is classified as Basket Maker III, or about A.D. 500 to 700. Fashioned with a remarkably even, beady surface, it carries both horizontal and vertical designs, each differing from the other. The colors used are red and black, making a sharp contrast with the ground.

The two Basket Maker sandals below it (*fig. d*), 9 inches long, are from northeastern Arizona and were woven some thirteen hundred years ago of fine cord made of yucca fiber. Each bears a complex pattern in red and black, fundamentally alike but differentiated in color and minor details. The Basket Makers seem to have made two types of sandals—one finely twined of cords, another fashioned of whole or partly shredded yucca leaves. They were perishable articles of clothing, yet much artistic finesse and maturity are manifest in these specimens, not only in the design but in the twined technique.

The three shallow baskets (*fig. c*), also from Canyon del Muerto, are all woven alike but have different decorative patterns. The two larger are Basket Maker III. The smallest, from Pueblo I Period, 800 to 950, is particularly gay with its several colors. Here the same ingenuity for working out a design is apparent that so skillfully adapted a geometric pattern to the rounded surface of pottery.

The "cradle" (*fig. a*) is a product of the Cliff-dweller people of Moki Canyon, Utah (Pueblo III, 1050 to 1300). It is 22½ inches high. The shape is highly complicated, but even so the two broad bands with their interlocking zigzag pattern are executed with absolute clarity. The fashioning of the legs shows extraordinary command of the technique. On the steep tricky paths among the canyons, this method of transporting and protecting young children must have been truly efficient.

The steady advance toward true textile technique is evident in *Pl. 170, fig. c*, a fragment of a burden strap woven of yucca cord, probably Basket Maker. It is 15 inches long and comes from Navaho Canyon in southwestern Colorado. The elaboration given to an article of such lowly purpose speaks well for the artistic feeling of these people. The bias zigzag is very effective on the narrow band.

The twined woven fabric of Basket Maker III (*fig. d*) shows still further advance, although it probably antedates the use of the true loom.[73] Stripes of various widths and patterns run across the unicolored material with no two of them alike. A similar fragment, now in the Southwest Museum in Los Angeles, is woven of the hair of buffalo and Rocky Mountain goat.

It was a general practice in the Southwest to apply strips of rabbit skin or feathers strung on a cord to a structural base such as that seen in *fig. b*. This foundation, made of yucca fiber, was for a small rabbit-skin blanket (Basket Maker or Early Pueblo), and traces of the strips of fur are still clinging to it. The solid workmanship in the piece is noteworthy.

In a much better state of preservation are the two feather blankets in *fig. a*, made in the same manner. They were found as shown, wrapped about the desiccated body of a child in Jemez Cave, New Mexico. The larger of the two, 34 inches long, inclosed the whole bundle, while the other covered the naked body of the child. Between were two deerskin robes, one heavier than the other. The three ears of corn were for the journey to the after-world. Both blankets show clearly the minute work involved in their manufacture. Infinite patience and a knowledge of all potentialities in the raw material were necessary to produce these articles, which after more than seven hundred years have still survived in good condition.[2]

About the 8th century cotton appears in the Southwest.[31] The introduction of this material furnished the early Pueblo peoples with a more workable fiber, and they made full use of it. It was undoubtedly raised in the locality where it was woven. The pieces illustrated on *Pl. 171* were probably made on the true loom.[38]

Our first cotton textile (*fig. a*) is a bag, 12½ inches long, found in a ruin near Montezuma Castle, Arizona. It is woven in damask technique with a white warp and black weft, the design produced by floating the warp thread. Here we meet again the interlocking motif that was seen in the pottery of this area. The date of the piece is approximately 14th century.

The larger lacelike fragment in *fig. b* is done in warp-weft openwork technique. It is 8 inches long, probably Pueblo III, and comes from Grant County, New Mexico. It shows a varied pattern composition in which oblique series of frets alternate with grille work. The narrow band above it is true lace.

The fragment in *fig. c,* dated in the 14th century, is unique, perhaps the finest extant piece of textile work from the medieval Southwest. It was about 48 inches by 30 originally and was a small robe or kilt found wrapped around a body in Grand Gulch, Utah. The piece is made in diagonal weave, producing a raised pattern in variations of frets, further accentuated by the use of yellow, black, and red.[38] Even in its fragmentary state, one can see how tightly the complicated pattern is knit into a single decorative scheme.

It seems appropriate to follow up these meager remnants with illustrations that show how persistently the talent of these peoples has continued. Although they now use different materials and new methods, it is safe to say that ancient traditions, even to some extent patterns, still survive.

A scene in Canyon de Chelly, Arizona (*Pl. 172, fig. a*), shows a group of Navaho women engaged in the manufacture of a blanket. The story goes that Antonio de Espejo, a Mexican merchant, obtained in 1581 four thousand cotton blankets in the Moqui (Hopi) towns.[36] The picture here is highly characteristic of the Southwest a few years ago. Unfortunately factory products have made a devastating inroad on the art during the last decades.

The large standing loom is an introduction from Spanish times, as are also the sheep and goats in the background, but the other essentials are little changed from pre-Columbian days. One woman is busy spinning, the girl beside her is carding, and the old woman with her back to us displays a finished blanket. The weaver is seated before the loom. She works without a sketch, carrying in her head the design, which, according to tradition, must be freshly inspired with each new web, for to repeat a successful pattern slavishly is to invite the gods to destroy one's inventive genius. The motifs generally have been handed down through generations, but they are strung together in an original pattern—as much a means of self-expression as words are to us.

An embroidered shirt from Acoma, New Mexico, dating from mid-19th century, is pictured in *fig. b*. This village, situated on a high table-land almost inaccessible, was one of the last strongholds of the Pueblo Indians, and here pre-Columbian patterns were preserved long after the Conquest. On the fine linen-like material of this shirt, motifs are worked which might have been copied from prehistoric baskets and pottery. The plain fabric with its colorful needlework is a mature expression of the textile art. Women's apparel from this same time shows a black base, with embroidery in red, blue, and green.

MEXICAN AND MAYA AREAS

The small fragments of textiles from the Mexican and Maya areas that have come to light in excavations are much too damaged to be representative of an art that must have been as highly advanced here as in other regions. There can be no doubt that these areas also had their beautifully woven and gorgeously colored vestments. Representations on stone and pottery should suffice as evidence, but we have additional proof, if needed, in letters, reports, and diaries of the *conquistadores*, which in many cases describe the attire of the dignitaries and chiefs in glowing terms. Lists also have been found of woven materials exported to Spain immediately after the Conquest. The cotton cloth of the Maya was so fine that it was at first mistaken for silk.[169]

The Tribute Roll of Montezuma pictures various types of blankets paid to him as taxes by certain districts of the country (*Pl. 173, fig. b*). From the sketches on this document, there would seem to have been stock patterns. Some carried involved all-over designs, others a central medallion on a solid color, while still others are spotted in imitation of a jaguar skin. Apparently the various types were differentiated with great care, a selective tendency that probably extended to the weaving of all articles of their clothing.

Although we have almost no pre-Columbian textile remnants from these regions, much information can be gathered from a study of their present-day fabrics. Even more stimulating, however, are the mantles, shawls, and shirts of forty or fifty years ago. At that time, as in the Southwest, commercialization had not spoiled the craft, and whatever the Indian made was still very largely a product of his own fantasy-world. Although European motifs were often used, the old manner prevailed in the technical approach, the feeling for color, and the significance of the decoration. Alien elements changed in the hands of the natives, and pagan symbols were blended among them into a splendid whole. Today, however, with the hordes of erratic souvenir-hungry tourists, the former folk art is rapidly becoming a dull and routine occupation. The white man's sense of time and money is penetrating into remote regions, and, as is only natural, merchandise destined for the market is made to suit the taste of the buyer.

On the other hand, his own costume is still very much a part of the Indian's life. Lilly deJongh Osborne, who came close to the soul of the native during the years she collected old Guatemalan textiles, told us about the Indian's habit of kissing a garment in parting from it after a deal. She also related an instance of a husband striking an old blouse, sold by his wife, to drive out any part of her spirit that might cling to it.[59]

The much worn *huipil* in *fig. c* was purchased a few years ago at San Antonio Aguas Calientes, Guatemala, from the girl who was wearing it. The name is derived from the Aztec word *huipili,* "my covering," and designates a woman's blouse. The colorful piece is woven in two strips, each about 12½ inches wide, and contains a number of medieval motifs worked on a dark blue ground. The two stripes that first strike the eye with their bold zigzag lines have six color combinations before a repeat, varying lavender and olive-green, deep red and green, and red and sky-blue. Lavender is the predominant note in the bottom stripes, and the two broad diamond bands are in a soft green set off with yellow and white. These tones are remarkably pastel, and the general effect is quiet, despite the great variety of color and pattern.

In *fig. a,* another scene taken from life, a woman of Santiago Atitlán, is pictured working on her hand loom. The photograph shows how simple the apparatus is even today. This condition, however, is rapidly changing, and the standing foot loom is taking its place. The modern outfit offers new possibilities and will radically alter an art that has changed little since the Conquest, the last to succumb.

ANDEAN AREA

The Andean Area is the most fortunate of all pre-Columbian regions in possessing a climate and customs which preserved a vast number of its extraordinary textiles. The dead were often interred in a sitting position, dressed in elaborate clothing and bound with a simple white cloth. At Paracas one strip of a winding sheet measured over 37 feet in length. On top of some of the bundles an artificial head was attached, made of cloth and stuffed. Features were added, sometimes cut out of metal, sometimes in the form of a mask (see *Pls. 203* and *208, fig. b*). The effect was much like that of a child's rag doll. Pottery and personal possessions went into the bundle, and food for the journey to the afterworld accompanied it. Some mummies were so well outfitted that they measured more than 6 feet in diameter. They were placed in caverns scooped out of the sand or within a wattled-wall inclosure, but especially honored persons were set among the gods in the temples, for the people believed the spirit of the deceased ruler or high priest remained to help them.[30] Although artificial mummification seems to have been occasionally practiced in Peru, generally it is the arid climate, especially along the coastal region, which has desiccated and preserved the mummy bundles. Though sometimes stained and rotted, they have proved a treasure-trove for the study of pre-Columbian weaving.

From the earliest recognized culture on the North Coast, the Mochica, only one important specimen has been authenticated, while on the Paracas Peninsula, about one hundred miles south of Lima, a single cemetery site yielded more than three hundred such burials. These contained—to mention only the textiles—magnificent mantles, tunics, headbands, loincloths, sashes, and bags.

In color, the tendency is toward strong contrast rather than delicate harmonies. From seven to thirteen hues occur. Red, yellow, and dark brown predominate, but blue, purple, green, white, and black are also used. In the more elaborate specimens, different shades of the same color enrich the scheme.[83] With the patina of the centuries on them, the fabrics present today a considerably more mellowed impression than originally.

In general it can be said that all techniques were known in all periods, although each period shows decided preferences. Thus, embroidery is characteristic of the Nazca and Paracas periods and tapestry, of the Coast Tiahuanaco. Also, different periods feature different color combinations.[8]

The deep-seated artistic sense inherent in the ancient peoples of the Andean Area is neatly documented in the selection of bobbins and spindles shown on *Pl. 174, fig. b*. Such a little tool, so insignificant in the eyes of modern man, who sees in it only a means to a goal, was for them a medium of self-expression. We have seen hundreds of such instruments in various museums but never two alike.

Made of very hard wood and painted at least in two colors, sometimes even incised with exquisite miniature work, they have in them the naïve charm of an unpretentious but balanced civilization.

Above them the hand loom from the Ica culture (*fig. a*) still has a partly woven bit of double cloth on it, showing how the work was set up. After seeing this crude outfit, we admire even more their refined patterns and technically mature fabrics.

A finished piece of double cloth (*fig. c*), found among the ruins of La Centinela in the Chincha Valley on the southern coast of Peru, shows this weave more clearly. Conventionalized fish and bird motifs, large and small, are ranged in an orderly fashion, with the elements alternating in natural light and dark tones. Interlocking frets form the borders.

From the earliest times that we know, various kinds of embroidery were practiced in the Andean Area, some of which are difficult to differentiate from brocade. Needles of thorn and copper have been found. The running pattern in *Pl. 175, fig. b,* a Nazca shawl, is an illustration of this type. It is done in wool on cotton. Conventionalized reptilian or fish motifs, their wedge-shaped heads clearly distinguishable, make up a fret pattern without any pretense to naturalism, which has an advancing rhythm.

Fig. a shows a fragment of a wool mantle from the site of Paracas. In the manufacture of such pieces, the sections to be filled with embroidery were sometimes woven in gauze technique so that the finished product would not be bulky. In both the square medallions and the border the embroidery stitch can be traced, following the contours of the body and face. In this respect embroidery as a medium is more liberated than weaving, for it allows a freer use of curves. The distortion of the human figure into a twisting attitude produces a lively pattern, and streaming hair represented by long light lines contributes to the feeling of motion and connects one motif with another. Each medallion is about 1½ by 1¾ inches. The thick heavy fringe attached to the mantle should be mentioned.

Whether Paracas fabrics antedate the Nazca or should be classed as contemporary is a question not yet settled. It should be noted that Paracas was identified as a site only about 1925. Therefore, many earlier pieces in collections, which probably came from Paracas, were classified as Nazca on the basis of their designs, familiar from Nazca pottery.[8]

Each set of steps in the right half of *fig. c* must have been woven and tie-dyed separately, then joined. In the left half, interlocking warp technique can be seen. The "patchwork" figures are loom-woven together on one edge and sewed on the other in a singularly modern pattern.

In the piece of a garment illustrated on *Pl. 176, fig. a,* wool embroidery in darning stitch completely covers a cotton base so that it appears at first glance to be woven. The figures with their angular lines are similar in style to those carved on the Gateway of the Sun at Tiahuanaco and place the textile in the Coast Tiahuanaco Period, about A.D. 800. Eight rich colors are used in the fragment, which is slightly more than 19 inches wide. Although the same figure is repeated in each horizontal row, the repetition is disguised through a varied color scheme.

Feline figures, 6¾ inches high, stand out from the light background of the Paracas mantle in *fig. b.* Countless diamond shapes embroidered in various colors make up each animal, producing a Paisley effect. The large creatures, alternately inverted, are arranged in horizontal rows, but the vertical line of the heads and the diagonal line of the bodies greatly diversify the design. The rich border shows a condensation of animal and geometric motifs.

Fig. c is a sample of polychrome embroidery from the Ica Valley, in Nazca style. A plain dark ground serves to set off the embroidered figures of the warriors. They are very much alike in costume, each wearing a fringed tunic and a serpent headdress and carrying two trophy heads on a staff. Reared snake heads curving like feathers from the headdress recall the metal masks of Chavin (see *Pl. 195*). The arrangement of the figures is worth studying for its subtle avoidance of wallpaper monotony: in each row every other one holds his trophies in his right hand, and a repeat of colors does not appear until the fifth. The oblique rows alternate in light and dark, but even here great variety in color and expression serves to offset the regularity of pattern.

The whole of an embroidered Paracas mantle, almost 10 feet long and over 5 wide, is presented on *Pl. 177, fig. a.* What strikes the eye first is the vitality of its pattern continuity and, in the actual piece, the contrast in colors. Only after a moment of sheer delight do we turn to the individual motifs and find two fish, generally one light and one dark, that seem to revolve with a deftly contrived centripetal effect. There is no regular repeat in the center field. The use of the same motif on the border against a different colored ground is far from monotonous; rather it augments the turbulence of the whole. It will be noted that the border does not run all the way around but that a patch containing one element rounds out each corner. Since the main field is not circumscribed, the whole composition is given more breathing space. The fish are worked in shades of blue, green, and yellow on a black ground in the center and a red one in the border.

In the section of the Paracas mantle (*fig. b*), the demon motif that makes up the entire decoration is dictated by the same imagination that embellished the pottery of the Nazca region, conditioned by the technique of the loom (see *Pl. 161, fig. b*). The bright colored figures, each about 7 inches high, stand out all the more sharply for being embroidered in wool on the blue-black cotton base. The square head is turned sidewise, and a fantastically tripartite tongue curves above it. One hand holds a staff upraised and the other, a device resting on the ground that resembles a stem with lima beans attached. In every other row the figure is upside down, which adds to the confusion of the pattern. The line of small vegetable shapes that is noticeable down the center of the photograph seems to run the length of the piece. A running stitch skillfully used makes the mantle reversible. It is a characteristic example of Paracas textiles and dates from about A.D. 400 to 600.

Although tapestry was used in the early periods of the Andean cultures, it occurs more frequently in the middle and late.[105] The two plates that follow illustrate fabrics woven in this technique.

The poncho, or shirt, in *Pl. 178, fig. a* is from the Nazca region in Coast Tiahuanaco style. It measures 45 inches wide and 41 long, and was made by sewing two lengths of cloth together, with slits left for the neck and arms. Plain stripes set off the densely patterned sections. The geometric designs and abstractions of animal and plant origin that form the individual elements derive from the Tiahuanaco, though loosened and stereotyped.

A detail from a tapestry band, which measures in its entirety 46½ inches long by 5½ wide, is reproduced in *fig. b*. It also is identified as belonging to Coast Tiahuanaco from the Nazca region. The field is red, and the body and legs of the animal are orange. A white limning closes the slits. The creature, 6½ inches long and probably a textile version of the puma, shows how ingeniously a figure taken from nature was translated into a woven design of remarkable power and integrity. We even accept without question the exchange of a paw for the tail. In the band, the individual figure loses somewhat its identity and becomes part of a flowing and colorful pattern.

The Late Coast Tiahuanaco tapestry with woven fringe (*fig. c*) is thought to have come from the Central or North Coast and could be dated around the beginning of the 11th century. It is done in Kelim technique in wool on a cotton warp and was probably part of a garment. (Compare the fringed ponchos on *Pl. 190.*) Colored birds, staggered in a step design, are woven in white, dark brown, pink, red, and tan on an orange ground and blend in mellow color harmony with the plain fields of soft red.

If tapestry weaving of simple rectangles and bands requires great technical skill, how much more is displayed in the complicated design of the fish on *Pl. 179, fig. a,* from the Central Coast. It is 21 inches long by 9 wide, in late style of Pachacamac, and is woven in Kelim technique. Its shape is well defined by the white outline, and stylized parts of it, such as the gills, fins, and tail, contribute a certain naturalism. But the weaver was not content with these additions alone; the backbone is added as a decorative feature, and extraneous designs and abstractions are used to enliven the entire surface. All these additional elements are kept in balance and proportion without endangering the primary effect. The colors are tones of brown and cream with touches of green.

In *fig. b* we have a square of wool tapestry, roughly 18 inches on a side, that is classified as Ica Period from the Nazca Valley. The simplification of every element shows how weaving, during the centuries, shed its involved patterns. The complicated techniques, however, remained, and Kelim, eccentric, and figure-8 weaves may be found in this piece. The human figure is used merely as a decorative unit and repeated unchanged. From an artistic point of view, the most praiseworthy feature is the narrow border of marching birds, representing stylistically a different tradition.

The square medallion in *fig. c* is done in tapestry technique, wool on cotton, with needle-knitted borders. A stylized condor is spread on the light field, while the two borders are decorated with conventionalized two-headed lizards, creating a moving pattern above and below the static figure in the center. Compared with the other two designs on the plate, the bird is executed with more detail than the little men just seen but it is far less animated than the fish. This piece is said to have come from the South Coast of Peru and was seemingly made after highland influence from Tiahuanaco had stiffened and formalized the fantasy-world of the weavers there.

Peoples who possessed such a penchant for traveling as the pre-Columbian population of the Andean Area needed bags for various purposes—from the simple cloth of the agriculturist to the Gobelin-like tapestry materials that were part of the apparel of a high functionary. In the three examples illustrated on *Pl. 180,* one finds embroidery, tapestry, and rep.

The tapestry bag with plaited cord top (*fig. c*) is probably the earliest in the group, and is identified as Coast Tiahuanaco in style. A spotted catlike animal serves as main motif in a design that is not only more intricate than the others pictured here but covers the entire surface of the bag. Even without the secondary and tertiary elements that are ingeniously placed to fill up the space, this figure alone would produce an animated and continuous pattern. In it something of the droll quality of the Nazca animals is evident, filtered and toned down through the centuries—to appear here at its best. The piece, with its gathered top, is subtle and sophisticated enough to serve as a modern theater bag.

Fig. b, a bag with embroidered decoration and needle-knitted edges and tassels, is in the same style but later in date. The design consists of a fantastically involved animal shape from Nazca weaving, frozen through highland influence into a rigid fretlike motif, its formerly vibrant rhythm exchanged for cold geometric exactitude. The plain section at the top as balanced against the fringe at the bottom reveals deliberate artistic sense.

Fig. a, 7 by 8½ inches, is a simple bag of loom-pattern or warp-pattern rep. It comes from the Central Coast of Peru and is said to be Inca in style, dated about 1400. The dominant color is deep red, and yellow, blue, and green are used in the design. This late piece has nothing of the involved convolutions of *fig. b,* nor does it show the suavity of *fig. c;* rather one finds in it evidence that even the artistic imagination of the Chimu people, usually so fresh and charming, dwindled during the high-powered Inca administration.

Brocade came to Europe from the Orient, and fabrics woven in this technique, whether imported or domestic, were always among those most highly prized there. The pre-Columbian dignitary also had his brocaded garments, some of them made perhaps before Europe knew of this complicated weave.

One fragment with a pleasing tapestry border and woven fringe is shown on *Pl. 181, fig. a.* The brocaded top comes out in an oblique series of interlocking feline heads, woven in mauve-pink wool on yellow cotton cloth. The border, with its interlocking frets in three shades of brown with cream, is executed with amazing clarity, and the combination of these two diagonal patterns with the narrow horizontal stripes is highly effective. The piece is dated after 900 and probably belongs to the beginning of the Ica Period.

The other example (*fig. b*), 39 inches by 28, is a single-faced wool brocade on cotton crêpe. While the provenience of the first is somewhat in doubt, the second was excavated in the Nazca region and belongs to the Ica Period, about 1100 to 1300. There is a distinct stylistic difference in the two, a difference of artistic concept. In the first, the whole gains life through the striking combination of its patterns and colors, while in the second, a realistic figure loses life through its repetitious treatment. Peculiar charm is added by the tiny light-colored birds in the border, one of the favorite motifs of the coastal region. Birds of all sorts appear in Andean art, from the little humming birds, depicted on Nazca bowls, to the ducklike creatures on bands of tapestry and the conventionalized figures hammered into metal-work.

Flat and cylindrical molds are good evidence that block printing, or the stamping of a design by means of a cliché of clay, wood, or, eventually, metal, was widely practiced among the pre-Columbian peoples (*Pl. 182*). Even though many of them may have been used for body painting and some for pottery decoration, we have textiles from the Andean Area that prove that they were also applied to fabrics. In some instances painting and printing appear in combination; others seem to have been painted to imitate block designs. Cut-out stencils of silver also have been found.

A complete poncho, probably Chimu, between 1100 and 1400, is illustrated in *fig. a.* It is in plain weave and decorated with painted figures that were outlined before they were filled in (especially noticeable in the lower four birds). The unevenness of the squares arranged in a V at the neck would point to free-hand painting; however, it must not be forgotten that since stamping was by hand and the amount of paint not accurately regulated, certain divergences might easily appear even in stamped units of the same motif. Sophistication is manifest in the placing of light birds on a dark ground in the yoke and dark birds on a light ground in the lower half.

As a design, the work is interesting, although the execution seems somewhat careless. Note the inverted bird in the upper right. The painting must have been done after the two strips of material were joined, for the bird in the center is split in two. Had the fabric been woven, this would have entailed fashioning half a figure on each strip, a procedure that would not have occurred under any circumstances.

Fig. b shows a painted detail from a band of coarse plain-weave cotton, said to have come from the Central Coast. In spite of the high degree of stylization,

WEAVING

the beguiling playfulness and softness of the spotted kittens can be enjoyed. Each is about 4 inches high. They are executed in tones of tan, brown, and white on a pinkish-tan field.

In *fig. c* we have a portion of a cotton cloth, also in plain weave, covered with an extravagant variety of decoration that involves four separate pattern themes repeated in diagonal arrangement. Considering the small size of the squares— they are less than an inch high—the clarity of the composition is remarkable. It must have been extremely difficult to keep so many little motifs in line and to fill in the solid colors without smearing. The excellent dye should also receive mention, for the colors are still bright. Stylistic elements of the Coast Tiahuanaco are evident, although the piece probably belongs toward the end of that period. Stamped or painted designs would seem more susceptible to outside influences than those that are loomed, for in a woven pattern tradition and technical principles are more deeply involved.

The production of delicate fabrics brought forth correspondingly delicate patterns. In *Pl. 183, fig. a* a fragment of a painted cotton cloth from Trancas, a Nazca Period site, is shown, the sheerness of which can be perceived in the photograph. The tiny birds, each about 1½ inches long, moving in opposite directions in alternate rows, must have been painted by hand. An absence of all rigidity of line, the usual corollary of mechanical devices, gives the piece especial charm. There is a healthy naïveté and play of fantasy in the design that make it the equal of many Oriental fabrics featured in art museums.

A net for the hair (*fig. b*), woven of maguey fiber, introduces us to the most fragile weaves, under which fall the laces, voiles, and gauzes. It is made in square-meshed netting with the design embroidered in double-knotted cross-stitch. The piece is identified as coming from the Central Coast and shows Chimu stylistic features. Nets such as this have been found on the heads of mummies *in situ,* and one has to admit that in few civilizations were the dead buried with such exquisite covering for their hair.

In *fig. c* a detail from a square-meshed lacelike gauze is reproduced that also comes from the Central Coast and is presumably Chimu. The designs are outlined and filled in with cross-stitch. Besides the human figure seen here, about 4½ inches high, animals enliven the decorative scheme. Airy fabrics such as these were manufactured for various purposes, ranging from fastidious hair covering to fish nets and from small bags attached to scale beams (see *Pl. 299, fig. a*) to veils.[84]

In *Pl. 184, fig. a* the familiar step-and-fret design is woven in gauze weave of cotton, giving the impression of drawn-work. The faultless transition from the plain section into the openwork pattern can be easily followed.[105] The piece is identified as Nazca.

The second example (*fig. b*) is probably Chimu and shows a combination of gauze with bands of plain weave and openwork. It is dated about 1300. The variation of tightly woven, fine-meshed, and openwork stripes is highly successful and so universally appealing that we can easily imagine the piece as a Sunday table cover in one of our own Victorian households.

The fragment of a poncho (*fig. c*) shows an unusual type of openwork which enhances the plain cloth through the lacy contrast of its squares. The border above the fringe is worked in tapestry weave in several colors and features the much stereotyped bird of Ica style, here almost lost in an interlocking-fret design.

It is not surprising that modern textile experts stand dumfounded before the manifold variety found in medieval Peruvian weaving. It seems as if technical hindrances did not exist for these people, nor any limit to their inventiveness.

The poncho in *Pl. 185, fig. a* displays the weft-loop weave, a technique used in our Turkish towels and terry cloth. In this photograph the fringe is parted to show the plain cloth between the rows of loops, but when worn the entire surface of the poncho presented a shaggy appearance. The slit at the top is the opening for the neck. A shirt of this type in such a good state of preservation is a rarity. What a striking garment it must have been when new, worn with accessories of metal, shell, or turquoise.

The foundation fabric in *fig. b* is woven with a cotton warp and wool weft in tapestry with spaced warps, giving an openwork effect. The tassels are of polychrome wool and are sewed on in groups.

Still more extraordinary is the complicated piece illustrated in *fig. c*. Here we have a closely woven tapestry in red, yellow, and brown, ornamented with a five-toothed motif in white and interspersed with openwork squares, over which are sewed tasseled rosettes of wool, fashioned separately—a prodigious task even for our machine age. The tassel colors are yellow, blue, and white; the rosettes, red and violet. These pieces probably come from the Central Coast and are Chimu in style. Contemporary Europe imported its choice textiles from the Orient, but they were less varied than those worn by the native chiefs in Peru.

Pl. 186 presents two caps, 5⅕ to 6 inches high, stylistically Coast Tiahuanaco. Both are made of wool with a knitted base (see top), into which the silky strands are knotted and then clipped in a manner not unlike our plush or velvet technique.

In the first (*fig. a*), a meandering geometric pattern characteristic of the highlands appears, while in the second (*fig. b*), conventionalized birds stand out clearly against the varicolored ground. The pointed knitted ends of the one and the four fuzzy pompons of the other, as well as their distinctive patterns, demonstrate that even where tradition dictated the shape, material, and motifs, a piece could still be individualized. The photographs show not only the evenness of execution and the fine texture of the wool, but give a fair idea of the many colors involved. One of these trig and colorful hats above an elaborate, loosely fitting poncho must have added considerably to the picturesqueness of the costume.

Although the Paracas textiles are among the earliest of pre-Columbian finds, they show some of the greatest finesse of execution. *Pl. 187* presents a detail of a superb mantle in soft henna wool of gauzy quality. The cloth is 46 inches long and 20 wide. A solidly embroidered border in rich polychrome with fringe is sewed completely around the edge, and the sheer body of the piece is covered with a pattern of mythical figures worked in a delicate running stitch in cocoa-brown. The design is made up of a series of double-headed monsters forming converging V's, covered with masks and other elements, all connected with one another. They leave diamond-shaped fields of equal size, in which the single main figure—the many-tongued creature seen in *Pl. 177, fig. b*—is placed without crowding. The line of heads at the edge should not be missed, especially the central one, like a heraldic motif. The angular build-up of the units has something of an incised carving about it, and the separate demon figure is slightly reminiscent of the Sechin stone (see *Pl. 99, fig. a*). The iconography of this early piece contains many of those fantastically stylized elements which were used throughout later centuries with little change.

Older than many of the textiles already seen is the justly celebrated ceremonial mantle from Paracas reproduced on *Pl. 188*. It is 54 inches long and 21 wide, including the border, and was found in a tomb with other fabrics and some gold objects as part of the funeral raiment of a chief or priest. The gossamer material, woven of cotton and vicuña wool, carries a design of puma heads and frets exquisitely woven into a continuous pattern. Delicate tones are combined in a never-repeating scheme: maroon, rose, and peach-pink with turquoise and azure-blue, green, yellow, and gold.

The real sensation of the piece, however, is the amazingly decorative wool border that contains an endless procession of ninety figures in twelve colors. It is about 3½ inches wide and wrought in a technique resembling embroidery and knitting—a lost skill that is known as three-dimensional knitting. The legs appear against a dark solid background, but above the waist the figures rise free. Their definitely plastic effect is achieved by a core of stuffing that varies in thickness. In its marvelous state of preservation, the border serves as a fascinating inventory of the elaborate costumes, headdresses, and jewels worn and the weapons used in that early day. The llama appears, haltered and laden with ears of maize; other cultivated plants are represented, and the puma and numerous mythological creatures, whose significance can only be guessed at today, crowd together in an overwhelming display.[84] The section chosen for enlargement is shown between the two arrows. In the detail (*fig. b*), the many-tongued demon of the preceding plate can be distinguished on the right, with the figure beside him turned under to provide more background. The looped rosettes that join the border to the mantle are also clearly visible here. This piece is said to be contemporary with the Nazca culture, which would date it around 500, or even earlier. It exhibits a perfection in technique and a fantastic richness in the conception of its design which in all the centuries that have followed have never been surpassed.

Because of their familiar shape, the ponchos on the next three plates are easier for us to understand than the many fragments we have seen. By their tangible presence they attest to the civilized apparel of this area.

The first (*Pl. 189, fig. a*) shows Ica traits in technique and design, although it comes from Ancon, a site on the Central Coast. This piece, as well as those that follow, is full size for an adult Indian. It is a very rare and an excellently preserved specimen of openwork, woven in a variant of Kelim technique with spaced warp,[105] already seen in the tasseled fragment on *Pl. 185, fig. b.* The bold painted diagonals are remarkably effective. Note that the weaving in the vertical bars is straight and tight, while in the horizontals the thread is loose, producing a wavy line that gives variety and softness to the cross-bar pattern. Only the tapestry border with its small moving animal motifs is solid. The cuffs have a quadruple fringe that repeats the colors in the shirt—dark blue, beige, red, and white.

Fig. b comes from Pachacamac, an immediate neighbor of Ancon to the south. Cotton cloth in plain weave, very thin, serves as base for the appliquéd designs. The condensed symbolism in the figure is characteristic of the coastal cultures, and it is presumable that these finely woven Chimu tapestry medallions were taken off an older material and applied on another in a later century, just as old laces are used on clothing today.

The poncho in *fig. c* comes from farther north, the Chimu site of Huaco. Rosettes and tassels add a characteristic colorful touch with their tones of red, tan, and brown. Below the decoration, the plain weave changes to openwork, fourteen double rows of it, and a tapestry border with a cleverly contrived interlocking-fret pattern completes the exquisitely finished garment.

Quite recently Peruvian archaeologists discovered in shallow walled-in graves at Paracas four hundred twenty-nine mummies.[145] In the bundles there were some rather plain funeral ornaments cut out of hammered gold, but the textiles found were of greater value. Mantles and shawls of delicate weave and stunning color combinations were unearthed, many of them in an amazing state of preservation when we consider the fifteen hundred years that have elapsed since their manufacture.

Extraordinarily well preserved is the poncho on *Pl. 190, fig. b* from this cemetery. It is a very large garment, measuring 50 by 38 inches, with a braided fringe 28 inches long at each shoulder and a 20-inch woven fringe along the border. Sometimes these shirts are so large that one suspects clothing was worn under them or that they were woven especially for the mummies. Figural and geometric motifs, easily distinguishable, are skillfully handled to produce a rich and mobile decoration. Note the difference in the interpretation of the same figure in the embroidered and the woven bands. The contrasts of the plain dark material with the colored and the smooth fabric with the rough fringe make the piece outstanding even among Paracas textiles.

The sleeveless poncho in *fig. a* comes from farther south and shows a pattern that marks the transition from Coast Tiahuanaco to Ica style. It is made of wool in a cloth weave, with borders embroidered in wool. The motif edging the monotone fabric is probably a stark conventionalization of a former cat pattern. (Compare with the bag on *Pl. 180, fig. b.*) It is now so condensed and unified, however, and so decorative that it does not occur to us to inquire into its origin. This piece also makes effective use of tassels and fringe, even if they are not so lavishly applied as in the other below it.

The four ponchos on *Pl. 191,* our last examples of pre-Columbian weaving, are especially noteworthy because they come from the highlands, where few textiles have survived the climate. All but *fig. a* are from Lake Titicaca, and two (*figs. b* and *c*) were found in a tightly covered stone box, which accounts for their excellent condition. All are made of vicuña wool in tapestry technique, with V-shaped yokes, and all feature in one way or another the checkerboard— as if this exact and organized pattern had become subconsciously the symbol for the tightly coördinated life under Inca rule.

It is possible that some of them were manufactured just after the Conquest; *fig. b* has a silver thread in the border, probably a Spanish innovation. But they possess generally stylistic features outspokenly Inca. We no longer meet the large mythological or symbolic figures of Nazca culture or involved geometric stylization. The application of the small square, the fret, and the step, among others, has become by now fluent and accomplished. The units are systematized, and there is no meandering of motifs. From the designs in *fig. b,* however, it is clear that ancient pattern elements of the Tiahuanaco culture persisted into later centuries, even into the Inca Period and beyond, as if a counterpoint in weaving threaded itself through all phases of the highland weaver's art. Here they too have become well-regimented decorative elements on a chessboard structure.

As a new motif of high rank the diamond appears (*fig. d*), executed with precision and somewhat suggestive of blanket designs in our own Southwest. Another new element is the suave arrangement of feathers on the same piece. Note also the human figures on its yoke, each wearing a shirt with checkerboard decoration and holding up a sketch of another. Figures are used in a different presentation on the lower border of *fig. b.* Their inclusion in such a design is considered by some also a mark of Spanish influence.

To appreciate the work fully, one must take into consideration the beautiful color modulations: the soft reds, vivid blues, and the olive-greens that are especially dominant in *fig. d.* In *fig. a* delicately conventionalized butterflies in rose and olive-green on a brilliant turquoise field enliven the rigidity of the pattern and individualize the piece.

An art so highly perfected and so vital to life in medieval America as was weaving could not cease to exist with the Conquest. The technical skill and feeling for design received new stimulus with the introduction of silk, linen, and sheep's wool from the Eastern Hemisphere. This meeting of two civilizations that had developed independently produced a blend, in weaving particularly, that has the fascinating quality of a fairy tale. The Spaniards, who embodied in their art influences from China, Persia, and other lands of the Near East, and the native American weavers, who achieved mastery by a very different road, turned out, especially in Peru in the 16th, 17th, and 18th centuries, tapestries which are today the cherished possessions of museums and collectors.

In style, some are strongly reminiscent of the Late Coptic. The human figure, so rigidly expressed or completely omitted in most pre-Columbian pieces, is now used more freely. New animals, such as horses and cows, and a new approach that encouraged the use of fruit and flowers in naturalistic form stimulated the talent of the native. Besides elements of European provenience, Levantine and Oriental motifs are sometimes blended into a beguiling potpourri. During these centuries an Hispano-American art flourished which surpasses all modern attempts at the neo-primitive, for here it was a true and spontaneous expression, not an artificial stumbling and stuttering in a highly technical age.

A post-Columbian tapestry poncho from the Lake Titicaca district in Bolivia is reproduced in *Pl. 192, fig. b*. In shape and general lay-out of design, it differs little from those we have already seen—even the V-shaped yoke outlined with squares appears. But the pattern in the yoke presents a stylized mixture of fantasy animals, flowers, and plants never met before. Even more striking are the dark stripes on the light base. The delicate motif woven into them actually has elements of a bird design, but it is organized into a floral effect with a continuity characteristic of European taste.

Much farther removed from the pre-Columbian atmosphere, both in shape and pattern, is the tapestry panel in *fig. a*. It measures nearly 8 feet by 6 and is all wool. Like an Oriental rug, it features as center a riot of flowers, with framing bands, each of which is made up of a different floral motif. Only the two lighter ones recall in their twining and winding elements pre-Conquest times; the others are well-digested decorative units such as appear frequently in Spanish colonial work.

Since there were no religious bans against using shapes of nature, as was the case in Islamic countries, all the European and Oriental motifs were at the disposal of the Peruvian weaver, and the result was especially rich and varied. Human figures, gesticulating dramatically, are introduced in the four small medallions. The couple on the left wear Spanish costumes of the 18th century— cocked hats, big boots, and pistols in their belts—while the other two seem to be Indians. Urns and baskets, infrequent in Peruvian weaving, show rococo influence. The Indian weaver's disinclination to repeat is manifest in the changes in the urns and birds and in the general color variations that disguise the inevitable recurrence. Pink, dark blue, yellow, and olive-green are the chief colors, each in several tones.[83]

A story-telling atmosphere pervades this exquisite and rare work of art, bringing to us the viceregal period of Peru. We can easily imagine this tapestry on the wall or floor of a proud and aristocratic palace of the 18th century there.

The textiles of the Andean Area reveal that the product can be highly complicated in pattern and intricate in technique even though the tool is primitive. The advance in this isolated civilization from the animal skins of the first hunting tribes to the Paracas mantle represents an achievement that is tremendous. The distance from this high grade of technical and artistic skill to our present-day production is far less. Not a single new type of weaving can be shown by modern industry. The hand-spun thread of the pre-Columbian natives was superior to ours in tensile strength, fineness, and evenness of quality. Furthermore, for durability of material and fastness of color, our production fails to show a great advance. We do not know how much would remain of our average wools and cottons after more than a thousand years in the earth.

VII

Metal-Work

WHEN Columbus pleaded at the Court of Spain for support of his expedition, he evoked the treasures of the East. The Admiral crossed and re-crossed the unknown ocean four times and touched upon the eastern shores of Central and South America, as well as the West Indies, but even the red-skinned population of these regions did not shake his belief that he was somewhere on the shores of fabulous Asia. As a token of the success of his undertaking, he brought back jewelry and small objects of gold and silver. By the time that Cortés's first shipments reached Europe, however, it was clear that it was a new world which lay beyond the seas.

The *conquistadores* could see on their first contacts with the natives that gold and silver had not the same value in the eyes of the Indians as in their own. It was not a medium of exchange for them but a resplendent material to be fashioned into articles for ceremonial and decorative use. Although the gold which Cortés collected consisted partly of raw metal, a great portion was already made up into objects—jewelry, statuettes, and utensils executed with artistic finesse. Even the unsentimental soldiers who took part in the Conquest were impressed by their beauty. All articles, however, had to be melted down into a more convenient form for shipping, and, at Montezuma's order, a group of the goldsmiths who had wrought many of the delicate pieces worked for three days casting the heaped-up gold into ingots and bars which were stamped with the royal arms of Spain. The more cautious of the soldiers ordered their share of the booty made into chains and other articles that could be carried on the person. Cortés had a small cannon made of gold and silver alloy. Upon seeing the greed of the Spaniards for the metal, Montezuma is said to have remarked, "The Christians must have a strange disease which can be cured only with gold."

But the thirst was insatiable. The lure of gold enticed other adventurers, and it was Pizarro who came upon the real El Dorado with its riches beyond the wildest dreams. In the realm of the Incas, gold and silver were used functionally. Besides "goblets, ewers, salvers, vases of every shape and size, ornaments and utensils for the temples and palaces," sheets of gold covered some of the buildings, dazzling as a mirage.[110] A fountain that sent up a sparkling jet of gold is described in one account, with birds and animals of the same material playing at its base, and mention is made of a golden ear of corn, sheathed in broad leaves of silver, with a rich tassel of silver threads. In some of the more northerly regions of South America, gold fishing hooks, tweezers, nails, spoons, and pins—even safety-pins—have been found.[9] So abundant was the metal that Pizarro, on his march into the interior of the country, ordered golden shoes for his horse as the iron was worn away. The picture of a small band of ragged Spaniards, marching in a hostile unknown land, their horses shod with precious metal, shows an illuminating paradox of the Conquest. Here, too, gold and silver were melted down and cast into solid bars of uniform standard. So great was the treasure that the Peruvian goldsmiths had to work at the task for a full month, ten times as long as was needed in Mexico.

By the middle of the 16th century, the importation of gold from the New World to Spain was so heavy that in the maintenance of her navy England reckoned with the booty seized from the Spanish fleet. In Spain itself, the enormous wealth proved unfruitful and transitory, and melted away in the hands of a corrupt administration.

Of the millions of dollars' worth of gold and silver that reached Europe in the Spanish centuries, we cannot trace a single object as an absolutely authentic survival of the Conquest.[71] Some of the extant pieces come from old collections, some from excavations, and many more circulate without data on their provenience. Even today, if worked gold and silver articles from pre-Columbian times are found by the ignorant population, they are apt to be looked upon only as a source of a few dollars, and it is fortunate if they are not melted down. A few of the specimens photographed for this survey have since disappeared, stolen and wantonly destroyed for the metal they contained. The "strange disease" still holds us in its grip.

The consensus of authorities gives credit for the early development of pre-Columbian metallurgy to South America. Indeed, according to some opinions many high cultural trends originated there and then worked north. This theory, challenging that of Maya precedence in antiquity, has many arguments in its favor. The Mochica, Chavin, Nazca, and Early Tiahuanaco cultures date at least within the first centuries of our era, and the earliest specimens shown in this chapter are believed to fall within this time. Most pre-Columbian metal-work, however, is generally placed after the turn of the first millennium.

"The golden land" of the Spaniards, the Inca Empire, comprised not only Peru and Ecuador but parts of Chile and Bolivia, and the art of metal-working extended beyond, into the regions of Colombia, Venezuela, Panama, and Costa Rica, where styles show local characteristics. Metallurgy is not believed to have reached the Maya and Mexican cultures before the 9th century—the 12th is more likely.

In both the Andean and the Interlying areas the mines were so situated that they could be worked by primitive methods. Gold was obtained principally by panning, while silver was extracted from surface mines. Besides these metals, copper, tin, mercury, platinum, lead, and iron in natural alloys are found in pre-Columbian objects.[71] The medieval Peruvians regarded their mines as living spirits and performed certain ceremonies in their honor. Those who worked them worshiped the hills that contained the minerals, and feasts were held with dancing and drinking to assure the benevolence of the spirits.[28]

Hammering, embossing, casting, plating and gilding, inlaying, sheathing, engraving, alloying, soldering, and welding were all processes known to the Peruvian goldsmiths around the 10th century. For these operations the use of hammers, anvils, furnaces, crucibles (probably made of pottery), and blowpipes was necessary.[70] It is interesting to note that comparatively few implements for such specialized techniques have been unearthed, probably because the excavated material up to now comes from grave sites rather than work sites.

Hammering, embossing, and engraving might be considered as belonging to the simpler methods, but the existence of cast and plated articles, of those with the design in an alloy of different color, or with inlaid lapidary material, shows real grasp of the medium and the achievement of highly specialized skills.

The *cire perdue,* or "lost wax," process of casting was widely employed. This method was essentially the same as that used for our bronzes today. It was known also in ancient Egypt and the Near East, then apparently lost to Europe in the first centuries of Christianity to be re-invented for the Renaissance shortly before Benvenuto Cellini. The perfection of this process in pre-Columbian America serves as a striking example of parallel development, when similar conditions produce similar results.

By this method the desired object was modeled first in wax or resin, some-times over a core of clay, and covered with a clay mixture. When this was fired, the wax melted and ran out of vents provided for the purpose, leaving a mold corresponding exactly to the wax positive. Molten metal then poured into the mold took on the desired shape, and after it solidified the covering was broken away. The rough castings were often hammered and burnished for smoother finish and sometimes welded together to form a larger object. The nature of the procedure invited the use of fine and intricate detail, accurately reproduced in the soft wax. The fact that only one object could be made from each mold would not appear as a drawback to the craftsman of medieval America, who apparently shared with the modern Navaho the conviction that the gods would destroy his talent if he servilely duplicated a piece.

MOUND BUILDER REGION

The objects in the first two plates were produced outside the bounds of our five areas, but are included to show the wide distribution of metal-working on an outspokenly artistic level. They come doubtless from a late period in Mound Builder culture but are presented at the beginning of this chapter rather than at the end, where they might appear as an anticlimax after the metal-work of the more civilized areas.

The ornaments on *Pl. 193, fig. a,* found at Hopewell Mounds, Ohio, were cut out of a hammered copper sheet with bone or horn tools. A surprising neatness of finish can be observed in them. Their geometric design is not only decorative but intricate in composition. The swastika in the upper right documents an instance of the independent invention of this form.

Fig. b shows shapes cut out of mica. They were excavated from graves of dignitaries of the Hopewell people and appear to have been used as ornaments on clothing. The material is a laminated substance, one that requires considerable skill to work, and was brought into the region by trade from Virginia and North Carolina.[31] Both pieces show amazing certainty in linear conduct. The eagle foot with its translucent silvery tone is unique—highly sophisticated in its stylization.

Fig. a on *Pl. 194* is part of a headdress fashioned of copper and, although damaged, is impressive because of its shape and symmetry. It comes from Nashville, Tennessee, and is 11⅝ inches long. The type appears fastened at the nape of the neck of a figure on one of the shell gorgets, also from Tennessee (see *Pl. 280, fig. a*).

The two copper sheets embossed with faces (*figs. b* and *c*) are from Spiro

Mound, Oklahoma. On the larger, 9½ inches high (*fig. c*), plastic effects were attempted, and every detail is sharply executed. Eyes and hair in particular are skillfully drawn, the eyes showing a manner of delineation quite different from the Mexican or Maya. The face in *fig. b,* with its half-open mouth, teeth, elaborate earrings, and the thin lines suggesting hair, bears a certain similarity to the early prints of Indian chiefs.

Fig. d, 10½ inches high and also from Spiro Mound, is cut away from the background, producing a sharp silhouette. Especially well executed is the section between the nose and chin. Technical superiority is evident in the feather headdress, with its harmonious line; although almost detached it is nevertheless an integral part of the composition.

ANDEAN AREA

The name "Chavin," as was already discussed in sculpture, is applied to an ancient culture that apparently once dominated the upper interior of Peru and in places reached into the coastal valleys. All four pieces on *Pl. 195,* classified as Chavin in style, came from the department of Lambayeque on the coast. This section, which lies some two hundred seventy miles northwest of the site of Chavin, received its name from the river flowing through it and was in ancient times a part of the Chimu Kingdom.

All specimens shown on this plate present variations of the same theme. Not only is the central subject recurrent, but the manner of delineation is definitely of the same iconography.

The plaque (*fig. a*) is 8½ inches high and was probably fastened to a headband. The standing main figure, holding a staff in either hand, is a jaguar or puma demon with tusks and a wrinkled muzzle. Its body seems made up of masks and intertwining serpent bodies. Secondary designs of puma and serpent heads fill all available space and make the effect of the whole confusing.

The same technique—a pattern pressed out in relief on a thin gold sheet— was applied in *fig. b.* It is 9¼ inches high and was part of a crown. Here again the main figure is an anthropomorphic creature with a staff in either hand. In the surrounding pattern we find the same elements as in the preceding piece, presented, however, with considerably more clarity. The human element is brought out in the smooth surfaces of the face, shoulders, and legs—a trick which sets off especially well the fine mask on the torso.

In *fig. c,* nearly 5 inches high, the main motif is transferred from the cylindrical shape to a plaque with cut-out outlines. The sixteen serpents about the head have not changed their position too much, and the mask in the center has all the details necessary to identify it as the same theme, crystallized by tradition and clarified by good workmanship. Here, however, with the edges cut out, a certain live and plastic impression is achieved that is not apparent in the other two. The deep corrugated embossing, extremely telling in the medium of gold, is especially well applied.

In *fig. d,* a gold ornament 6½ inches high from the same region, appears the quintessence of the type. The main motif is loosened, and a remarkable lightness has been gained by cutting out the background. This mask has lost its fangs, otherwise the features are the same, perhaps the most clearly expressed of all. Entwined serpent bodies serving as frame for the head produce a highly decorative effect.

The transplantation of the same theme into different media by different cultures is illustrated in *Pl. 196.* The plaque (*fig. a*), said to have come from Pachacamac, shows influence of the Coast Tiahuanaco and Chavin styles. A thin silver sheet was cut out to the desired shape, then lightly embossed. It contrasts interestingly with the jaguar masks of the preceding plate. Hollow eye sockets and an open slit for the mouth line are effective in their negative emphasis.

The silver stirrup jar (*fig. b*), perhaps from the Mochica culture but with strong Chavin influence, presents an anthropomorphic jaguar god in the round. About 13 inches high and hammered of high-grade metal, it was made in several parts and soldered together. Characteristic features of the jaguar demon seen on the preceding plate appear: the eyes outlined in heavy loops, the curving eyebrows that flare at the ends into cat's ears, the bared teeth with four huge tusks which stand out even more prominently through plastic presentation. The snakes, however, do not appear, and more anthropomorphic elements are brought into the composition. The two rows of teeth are clearly defined as human, although stereotyped, and appendages are attached suggestive of human ears. That which in the other examples was a lively play with lines, producing a vibrant whole, has become in the silver piece merely the expression of a remote idea. Little feeling for the material is apparent. The shallow corrugated lines on the top suggest pottery, while the deep groove above the eyes would be more effective in stone.

In *fig. c* we have the same subject carved in the round from wood—a staff or paddle head probably of Late Coast Tiahuanaco style. Much similarity to the silver jug can be detected. The channel below the eyes, which shows up clearly at the right in the photograph, is deep and particularly expressive in the softer material. The headdress, only suggested in *fig. b* and simplified in *fig. a,* is here worked out into an animal-mask. Shell or bone inlay gives good emphasis to all the carving by the introduction of a contrasting material. The four fangs should be mentioned as a feature consistently present.

In medieval America earrings were a distinction allowed only certain ranks, and the piercing of the ears was a ceremonial occasion. As the wearer grew older and the lobes stretched, his ear ornaments became larger and larger. The derisive Spanish name for the Incas was "long ears."

The four earrings shown on *Pl. 197, fig. a,* were found at Chongoyape in Lambayeque, the same site where some of the other pieces of Chavin style (*Pl. 195*) were discovered. They are all of gold, with the largest slightly over 5 inches in diameter. In each case the design was pressed into the metal, then cut out and soldered to the tubelike cylindrical section, which was inserted into the lobe. In two of them the decoration consists of rectangular serpent heads made up largely of straight lines; the other two, representing bird heads and beaks, have more convulsive contours.

Fig. b presents another object of personal adornment, a necklace identified as belonging to the Mochica. In its present arrangement it is about 16 inches long and composed of thirty graduated heads, the largest about 1½ inches in length. The features are slightly diversified, but each wears a puma headdress, and all are hollow behind and perforated along the edges for attachment to cloth. A chief with such a golden string sewed to his colorful poncho must have presented a picturesque appearance. The Scythians of prehistoric Asia—known as the best metal workers of their time and the diffusers of many metallurgical inventions into Europe—also combined textiles and metal in the same sophisticated manner, ornamenting their tunics with small golden objects.

The magnificent ceremonial knife illustrated on *Pl. 198, figs. a* and *c,* was found with other remarkable gold and silver objects quite recently at Illimo, near Lambayeque, on the northern coast of Peru. The treasure came from funerary tumuli in which several Chimu dignitaries were interred. Their graves contained, besides this piece, gold cups, some with repoussé figural decoration and others with turquoise incrustation (see *Pl. 201*), as well as gold funerary

MEDIEVAL AMERICAN ART

masks, simple beakers of gold, spoons, bead necklaces, earrings, pins, bells, timbrels, and personal ornaments of gold and silver. This sensational hoard, which apparently had escaped the busy digging of intruders and robbers for centuries, constitutes both in value and artistic importance the greatest single recorded find made in South America since the *conquistadores* laid hands on the metallic wealth of the Inca Empire.[164] It is fortunate that this and that other all-important treasure from Tomb 7 at Monte Alban in the Mexican Area, remained undisturbed until scientific handling could be assured.

The Chimu people, like their predecessors, the Mochica, were characterized by a cruel and warlike spirit. According to some sources, they practiced human sacrifice, a custom with which this knife might be associated. Its elaboration points to ceremonial use. It is about 17 inches long. The figure above the half-moon-shaped blade has been identified as the Chimu demigod, Naymlap, and shows him with an ornate headdress, the two outer bands of which, wrought in filigree, give the effect of an aureole. Eight pieces of green turquoise stud the arc and two more, his earplugs; these, together with the two wings that extend from behind the arms, are legendary characteristics of this mythical figure. The beaded edge, remarkably well preserved, is carried into the smallest detail, appearing even on the minute exquisite birds suspended from either end of the aureole. The semicircular outlines of the headdress and the blade form parentheses which seem to inclose this perturbing symbol.

Even more decorative detail appears on the back of the statue (*fig. c*). The bell shapes in the fringe along the edge of the shirt and apron, as well as the eight dangling pendants outlined with rows of globular beads, are all intact. With his wings and the birds hanging from his headdress, he might be an Icarus of the Chimu people. According to legend, he gave himself wings with which to fly to heaven.

In *fig. b* further evidence of the settled iconography of this region is discernible. It is part of a gold ear ornament, 2½ inches in diameter, from Jayanca, near Lambayeque, in the heart of the Chimu Kingdom. The main characteristics of the former image are present, and doubtless the same personage is represented.

Superb craftsmanship produced the piece in *Pl. 199, fig. a,* a gold cup, 5 inches high, also Chimu. The embossing of the figure is very shallow, but a bolder pattern was applied in the shell-shaped ornament just below the rim. These two kinds of relief effects—protruding shells and flatter figure—add to the

‹ 246 ›

artistic value and interest of the piece. Although the pose of the figure is some-what different, the wing-shaped eyes seen in the Illimo knife reappear here. This cup, as well as those on the following plate, is of an unexpected thinness, yet faultlessly made. A number of them have been unearthed in a relatively excellent condition.

Fig. b shows another hero-god with outstretched arms and elaborate gar-ments, repeated on the divided surface of a gold plaque. This Chimu ornament comes from the vicinity of Chan-Chan and is about 3½ inches high. Here again the shallow repoussé of the figures is well contrasted with the more pronounced dots that ornament the frame.

The figural decoration of a large earplug (*fig. c*) demonstrates the same ideology and technique, with the additional interest of cut-out outline and per-foration. Three of the four figures wear a modified aureole headdress, not so elaborate as in the Illimo knife. The central personage holds in his left hand a cup shaped in the round and in his right a bag with dangling pendants. Other disks are attached as ornaments elsewhere. Note the long bar, with a monster-head at either end on which the chief character seems to ride. Originally the plaque was mounted on the front of a very large earplug and surrounded by an exquisite frame of beaded gold (see *fig. b* on the preceding plate). Behind it was the tubular section, also of metal, that was inserted through the lobe of the ear.

Cups were common all over the Andean Area. Their decoration varied, however, according to district, and silver and gold, or even wood, were used as material. The shape is characterized by a flawless dignity of line. *Fig. a* on *Pl. 200* is of gold, about 5 inches high, and is said to have come from the high-lands, while *fig. b* is of silver and from the coastal district around Ancon. The silver beaker flares gracefully from the base and is covered with repoussé de-signs of cats and other patterns. The gold cup is broader, has straighter sides, and a single protruding band is its only ornament; its simplicity of style is typical of Classic Tiahuanaco.

In *fig. c* two gold beakers and cup-shaped earplugs demonstrate a variety of patterns. The two larger pieces are 5¼ inches high, and were fashioned of gold hammered over clichés, with the bottoms soldered on. They come from the Chimu Period of the Lambayeque region. In the cup on the right, only a frieze is used above an embossed double band, which employs, inverted, the bird fig-ures common in the decoration of Chimu pottery, textiles, and stucco work. The fact that the birds are in a natural position when the piece is turned upside down gives reason to believe that some cups may have been kept inverted. The more elaborate ornamentation of the piece on the left shows the familiar stunted figure with semicircular sunburst headdress, placed within a geometric border of frets and other elements which have some suggestion of masks.

The ear ornaments, 2¾ inches high, have a pleasant curving form and are very finely incised or engraved with an oblique spiral design that leaves only a narrow ribbon-like strip undecorated. Again we find a squat human, this time in profile, repeated at measured intervals within a border of frets. The design is lucidly carried out within the limited space allotted it. Extraordinary feeling for the medium is shown in the use of plain bands to relieve the incised design as well as in the cast beads along the edge, soldered together and applied with unerring precision.

In the gold and silver cups on *Pl. 201,* still more variety is displayed, not so much in shape, which seems to have been more or less standardized, as in decoration.

The main interest in the two gold pieces from the Illimo treasure (*fig. a*) lies in their incrustation with turquoise. In spite of a certain divergence, very slight, in the border patterns, it is clear that both were manufactured on identical principles; even the soldered sections added at the bottom are similar. The beaded setting which incases each stone is a graceful artistic solution, as it not only holds firm the colorful material but brings plastic variety into the composition.

The silver cup (*fig. b*) is said to have come from the Piura Valley in the realm of the Chimu. Motifs characteristic of this culture embellish the piece, applied with a fine feeling for pattern. Human figures are blended into the oblique band of birds, fish, and symbolical objects as in a tapestry, where all elements are subordinated to the general scheme. It was much more difficult to execute the pattern within these winding mounting ribbons than in the horizontal line more frequently seen. The damaged edge, like crumpled paper in appearance, gives an excellent idea of the thinness of the metal.

In *fig. c* the tall gold ceremonial cup, 12⅔ inches high, comes from the northern coastal region of Peru. Its narrow chimney-like cylinder flares slightly toward the top and is finished with a fine beveled lip. The sharp protruding line of the jaw gives the feeling of a goblet and marks off the elongated neck below, which offers a good grip. Such faces always show the angular U around the mouth, indicated by a single downward-curving line, and the nose is always aquiline and sharply modeled. Cups of this type are found quite frequently in excavations even today, after four hundred years of treasure hunting.

In *Pl. 202* three different interpretations of the human figure from districts near one another are offered for comparative study. In the first illustration (*fig. a*), it is embossed on a gold cuff, about 5¾ inches high. Seemingly each figure was hammered from the same cliché. The heads are large, with the main features of the face clearly indicated, while the body, arms, and feet are small in comparison and sketchily done. No framing motif or additional decoration is combined with this puritanical trio, but their placement with ample breathing space shows artistic deliberation. Stylistically this piece might belong to the Mochica culture; however, such cuffs were also found in graves in the Ica Valley south of this region.

The small gold statuette, 2½ inches high (*fig. b*), is from the Chimu culture. Except for the two hammered gold disks in his hands, it is cast in one piece. The nose is pierced for an ornament that has disappeared. As on the cuff, the head is disproportionately large, a common characteristic throughout pre-Columbian art, and some details, such as the navel, are so sharply brought out that we may assume for them, too, especial significance. Despite its static build-up, the figure has life and in its communicative appeal will stand comparison with the turquoise and silver statuettes on *Pl. 258*. There is a hook in the back of the head, probably for suspension.

Still more ingratiating is the Chimu doll of silver (*fig. c*), which was put together of several sections of hammered metal and is, therefore, hollow. In his hands he holds a cup with a face design like that discussed in the preceding plate. The act of drinking is well conveyed to the onlooker through his movable arms. There is a toylike quality in the piece that is sensed immediately, which gives us a new angle on the mechanical versatility of these people and the scope of their imagination.

Masks were composed of semiprecious stones in the Mexican Area; in the Andean, something on a similar order was fashioned out of metal. As mentioned under weaving, the use of masks on mummy bundles seems to have been quite general here, but we find outspoken plastic differences in pieces from different regions.

Both specimens on *Pl. 203* appear to have come from the North Coast and are characterized as Chimu in style. In such work the Chimu people show an advanced and articulate artistic expression, frequently superior to that of their southern neighbors. A mature—we might also say aristocratic—mannerism is evident when these masks with their sure lines are compared with some of the pieces from the Ica Valley, for instance. The plastically composed and positive expression is there flattened into a geometric design and the arrogant mouth, generally closed in Chimu pieces, is opened to show teeth that are primitively embossed.

The mask in *fig. a,* 6 inches high, is hammered out of very thin gold, while that in *fig. b* is made of base silver. The latter, found among the unpublished treasures of the British Museum, is extraordinary, not only in design but because its accompanying materials are still intact. It is made up on quite different lines from the piece beside it. The eyes represent monkey heads, lending it especial interest. Feathers denoting a beard offer proof of the importance of the personage, for beards were allowed only rulers, high priests, and chiefs. A brocaded or embroidered band frames the mask and once served to bind it to the mummy pack.

Veritable statuary is presented on *Pl. 204,* shaped with a beguiling blend of naïveté and realism. *Fig. a* is a silver alpaca of Inca style, 12 inches high. Plain surfaces are used for the head, but the rest of the animal is fashioned from a sheet of metal hammered in corduroy welts to convey the impression of its long woolly coat and even the contours of its body beneath. Its pose is natural and quiet; its realism, accentuated by the disdainful expression of its face, one of the beast's characteristics.

The small figures in the group (*fig. b*) come from the Titicaca region. The man and woman are cast in solid silver and decorated with inlaid golden bands and eyeballs. Their postures are uniform, with only the heads showing a slight difference. He wears earplugs and a high headdress; she is distinguished by long hair that is parted in the middle and falls over the back. The silver llama, about 9 inches high, is cast in several pieces and soldered together. In some cases, as many as ten to thirteen separate parts were used to make up such a figure. The tips of the cleft hoof and the scalloped edging of the blanket are of gold, while the blanket itself was inlaid, probably with turquoise or some other semiprecious stones to give the ground tone.

In *fig. c,* a copper statuette 4¼ inches high from near Cuzco, the humorous element is introduced, more frequent in Andean art than in Middle American.

A little hunchback figure is depicted, clinging to the back of a llama who seems to endure him with reluctance. The animal's legs, caught in slow motion, add to the realism of the portrayal.

An alpaca or guanaco, about 4½ inches high, is presented in *fig. d.* The piece would seem to have been cast by a worker of considerable experience, for the silver alloy of the body and the gold of the head are beautifully joined. In contrast to the animal above it, the pose is lively, with its turned neck, bent knees, and raised forefoot all suggesting motion.

The medieval peoples of the Andean Area had such a highly developed sense of decoration that they ornamented even their tools with human and animal figures in a way which would not occur to us with our utilitarian approach. These pieces radiate the same charm that marks some of the pottery and also show the enjoyment of these peoples in their implements, partners in their craft.

A bronze knife is pictured on *Pl. 205, fig. a,* with a golden bird, probably a flamingo, perched on one end and a serpent crawling along the back of the blade, its reared head especially clear. The total length of the piece is 5½ inches. The blade is very thin along the cutting edge and at the point and must once have been quite sharp. Both serpent and bird were cast separately, the snake being welded to the blade, while the bird, of high-grade gold, was set into a socket in the end of the handle. It is believed that the working of bronze originated in the Classic Tiahuanaco Period and was introduced to the coast with the spread of that culture. In some cases the natural material appears to have been used, in others there is evidence of alloying.[10] In this connection, it is interesting to note that a large sheet of tin was discovered at Machu Picchu.

Close to the first piece in idea and execution is another unusual knife (*fig. c*), only 5 inches long, which was found by Dr. Bingham on his expedition to Machu Picchu. Humor and keen observation are manifest in the attitude of the boy as he lies on his stomach in his peaked cap and short tunic, waving his legs and dangling a large fish on the end of a thick rope.

The same qualities are apparent in the bronze chopper with a man and llama on the top of the handle (*fig. b*). Although corrosion has blurred the details, the piece gives a good idea of the originality used in the decoration of these implements.

It will be noted that some little figures on these bronzes have a practical application: the pointed ends could be used as awls for boring; the flattened surfaces, as adzes; the rounded parts perhaps for burnishing. All are probably Inca and late in date.

The bronze knife in *Pl. 206, fig. a* may have been used for cutting, scraping, and chopping. The shape of the blade recalls the Illimo ceremonial knife (see *Pl. 198*)—a form which is said to have persisted long after the Conquest. It has been compared to the Eskimo woman's knife. A llama head with a long neck forms the handle, 4½ inches high. Delicate inlay work, admirable from point of view of design as well as technique, decorates the piece, with the laconic drawing of the llama in the second square particularly worthy of mention.

Inlay work on a larger scale is seen in *fig. e,* a staff head of bronze, 3⅝ inches high, representing a bird. Fashioned in the shape of an adze and decorated with stripes of copper and silver, it presents a skillful blending of the practical and ornamental. The parallel strips of metal by no means give a naturalistic representation of a cormorant's feathers, but the idea of the colorful creature is nevertheless well conveyed. Its legs are executed in high relief. A handle, probably of wood, was attached.

Fig. b is a small bronze spoon, pictured here in its actual size. It may have been designed for handling valuable powder or medicine, or as a ceremonial gift. The chewing of coca leaves mixed with lime was a habit long-established in the Andean Area and the little implement may have been used for measuring a dose of this. The pointed beak and tail, however, suggest its association with a craft.

Fig. c is of special interest because it is said to have been found in El Salvador, although it is typical of the Andean Area. It may have traveled all this distance by trade, or it may be an imitation or copy of an Andean piece made somewhere along the route. As small as they are (the whole tool is only 2¾ inches long) and even in their corroded state, the figures of a parrot and monkey are clear.

The copper awl, or pin, with a rattle handle (*fig. d*) is about 5 inches long and might be of Chimu provenience. In the openwork all around the domed top small human figures are wrought in an ingenious pattern—an unusually fine bit of casting.

In *Pl. 207* we reach a high point in the metal-work of this area. With technical problems no longer a matter of concern and with totemistic representations stylized to a high degree, the objects approach very closely what we term *objets d'art.*

In *fig. a* is pictured a group of small gold articles of unknown provenience but Chavin in style. Superior workmanship is manifest in all of them. Each bead in the necklace is composed of one solid and one openwork band, which, in turning one against the other, brings an unusual play into the design. The two objects at the top of the plate are identified as scrapers of cosmetic oils. The left one, 3½ inches long, is decorated with a human figure seated on an openwork base and blowing a shell trumpet; the right one has a tiny bird on top. Both are hollow and are composed of several pieces.

Condor heads in good Chavin style (see *Pl. 197, fig. a*) are embossed on the disk on the right. Even more fluent, however, is the decoration on the other dishlike ornament with its bulging center. Here the sinuous and interlacing ribbons resolve themselves into a feline mask in the medallion (inverted in the photograph). Note the two snake heads that make up the lower jaw.

The group is the product of a civilized people; there is nothing vacillating about the work. Material, shapes, patterns, and figural ornaments are homogeneous, all of one culture that had the power and the time to digest everything here expressed into one artistic language.

The two shallow plates and the pitcher with a stirrup handle (*fig. b*) come from Huarmey Valley on the coast of Peru and are made of an alloy of 64 per cent gold, 30 per cent silver, and 6 per cent copper. The pitcher was fashioned from two semispherical parts and the stirrup section. It is decorated with an interlocking fish pattern, one favored in Chimu pottery and textiles and well adapted to a rounded surface. The eye dot is the only globular detail in an angular composition. The two plates, about 8 inches in diameter, are simple in shape and ideal in proportion. The slanting-Z element, interspersed with dots, suggests a writhing serpent body and attains staccato rhythm. But here, as in the case of the pitcher, the totemistic significance of the motifs has lost its vehemence and become primarily decorative in character. Probably made between 1300 and 1400, the forms are the result of the refinement of centuries.

As stated at the beginning of this chapter, it would appear that metal-working was first developed in or around the Andean Area. From here, certain pieces may have found their way into very distant regions where they fructified the local arts.

In *Pl. 208, fig. a* the golden breastplate, 5¼ inches in diameter, is said to have come from the highlands of Peru, although disks like these are actually more common in Ecuador and even farther north.[123] Stylistically it is classified as belonging to pre-Inca times, because of the resemblances to both Chavin and Tiahuanaco styles. The plaque, with its involved decoration, is not of high artistic quality, but the organization of its symbols into an apparent scheme gives good reason to argue that some kind of a system is involved in the piece. According to certain interpretations, the large face in the center represents the sun and the intricate characters on the rim stand for the various months of the year.[96] This is particularly noteworthy since the Andean Area is not known to have had any calendar comparable to the Maya or Mexican.

Interesting discussion centers about the gold disk in *fig. c.* It is said to have been found in a vaulted tomb near Zacualpa in the highlands of Guatemala under circumstances that would date the burial around the 10th century.[69] It can be seen that it bears some similarity to the foregoing piece, although in its crushed condition details are indistinct. Its style has been analyzed as combining elements of Chavin and Middle Chimu.[60] However, it has also been pointed out that it contains features of the Mexican Tlaloc, a circumstance that would suggest its manufacture nearer the place where it was found. It is 5 inches in diameter and shows another face when inverted. The eyes in the center are easily distinguished and the hanging tongues and the mouths, one wide with fangs and the other narrower with teeth, can be recognized after a moment's study. The rim is narrow and plain. Little calendrical content can be read into this second piece. The first plaque with its series of involved symbols would appear to antedate it.

Fig. b shows embossed silver ornaments from Cuzco, which may have been applied to mummy heads. The round one is considered an ear ornament; the almond-shaped one, 4⅞ inches in length, was perhaps for the eye. They are crudely executed with not too interesting patterns. On the second, two animals are roughly drawn in repoussé. Both are probably Inca, examples of a late and mass-producing culture.

More artistic deliberation can be discovered in the fragment in *fig. d,* taken from the same tomb at Zacualpa mentioned above. It is a piece of a small gold plaque, 3¼ inches in diameter, featuring a bird framed by a composite border design. The center and the rim seem to have been beaten out separately in two pieces, then welded together; the break follows the line of fusion. The design is very unusual. Dotted lines on metal-work are primarily a characteristic of the Chimu or their neighbors. The delineation of the bird, however, has no stylistic affiliation with any known culture; Dr. Lothrop recalls only designs on Managua-ware pottery from Nicaragua that might be said to resemble it.[69]

Animal representations of late cultures of the Andean Area are shown in *Pl. 209.* The gold beard-tongs, or tweezers (*fig. a*), is about 2½ inches high and from the Central Coast of Peru. In the droll and well-executed scene on top of the instrument, two monkeys sit nibbling, as if perched there only for a moment.

The gold disk (*fig. b*), perhaps an earplug, is about 2 inches in diameter and identified as Chimu. It shows a flock of monkeys encircling a central figure portrayed in the round. The intermingling arms and legs and the curling tails are used to the best advantage to create a decorative design.

A pair of humming birds decorates the gold ear ornament from the Ica region of southern Peru (*fig. c*). The piece is 1¾ inches in diameter and presents the subject in perfect three-dimensional plasticity. All the grace and volatility of these colorful creatures have been transmitted in this diminutive representation.

Fig. d, slightly enlarged as shown, doubtless had symbolic content. Its provenience is unknown. The condor head with its static strength of a totem is reminiscent of Tiahuanaco or Coast Tiahuanaco. But the realistic creeping attitude of the little amphibian suggests cultures north of the Inca realm. Birds, amphibians, and reptiles attracted generally great interest because of their affiliations with the sky and water. The ability to fly or to live under water always has had a fascination for the human. Its association with supernatural power is still more evident in the cultures of Ecuador, Colombia, and the Isthmus.

INTERLYING AREA

Although certain similarities in technique and ideology were spread over the Andean and Interlying areas, outspoken stylistic characteristics can be found in the different cultural regions that are clearly indicative of their locality.

An example of this is seen in the Bat-god (*Pl. 210, fig. a*), a figure strange to the iconography of Peru. The piece came from the Tola Islands in Esmeraldas, in the northwest corner of Ecuador. Quito, the capital city of this once independent nation, fell under the domination of the Incas for a time, and it is known that certain of its districts thereafter produced chiefly bronze tools for the Empire. There was no time for Inca influence to go deep, however, as the Conquest soon put an end to it. The culture of Ecuador seems to have been allied more closely with the north; the figure of the Bat-god extends from here through the Isthmian region and into lower Middle America (El Salvador and Honduras), where we have already seen it on pottery.

This piece records, in a cruder edition, the same technical achievement that we saw in the Andean Area. It is 9½ inches across and cut in the shape of the deity out of one piece of medium-thick sheet gold, with the details embossed. The outline of the wings is irregular, the rows of dots unevenly applied, and the sides unsymmetrical. The body is compressed and the legs are only indicated, doubtless deliberately, so as to throw full emphasis on the head. This part is executed with a definite feeling for the use of various planes. It was made separately and joined by soldering. A new manner of representation is revealed in the treatment of the eyes and nose. Although the face of the god is stiff and inarticulate, the plaque has the compactness and vigor of all true primitives.

The mask (*fig. b*), also from Esmeraldas, is made of bronze with a low tin content and is about 7½ inches long. The hollow eyes and mouth are unusual and add a fantastic touch. Two tusks protruding from the lower lip offset the human features. In impression, the piece recalls masks of modern Latin America.

Fig. c is a bronze disk, 13½ inches in diameter, from the Manabí district of Ecuador. In contrast to the plain bowl-shaped rim, the center carries an embossed face, hammered over a mold. The dotted lines seen in *fig. a* appear here in the headdress as a more organic part of the composition. Such pieces were probably used as breast ornaments, although it has been suggested that they were gongs.[54] While the material from Esmeraldas (see also *Pl. 151*) is stylistically quite distinct from the Peruvian, showing relationship with the north, that from Manabí has been linked with Peru. Both sites are presumably pre-Inca.[8]

The breastplate on *Pl. 211* offers a much riper example of the Bat-god concept. It is 13½ inches across and came from Esmeraldas. The bat head, thrust savagely toward the onlooker, was hammered out separately and joined to the beaten plate. Although the noseplug seems to pass through the septum, it was in reality two separate pieces soldered on either side. Embossed patterns, the meaning of which is unclear, ornament the background of the middle field. Four uniform human figures are placed on the sides, their large headdresses worked out with crude but decorative detail while embossed legs suggest their bodies.

A human face surmounted by a helmet-like headdress appears on the small gold plaque from Ecuador (*fig. b*), about 4 inches in diameter. The composite animal frieze on the rim is made up of bird and monkey elements, very decorative in their stylization.

While the Bat-god was represented in the two preceding plates, first with the contours of a body, then surrounded by a stylized abstract pattern, the head of the deity on *Pl. 212* seems almost subordinated to the elaborate independent decoration that surrounds it. This golden ornament is 14 inches across. The head in the center, even though somewhat modified, shows enough similarity to the other two to be identifiable. The strong plastic effect still prevails. It also was fashioned separately by hammering and stands out 1½ inches from the background, to which it was joined by a fine bit of soldering. Highly interesting is the middle section where four double-headed alligators—very animated, with their upturned snouts—appear in faultless repoussé. Dots and triangles represent the scales.[34] The embossed lines are attractive in themselves, with their alternating courses and lively changing shapes. The design has the appearance of quilted work of remarkably even quality. The outer edge of the breastplate is slit to represent feathers. Their plain surface, vibrating and shimmering, adds a new decorative variation, which makes the piece most striking in its artistic balance.

With Ecuador we leave the territory which could have received first-hand artistic impulses from the center of the Andean Area. In Colombia we shall notice not only the ideological change, perceptible in certain Ecuador pieces, but also utter differences in technique and construction, involving primarily cast objects, the manufacture of which was undoubtedly a later achievement than cold hammering and soldering.

A semicivilized concept is manifest in the gold ornaments in human shapes (*Pl. 213, fig. a*) from the region of the Chibcha people. This powerful tribe resided in the highlands of the Cordillera Oriente, one of the rich gold districts of Colombia, and resisted the Spaniards valiantly at the time of the Conquest. Isolated not only from attack but also from many outside cultural influences, they were inferior to the Incas in their social and artistic development. Their gold work and other minor arts reveal a mixture of individual traits with peripheral designs borrowed from neighboring cultures.

The five pieces in the middle of *fig. a,* which were probably fastened to robes, show a uniform technique. The center figure is about 5 inches high. The gold background cast in one flat piece was intended to represent the outlines of a human body considerably simplified; features and other elements were applied in gold wire where a suggestion of detail was deemed necessary and separate dangling ear pendants were attached by links. By comparing the posture of the three central figures with *Pl. 218, fig. c,* an obvious similarity will be noticed. This Chibcha type will appeal to the neo-primitives of our own day. The two flanking figures are solidly cast in an axe-shape, the blade section serving as lower half of the body and the heads and arms forming the top. This form could derive from earlier similar shapes in stone, which, indeed, might have served as the first positives for molds. (Compare *Pl. 237, fig. a.*)

The pre-Columbian peoples had a predilection for bells of various sorts, sometimes without clappers, sometimes with pebbles or pellets of clay inside them. Tinkling ornaments of shell or metal were frequently attached as a fringe to garments, as pendants on jewelry, or to the legs. The two gold bells in *fig. b,* the taller 2½ inches high, come from Colombia. They were cast, with the exception of certain wire decorations which may have been soldered to them. In the smaller, a tiny figure is seated on top of the bell; in the larger, the body of the animal serves as the bell-jar. The contrast of plain surface with twisted and composite wire decoration shows an advance over the Chibcha figures. Both are inarticulately crude in style, however, when compared with other Colombian ornaments.

A rare piece of gold work, said to have come from La Guaira, Venezuela, is pictured in *fig. c.* Although this region is outside our five areas and the archaeology of the country is only now beginning to be organized, this striking image should be included here as evidence of the widespread metallurgical knowledge below the Isthmus and as an example of still another style. The figurine stands about 5½ inches high. Cast parts are fused with hammered surfaces, and some of the lighter decorative elements, made up of coiled wire and nail-head shapes, may have been soldered on, while others were doubtless cast with the main body. The subject of the piece is an anthropomorphic figure with ferocious tusks and button-like eyes (discernible in the diamond sector directly over the teeth). An extravagant headdress is featured, with frondlike plumes and two stylized animal profiles on either side. Two solid beaks jut forward over the creature's forehead. It may be presumed that local stylistic elements mingle here with foreign motifs, already stereotyped when taken over.

All the flasks on *Pl. 214* are of gold and come from Colombia. The largest (*fig. a*), about 7½ inches high, shows a male figure embossed on one side and a female on the other. The shape of the vessel is pleasing, with the curving lines of the sides well balanced by the bulging bottom and heavier shoulders. No hesitancy is apparent in the execution of the neck, although it too was difficult to fashion. The form is living; the most static element is, perhaps, the fetish-like image in the center which changes the mood of the piece. We shall meet this rigid figure stepping out into the three dimensional (see *Pl. 218*); even then its ineloquence does not disappear.

The flask in *fig. b* is a variant of the one beside it. Instead of the concave line that serves to lighten the latter, this piece has convex sides, adding corresponding bulk, and an onion-shaped neck that harmonizes with the curves of the body. The composition of the human figure is more or less identical.

The two smaller flasks in *fig. c* likewise seem to have presented no problems to their makers. Even to our eyes they are perfect in their proportion, the shapes are civilized, and the execution is faultless. The piece at the left, about 4 inches high and in the form of a gourd, has a jovial rotundity suggesting the flesh of a living plant. It could have been suspended on a ribbon by the two loops on the sides. The flask on the right has absolutely no decoration and its surface is smoothed and burnished. Shaped with consideration, its contours bring to mind an almond or some delicate exotic fruit.

The Quimbaya people, who inhabited the region of Antioquia on the Cauca River in the northwestern part of Colombia, were among the most skillful gold workers of medieval America. Pure gold or gold alloyed with copper was used, and broad polished surfaces, enlivened by intricate relief work of coiled wire and neat braided bands, characterize their art.[70] It is noteworthy that no air bubbles are present in any of this cast work and that there is no evidence of a period of experimentation.

Pl. 215 and those following take us into a strange fantasy-world where human elements are blended with animal shapes and decorated with what appear to us abstract or geometric motifs.

The pendant (*fig. a*) is a rare specimen of craftsmanship, even among the works of the Quimbaya culture. The main part is only about 3 inches high, but the piece appears much larger because the bird heads extend for an inch and a half. The principal elements are strongly plastic, with all minor detail abbreviated. A human head and shoulders are easily distinguished, but all human likeness is dispensed with below, where the figure blends into twin bird bodies with sharply delineated heads and beaks. The elaborate headdress with its two bell-shaped ornaments and the winglike wire spirals on either side will be seen again on the next plate. There was apparently no intention even to suggest arms, and the hole in the chest is impossible to interpret realistically, although it is of value in balancing and lightening the design. A realistic tendency is again evident in the compact bodies of the birds, with which the human figure merges so smoothly that the point of fusion cannot be defined. Although the eyes protrude too far and no bird ever wore such a plaited "harness," it is just this part of the faultlessly cast pendant that needs no interpreter; so expressive is it that we accept it without question.

The same type of semicircular nose ring as that worn by the figure is shown in *figs. b* and *c,* 4 and 4¼ inches wide respectively. These come from Antioquia, where they seem to have been quite common. The rows of openwork, fashioned in a highly complicated technique, look as airy as if made in crochet but are quite solid to the touch. Remarkable continuity is observed in the composition. On comparing the two pieces, it is interesting to note that the creature on the top edge of the first has degenerated in the second to a mere zigzag.

A diminutive idol, 2½ inches high, with a head composed of stylized animal elements placed on a human body, is the subject of *Pl. 216, fig. a.* It was cast of gold in several pieces and reveals full command of the technique. The emphasis is laid on the ornamentation of the upper part and the face is almost submerged. However, a wedge-shaped alligator-like head is discernible with a grinning pointed mouth, on top of which, at the apex, is a tiny rounded snout and perhaps eyes close to either side. The two bell shapes noted on the preceding plate are still more prominent here, and similar wire coils sweep upward as if in an elongation of the mouth. The hands of the idol, the five fingers well defined, grasp ceremonial bars. Below the belt, plain flat sections are used to signify the legs, and a complete departure from realism is reached in the feet with their eight toes. The small piece shows unexpected deliberation in its composition. From the point of view of design, the smooth lower part with its flaring base counterbalances the bell-shaped ornaments on the top, and the broken elements are concentrated between them.

Further disintegration of the human figure is shown in *fig. b,* about 10 inches high, another Quimbaya gold breast ornament. The leg sections are now merely two vertical sheets of metal, and the feet, with no suggestion of stance, have become a single finlike appendage, with the toes a series of numerous incisions. Five birds are ranged across the breast on a gold scaffold, producing a second plane. On both ends of this support, conventionalized "flowers" of wire form a motif that appears also in *Pl. 218, fig. d.* The bell-shaped elements at the top are more pointed than in the idol beside it, and the two slender winglike compositions at either side narrow as they mount, thus augmenting the vertical effect. Their lines remind us of those in medieval European manuscripts where the Gothic tendency saturates even the angels' wings.

The transmutation of the central anthropomorphic figure into an abstraction is fully realized in the three pendants of Quimbaya type shown in *fig. c.* The tallest is about 10½ inches. Such ornaments must have been manufactured frequently, for a number of them have been found showing very slight deviations. This would help explain the high degree of formalism involved in them. All three examples illustrated here show to an identical degree the boiling down of naturalistic elements into flat, round, and coiling units. The headdress "bells" are no longer laid horizontally, but are tipped forward; the mounting "wings" have become tight cautious coils, and the wire elements are multiplied, with the topmost spiral the largest. Instead of arms with ceremonial bars as in *fig. a,* we find here only two sticks, like elephants' tusks, issuing from the center, and the fingers that grasp them are denoted with wires, sometimes five, sometimes only three to a side. Nose and eyes can be inferred in the thimble-shaped protrusion beneath the bells and the two screw-head shapes at either side of it. A zigzag pattern decorates the base in complete disregard of its derivation. The nose piece with its four spirals is a new element, as is also the double whorl below it, but all their number does not bring new charm to the whole.

The circle of conventionalization that started with the first figure on the plate is closed with these ornaments. Both *figs. b* and *c* branched out from the same idea, and which of them has more conventionalization depends on the evaluation accorded certain elements. Only by looking at *fig. a* can we trace faintly the impulses which fathered such pieces. It is worth noting that this type of ornament is conceivable only in metal, proof of the deep-rooted feeling these artisans had for the medium.

Fig. a on *Pl. 217* shows a knife-shaped pendant about 11 inches high from Popayan, Colombia, south of the Quimbaya region. It is made of an alloy base of gold, silver, and copper, with a thin plating of fine gold, the process of which is still problematic. The central anthropomorphic figure and the four small beaked creatures were cast by the lost-wax process and are hollow behind, while the thin knife blade below was probably hammered from cold metal. The variously executed sections were joined by soldering. A circular nose pendant and three bead necklaces decorate the main figure, whose body is outlined and divided by delicate beading. Its legs are short and out of proportion, the knees encircled by tight bands frequently met with in Colombian work (see next plate); the screwhead eyes are already familiar. The hanging mass of feathers on the headdress counterbalances the upward sweep of the knife blade, and the approaching finger tips of the main figure contrast with the outward-turned palms of the smaller ones. Tactile variation is furnished by the flat "bird-monkeys" and the finely executed geometrical pattern of the openwork nimbus. A heavy loop is soldered to the back for attachment.

This piece shows influence from both the north and south. The general idea of the figure above a curving knife blade recalls the Illimo knife of Peru (see *Pl. 198*), while the divided crest and the multiple fingers and toes—perhaps symbolizing supernatural power, as do the many arms of Hindu deities—suggest the work of Panama and Costa Rica. Its date would probably fall between the 11th and early 15th centuries.[16] In its general aspect the ornament is unique and presents a crystallization of the "primitive" that is exemplified in the more familiar African wood carvings. Nothing in this piece is completely realistic; elements of life, of fantasy, and abstractions combine in frozen flamboyancy.

In *figs. b* and *c* we have variants of the same theme, also from Colombia but on a lower artistic level in both composition and decorative effect. *Fig. b* introduces an amphibian element that we shall encounter more and more frequently as we proceed toward the north. In this piece the human face is square when compared with the V shape of *fig. a,* and the eyes and mouth are represented by depressions on the surface in contrast to the protruding elements of the larger piece. Wings replace the arms or forelegs, and the "knife" section is tapered down until it resembles a tail. The nose rings are identical, and the headdresses, especially in the inner geometric arc, show similar design.

In *fig. c* human characteristics again predominate, although the face or mask is strongly reminiscent of bird features. The openwork in the headdresses just seen has here been transferred to the blade, and the feathers are again more realistically portrayed than in the conventionalized presentation in *fig. b*.

Besides the general idea, all three pieces have in common the beaded trim which ornaments the body of each central figure. It conveys the most realistic suggestion on that one with amphibian qualities (*fig. b*). On the plate just preceding, we can trace the stylization of an anthropomorphic figure into abstraction; on this, we may be confronted with steps toward the personification of an idea, perhaps of the Crocodile-god.

The golden plaque on *Pl. 218, fig. a* bears a subtle relationship to the pendant from Popayan in the curving outline of the upper section and in the bird heads and tails with their perforations at the sides. It is well proportioned, with the broad base line successfully carrying the weight of the whole. The seven embossed figures, with headdresses little more than suggested by beaded aureoles, are uniform, but the central personage—who is leaning forward as if from a balcony—and the two just below him are represented in different attire. He wears a three-dimensional headdress somewhat similar to that of *fig. c* on this plate. There is a ring in his nose for an ornament that has disappeared, which, from the general design, may have extended into the blank space below. The two figures at either side wear headdresses in the form of birds that show marked similarity to the next piece. Cautious craftsmanship is seen in the small supporting sections, which, nearly unnoticed, strengthen the most fragile side parts. The hooks at the bottom may have served to affix it to another material or have held dangling pendants. Mention should be made of the plaited edging, outlining the entire plaque.

Interest is due the gold breastplate in *fig. b* for its rare subject matter—a tower with four birds of prey sitting on the top. It is about 6 inches high and is identified as coming from the Quimbaya region. A kind of artistic shorthand is employed to record the birds. Only the heads received real emphasis; the bodies are practically non-existent, and the claws are depicted in relief, artistically less powerful, although there would have been space for bringing in more details if desired. In this respect, the composition recalls the bird figures of *Pl. 215, fig. a.*

Fig. c is a gold figurine from Antioquia, done in the lost-wax technique of which the people in the Quimbaya region were such masters. It is 6 inches high and presents a female figure. She wears the tight knee and ankle bands that have been noted elsewhere and a crownlike headdress with two beak blades and wire spirals at either side. A large lunate pendant hangs by two rings from the nose, covering the lower part of her face, and two others, circular in shape, are affixed to the hands.

There is considerable resemblance between this figure and one 9 inches high shown in *fig. d.* This statuette wears a conical headdress, and the hands, which are in the same position, hold spirals of gold wire suggestive of flowers. The nose is pierced and doubtless once carried an ornament. Even if the proportions are not in accordance with our ideals of beauty, the body is young and vibrant; the shoulders and knees have the static elasticity of the prehistoric sculptures of other great early civilizations, and the slim waist would satisfy the fashion designer of our own day. As in so many South American representations, the legs are short.

Both pieces have the same tapering base which might have been attached to a staff or other similar object. Both have the qualities of an idol, emphasized by the presentation of a figure completely nude, with jewelry and ornaments. A discussion of the reasons why so many idols of prehistory are thus represented would require too great a digression here; however, it may be pointed out that their symbolism is connected with fertility rites and goes back to the earliest times of mankind.

The technique and artistry of the Quimbaya region reach their peak, perhaps, in such pieces as those reproduced on *Pl. 219*. The modesty of subject, the immediacy of the representation make them not only easily understood and enjoyed, but give an insight into the more relaxed moods of this people when they were not weighed down by a mystic-totemistic sorcery. Nothing conveys their inherent talent and keen nature observation so simply and with so much naïve charm as these pieces. Despite a certain stylization, which is apparent, all embody the spirit of life.

The gold staff head representing a pelican (*fig. a*) manifests lively realism and technical assurance. It is 5 inches high and was cast in several pieces, then soldered together. Eyes, beak, claws, and tail are fashioned skillfully and simply; neck and legs are static. As in all good sculpture, not all the elements have the same quality of motion. The openwork of the breast contrasts with the solid surfaces and makes the piece appear lighter in weight. Even the unevennesses of tone due to soldering seem to enhance its animation.

Fig. b is a golden staff head, about 8 inches long, from Monteria, Colombia. The five birds standing in a row on a latticed bar are humorously appealing. Heavy, weighing more than one pound, the piece nevertheless gives the impression of lightness: the birds are alert, as if about to take flight from a riddled crumbling log. The use of a lattice pattern for the base prevents this subordinate element from distracting from the focus of interest. From the technical as well as the plastic point of view the work is outstanding. It was made by the lost-wax process; the base and the lower lines of the bird on the extreme left show best the great skill essential to its execution. Both birds and base are hollow, yet so solidly cast that not one beak or section of the bar can be bent.

Two more staff heads are seen in *fig c,* executed in the same technique. In the diminutive dog, shown in actual size, there is a broader use of openwork.

METAL-WORK

The animal has a toylike charm, and its expression is droll and humorous. Still more humor is discernible in the human figure beside it. The little man is seated on a low chair, blowing on a trumpet—a common musical instrument throughout medieval America—and shaking a rattle with his right hand. His left arm is realistically modeled; it is part of a living body engaged in making music. The sense of tone is rarely present in representations of musicians of any age or region, but this little man seems surrounded by the din he is creating. The decorative bands around the crown and on the edge of the brim of his broad hat are clearly marked, corroborating the description of the earliest Spanish writers regarding the picturesque headgear of the natives.

These are some of the rare pieces of pre-Columbian metal-work completely plastic in radiation, released from any remnant of two-dimensional tradition which cut its shapes from sheets of metal.

The jewelry and metal trappings of chiefs included far more impressive objects than the golden staff heads just shown; headgear, more ornamental than protective, was also made of the precious metal. The crown from Antioquia (*Pl. 220, fig. a*), 6 inches high, was cut from a sheet of beaten gold. It is rare, not only because of its perfect state of preservation, but also because it has more decoration than most of the extant crowns. An embossed geometric pattern covers much of the surface, but the feature of the piece is the concise cut-out representation of a soaring condor. Little scrolls moving upward from the outspread wings add to the feeling of height.

Headgear of considerably greater weight (over twelve ounces) is pictured in the massive gold helmet from the Quimbaya culture (*fig. b*). It was fashioned in semispherical form, full-size and shaped for a human head, with repoussé decorations hammered in afterwards. Such gold helmets from pre-Columbian America are infrequent and most of them bear convulsive animal or geometric patterns. This casque is a rarity on account of the single female figure embossed upon one side. It is a crude representation to our eyes, but there is no denying that it is well placed within the space accorded it and the design shows vigor. The hammered dots and lines curving away from the head may be the conventionalization of a great headdress extending across the upper field and ending on the opposite side of the piece. This conjecture is supported by the position of the hands, which appear to be clasping the edges of the huge ornament. (Compare *Pl. 148, fig. e*.)

Headbands, crowns, and helmets of solid gold have been found in Peru,

Ecuador, Colombia, and Panama; north of this, there is no record of this type of headgear. In Mexico, the inventories of the loot at the time of the Conquest mention wooden helmets, gilt-edged or sheathed in gold and combined with feather-work and stone mosaic.[70]

Another gold helmet, about 4¾ inches high and weighing eleven ounces, is pictured on *Pl. 221, fig. a.* It comes from Darien, Panama. The surface of beaten gold is divided into four equal fields, each embossed with a double-headed crocodile. So precisely is the subject pattern repeated that we may presume its application by the use of a cliché. The realistic impression of the amphibians is offset by a second head where the tail should be.

That there was no intention of producing a record true to life in these helmets is doubly clear in the next piece (*fig. b*), from Coclé, Panama. It is made of thin beaten gold and weighs slightly less than eight ounces. Here the entire surface is covered with a highly stylized pattern of similar ideological content, showing repetitions of the double-headed Crocodile-god, one in the center of the photograph and two others on the sides. The tendency was to cover all available space. Human, reptile, and geometric elements are condensed, and in the restless crowded texture we discern mainly the vibration of a positive decorative talent. Note the perforations around the edge for sewing in a lining.[70]

Panama and Costa Rica used techniques similar to those of Colombia, but their art shows definite local motifs. In studying stylistic divergences, however, it should not be forgotten that until 1903 the territory known today as Panama formed a part of Colombia. Throughout the Isthmian region, the same veneration was bestowed on crocodiles and alligators that rattlesnakes received in the Maya and Mexican areas. The aborigines fought them and made use of their bodies according to the traditions of the land; but they also incorporated them into their fantasy-world, elevating them to the symbol of a god. We find them partly realistic, partly stylized, embossed in relief in curious patterns, or, as they appear on this plate, cast in three dimensions. Other reptiles, such as frogs, lizards, and turtles also occur frequently.

Pl. 222, fig. a, about 4¼ inches long, is now in the Museo Nacional at San José, Costa Rica. It is made of eighteen-carat gold and weighs about two ounces.[65] In style it appears to be an offshoot of the Chiriqui culture. The alligator or crocodile is pictured here quite realistically, with human prey; the man's head with earplugs, his body, arms, and legs are clearly depicted. As will be seen, this rare presentation may furnish a clue to problematic elements in many of these pendants.

The gold alligator from Coclé (*fig. c*) is 7 inches long and quite massive. It was cast in one piece with an open channel underneath that held the core around which the molten metal was poured. Small eyes on the under side show that, heavy as it is, it was attached to another material. The body of the creature, with its bulging eyes and creeping posture, is quite naturalistically observed; there are even certain suggestions of muscular build-up. On the other hand, the tail, with its divided curling flukes and the bars and rings on either side, is completely unrealistic. The same is true of the object carried in the reptile's mouth, which is probably a highly conventionalized human body. Upon comparing it with the piece above, we can discern the great loops of the earplugs; the element beside them may represent a waving arm, and the toothed edge in front, the feet, with the pattern then doubled in mirror fashion for the sake of symmetry.

The twin reptiles in *fig. d,* about 3½ inches long, are of gold and also come from Coclé. The protruding eyes, sharp bared teeth, springy elastic legs require no explanation; they testify to the talent of the goldsmith who wrought the piece. Cuneiform depressions along the bodies represent the markings of the reptiles. Their curling tails have decorative effect, although the position is not natural.

We should compare the objects in their mouths with those in *figs. a* and *c* to see how much change could occur in one motif within the frame of a single idea. Considerable difference can also be noted in the treatment of the tails and scaly surfaces of their bodies. Such a combination of good naturalism with strange symbolism is one of the main characteristics of medieval American art and complicates not only the problem of interpretation but the analysis of style as well.

The shark pendant (*fig. b*) comes from Chiriqui, Panama. It is about 4 inches long and was cast in one piece. Of brilliant yellow gold, it reveals a smoothness and elegance that are extraordinary, even among the many other faultless pieces from this region. In the lively representation of the body even the glutinous quality of the skin can be felt. The rings at the ends are for suspension.

The two embossed gold plaques from Coclé on *Pl. 223* show a mastery in technique and stylization such as we have not met since certain early cultures of the Andean Area.

In *fig. a,* about 8 inches in diameter, there is a similarity in build-up—even though the decorative effect is different—to gold work from Chavin, Lambayeque, and, to some extent, Tiahuanaco. These older pieces are perhaps quieter in their stylization, more suave in linear conduct—more civilized, one might say; in the specimens from Coclé, the expression is brought out with brutality, a cruder plasticity, but certainly with primeval vigor. It is interesting to find the same ground idea depicted in *fig. a* as in the Gateway of the Sun at Tiahuanaco (see *Pl. 46*), the Chavin stone (see *Pl. 99, fig. b*), or the gold plaques of Lambayeque (see *Pl. 195*). The figure in the Coclé piece has the same frontal pose, with arms outstretched, each holding a staff; the elaborateness of the headdress, the emphasis on the belt which resolves into a fantastic animal on either side, the exaggerated teeth, and the decorative presentation of the feet all register a certain relationship. Technical aptitude is shown in the extraneous elements added for decoration, in the palms, the feet, and the grooved bodies of the monsters, for instance. All contours are sharp and angular in contrast to the rounded corduroy effect of Lambayeque work.

Still more enjoyment in the command over the material is visible in the other gold disk (*fig. b*). This one is slightly larger and shows two identically gesticulating figures with bodies more or less human and heads like birds. The extravagant belts that sweep to the edge of the piece are suggestive of the flowing plumes of a tail and an instance of the exuberance in technique, for the same idea could have been conveyed much more simply. In spite of a certain crudeness in the delineation, the power and movement in the design are immediately sensed.

Both culturally and artistically, much is unbalanced in the Interlying Area, but for this very reason these examples are especially important to our survey as artistic milestones on the way up from the south. Because their language is so sharply minted, it is easier for us to approach through them the works of other cultures whose expression is less articulate.

The same vigor and the same enjoyment in ever-changing plastic surfaces, already met in larger specimens of Panama, are even more apparent in the jewelry shown on *Pl. 224,* all from Coclé.

The first gold pendant (*fig. a*), 2 inches long, is fashioned in the shape of an insect. Its head and thorax are cast in gold; the abdominal part is made up of light translucent quartz. Two hooks for suspension are at the tip. The casting and handling of such small and delicate details may be regarded as one of the triumphs of the lost-wax process.

Fig. b is a gold cuff that was found on the arm of a skeleton in one of the richer graves at Sitio Conte in the Coclé region. It is of thin sheet metal, and the pattern, hammered in over a cliché, shows two crocodiles, each with a bird perched on its tail. The hind legs of the amphibians are omitted, but the fore-feet recall in their gesture the second gold plaque on the preceding plate. The headdress, too, and the sharp contours and decorative depressions of the general pattern show similarity. Cuffs of gold, silver, and copper are not common in medieval America but they have a widespread distribution.[70]

The gold pendant with four curly-tailed animals (*fig. c*)—probably alligator cubs—measures only about 2½ inches in length. Miniature animals with elongated and curling tails were quite common in Panama and have been found made of agate also. Here the alert little creatures are placed side by side, coalesced in such a way that they stand on a total of only ten legs, the front five of which are clearly visible in the photograph. The pendant was cast as a unit, and part of the clay mold still adheres to the under side.

The combination of two or more different materials in one piece is always a sign of superior workmanship—when skill has leisure to play with its medium. In medieval Europe ivory, rock crystal, and mother-of-pearl were framed with metal by Benvenuto Cellini and his followers. The combination of metal and semiprecious stones, such as serpentine and opal, besides the quartz and agate already mentioned, appears frequently in the jewelry and other small objects of the Interlying Area. *Fig. d* shows an impressive pendant of solid gold, 4¼ inches long, representing a fantasy animal whose body is a fine dark emerald. In this unusual and fascinating piece, the same skill already observed is apparent, perhaps to an even higher degree. Stylized elements, like the bifurcated tongue, are combined with such expressive naturalistic details as the springy legs, and virtuose embellishments—products of pure fancy—are added, such as the "cog-wheel" at the end of the tail and the dangling pendants at the back.

Of the four objects on this plate, three were cast, one was hammered, and two of them were fashioned in combination with precious stones—no mean achievement for a semicivilized people.

Casting reached such perfection and routine on the Isthmus that metal-work complicated in both structure and decoration was turned out as a matter of course. And if these products are not especially appealing to our eye, the reason should be sought in the obscurity of the concept rather than in any technical ineptitude.

Pl. 225, fig. a is not only interesting as a piece but also because of its material. It was made of an alloy of gold and much copper, a mixture now generally called *tumbaga* (from the Malay word for copper) and easier to handle than gold alone. As gold was more plentiful than copper in these regions, the combination must have resulted from considerable experience in working with the metals and observing their durability. The gilded *tumbaga* pendant shown here is about 5 inches wide and 3½ high. After seeing animals in groups of two and four, we now have two warriors, mirror images, one of the other, standing with bowed heads side by side, their toes clinging to a thin metal rod. They wear conical caps upon their heads and over their chests hang necklaces of several strands. Across the body of each runs a braided "bandoleer," which supports at the hip a tiny bird. One hand grasps a paddle-shaped club; the other, a bundle of spears. The twin figures are joined at the shoulders by three small knobs, from which, suspended by a braided cord, hangs a human head. Originally two other heads (the left one is broken off) hung from the lower ends of their weapons. The statuette evidently depicts the return of victorious warriors, carrying their battle trophies. There is doubt as to whether this type of work originated in this area; compare it with the stone carving of the "dual officiants" (see *Pl. 97, fig. d*).

The next illustration (*fig. b*) shows a somewhat similar gold pendant that is said to have come from Colombia. It is about 4 inches wide and presents an octette of flageolet players—twin major figures and six smaller editions of the same type. Whether they are human or animal cannot be determined; their posture is that of men, but their faces and clumsy feet are rather animal-like. Considering the many open spaces between the constituent elements, the whole piece is remarkably compact.

Fig. c, from Costa Rica, is an interesting parallel to the first piece. Here the twin figures walk hand in hand. There is a suggestion of the war clubs in the bars at the sides; on the other hand, the wire coils that decorate the heads and form the hands connect them also with *fig. b*.

The east coast of Costa Rica was first discovered by Christopher Columbus on his fourth and last voyage. Port Limon lies today on the bay in which the Admiral's exhausted men rested and repaired their ships in 1502. The Indians were not hostile toward the newcomers, but rather were disposed to barter their goods; they even made presents to the Spaniards of fruit, animals, and gold ornaments. The name "rich coast" was thus given to Costa Rica with reason, for, when compared with those first touched by the Spanish ships, it was a country with an abundance of metal objects. The inhabitants are reported to have known the arts of weaving and casting gold. They were clever wood and stone carvers and no mean potters.

An interesting compositeness is evident in the next specimen from this region (*Pl. 226, fig. a*), a gold pendant about 4 inches high that undoubtedly shows a blend of local and imported ideas. At least three different creatures are incorporated in this symbolic piece: the main motif is a condor with flattened wings and tail; two grinning reptilian heads branch to right and left, and a heavy bovine animal gazes out from the breast. The use of smooth cast surfaces is striking, revealing a sure feeling for the medium and a grasp of the technique.

Beside this pendant we show one typical of the Quimbaya district of Colombia (*fig. b*) to indicate how far the threads of influence stretched. Some affinity to the Bat-god (see *Pl. 210, fig. a*) is evident in the squat body with drawn-up legs posed between the outspread wings, and a certain relationship with the plaque in *Pl. 218, fig. a* can be discerned in the rounded sections at the top, the broad flat base, and the cut-out bird heads at the sides. At the same time a similarity of idea between the two figures on this plate will be noticed, even though they come from widely separated regions. This likeness extends not only to the form but also to the build-up of the central bird head, presented in the round with profile silhouettes on either side. Each, however, speaks its own language. The fine stylization and superior workmanship in the second let us forget for the moment to delve for the complex idea behind it, while in the first, a less-refined execution and bolder delineation emphasize its puzzling qualities.

The cast gold figurine, 2¾ inches high and from Panama (*fig. c*), shows a little man carrying a pipe or blowgun in his left hand and in his right an object as yet undefined. Reptile heads seem to be represented in the protruding elements of his headdress. Flattened surfaces, such as those in the arms and feet, appear frequently also in Costa Rican work, but it is undecided where this manner originated. It contrasts effectively with the rounded body and head, bringing out the sheen of the metal. The braided headband and twisted belt likewise add variety to the composition. The hands are interestingly stylized.

The gold rattle or bell in the shape of a seated man (*fig. d*), shown in actual size, comes from Costa Rica. Its utilitarian purpose prescribed the bulky shape. One feels, nevertheless, more life in this figure than in the little man just described; even a touch of humor is apparent. The piece was cast in several parts and one line of fusion is visible at the belt.

MAYA AND MEXICAN AREAS

Nicaragua, Honduras, El Salvador, and Guatemala are poorer in metal objects than the areas just discussed. The gold figurines and ornaments that have been taken from graves here, particularly those dated from the 13th century on, bear, for the most part, characteristics of Costa Rica, Panama, and Colombia.

Figs. b and *c* on *Pl. 227* are cast copper bells found in the Maya Area. Both have a fine definite tone, proof of good clean casting. *Fig. b,* a little over 3 inches high, comes from Honduras. It has a grotesque face as decoration, with the slit of the bell serving as a mouth, through which the clapper, a pebble or clay pellet, may be seen. Excellent use was made of the available surface. The same drollness pervades the turkey bell (*fig. c*). This piece was found in British Honduras, near the border of Guatemala, and is also about 3 inches high. There is a naturalistic quality about the representation that can be universally understood, although the details are not carried out all over the piece.

The copper mask in *fig. a,* about 5½ inches high, was identified as belonging to the Tarascan culture of Mexico. Note the vast difference between this and the one of bronze from Ecuador (see *Pl. 210, fig. b*). In the latter, the expression is rather grotesque, the work bold and rough; here a symbol of death is cast with such finesse that it appears modeled. The subject is Xipe-Totec, God of the Flayed. His closed eyes and sagging mouth, the two braided lines running down the face to hold up the skin of the cheeks produce a remarkable intensity. The piece has something in its plastic make-up of an early Romanesque sculpture.

The Codex Mendoza (see *Pl. 269*) offers pictorial evidence that gold formed a part of the yearly tribute paid by the southern provinces of medieval Mexico to the Aztec kings. Names of the towns levied and the quantities exacted are recorded in glyphic signs, a list which was of great assistance to the progress of Cortés during the Conquest. The gold was delivered in gourds or cane tubes, or cast into bars. Manufactured articles in the Codex Mendoza include diadems, headbands, bells, breast ornaments, earplugs, labrets, and round beads.[121] Diaz records that gold, silver, and other metals, as well as precious stones and jewelry, were sold daily in the great market at Tenochtitlan. The Aztec goldsmiths' center was a town not far from the capital and the artisans were famed throughout Mexico. One might say that the intervening goldless region between Mexico and the south served as an insulator and a refining filter as far as stylistic influences are concerned. More problematic is the acquirement of the technical knowledge that enabled these people to produce autochthonous shapes in metal on a par with their other arts that were developed over a far longer period.

It is in the region around Oaxaca that the most elaborate pieces of jewelry in the Western Hemisphere have been excavated. Nearly a thousand miles by airline from the nearest archaeologically established metal-working center (Costa Rica), the Zapotec and Mixtec inhabitants of this section made use of all the techniques known to the southern areas, applying them in a vigorous and individual manner, and invented new forms.

The gold ring from Oaxaca (*Pl. 228, fig. a*) is an example not only of virtuosity in casting but also of increasing refinement in artistic taste. At its greatest length it is about 2½ inches, slightly less than pictured. In the body of the ring, whorls and beading have been combined against a solid background. The ornament on the shield, expertly cast in separate parts and soldered to the base, represents a descending eagle, symbol of the setting sun, bearing in its beak the glyph meaning "precious" or "jade." Five minute drop-shaped bells, which tinkle as they strike one another, hang from the pendant and two more dangle from the bird's outspread wings, making the piece sprightly. The cast wire work of the wings and feathers above the head has been individualized and brought to a higher artistic level than we have met before. When compared to the much cruder specimen that follows, this work shows obvious development.

The copper ring, about 1¼ inches high (*fig. b*), is said to have been found near the border of El Salvador and Guatemala. It was made by the same technique as *fig. a,* but there is little comparison. The difference may be accounted for in part in the 500-odd miles that stretch between the places where the two pieces were found. The cruder material is also partly responsible, and the layout of the features would indicate a lower level of craftsmanship. Its chief interest lies in its material and in the unique design.

A gold ring from Oaxaca (*fig. c*), about 1 inch high, shows the most delicate execution in this group. The narrow lacelike band is composed of two double wires that frame a series of the ∽ motif. A design of the feathered serpent, daringly unconfined by a rim, replaces the shield, and a tortuous movement pervades the entire piece.

The ring in *fig. d,* only seven-tenths of an inch in diameter, is of a type quite usual in Oaxaca. It imitates filigree but was produced by the lost-wax process. The fashioning of the model in wax gave opportunity for inventive play with curving threads and globules. In the tiara-like construction a series of double loops, very characteristic of Mexican gold work, is used to form a glyph, and another symbol is applied directly below it.

Fig. e, the last of the rings, is among the most exquisite examples of this technique. It is about 1 inch high and belongs to the Oaxaca type. In the illustration it is shown in a horizontal position to bring out the design more clearly. After a moment of observation, we recognize the contours of a human profile at the right edge. The large nose and mouth and the eye appear first, then the earplug and headdress. After that, it is easy to find two hands nearer the center of the ring, one extended in a normal position as if in a gesture, the other placed above the head for the sake of symmetry. Four fingers are clearly executed, with even the nails suggested by small globules, and the thumbs, widely separated from the rest of the hand, hold the central panel. Dots are also used to delineate ornaments on both wrists, as frame for the headdress, and on purely decorative sections of the ring. The various framing motifs are distributed in such a way that they strengthen the center.

Our approach to the crowns, helmets, and rings of medieval America is made easier by the fact that we are accustomed to these shapes in our own civilization. But when it comes to earplugs, lipplugs, and noseplugs, we are hindered in our appreciation by unfamiliarity with their use. Nevertheless, many of these pieces are works of art and excellently contrived from a technical point of view.

The labret, or lipplug, from Oaxaca (*Pl. 229, fig. a*) measures about 2½ inches, including the tongue. It represents a serpent head, at the base of which is a plain section that was inserted into a slit in the under lip. Smooth solid surfaces have been well used. Twisted wire and series of globules, characteristics of Zapotec-Mixtec work, ornament the top of the head.

The smaller lipplug below it (*fig. c*) also comes from the Oaxaca region. Here again appears a serpent with outlashing tongue. There are less broken surfaces than in the first example. Each detail is outlined with a fine ridge. This ensemble play of wavy lines gives not only a higher artistic touch to the piece, but removes it deeper into the world of fantasy. Delicate perforated work adorns the outer edge of the plug proper.

Fig. b shows a plain headband and a feather of gold from Oaxaca. The diadem is oval in shape, with the rim wider in front than in the back. The feather, a little more than 13 inches long, carries a loose design in repoussé. Both objects were found together and the feather may have been worn affixed to the headband. The simplicity which permeates these pieces is not without subtlety. It would seem to be more characteristic of Chimu culture than of the area in which the articles were found.[60]

In *fig. d* a piece from the famous treasure is shown that was discovered in 1932 in the Mixtec burial of Tomb 7 at Monte Alban. This sepulchre contained nine skeletons decked in all the pomp and riches due kings or high priests and yielded over five hundred objects. The bracelet is of normal size and executed, like so many of those here considered, in repoussé. Two endlessly intertwining serpentine lines make up the pattern, with less protruding dots, doubtless eyes, between the convolutions. These are the same decorative elements that appear in the Chimu "plates" (see *Pl. 207, fig. b*), but are used here with greater force and assurance. The gold is of an amazing thinness and shows neither breaks nor cracks, proof of excellent workmanship.

Every one who enjoys jewelry will immediately grasp the beauty of the necklaces shown on *Pl. 230*. The first (*fig. a*) is of gold and from Tomb 7. Each section is about 2½ inches long. Jaguar teeth are represented in the corrugated units at the top,[23] and a moment's consideration of the entire row of thirty-nine will demonstrate how well the grinding jaw is suggested. It will be recalled that in the art of this area especially a warrior's head usually protrudes from the gaping jaws of an animal headdress. The loops and rings are precisely executed and divide with their faultless line the smooth surfaces. Each bell is slit and tinkles softly when it strikes its neighbor.

Fig. b shows a necklace of Toltec workmanship found near Texcoco. Fashioned of an alloy of silver and copper, it is much corroded and appears dull beside the shining gold of the others. However, the beautiful graduation of the beads justifies its presentation here. They run from about the size of a pea to that of a hickory nut, more than an inch in diameter, with the largest cast in two halves, then soldered together. All are hollow and astonishingly thin.

Another of the treasures from Tomb 7 is the gold necklace in *fig. c*. It is designed on the same general plan as the first but has enough individuality to be included beside it. Instead of the flat tier of golden jaguar teeth, here there is a row of plain round beads, between which pear-shaped drops are strung. From these, without an intervening element, hangs a smaller bell. Twenty-eight of the pendants are uniform, while in the three in the center the lower bells are smaller. In comparing the two necklaces, both a consistency in type and a divergence in detail will be noted, evidence again of the nuances the goldsmith was capable of creating.

The gold pectoral on *Pl. 231, fig. a* also comes from Tomb 7. It measures 4½ inches in height and weighs a little more than three ounces. While it looks as if it were fashioned with wires in filigree technique, it was actually produced by the lost-wax process. The piece is usually called the "Jaguar-Knight." He probably represents the Death-god, wearing a buccal mask in the form of a jaw-bone, held in place by a double cord that passes under his nose. Above the fore-head is a helmet, formed by a blend of jaguar and serpent heads and surmounted by feathers and round medallions which were of plaited paper. Two serpent heads protrude from his large earplugs. Bells are attached to the lowest strand of the necklace, and a pendant features an eagle swooping downward with out-spread wings. In connection with this motif, it is interesting to remember that the descending eagle symbolized the west, the point of the setting sun, or the end of life.

The neck of the deity rises out of a flat plaque instead of a body, on which glyphs are outlined in the same technique that is used in the headdress. These are far from symmetrical in their linear distribution, but nevertheless fulfill a decorative purpose. Dr. Caso believes that the piece commemorates an impor-tant mythological or historical event.[25] The whole portrayal of the god attacks us immediately through its expressive presentation of the power of death.

A pectoral from Costa Rica is shown in way of comparison in *fig. c*. Though here the human element is practically non-existent, certain details of the two bear relationship, while others, namely, the crescent "bird heads" at either side of the head and feet of the main figure, as well as its numerous toes, hark back to the south of Panama.

The gold statuette (*fig. b*) is supposedly a portrait of Tizoc, who stood at the head of the Aztecs from 1481 to 1486. It is believed to have been a gift from him to a contemporary lord at Texcoco, where the piece was found. The figure is 3½ inches high, and its gold content is said to be over twenty carats.[128]

If it is a portrait, we certainly do not discover many individual characteris-tics in it. The stocky figure sits in a tight pose. This position would simplify the shape for casting; but the same squatness occurs also in pictorial representa-tions of the king where such technical considerations would not influence the delineation. He wears the royal crown decorated with plumes. A slender tubu-lar object adorns his nose and a lipplug (see *Pl. 229*) protrudes from his chin. A string of large beads arranged on his chest ends in a circular disk, similar to the one shown on *Pl. 234, fig. a,* but with a top piece added. Studded bracelets and anklets decorate the arms and legs, and in his right hand he holds a baton of command.

In the back, extending over the hair, crown, and feather headdress, is the symbol of a wounded or bleeding leg. This is Tizoc's glyphic identification and always accompanies his figure in the several codices and stone carvings where he appears. His name is a combination of *zoc*, "bled," with the prefix *ti,* signifying "the bled one." Interwoven in a wire-work design on the back, which gives the impression of a mantle, is the date glyph for 1481, conforming with the year of the election and elevation of the ruler. He was the seventh in line of the Aztec dynasty, of which Montezuma II, ruler at the time of Cortés's arrival, was the ninth.

From an artistic point of view, the piece has not the exuberance characteristic of Zapotec-Mixtec gold work. It speaks stylistically a different language, although it was made by the identical technique that we have seen used so profusely in the companion pieces on this plate. A rare survivor of gold work from the inner circle of the Aztec Empire, it helps us visualize the quality of the golden hoard that disappeared in the Conquest.

With the gold pendant on *Pl. 232,* also discovered in fabulous Tomb 7, we reach the highest achievement of the goldsmith's art in medieval America. It is 8½ inches long and was probably used as a pectoral. Several pendants exist, discovered earlier than this one, that might be regarded as forerunners or provincial examples of the same idea; one of these has a plaque with figural content at the top and three simple loops holding bells. However, they contain fewer elements than the piece illustrated and are far inferior to it in execution. All of them are said to have come from the Tehuantepec region, more than one hundred fifty miles south of Monte Alban, and are allegedly of Zapotec manufacture,[121] while this one, from Tomb 7, is of Mixtec origin according to Dr. Caso's classification.

This masterpiece, produced by the primitive implements of the pre-Columbian goldsmiths, could not be surpassed, either in design or in technique, by the use of modern equipment. It is built up of seven units, each different in shape and content, loosely connected by links and separated far enough so that each element is accorded the emphasis due it. There is no repetition—rather a sequence, planned with unparalleled artistic deliberation. The angular plaque at the top, massive in background and largest of all the sections, is followed by a disk, also with a massive back. The third part is openwork in a squarish frame, and the fourth is made with the same technique within a narrower space. Next come four "cockades" with very little openwork, followed by four hollow balls. Bells in elongated drop form constitute the seventh element, providing an effective contrast to the solid top piece.

In spite of the general horizontal trend in the design of each of the first four sections, there are always connecting lines that direct the eye on to the next. The progressive loosening of the respective parts, from the angular plaque to the dangling bells, is so subtle that the vibrancy of the piece can be felt, even though it is fastened to the black velvet holder in the museum.

The pectoral embodies an indigenous cosmic representation.[25] The rather macabre ball game of the gods across a grinning skull at the top is the glyphic presentation of the nocturnal heaven with stars. On the second section is the sun disk, and below it is the moon, symbolized by the "flint knife." Finally, the earth-monster is shown, with open jaws, fangs, and a forked tongue. Feathers—ceremonial ornamentation—are represented by the cockades, and the bells at the bottom are symbols of the music of life.

The gold mask of the god Xipe-Totec (*fig. b*) is also one of the finds from Tomb 7. It measures nearly 3 inches in height and weighs slightly more than three ounces. Its precise use is uncertain; it may have served as a belt buckle or a clasp to fasten the hair, or even as an ornament on a necklace. Xipe-Totec, as has been mentioned under sculpture, is the God of the Spring. But, since the skin he wears is also similar to the thin sheet of gold which jewelers used to cover wooden objects, he was also regarded as God of the Jewelers. Drooping eyelids and a sagging mouth, shapeless without indication of lips, express the flabbiness of the flayed skin. The four cords on each side of the head that served to hold the skin in place are executed with such skill that they seem as pliant as twisted cotton. Stepped and V-shaped lines applied around the eyes denote face painting, and a dangling nose ring, earplug disks, and a band which fastens the hair complete the adornment. The band seems higher on one side, indicating that the wearer is a warrior, and has the characteristic tuft of the military class.[25] The chimney-like opening at the top was for additional ornament, probably feathers.

It was inevitable that the often bloody ceremonies of these people should be expressed in their art, and this mask, with its terrifying and complex associations, so utterly strange to us, conveys much of the atmosphere of pre-Columbian Mexico. We are forced to ponder the spiritual world that inspired it, so un-Christian yet so expressive in its art that even we can grasp something of its significance.

Realism is blended with symbolism in such a masterly way that we cannot define where one begins and the other ends.

Our last gold necklace (*Pl. 233, fig. a*), another gem of the Oaxaca type, is 20 inches long, with cast beads featuring turtles as the main element. The delicate wire loops and bell pendants, one hundred twenty in all, are similar to those seen on *Pl. 230,* yet produce a different effect, with three of the pear-shaped pendants hanging from each bead. Of all the necklaces shown, this one gives the smoothest and most solid impression and is actually the heaviest in weight. All the Oaxaca necklaces attest to a long road of civilization—from the shiny colored pebble-stone string to *colliers* such as these, highly sophisticated and technically impeccable.

Although the Tribute Roll of Montezuma and the contemporary writers of the Conquest mention towns in what is today Vera Cruz as paying tribute in gold objects, few examples from this region have as yet come to the fore. It was probably customary here also to bury with kings, priests, and chiefs, their jewelry and other personal effects, but so much movement has passed across this territory since the landing of Cortés that the ground must have been pretty thoroughly combed over at an early date. However, little surveying has been done archaeologically, and no one knows what still remains in these "hot lands." The few gold plaques that are known lean in composition toward the Oaxaca style, showing generally a more or less plastic head, sometimes with shoulders and arms, that flattens down into a plain sheet with a raised rim.

Among the newer acquisitions of the Museo Nacional in Mexico, however, is a red-gold plaque from Vera Cruz (*fig. b*), about 2 inches high, which offers a contrast to the type just described. A seated figure with elaborate headdress is represented, holding an object with both hands. Legs and feet are depicted with the same clarity and emphasis as the head and shoulders. This is the only case known to the writer in which a plaque of any pre-Columbian area contains the entire human figure cast in relief. The head is part and parcel of the piece, emphasized by its uneven upper rim but firmly tied into the framework of the plaque by delicate reeding edged with diminutive circles. The bird-mask, with its solid and irregular line, and the two rosettes on the corners retain their customary shape. A row of teeth that marks the animal jaw of the headdress and the beads of the necklace effectively frame the face of the man. Note the cape that falls in folds behind the figure. The lower third of the plaque is devoted to a glyphic representation, in which a segment of a circle—suggestive of a shield

—irregular step-frets, and five dots are discernible. Judging from the concavity in the object the dignitary is holding, it may have been inlaid, and it is possible that the background also contained either inlay work or enamel.

The figure does not show great individuality in its features. There is nothing ferocious in the expression; rather it seems somewhat contemplative. The only reminders of the more familiar type lie in the filigree wire elements and in the raised edge that frames the composition. To execute this small and difficult subject represents an achievement in casting; but still more important for us, from an artistic point of view, is the sympathetic air of the piece. Saville illustrates a 4½-inch gold ornament which shows stylistic affinities to our plaque. It was found at El Tajin and had Nahua glyphs on the back.

Pl. 234, fig. a takes us about one hundred twenty miles northwest of Oaxaca into the neighboring state of Guerrero, where at Texmilincan this solar disk of beaten gold, 6 inches in diameter, was found in an ancient sepulchre. Classified as a product of the Mixtec culture,[3] it is important not only as evidence of the wide influence of these people but also because of its complete dissimilarity with Tomb 7 specimens said to belong to the same culture. The fact that it was discovered near the border where the Aztec language meets the Mixtec may explain somewhat the great stylistic and technical differences between it and the Oaxaca pieces. Besides the gold disk, the grave contained earrings, bells and blades of copper, small onyx vases, fragments of jade, and a small turquoise mask.[98]

The disk is ornamented with the intertwining bodies of two feathered serpents in a design similar to that on the well-known stone ring in the Ball Court at Chichen Itzá. It is divided into two sections, and a narrow embossed edge marks the inner and outer margins. The more important elements—the heads, from which two human figures emerge, and the rattles bound with plumes —occupy the outer circle; the inner half contains the finely laid and artistically stylized serpent bodies, the scalelike markings forming an unbroken rhythmic circle. The crossing of the two bodies is smoothly and effectively solved. Slight differences in the two reptiles indicate that a full cliché was prepared for the embossing of the disk. The fret-scrolls resemble the main pattern of the Ulua vases. Caso designates the piece as pre-Aztec because of the *atlatls* wielded by the small human figures, a weapon which antedates the bow and arrow supposedly introduced by the Aztecs. Its disk form and the suave and undulating lines of the serpents recall certain admired Chinese jades.

A suggestion as to the use of this disk is offered by the ornament seen in the Tizoc statuette (*Pl. 231, fig. b*). Gold figures have also been found in the

Totonac region wearing a disk-shaped jewel hanging from a necklace, and the large pottery statue from Mexico (*Pl. 119, fig. b*) is depicted with a circular ornament framed by carefully plaited paper. It would seem that thin gold sheets were often combined with other materials, such as feathers, paper, wood, semiprecious stones, or woven stuff.

The three pieces in *fig. b* are spectacular examples of such a combination. They are the frames for eyes and mouth of a life-size mask, probably originally mounted on a base of wood, and were dredged from the bottom of the Sacred Well at Chichen Itzá. As has been described, boys and girls, ceremoniously adorned, were sacrificed here to the Rain-god, and pilgrims cast valuables into the water to secure the benevolence of the deities. An inventory of objects brought up through the operations of the late E. H. Thompson lists other masks, one of which is given as of solid gold and 7 inches in diameter. (Compare the Chimu mummy masks on *Pl. 203.*)

The embossing is unusually shallow, little more than faint ripples, yet clear enough to define the theme. Two ovals in a zoömorphic pattern ornament the mouth, edged with a series of blunt hooks suggestive of plumes. Each of the eye frames is decorated with a cut-out stylized figure of the feathered serpent, facing toward the center. The open mouth with fangs and an exaggerated forked tongue are clearly visible, particularly over the one on the right. Four rings mark the rattles at the opposite ends. The great loops formed by the sinuous writhing bodies, furiously waving plumes, and lashing tails lend superb fluency to the composition. Both clarity and a feeling of motion are gained by the spacing of the various elements and the lacy arrangement of the openings.

Like the preceding disk, the piece technically is not complicated; its remarkable feature lies in the conception of the design. Here the feathered serpent, an ever-recurrent theme in medieval American art, comes to its most flamboyant expression. So powerful is the purely decorative effect that without attempting to fathom its symbolism, we recognize in it the hallmark of genius.

In the transformation of Late Romanesque into Gothic in different regions of medieval Europe, art-history is presented with a spiritual as well as a stylistic problem, which is still to a certain degree unsolved. With incomparably less data at its disposal, pre-Columbian archaeology is confronted with a problem even more obscure. Although valuable contributions on the subject of metallurgy in medieval America have been made within the field of general survey and analysis as well as in specialized laboratory investigations, too few pieces of metal-work have been excavated under scientific conditions to establish a sequence of styles such as has been built up for pottery in a number of our regions.

The evolution of design as revealed in these pottery sequences is of uneven value as far as gold is concerned. In the first place, some prolific metal-working centers produced no top-rank pottery; in the second, one of the highest cultures, the Maya, had practically no gold until its late and final period. In the Andean and, to a certain extent, the Interlying areas, metal-work developed technically and stylistically in pace with the other applied arts. In the Mexican and Maya, however, it came as a new and attractive medium into the dexterous hands of an already artistically conscious people who made use of it in their own way. Their iconography was already articulate and well developed; the craft did not have to grope its way through primary processes.

Much of the surviving material comes from the so-called middle and late epochs of various cultures, which had their periods of flourishing and of decline. The influence of their art traveled far, at times to sections where technically the people had not advanced to as high a level. This resulted in peripheral versions. Also, stylistic trends were sometimes better preserved in geographically pocketed districts than in those that lay along the main arteries of travel, producing a shift or lag in chronology.

The tribal talent of the various pre-Columbian regions was so strongly individual that the application of the same techniques yielded very different effects, and, as paradoxical as it may seem, the mastery of the most complicated technical processes did not always produce the most highly artistic results. The first Lambayeque plaque (*Pl. 195, fig. a*) and the mask from Chichen Itzá (*Pl. 234, fig. b*) were both worked from thin sheet gold in repoussé; but while in the former the symbolic content is rigidly held down by spiritual inhibitions, the Late Maya piece shows amazing maturity and facility of expression. The disk form was used for both the ear ornaments (*Pl. 197, fig. a*) and the solar disk from Texmilincan (*Pl. 234, fig. a*); the scroll designs of the Lambayeque pieces are balanced and pleasing, but brief study will show the far superior and more subtle values of the Mixtec specimen, in spite of its more regular form. The Chibcha figures (*Pl. 213, fig. a*) have the same build-up as the mask from Monte Alban (*Pl. 231, fig. a*) yet show technical infancy and a helplessness in expression when compared with this masterpiece of international esthetic worth.

Of the two main problems presented by a study of the metal craft of medieval America, the technical will be solved much before the stylistic, for technological analysis in our age has advanced far more rapidly than our ability to penetrate the spiritual complexities of a vanished and alien world.

VIII

Jade and Other Semiprecious Stones

THE attachment of man to stones of unusual color and shape is as wide as the world and as old as civilization. Amulets, bracelets, beads, and ceremonial objects made of some kind of lustrous stone occur generally among prehistoric peoples, and the popular costume jewelry in our department stores, vying with expensive jewels, shows that even our enlightened era still feels the fascination. We are familiar with the ornaments shaped by the early artisans of the Near and Far East, but have had little opportunity to appreciate the skill and artistry of the lapidary of medieval America, although here, after pottery sherds, semiprecious stones are the tokens most commonly found in excavations from the higher cultures.

Among the stones used in medieval America were jade, turquoise, rock crystal, and serpentine, as well as amber, onyx, jasper, and agate. Of these, the jade work stands first in quantity and in its artistic quality. The finest carving, however, is confined to the Mexican and Maya areas, where the styles are frequently so interrelated that they will be presented here as if from one vast region.

The Southwest and the Andean Area had no jade but used turquoise, a material also esteemed in the other areas of high culture, as will be seen in the chapter on applied arts. In the Southwest, the worked shapes are more or less simple, generally with little or no elaboration, and do not represent as high an artistic invention as the craft in the other areas. However, the stones are put together in a tasteful and appealing way and show inimitable color sense, whether in the working of single pieces or the juxtaposition in a string of beads. In the Andean Area, turquoise was delicately carved into figurines and vessels and was used also in inlay and mosaic-work. It is comparatively rare, probably because gold held more meaning for the Children of the Sun. The absence of carved jade in both of these regions is an argument against any intensive intercourse between them and the Mexican or Maya areas in the first half of the Middle Ages; otherwise, some traces of the jade cult would surely have found its way hither, just as metal from the Interlying Area reached the land of the Maya as civilization spread.

Besides its rarity and beauty, jade had a deep symbolic meaning for the Maya and the Mexicans. The Maya word for it was *tun*. The Nahua name *chalchihuitl*, or "green stone," carries an association with "grass" or "herb," emphasizing the color which is the symbol of life itself. It is known how Montezuma, on seeing the great delight with which his gifts of gold were received by the Spaniards, promised them more valuable presents for the following day, and how disappointed Cortés was when "some green stones" were proffered on this occasion. Although the offering was an anticlimax to the Spaniards, to the Aztecs it really comprised their most choice possessions.

The word "jade" is of Spanish origin and, contrary to general belief, is closely connected with the discovery of America. The Chinese names (*yü* for white jade and *pi yü* for the green type) clearly have nothing to do with our term.[88] In European literature the first mention of the stone occurs in the work of Monardes, a physician of Seville, in 1565.[147] He calls it "piedra de hi*jada*," the hypochondriac or colic stone, from the Spanish *hijada*, meaning "loin." The Indians believed it efficacious for certain disorders and passed on their tradition to their conquerors, together with other exotic remedies, drugs, and foods of more actual value. Medieval Europe, even prior to the Conquest, was wont to prescribe pulverized stones mixed with animal or plant extracts for certain illnesses—a practice handed down since the times of Babylon and ancient Egypt. *Piedra de hijada* included carved or shaped stones varying in shade from a very pale to a blackish green. The mineral content was of no importance; the stones were selected on the ground of their appearance, color, and tactile qualities.

Although known in Europe since the Conquest, jade may be said to have first impressed itself on public consciousness after the sack of the Summer Palace in Peking in 1861. Before that time, all worked green stones with a luster were popularly put under the general heading of jade. It was only after Chinese jade objects began to appear in greater quantity in the European art market that the necessity arose for a more exact differentiation between the different types of stone, and the classification was undertaken on a chemical basis.

While the word "jade" was coined by a Spaniard to designate a pre-Columbian importation, the term "jadeite" was invented by the French chemist and mineralogist, Augustin Alexis Damour, after the opening of China. With the aid of chemical analysis, two separate types were distinguished; both have a high silicate content, which makes it possible to mistake one for the other. The first, nephrite, sometimes called "true jade," is a lime magnesia iron silicate. It has a wide range of colors and a waxy sheen. To the second category belong jadeite and the subgroup, chloromelanite, silicates with alumina and soda content. Jadeite is often pale, but it may run to brilliant greens with a vitreous luster; chloromelanite is a darker shade, frequently almost black. Thus, the much misused term "jade" covers two types of stone; it is a cumulative expression and will be used in this survey to denote all those stones of high silica content which were called *tun* by the Maya and *chalchihuitl* by the Aztecs.

Recent investigations with the spectroscope show a definite mineralogical divergence between the jades of America and those of the Orient. The American jadeite contains always a large amount of diopside, not found in the jadeite of Burma and China. Phosphorus, nearly always present in Oriental nephrite, was entirely lacking in all the thirty-odd pieces of American origin examined.[101] These modern scientific tests should finally put to rest the false and fantastic ideas that jade is not native to America and must have been imported from Asia.

Substantial evidence of the autochthonous origin of jade in America existed along several lines long before scientific investigations began. The Tribute Roll of Montezuma, which served Cortés so effectively in locating regions where gold was produced, contains place names in which the Aztec glyph for *chalchihuitl* occurs, suggesting that the green stone was to be found there. The quantity of pre-Columbian jade extant, either undocumented in circulation or found by excavators, testifies further that the stone was fairly common, though the finer types seem to have been rare and may have been traded from one district to another, even occasionally reworked. In the Museo Arqueológico in Guatemala there is a magnificent block of it, weighing about two hundred pounds, that was excavated from the pre-Columbian site of Kaminaljuyú by the Carnegie Institution of Washington in 1937. Sawed and chipped at various points, it shows the marks of the lapidary, made apparently to determine the color grain and to remove smaller pieces for working.[165] Pre-Columbian jade objects which have turned up in Honduras, El Salvador, and Costa Rica frequently vary enough in color and quality to make one suspect different local deposits. Jade has been reported from several Mexican states, chiefly in the form of nodules in the beds of some of the rivers, notably in Hidalgo, Guerrero, Puebla, Oaxaca, Chiapas and Vera Cruz.[86] Furthermore, jade has been found as far north as Alaska and as far south as Brazil; and, what is known by very few, true nephrite has been discovered in our western mountain states, in California and Wyoming.[51]

Thus, archaeological, historic, and mineralogical evidences combine to prove beyond doubt that the jade of medieval American art is as indigenous as the limestone used for Maya temples. Contrary statements may be considered as misconceptions, smuggled into general opinion. Before any serious research was conducted, fanciful theories were already widely circulated, particularly by those fantasts of archaeology (all too frequently Teutonic) who persist in trying to link Babylonian astronomy and Greek mythology with the past of medieval America. Little has been known about jade in America simply because no systematic investigations were begun until very recently.

The stone was esteemed in the Maya and Mexican areas as a mark of rank and was worn by the hierarchy. Most of the pre-Columbian objects fashioned of jade were personal ornaments, amulets, masks, and figurines; in the Early and Great Maya periods we find cuffs and anklets also represented. Its masterly carving and polishing is one of the amazing accomplishments of these people. How such delicate lines and fine contours could have been executed without the use of metal chisels and drills is difficult to imagine. The work was done with primitive implements, probably of hard stone. Indeed, by the time they had succeeded in shaping their tools, they were well on their way toward mastery in the carving of any subject.

As jade was very precious, the smaller pieces were often used in their natural shapes to insure as little waste as possible. The larger stones were split along the grain or sawed into units with at least one flat surface, probably by means of cords and abrasive powder. For boring and cutting both solid and hollow drills of bone, stone, or other hard material were used, revolved in the manner of a primitive fire-making tool. The limitations of these drills were overcome in ingenious ways. To form depressions, the lapidary might bore several holes side by side and then rub the cavity smooth. The hollow drill held at a slant would produce the segment of a circle. Straight lines were often achieved by sawing with cords or rubbing with wooden or stone implements. The work was polished with abrasive powder or wood. It required great patience and skill to smooth the carved surface and rough edges without injuring the shape or blurring the sculptured details. The time element, however, was never a consideration in medieval American art, and pre-Columbian craftsmanship can scarcely be understood without keeping this in mind.

The development of several distinct methods in handling jade can be observed, just as in the sculpturing of stone or stucco, and local preferences and styles suggest themselves. The color and shape of the material often gave inspiration for the subject and design to be followed. We shall see pieces where the natural form of the stone was used without change as sculptural frame. Again, usually in later times, the edges were chiseled and polished off to form a basic outline, before sculptural embellishment began. Fetish-like three-dimensional subjects are found, and figures composed in relief; some designs flow to the very edge of the irregular stone, while others are placed within the restricting frame of a medallion. Oftentimes the color grain was used to good effect to highlight the plastic contours, and admirable efficiency developed in combining and calculating defects to sculptural advantage.

The great importance of carved jade in setting and transmitting style should be stressed. So deep-rooted was the veneration for the green stones that even after the late introduction of metal, it persisted, as we have seen, until the Conquest. Thus the working of jade covers the time-span of the civilization discussed in this survey. Styles in carving and changes in technique were exchanged from one region to another by means of the prized and easily handled jades, and stylistic influences can be noticed in distant and peripheral districts, much as one hat from Paris has been known to change the fashion in many a provincial town. In view of this complicated exchange, no attempt has been made here to try to classify the various types presented into a tightly knit series for the sake of chronology. Nor would a precise mineralogical differentiation be productive from our point of view.

The associations connected with jade in the culture of medieval America go far back, beyond the time on which we have any adequate archaeological data. The artistic impulse of peoples of prehistory manifested itself much earlier and in a more articulate manner than most of us would expect. Jade beads are found in the earliest graves. The custom of putting a piece of jade in the mouth of the deceased—it stood for the heart and was supposed to help him on his way to after life [151]—shows that symbolic meaning was attached to it. In China also, carved jade was placed in the mouth of the dead as a tongue piece. This does not imply any connection with the American practice, but points only to the very old use of this stone in both civilizations and to the fact that the formative periods of each go back into a distant age when no metal was known.

MAYA AND MEXICAN AREAS

The Leyden plaque and the Tuxtla statuette (*Pl. 235, figs. a* and *d*), bearing glyphs interpreted as belonging to Cycle 8 of Maya chronology or about the 4th century of our era, have been considered two of the earliest dated objects found on this continent. It is quite probable that both pieces were moved not once but a number of times hither and yon before they came to rest in the spots where they were discovered.[91]

The Leyden plaque (*fig. a*) was unearthed near Puerto Barrios, Guatemala, during the digging of a canal in 1864, and is now in the Rijks Museum at Leyden, Holland. It is of a very pale jade of fine quality and about 8 inches high. On one side of the smooth celt-shaped plaque is a column of hieroglyphics, characteristic of the archaic or early period of Maya art and not yet identical with Maya codex technique. On the other, a dignitary is shown, standing on another human whose uplifted and backward-turned head and upswung feet are clearly incised. The delicate tracery of the balls, tassels, and curlicues in the elaborate ceremonial costume is fluently drawn. Horizontal lines in the belt and the flaring jaws of the serpent headdress divide and clarify the design. The three-quarters pose seems natural and is delineated with assurance. Dr. Morley reads the date as A.D. 320 and from the position of the figure associates the piece with early Tikal.[90]

The Tuxtla statuette (*fig. d*) was plowed up in a field near San Andres Tuxtla, in Vera Cruz, Mexico, about 1907, and is now in the National Museum at Washington, D.C. This jade, 6 inches high, is of a darker tone. Here the outer layers of the stone have been shaved down to a somewhat clumsy but definite shape, and plastic expression has been attempted. The eyes and nose are human, the eyes achieving an alert penetrating look, which is one of the statue's powers, by the simple means of bored holes. The jowl line is brought down deep and broad and shaped as if in a grin. Fantastic elements appear in the lower part of the face where the mouth or mouth mask is shaped like a duck's bill, with incised marks on either side of the center line in realistic representation of the bird's nostrils. The lines starting at the shoulder level and curving down each side are suggestive of folded wings or of arms covered with a cloak. Clawlike hands emerge from them toward the bottom of the piece. (Compare with *Pl. 68, fig. b* and *Pl. 132, fig. b*.) Recently doubt has been cast on the interpretation of the glyphs as Maya; it has been suggested rather that they are Olmec—as yet undeciphered.[154] This, however, in no way detracts from the intrinsic strength of the figure. Regardless of its origin, it carries within itself the concentrated energy of truly primitive art. Its remarkable tactile quality—that appeal to the hand to grasp and fondle it—is naturally more apparent in the statue itself than in the photograph.

These two specimens of pre-Columbian lapidary work exemplify the same two tendencies noted in sculpture: in the first, the stone serves as a background for the delineation; in the second, it is shaped in the round, into a three-dimensional object. It is noteworthy that in pre-Columbian jades the manner of delineation, that is, the convention of representing the eyes, ears, nose, and the like, never became restricted to a single style. The eyes, for instance, seldom show the double-rimmed lids and convex eyeballs of realistic Greek interpretation; the nose is sometimes wedge-shaped, sometimes "hammer head" like an inverted T, sometimes bulbous; ears may jut out into handles or be reduced to an incised spiral.

The next three pieces show, primarily, subtly worked shapes. The first (*fig. b*), 5¾ inches long, is probably a pectoral. It bears a lozenge of Maya glyphs, identified as quite early in type, incised in a frame at either end of a fine light green jade bar. It is highly polished and evidently was finished with great care.

In *fig. c,* a recumbent human figure is scratched on the surface of the stone. In his outstretched right hand he carries a torch or perhaps a weapon, while the left grasps some object. His headdress is subdued and apparently is not Maya. The square mouth also bears out the impression that we are dealing here with a different regional tradition. The even rim around the entire piece suggests that it may have been a palette.

Fig. e, a small idol from Uaxactun, takes us again into the field of the three dimensional. Here a seated human figure is represented with a disproportionately large head and bulging eye. As we have noticed in other categories of pre-Columbian art, the head and upper part of the body are often emphasized and more realistically treated than the lower half of the figure, which may be dwarfed or barely suggested.

Pl. 236, fig. a presents a sculptured stone slab, Stela I from Copan, dated 677, and shows an early style, often considered related to wood-carving. Note the hieratic position of the hands holding an ornate ceremonial bar. An interesting resemblance is found in *fig. d,* a jade plaque of fine quality which was unearthed during the building of a railroad near the city of San Salvador. The hands are placed back to back, as in the stela—though here they support nothing —and the headdress is an animal-mask. The feet, however, are not pointed outward in the traditional Maya pose. The subject covers the entire face of the stone—only in the beading on the top is the even outline broken. High and low planes, smooth and broken surfaces are well utilized for clear delineation.

The head is square, the mouth thick and widened, the nose and eyebrows carved in one with simplified lines. A necklace and the edges of a tunic are emphasized, and drapery reaching to the feet is suggested behind. (Compare with *Pl. 69, fig. c* and *Pl. 82, fig. c.*) Despite the fact that there is a suggested level beneath the feet, the figure does not seem to stand but gives the impression of being suspended.

The two pieces in *figs. b* and *c* show more plastic consideration; even though the right edge is a straight and static line, on the left, use has been made of a more defined language of sculpture. In the first, a human figure is depicted, arms crossed, head turned to profile; along and above his forehead rests the snout of a water monster that lies folded over on itself. (Compare with *Pl. 139, fig. b.*) The piece is 6½ inches long and comes from Kaminaljuyú. The jade is very fine and its tactile quality here comes forward. It is pierced at both ends so as to hang face downwards.

A somewhat similar figure is presented in the whitish bar from Quiriguá (*fig. c*). Its arms are also crossed and the legs are represented in the same dangling position. But with its simpler headdress, the whole piece is easier to grasp.

The universal appeal of charm stones is exemplified in the large breast bars from Venezuela, approximately 12 inches long (*Pl. 237, fig. b*). In this case the carefully shaped and smoothly polished pieces of slatelike texture—said to be symbolic of the Bat-god—were apparently worn as ornaments. They are light in color and weight and are extremely pleasant to handle. The shape in itself has dignity and accents the beauty of the stone. Very early Chinese jades were treated in the same manner, the lack of any embellishment serving to enhance their significant form and fine color. Here might be mentioned also the bird and banner stones of Mound Builder culture which show real feeling toward balance in form.

Fig. a is a bluish jade from Costa Rica, about 7 inches high. On the upper half a masked figure is carved, terminating in an undecorated blade which, perhaps because of the contrast, makes the whole into a shapely and pleasing piece. The deep eyes may have been inlaid. The crossed hands are depicted in an abbreviated manner. Two stylized intertwined serpents, the heads of which can be seen on the sides, make up the headdress. This same type appears on two jades found in El Salvador, as well as on a piece dated mid-7th century from Copan (not shown here), and is very clearly represented in *Pl. 247, fig. a.* The tonguelike affix before the mouth and the lines suggesting a shoulder remind us of the

Tuxtla statuette. Several similar jades are known to have come from the Nicoya Peninsula, a district that produced also a high grade of pottery (see *Pl. 145, fig. a*).

Fig. c is unusual because of its modeling. The heavy rounded section at the top flattens out into a shape like a police whistle. How important this section is in maintaining the subtle balance of the piece can be seen by blocking it off with the hand. The plastic contours of cheeks, eyes, and nose are brought out with assurance and simplicity. Mouth and jaws broaden into the same duck's bill seen in the Tuxtla statuette, with a contrast as effective as that in the blade at the left of it. Perforations to suspend it as a pendant or attach it to another material were bored in each edge just below the eyes.

Realism and the humor of a caricature are manifest in the carving from Oaxaca (*fig. f.*), about 3 inches high. Here once more the stone was the medium for only an engraving and even the unused sections before the face and behind the head were not carved away. The lower half of the body has been neglected to emphasize the sharp and clear-cut profile of an elderly smiling man, who appears to be seated with his forearm laid along a horizontal rest. Features, headdress, and earplugs are well defined and remind us of the Monte Alban *danzante* type seen in *Pls. 57* and *91*.

Fig. e, 3¼ inches high, is actually more akin to the Monte Alban slabs in manner of carving. Mouth and nose are depicted in a kind of sculptural shorthand and lean toward the Olmec in type. The piece shows a full figure sitting cross-legged. At the bottom center can be seen a miniature hand resting on a knee that depends largely on the contour of the stone for its shape. The necklace and tulip-like earplug were apparently considered of greater importance than the realistic representation of the body. The face has expression and is the *raison d'être* of the whole piece.

Fig. d shows a much more settled manner of depiction. Here also main consideration is given to the face, but the composition of the whole figure is more distinct. A careful study of the stone before carving is evident in the placement of the subject and in the clever use of the light streak in the jade to emphasize the shoulders and the lower part of the face. The lines of the forehead, eyes, nose, and mouth are executed with a sure and routined hand. This piece has a compact robust appearance, multiplying several times the effect one might expect to find in such a small space. The brain that conceived it had a definite idea of what it wished to represent and was able to impart the inspiration to the simple tool.

The serpentine plaque in *Pl. 238, fig. a,* about 6 inches high, may be considered as late in style. It shows Tlaloc, Rain-god of the Aztecs, as an older man with heavy headdress and earplugs with pendants, holding a serpent in his left hand and in his right, a symbolic object. In contrast to the earlier figures, he stands firmly on the ground. The background is filled in with explanatory symbols such as usually surround Aztec figures in the codices—appendages which are decorative, though they make the piece more difficult for us to understand.

Fig. b, somewhat over 5 inches high, was found at Teotihuacan. It presents a seated chief in full regalia attended by a smaller figure in the lower left. In the upper left is a demon in the jaws of a serpent. The central figure, with its elaborate feather headdress, is a hieratic representation, very detailed but less liberated as a sculpture than a number of other less-pretentious pieces here shown. Note the bar-bead pectoral and the jade mask on his belt. Considerably greater sculptural vivacity appears in the subordinate characters. Dots, circles, and curving lines are evidence of ingenious work with round drills. T. A. Joyce connects this carving with the style of the "celebrated site of Copan," [56] but stylistically it is nearer the reliefs of Piedras Negras and Yaxchilan. The speech scroll that appears before his face is associated with the Toltecs.

The plaque in *fig. c,* shown in actual size, is carved from a stone of good quality and high luster. Here the face is presented in full front. Almond eyes, beaklike nose, and grim mouth identify it as typically Maya. The body is facilely and economically done, and the placement of the figure within its allotted space is perfect. For the first time in this chapter a raised carved frame appears, well within the margin of the stone itself, with the flowing plumes of the monster-headdress effectively utilized for the upper part.

A comparison of the two pieces (*figs. b* and *c*), both Maya, demonstrates the considerable stylistic divergences which existed in various regions of the same folk, not necessarily widely separated in time. The gestures are similar but reversed. Facial differences could be analyzed, going deep into detail, but here it will suffice to call attention to the different execution of the eyes and mouths. In relief, a profile lends itself to sharper characterization than a full face, but even aside from this, each piece speaks its own language. The technique of the one might be called pointillistic and of the other, impressionistic.

In *fig. d,* nearly 4 inches high, costume and gesture derive from another tradition and another region. The round heavy-lidded or half-closed eyes, apparent also in the mask, are characteristics of Oaxaca. The broad necklace is well brought out and the monster-mask headdress that frames the face shows real virtuosity in the carving of complicated scrolls, curves, and undulating lines. The nostrils of the animal, conventionalized, can be discerned in the swirls just above the forehead. By adding the small feather sections at either side, the carver has skillfully suggested a full swaying feather ornament.

One of the several sculptural directions taken by jade carving seems to have placed more and more emphasis on the head. In all the pendants on *Pl. 239,* the head was given the main consideration, although in *figs. a* and *b* a body, dwarfed and out of proportion, is also indicated.

Fig. b, about 5 inches high, is composed largely of curving lines. The introduction of the horizontal in the "coffee-bean" eyes and mouth and in the arms brings the face out of the swirling ornament and rim of suggested plumes. The round knees and tab of the belt are so executed as to complement the pattern formed by the eyes and open jaw of the monster-mask.

The face in *fig. a* is definitely framed by double and triple parallel lines which indicate the headdress and show the arms in ceremonial gesture, a pose, as in *fig. b,* that is physically impossible but has decorative value in the design. Circular earplugs and a "choker" necklace of large beads cut the rectangular surface and harmonize with the scrolls in the headdress and the eyes of the monster-mask. A new feature appears in the two "concealed" profiles at the upper corners of the stone. Such faces occur in jades from the Guatemala highlands and from El Salvador, as well as the Olmec region. Maler mentions superimposed heads on stelae and other sculptures at Tikal,[75] and Means speaks of "hidden faces" in monumental stone carving from the Andean Area.[84]

The work in *fig. c* shows much more virtuosity in the deeper carving and deliberate contrasting of high lights. This piece is less than 1½ inches high. The face is the bulbous-nosed, heavy-lidded Oaxaca type, with even the eyes of the monster on the mask half-veiled. The use of round and curving lines throughout results in the absence of real "center" in the design; the effect is that of a delightful arabesque. In Copan, beneath Stela 3, dated mid-7th century, some jade pieces were found which show a certain similarity to this in build-up.[143] It would seem that in many early jades the lapidaries were content if they could place a face in the middle of the stone—then whatever surface remained was filled in with condensed symbols.

Fig. d is carved on a thin brownish slatelike stone. Here the idea has flattened down or thinned out to a degenerate and simplified expression. A monster-mask with especially ferocious fangs is recognizable just above the forehead of

‹ 293 ›

the human face. Little of the power and skill which created its numerous fore-runners is apparent in the carving.

Fig. e, only 2 inches wide, shows a head in profile, emphatic in facial lines but with the headdress less clearly worked out. The intertwining elements may be a conventionalized representation of a sinuous serpent body and a serpent's vertical jaw is visible behind the head. Center is given to the design by the earplug, the sharpest element in the whole. Details in this piece bear little relation to others on this plate and may indicate a different region of origin.

The profile in *fig. f* is liberated from all its wrappings. Although the natural shape of the jade was evidently the starting point for this design, it has been completely subordinated to the composition. The subject fills the entire stone and all irrelevant material has been pared away. The face, with its hooked nose and curling lips, is the feature of the piece. As there was apparently no space above the forehead for the headdress, it sweeps behind. Only a tuft of feathers remains of the familiar trappings; mask and round earplug are here absent. The material is good crystalline green jade, and the streak of lighter coloring, which extends from the forehead in front of the eye, beside the nose, and down the cheek, has been well utilized for plastic effect. The expression of the eye, which is bored through the stone, is greatly enhanced by the wing-shaped groove under it. A flamboyant rhythm permeates this piece, particularly noticeable when it is compared with the others.

The first two pieces on *Pl. 240* show persons engaged in activities not clearly definable. In *fig. a,* slightly over 4 inches high, an old man is seated with knees up and fingers outstretched, evidently concentrating his attention on one point. The edge of the stone is cut to conform with the elaborate carving which surrounds him, the lower part of which seems to represent a serpent in profile.

The figure on the whitish jade (*fig. b*) has Oaxaca-type features. He holds in his right hand an implement that resembles a stylus or quill, and in his lap, a good-sized jar, perhaps of paint. There is tension in the half-raised hand, and the gesture of the whole figure shows real working activity. A large monster-mask appears above him, perhaps part of his headdress. The original edge of the stone seems to have been left to a certain degree, though shaped to symmetry in the lower portion. Note the similarity of action in the top figure on the page from the Dresden Codex, *Pl. 266.*

In the four pieces that follow, the definite placing of a figural composition within a frame is evident. All the faces are typically Maya, though far from stereotyped. In the first three, the feather headdress overflows the frame, each in its own manner. The feathers in *fig. c* are horizontally placed; in *fig. d,* the edge of the stone is utilized as outline for the headdress which flows backward and down. The inner rim of the frame here is interestingly interrupted on a level with the thighs. Although the warrior in *fig. e* is confined within his frame, it is clear that he was only a part of a larger carving, for a fragment of a grotesque mask can be made out on the right. This pendant is 2¾ inches high in its present state and of a brilliant true "jade green." Note the pectoral that the warrior wears, like the piece shown in *Pl. 241, fig. h.* In each of these jades the pose of the hands is individual, but all show ceremonial gestures.

In the last pendant (*fig. f*), about 5 inches at its greatest height, a fine springy rhythm enlivens the figure who is apparently making an offering. The glyph before his mouth is as yet undeciphered. He wears an antlered headdress, unique in the jade carvings illustrated in this survey. The style has been identified as Ocosingo, or Tonina, from central Chiapas. The piece is a perfect medallion, with the subject placed, unbroken and uncrowded, within the given space and framed by an even rim, bearing its own subordinate decoration.

These last two pendants, though clearly in the style of the Old Empire—particularly reminiscent of Palenque—were dredged from the Sacred Well at Chichen Itzá. Possibly they had been handed down through generations before they were cast into the water as offerings to the Rain-god. We have a somewhat similar custom in passing on the amulets, lockets, and crosses of our forebears.

The Sacred Well at Chichen Itzá has proved a repository of objects from widely diverse regions and times, providing invaluable information on the interrelation of cultures in Middle America since the 12th or 13th centuries.[150] Recently some amazing finds of jade were made in southern Vera Cruz and vicinity, where a great number of worked pieces were discovered, representing several styles and types.

The emphasis on the head with the subordination of every decorative motif is unmistakably evident in *Pl. 241. Fig. a,* about actual size as shown, illustrates very well the use of the round drill. The human head, which is carved here in low relief and placed within a triangular-shaped stone, steps out into three dimensions in *fig. b,* and the unrelated or medallion rim of the first has been fashioned in the second into ears and a thick neck. A head of the same tradition appears in the thumb-nail sketch from the Guatemala highlands (*fig. c*), about 1½ inches high. The jade is a clear limpid green, but the carving is weak and unclear in detail, perhaps because it is so minute. These three pendants all show similar features: the almond eyes, rounded nose, and drooping mouth are Maya; the tall headdress with curling ends suggestive of maize leaves and, in *fig. b,* the arrangement of the hair in pompadour fashion are not only Maya but Maize-god attributes as well. *Fig. f,* although said to have been found at Monte Alban, possesses a number of the same characteristics. Here the rim has entirely disappeared and the face has a full expression, the result of a routined sculptural interpretation.

The fragment in *fig. e* shows an advanced technique in its use of sharper relief. The face itself is framed by the open mouth of the animal on the mask. Above is a considerable headdress. Although Mayoid in style, the features show another manner of carving.

Fig. d, 3 inches high and found in the Sacred Well at Chichen Itzá, is carved from an unusually fine apple-green jade. Here the head was sculptured out of an oval stone into a three-dimensional representation. The monster-mask, which appears foreshortened and is treated plastically, extending toward the back, is rather less defined than the clear-cut face with its somewhat vacant expression. Typically Maya is the receding chin, more readily seen here than in the first three specimens. Glyphs adorn the edges and even the back, which is flat.

In *fig. g* the stone again becomes the medium for a relief, with the edges trimmed to produce a symmetrical shape. The monster-mask here takes the form of a casque and the rim below the chin is worked out into an evenly executed collar, which, with the emphasized earplugs, helps balance the composition. The prominent jaw contrasts sharply with the almost chinless figure beside it. A similar type, though more uncertain in execution, was found in El Salvador.

A square shape and a predominance of straight lines lend a stern expression to *fig. h.* Compare it with the preceding head—a similar shape in which curved lines are the rule. The expression is quite conventionalized. He may be wearing a stylized headdress or the lines at the top may indicate hair. This pendant is 1⅔ inches high and was found at Zacualpa.

Pl. 242 presents larger pieces of carved stone. *Figs. a* and *b* come from Copan, Honduras, a Maya site that produced several styles during its existence. Some stylistic differences are manifest in these two statuettes, though the oblong shape and ceremonial posture, by now familiar, show a uniform idea. The first (*fig. a*), 7¾ inches high, is rounded and more squat in form, and the face is set off from the body, masklike, by sharp contours. There was apparently no attempt to adjust the shape to the imperfection in the stone (left) and the bent leg is merely carved across it. In general effect the piece is reminiscent of the stone carvings called *tortugas* or "turtles," at Quiriguá.

Fig. b is more elongated and angular, with the stone apparently cut to the contours of the figure. The carving is more simplified and the details are generalized. The man wears another type of headdress, with the wide-open jaw of the serpent extending above his forehead. It may be remarked that neither of these Maya jades shows the strongly almond-shaped eye. The designated pupils in *fig. b* are unusual.

Fig. c is another of the remarkable finds made by A. Ledyard Smith at Uaxactun. The figure, $10\frac{1}{2}$ inches high and devoid of all decoration, is seated in somewhat the same pose as those above it, but with the hands crossed over one another. The same stereotyped expression is evident as in the other two, but here more clearly perceived, perhaps, because of the clear green of the material. This piece, however, is not a mere lump of stone fashioned in the semblance of a human, but a real three-dimensional statuette. The eyes may have been inlaid and there are traces of red in the eye sockets and mouth. Noteworthy are the incised fingers and the "eyebrows," associated with Olmec traits (see the next plate), and the numerous piercings, apparently for added ornament. The absence of a headdress is another non-Maya feature.

A kneeling woman is represented in *fig. d*. The shape, the dark-toned material (a green diorite), and the economy of detail are typical of Aztec work. In this small piece, about 3 inches high, the head has received all concentration to the detriment of the body, which is little more than a rounded base with arms suggested at the sides and small feet extending to the rear. The static effect of the carving, created primarily by its solid shape, is augmented by the empty eye sockets, which were probably once inlaid, as was the medallion on the breast.

The statuette in *Pl. 243, fig. a*, $4\frac{1}{4}$ inches high and said to have come from Vera Cruz, is of an agreeable pale grayish-green color. The little figure has tattoo marks over his body. His ears are pierced for ornaments but he does not wear a headdress. The pose is more relaxed than in the pieces on the opposite plate and he appears to be blowing on some instrument, perhaps an ocarina. A hole is bored up through the center of the stone, possibly for mounting it on a staff.

We now come to that puzzling manifestation of medieval Mexican art, known as the "baby face" or "tiger mouth" type. It is a characteristic tentatively assigned to the mysterious Olmec people, who are believed to have inhabited a part of the state of Vera Cruz, south of the city of that name, as well as the contiguous areas of Tabasco, Chiapas, and parts of Oaxaca. Olmec is said to mean "dwellers where rubber grows." They exerted an influence on the Maya art of Cycle 9 (A.D. 435 to 830) and again, in the New Empire, on the art of Yucatan with its strong Toltec infusion. This art and culture are now called La Venta, after one of the sites where it occurs in most characteristic form.

"Most typical of Olmec art," as J. Eric S. Thompson writes, "are the treatment of the muzzle and mouth in anthropomorphized representations of the jaguar and the blending of these feline features with those of a youthful deity. The characteristics . . . are: the flaring nostrils at the base of a narrow nose, the muzzle shaped like a croquet hoop, the triangular or square appendage from the upper lip, the uptwist of the lower lip to follow the line of the upper lip and muzzle, the nick in the forehead." [154]

The tiger-mouth deity (*fig. b*) has an interesting mixture of human and animal features. As fantastic a creation as it is, it was, nevertheless, like other representations of medieval American iconography, clearly defined in the imagination of the carver. The headdress with its hanging ear-flaps is skillfully worked over the head with a facile touch, and not only patience but very mature technical skill are shown in the execution of the minute details in the face. Ferocity in the general impression is neutralized by the childish roundness of the forelegs that end in human hands, the ribbons tied at the neck and wrists, and the tassels flaring at the back. Note the medallion with a cross on the breast, similar to that on *Pl. 235, fig. c.* This photograph brings out the brilliant luster of the stone.

Fig. c shows a representation a little more on the human side. At first glance, it might be taken for a child, with its soft square face and hanging jowls. The over-developed mouth, however, with its moustache-like addition, and the stumpy nose are rather elements of fantasy or symbolism. A band around the forehead and ear-flaps are the only ornaments. From the shoulders down, the body is condensed into a cubical shape which, with hands tip to tip and the stubby feet only indicated, is in sharp contrast to the clearly developed and alive expression of the face.

The same idea prevails in the last piece (*fig. d*). The face has the same exaggerated features and the body is even more out of proportion. The only real carving in the figure was in the shaping of the chin, mouth, and nose—the symbolic elements; the rest that was plastic in *fig. c* is here only incised. It has slanting eyes that are distinctly crossed and "cockscomb eyebrows" that are somewhat similar to those in the little naked idol on the opposite plate. Here the forehead shows the deep V-shaped nick, a characteristic of the Olmec.

Pl. 244 presents two necklaces fashioned by the medieval American lapidary. Beads, especially from Oaxaca and Guerrero, were much in demand as objects of trade over a wide area. The first (*fig. a*) is of graduated translucent quartz and comes from Chichen Itzá. Rock crystal is recognized as one of the hardest stones and the beauty of the shaping and the polish, as well as the skillful uniform boring, are admirable, particularly so when it is remembered that the pre-Columbian worker had only simple tools at his disposal.

In the jade necklace (*fig. c*), the beads are neither so even nor so regular but the quality of the stones is very good. The color ranges from a marbleized dark gray to a light greenish crayon gray. Some of the very different shapes may have been added later, as the arrangement with the pendant—upon which a face is suggested with a few essential lines—is recent.

The broken circular disk in *fig. b* is of an unusually fine jade color and demonstrates great technical ability, both in the carving and in polishing off the undesired sections to produce such a difficult form. It would have been task enough to cut down the stone into a circle, but to bore the hole in the center was a still more risky matter. The thin flat body and the ring shape are responsible for our having only a fragment, but even this shows the delicacy of the work. An off-color cement used in restoration makes the seated figure at the edge rather unclear in the photograph. Nevertheless, it is apparent that only a gifted and experienced craftsman could have conceived and produced the design. A staccato rhythm is created by the interspersing of figural and decorative motifs.

The following plates unfold before us a variety of shapes and color, techniques and expression, a range in region and time, but all show clear envisaging of the subject and command over technicalities.

All examples on *Pl. 245* measure from 2½ to 3½ inches in height. *Figs. a* and *b* are conceived on the same general plan: an idealized elongated head shape, executed without any decoration but highly plastic. Their ears are conventionalized to the simplicity of handles, and the slightly opened lips have a greater or lesser tendency toward the Olmec tiger mouth. The first piece has more life than the others; there are no eyeballs, but it has a live and penetrating look. The upward lines between the eyes are carved deep with considered sculptural effect. To us the cheeks appear swollen. The thickened nose combines with the upper lip and probably carried a nose ornament.

The two figures below these (*e* and *f*) are related to them. Both show artificial deformation of the skull to an even greater degree. Both have a narrow rim under the chin. *Fig. e,* however, has a quieter facial expression and more realism, while *f* is made uncouth for us by exaggeration in the eyes and mouth.

The rounder shapes in *figs. c* and *d* reveal grotesque humor. Whether they represent a crying baby face or a mask of some fantasy-world, the force of expression in these small pieces cannot be denied. Pronounced angles in the upper lips give them both outspoken tiger mouths. Note the incision work around the eyes in *fig. c* that may have denoted tattoo or paint. The mouth is hollow; in *fig. d* it is only deepened. Here luglike ears occur, similar to those in the group just described.

It should be pointed out that where a human face with Olmec features appears the dome of the head is bald and without headdress. This observation holds for the great number of jade pieces which we have studied.

Fig. h presents a profile view of a pendant with characteristic Maya ornamentation around and above the face. It is carved from a light jade of better quality than most of the others on this plate and is executed in a very different manner—much more decorative and flamboyant.

Fig. g has the same hanging lower lip, half-closed eyes, and rounded nose. The straight lines above the forehead are similar to those in *fig. d,* but while the piece in the upper row has an articulate expression, this one is stoically uncommunicative. It is a mask in shape, quite deeply hollowed out in the back. Acquired in El Salvador, it is a mottled light green flecked with gold, a material seen so frequently in jades thereabouts that we may speculate on its local origin, perhaps around the region of San Miguel.

The pectoral in *Pl. 246, fig. a* is 3¼ inches high and of the finest quality jade, a deep rich green in tone. From several points of view it is unique. The unusually plastic head does not occupy the entire stone and flat surfaces extend on both sides. Again the skull is dome-shaped, but the arrangement of the hair in locks, incised in turn with fine lines, does not occur in any other known pre-Columbian work. There are masks in the Museo Regional of Merida, Yucatan, and in the Musée de l'Homme in Paris, on which locks of hair are indicated, and there are also stucco reliefs where the same detail is implied, executed, however, with incomparably less artistry. Especially remarkable is the treatment of the eyes with their slight cast, revealing deliberate use of the effects of light and shade. Flattened circles in the iris catch a luminous reflection and deep incisions above the eyeballs serve to intensify the gaze. The tiger mouth is so discreet that it is little more than a disdainful droop. A finely chiseled nose with a pierced septum is evidence that the carver could be realistic when he chose. The ears are delicately sculptured, and decorated with earplugs. On the left the two glyphs, as yet undeciphered, appear to be Olmec; Joyce reports traces of two others, one on each side where the stone is broken off, and estimates the piece therefore as having been originally at least 6½ inches wide. Because of its technical and artistic superiority, he places it at the highest period of Copan. However, the non-Maya glyphs and Olmec features would remove it rather to that region where Maya and Olmec art meet. The face has real spiritual content. Its penetrating forcefulness and mysterious beauty combine to make it a *chef-d'œuvre* among pre-Columbian jades.

Strong kinship in ideology and appearance can be discerned in the companion piece (*fig. b*), a profile carved in relief on a shield-shaped stone, one corner of which has been broken off. Here also the subject does not take up all the available surface. On the upper edge and again under the chin smooth sections are left that emphasize the passive frame into which the head has been placed, balanced. The carving is very shallow. In front of the sculptured forehead, a second head appears, lightly incised in the margin, and a third is found facing out of the top line of the shield, with the forehead of the main head forming its chin. On the cheek of the main face are outlined two minor profiles, facing each other—from their design and position possibly representing tattoo. These faces all show strongly Olmec features. It is possible that some of these subordinate profiles were cut into the stone later. The hollowed-out eye and the vertical lines in front of and behind the ear in the large head may have been inlaid.

Each of the four small heads shown on *Pl. 247* differs in style as well as in the quality and color of its material. Three different ways of carving the eyes are evident. In *fig. a* the stone is alabaster-like. The most distinguishing features of the piece are the serpent headdress and the execution of the eyes and mouth. Eye sockets and lids are lifted out of the stone and a channel carved all around them, giving the coffee-bean effect familiar from pottery. The two condensed intertwined serpents are a rare decorative addition as headdress, on which incision is utilized in contrast to the strongly plastic face. (Compare with the headdress on *Pl. 237, fig. a.*) Ears are indicated by a coil, and the distended lobes are bored with large perforations.

Fig. b breathes a martial air. A singularly hard-bitten expression is given the face by the deeply cut crescents that outline the nose and suggest eyebrows. The nose is broadened and flattened into a triangle and nostrils are indicated by shallow round depressions at the base, produced by the same method that bored the iris in *fig. a* on the opposite plate. The mouth, represented by a broad curved band, tending downward like a drooping moustache, and the lug-shaped ears lean toward the Olmec. A helmet rather than a headdress is suggested by the lines that divide the head into three sections. Compact, succinct, and vigorous, this little piece, not 2 inches high, has the vehemence of a portrait.

Fig. c presents a more realistic head. It is about 2½ inches high and cut from pale jade in an acorn shape that must have been difficult to carve. The face has considerable plastic detail, and, in comparison with the straight lines of the others, its peaked outline is striking. A unique feature is the pointed helmet, fashioned in perfect symmetry and counterbalanced by the natural almond shape of the face. The deep-cut rim of the headdress produces a pleasing shadow.

Fig. d can be regarded as the product of a lateral development, with similarities to the Olmec heads on *Pl. 245* and to the square baby faces of *Pl. 243*. No headdress, no hair, no helmet, no ears even are indicated; the nose is only half-heartedly three dimensional, and two holes are drilled through the upper lip for nostrils. This conventionalized face has, however, an indisputable mystic radiation. Here we approach the complex idea of the fetish, in which not the simplified sculptural representation was of importance but the magic power which was attached to it and lay behind it. The piece was bought at Chichen Itzá but may have traveled a considerable distance from its place of origin.

In the next three plates larger masks are presented. *Pl. 248, fig. a* is a pale sea-green jade about 4½ inches high. It represents Coyolaxhqui, sister of the Mexican War-god, Huitzilipochtli. The image, in itself far from sympathetic, seems to be weighed down by the bulk of the stone. The face proper is nearly square and appears stretched between the earplugs. An inert headdress and cumbrous ornament increase the heavy impression. The milky color, the expressionless slit eyes, and swollen lips all combine to give a feeling of deadness to the subject.

Fig. c below it, 7⅛ inches high, shows technically a new approach. The use of several planes in the execution of the mouth and forehead creates sharp contours, utilizing the effect of light and shade. Incision underlines certain sculptured details. Deep bored holes used in the eyes and nose intensify the fierce and demoniac expression.

Fig. d is rounder but has similar features in its build-up. The protruding forehead and mouth are evident, but the general surface is smoother. The drooping mouth is simplified into two bands, and the headdress, fully executed in the piece beside it, is here only suggested by the flamelike middle section. Slight markings denote ears that are not represented on the other at all. The eye sockets may have been inlaid with another material, as cavities for affixing it are visible in the inner corners.

Fig. b, about 4½ inches high, is the quietest among the four on this plate and the most human. The stone is agreeably rounded and polished. All features are in proportion. The mouth and nose have not the unnatural emphasis seen in the masks below it and only the raised upper lip with its suggestion of the tiger line shows relationship to them. Here the decoration on the forehead—plastic in the other pieces—is only incised, a deterioration of the same motif, probably indicating, with the other lines about the face, tattoo or paint.

Pl. 249 demonstrates how powerful artistic concepts of certain pre-Columbian periods were stereotyped into formulae through frequent repetition. The mystic quality of the work diminishes as the lapidary approaches naturalism.

Figs. a, b, and *d,* all Toltec in style, range from 6 to 10 inches high and are variations of the same theme with few divergences. The heraldic shape of the masks is similar, and a complete absence of decoration is common to them all. The eyes in general suggest the coffee-bean type, but the slits are widened and shaped to resemble more nearly an eye socket. Particularly good workmanship is manifest in the first.

Fig. c, about 9 inches high, is executed in a different sculptural manner. Eyes and nose are less pronounced and even the protruding mouth does not show the sharp contours of the companion pieces. A rim above the forehead—which will be met again on the next plate—points to another provenience.

Fig. a on *Pl. 250* is a round mask and, as such, is quite rare. It is a Xipe-Totec representation, seen also in sculpture and metal, executed here in a very dark stone with a high polish. An unusual feature is the hair, divided in the middle and stylized with even strokes. The piece is 4¼ inches high.

Fig. b may be an unfinished carving. Better than any of the other illustrations it shows the technical approach of the lapidary. Marks left by hollow drills of various sizes can be seen in the eye sockets, and a print of a "reverse" is still visible on the left, below the nose. Nostrils are indicated by segments of a circle; the mouth is but a sawed line. The headdress is only outlined, and the circles drilled at the sides may be the beginnings of earplugs. After comparison with the piece beside it, it becomes evident how much contour and expression could be given by further working; note especially the similarity of the noses.

Fig. c, 4¾ inches high, also has the rim above the forehead. The mouth is somewhat open. The vaguer expression is the result of the standardization of a sculptural manner.

The mask in *fig. d* is very large, 18 inches high, and of bright green serpentine. It probably represents a dead warrior. An unusual feature is the lolling tongue, which is sometimes suggested but seldom executed with such realism. The depiction of the row of upper teeth is also unusual. Otherwise in sculptural build-up the mask is quite similar to the Toltec type.

The small objects on *Pl. 251* exemplify the broad skill of the lapidary in many regions. In *fig. a* we find the jaguar head that has appeared on so many headdresses with symbolic intent carved in a more natural form. It is not surprising that the little piece, about 3 inches high, exhibits such good workmanship and realism in expression, for it comes from Piedras Negras, a site which had the ripest plastic talent. The jade is a mottled apple-green and of finest quality. There are glyphs carved on the back.

The beguiling monkey head in *fig. b,* about 4 inches high, is said to have come from the state of Puebla, Mexico. It was here that influences from the distant tributary states met the inner circle of Aztec iconography. The piece is made of obsidian. This material was commonly used for sacrificial knives, daggers, and other sharp-edged implements, which the pre-Columbian lapidary split off from "cores" with great dexterity. But the shaping and polishing of this figure with its many rounded surfaces must have required especial skill and patience. It has fine tactile quality. Although the eyes have lost their original inlay, they still have a live expression even with rough blank sockets.

Fig. c is simpler in its carving but telling in its effect. This is one of the rare cases in which the inlay has survived. The white shell in the eyes, with red dots for pupils, augments the bizarre effect of the whole little mask. Compare the grotesque nose with that of the large pottery figure at Oaxaca (see *Pl. 124, fig. c*).

In *fig. d* only the main contours of the amphibian are plastically executed;

all surface representation is done by shallow incised lines. This example, better than many others, demonstrates that the pre-Columbian carver saw nature in his own way and did not hesitate to apply incision, relief, and even three-dimensional sculpture on one and the same piece. What merits special attention in this carving is the contented expression in the face, achieved obviously with intent.

The serpent fan handle in *fig. e,* about 5 inches long, is another of the gems found among the treasures of Tomb 7 at Monte Alban. The jade is very fine, both in luster and color. Not only is the sleek creeping quality of a reptile well caught, but excellent skill is shown in the cutting: to chisel out, shape, and polish so perfectly the slender cylinder required great deftness. Here is proof that the Zapotec-Mixtec region, so different in its stylistic language from the Maya, was also master in the technical field.

The jade hand (*fig. f*), perhaps a votive offering, comes from the Ulua Valley in Honduras, a region which held several strong Maya characteristics, as in a pocket, when they had disappeared elsewhere. The quality of the stone, milky in tone, is fine. An amazing command of technique is displayed in the living gesture in all the fingers, whether opened or closed. The piece is truly three dimensional; even the knuckles are worked out on the back.

Full standing figures carved in jade are rare in medieval American art. Of the three on *Pl. 252,* the first to our eyes seems somewhat ponderous, the second, rather grotesque, while the third is the most perfect in expression. Certain features of the Olmec type can be discerned in all of them; not one has any headdress and the luglike ears and bald dome prevail. A truly Olmec mouth, however, appears only in the last.

Fig. a, about 20 inches high, is one of the largest pre-Columbian jades ever found. Hands and legs are stiff in execution but the contours of the chest and cheeks are ably worked out. The neck is not so deeply defined as in the others, perhaps for fear the head might break off, but it nevertheless sits naturally on the massive shoulders. Glyphs are inscribed on the belt and the edge of the kilt. The eyes may have been inlaid, as there are depressions in the inner corners. Here we must admire the skill which was able to carve a statue of such dimensions without breaking the stone.

Fig. b is only about 5 inches high and stands in a more vivacious pose. The elongated head is by now familiar but the pointed beard and prominent teeth are unusual.

The statuette shown from the side in *fig. c* and from the front in *fig. d* is 9½ inches high. Of the three, this one is made of the best jade and, as carving, it is the most articulate. The contours are smoothly rounded and agreeably plastic. He stands without support, with slightly bent knees, a posture that gives the figure more elasticity. The hands seem to have held a separate object.

After seeing the standing figures, it is interesting to observe that the seated pose offered more opportunity for variation. All the statuettes on *Pl. 253* have more life in pose and expression. The position of the man in *fig. a* recalls that of the jade from Uaxactun (see *Pl. 242, fig. c*), but here the limbs are freed from the mass of the stone. A close cap is suggested, the only indication of headdress among the seven figures in this display. The face has strength and authority; tattoo or paint may be indicated by the incision work, which intensifies its severity.

The material of *fig. b* is pyrite, an iron ore with a metallic luster, very difficult to work. There is some similarity here to the baby faces of *Pl. 245,* but the eyes slant downward and the face does not show the same plasticity. The tiger line in the upper lip is pronounced—note the depressions made by the round drill in the angles of the mouth. Stumpy arms and legs add to the amusing impression.

A completely different language of expression is manifest in *fig. c,* about actual size as shown, which comes from the Ulua Valley; evidence that the people of this region had excellent plastic feeling and a correspondingly able technique has already been seen in the marble vases. This figure is bearded, with a fringe of moustache at the corners of his mouth—a rarity in Middle American sculpture—and shows relationship to *fig. b* on the opposite page, the only other bearded one in this group. The forward thrust of the elongated head and the wide shoulders dominate the impression. Different planes of the face are sharply contrasted and add to the power of attack on the onlooker, despite the relatively small size of the piece. His hands are well worked out, but the feet are only incised.

In *fig. d,* the statuette, 4¼ inches high, is sculptured from the finest green jade. The pose is the freest represented here and harks back to Maya statuary (see *Pl. 81, fig. b*). In his right hand, the figure holds a plant, in his left, an unidentified object. The head shape and many of the other features are quite similar to those of the standing statue in *figs. c* and *d* on the opposite page. Again, in this example, the Olmec mouth has no repelling effect.

Besides their different poses, these four little figures also manifest diverse spiritual content. The first is intent and has poise; the second is droll and restrained; *fig. c* has an aggressive, almost ferocious air throughout, while *fig. d,* the masterpiece, displays an aristocratic refinement, imparted with grace and subtlety.

The heavy jade vessel on *Pl. 254, fig. a* is carved in the likeness of the Rain-god, Tlaloc.[25] A little under 9 inches high, it weighs ten pounds and three ounces—a compact piece of rather dark, pleasantly green stone. As the verdure brought by the rain was symbolized by the color, one can readily understand why this beautiful block of precious material was used for an image of the Rain-god. The deity's upper lip has the tiger line, and his fantastic tongue may represent falling water. A hole bored just behind the tongue is visible in this picture. His bulging eyes and knoblike nose are fierce and powerful enough to match the heavy sculpturing of the lower features. The ears, with their straightened lines and the convolutions indicated by an incised S, serve as handles. Below the prominent head, a body, hands, and legs are suggested. The hands can be seen on either side under the ears, holding upright some object. Other details of figure and dress are reduced to geometric patterns. A finely rounded rim finishes the vase effectively.

This piece shows a transmutation of a utilitarian shape into the likeness of a mythological being, such as was also seen in pottery. Much in the composition was dictated by ritualistic iconography, but it required remarkable talent to realize it in such balanced form.

The unique statue in *fig. b,* 7½ inches high, was cut from a rather pale mottled jade of fine color (called wernerite) and is unbelievably smooth over the entire surface.[44] The figure has been identified as Toci, Mother of the Gods, from whom the deities sprang full grown. The goddess is shown clasping her buttocks in the typical crouching position of Indian women in childbirth. Her labor is conveyed by the cramped expression, the prominent collar bone, and straining lips. The face of the small figure is mature and the animal paws give to the birth a symbolic significance.

On every side the piece is equally worked out. Straight hair, only partly visible in this illustration, hangs halfway down her back. The ears are unusually realistic. Holes are drilled not only in the earlobes to hold jewelry, but in the feet, body, under the chin, and into the hair, indicating the application of other materials for ornament. When photographed, the statue was tilted forward to stand the figure in a natural position which was probably achieved in pre-Columbian times by additional props, since then disappeared. A monumental quality is embodied in the small piece; despite its harrowing theme, it has dignity and austerity.

Two objects cut from rock crystal, a hard yet easily cracked stone, are presented on *Pl. 255*. The goblet in *fig. a* was found in the celebrated Tomb 7 at Monte Alban. It is about 4½ inches high and 3 in diameter and is carved from a single piece. Its shape is pleasingly proportioned, the polish fine and smooth, and the edges are perfectly rounded. The base was hollowed out to about a third of its height, enhancing the delicacy of the whole, and the translucent material was worked up into a frosty tone. The piece gains dignity by the omission of decoration; there is life enough in the undisturbed play of changing light caught and reflected through the rounded surface.

The life-size skull (*fig. b*) is realistic in detail. Crystal, here polished to a glassy finish, is remarkably effective for this gruesome subject.

Pl. 256 offers other examples of a most remarkable technical skill in working hard and brittle materials. The life-size representation of a frog cut from rock crystal (*fig. a*) speaks for itself. Its naïveté and humor are so eloquent that we have only to enjoy it, unhindered by strange ideology. Reflections are subtly utilized to give it life. Even though unnaturalistic in many details, it appeals to us through the universal language of straight-forward sculpture, the language of toys.

The crystal man in the moon (*fig. b*) is so sophisticated that one may question whether it is a product of pre-Columbian times. According to some writers, the theme was not strange to medieval America: a jade representation, found in a tomb near Quiotepec, Mexico, was reported in 1916.[53] Seler points out that similar figures are found in Zapotec codices, and de Rosny described a sign of the month as "a crescent to which is attached a face in profile."[116] Even if the carving was made after the Conquest, this should not lessen our enjoyment; the illustrations in this chapter have already demonstrated that the pre-Columbian artist possessed the ability to execute such a piece before contact with the white man's civilization.

The model of a temple-base, 8 inches high (*fig. c*), was carved from one flawless piece of obsidian. The evenness of detail is particularly worthy of mention; note the stability gained by cutting the lowest terrace on a slight slant, while the sides of the other four are more nearly vertical. On the top is a depression which suggests additional decoration.

Fig. d is an eccentric flint, a type of object generally found in the region of the Maya Old Empire, frequently in votive caches. Creatures such as the dog, snake, bird, and scorpion are represented, but some pieces defy interpretation. They must have had some ceremonial significance, since no practical use can be divined for such fragile and irregularly shaped objects. The piece here illustrated is said to have come from near the border of Guatemala and Honduras. It is about 7½ inches long and less than one-quarter of an inch thick. To chip off the stone to this bizarre outline, depicting profiles, headdresses, and ceremonial paraphernalia, must have involved expert craftsmanship.

Fig. a on *Pl. 257* is a tripod vase from Tomb 7, Monte Alban, made of a kind of onyx which the Mexicans call *tecali*. This material is well adapted to carving and, like alabaster, can be reduced to sheets so thin that light shines through them; after the Conquest, windowpanes for churches were sometimes made of it. Like the crystal goblet from the same tomb on *Pl. 255,* this vessel has no decoration of any kind; both depend on their pure shape and unadorned surface for artistic effect. The whole interior is hollow and the walls are extremely thin. When the photograph was taken, an electric light was placed inside (the wires were painted out in the print) to give an idea of its translucent quality.

The miniature vase of grayish-green jade from El Salvador (*fig. b*) is only about 2 inches high, but considering the much harder material from which it was carved, the accomplishment is considerable. Its fine spherical shape would in itself excite admiration. In contrast to the onyx vase, the surface is covered with a meandering pattern, probably a stylized serpent body, with the characteristic lattice-and-bar motif of the Maya. The rim is very symmetrical and well rounded.

The remaining specimens are again of Mexican onyx and are said to have come from the Isla de los Sacrificios, situated just outside the modern seaport of Vera Cruz. This region was inhabited by the Totonacs, skillful stone carvers, as other plates in other chapters have already shown. The first of the two (*fig. c*), about 13½ inches high, is carved from a creamy-colored stone, with brown and yellowish veins that accent its vertical lines. Especially noteworthy are the fine line of the fluting on the body, ending in scallops, and the perfect execution of the double rings above them. The combination of incised symbols on the neck—the circles for "jade" or "precious," the fret-scrolls for "liquid"—occur often in

Teotihuacan and Aztec glyphs and has been interpreted as signifying sacrificial blood.[25]

The vase with the lizard (*fig. d*) is about 9 inches high. While the fluted vessel, with its glyphs and mystic associations, is composed and uncommunicative, this piece has an outspoken naturalistic accent. The little creature, its head raised inquiringly over the edge, introduces a comic touch. There is excellent balance in its position, even when viewed from another angle. The bases of each, as well as the use made of the veining in the stone, are completely different.

ANDEAN AREA

This chapter would not be complete without some contribution from the Andean Area. The little Mochica masterpiece on *Pl. 258, fig. a* is of mottled greenish turquoise and only 2¼ inches high. The head and headdress appropriate nearly two-thirds of the piece, but it is this disproportionate presentation that gives to the figure the charm of a good fairy-tale illustration. His face has the preoccupied expression and composure of some one doing something important, and his outstretched hands holding the offering have the gesture of willing and friendly giving. The gift in his right hand appears to be two shells sealed together, a contrivance often used to hold a treasure. As a visible sign of his ceremonial occupation, he is wearing a puma pelt, the head of which serves as headdress—its forepaws hang at the side of the ears and the hind feet and tail are worked out on the back of the statuette.

How standardized were certain plastic features, regardless of material, is demonstrated once more in the panpipe player of cast silver, 6¾ inches high, also from the Mochica culture. Here the headdress is more elaborate, the costume more detailed, and the fingers of the little man are more clearly defined. His carriage, however, the length of dress, the feet, and especially the delineation of the features are identical. Even such a small detail as the eyes is expressed with the same lines and convexities, whether in stone or metal.

Below it (*fig. c*) is a small cylindrical vase of turquoise. The stone has a good even color, and the matt surface gives it tactile charm. Its decoration appears abstract and geometrical, although a symbolic serpent body and monster-heads of Chavin style can be discovered in it. Balance appears in the decorative elements, but beyond that the piece makes no great appeal to us. The ingratiating little Mochica gift bearer and this small impersonal vase show the difference in artistic temperament between two early cultures, in regions not far from each other, both in the north of Peru.

The tools of the pre-Columbian lapidary were less advanced than those of the Chinese. Nevertheless, numerous pieces of medieval American jades can compete in beauty and interest with those of the Orient. Amazingly varying styles will have been observed in these pre-Columbian pieces, although a relatively small range is discernible in technical development. Modulations in taste seem to have influenced the styles over wide regions from period to period. As documents that would help reconstruct the sunken cultures, these small pieces are not of primary importance; their artistic appeal, however, is so obvious that they can be enjoyed *per se*.

Jade was singularly adapted to cult purposes here. Even while still unworked, it presented with its frequently mottled tones the broken surfaces which the Maya deliberately created in their sculpture and pottery. Its extremely pleasant tactile quality, the great variety in color, the suggestive shapes in the raw material all inspired the lapidary not only to bring forth objects of high craftsmanship but to imbue them with a mystic content.

IX

Murals and Manuscripts

PRIMEVAL man scratched and painted on cave walls pictures of the animals upon which he depended, probably as a magic ritual to assure success in the hunt. Here began the art of recording on a two-dimensional surface, a form of expression which has passed through more changes than architecture, sculpture, or any of the applied arts.

As long as the walls of caves served as medium for the animal and human contours, this art had a universal quality. Later, the picture was drawn on animal skins or sheets of plant composition and each civilization created its own pictorial language. In the beginning, each symbol stood for one concept, such as sun, moon, rain, death. Gradually, characters taken together developed into hieroglyphic writing. As the culture became more complicated, the ideas broadened in their association to cover the needs of a growing perception and the writing became more and more fluent, often achieving the state of cursive script.

For this reason it might be said that the recording symbols of a people reveal the grammar of its mind, the whole process of thinking, as fundamental as speech construction. The sequence of the symbols—their arrangement to express a thought—is also peculiarly individual with different civilizations, a revelation of the manner of their approach to an idea. This is a difficult point for us to grasp, for, as most of the languages with which we are familiar are basically related, we seldom have to deal with an absolutely different ideology.

In some civilizations writing developed on the flat surface of the sheet, scroll, or folder, while in others it was inscribed on stone tablets, clay, wax, or metal. Egypt recorded on pages made of papyrus reeds, and young Christianity used animal skins for the scrolls which passed on to posterity the words of the Gospels. Paper, as we know, is a Chinese invention. Ancient as is the practice of writing, the present shape of the book is relatively young. We do not find pages bound into book form until the 11th century, and at that time the written word was at least four thousand years old.

In pre-Columbian America the origins of writing cannot be traced so far back. We do not even know the circumstances of its creation, although it may safely be stated that it was more recent than in the Eastern Hemisphere. In the Southwest, there was some method of communication before the Conquest, but little is known of it beyond the fact that crude signs were cut on the bark of trees to register the time-count.[169] In the Andean Area, counting, records, and communications were effected with the help of the *quipu,* an ingenious invention of cords of varying colors, thickness, and length, in which knots were tied at certain intervals (see *Pl. 299, fig. b*). It is possible that these people might have developed writing in time, as China also had a method of knot-recording before written characters appeared. The scope of the *quipu* is still a matter of conjecture; in the Inca dramatic legend "Ollantaytambo" it is read as a message.

Only the Maya and the Mexicans had developed systems of writing. These were idea-associative in mental structure and pictographic in appearance. Like the early European codices, which treat most frequently of dogma, legends, history, and astronomy, the writings of medieval America pertain chiefly to calendrical, religious, and historic matters. The gods intimately connected with agriculture and fertility were of great importance—as is generally the case among people whose existence depends upon the size and quality of an incalculable harvest—and the pictorial representations of these deities always retained certain attributes from nature. In addition to those gods who grew out of the life of the common people, there was another group embodying the more esoteric ideology of the priestly caste. Gods ruled each day or period, as indeed they once dominated our own, judging from the names of our days and months, and the figures of many of them came to stand for the time-span over which they presided.

It is believed that after A.D. 889, when the Maya custom of erecting dated stelae was abandoned, the records were kept on the more easily handled codices, or manuscripts. The material used for these was deer hide or a "paper" made from the maguey; the surface was covered with a very thin lime wash to receive the text. In Mexico, glyphs were painted in red, blue, green, black, white, yellow, orange, brown, and purple.[169] Most of the primary colors appear in different shades, a sign of refinement in color appreciation. All figures and designs were outlined in black, which bound the different pictorial elements into one composition. A fine brushlike implement was necessary to make the slender contours of this writing and the work could have been executed in hardly less time than was required for the miniatures of medieval Europe.

The extant codices consist of a single long sheet, folded like an accordion, or *leporello.* Each page is 6 or 7 inches from top to bottom, and the unfolded manuscript has been known to measure as much as 34 feet. At each end were covers of wood or hide to protect the contents. In one instance—the Codex Vaticanus B in the Vatican Library (see *Pl. 267, fig. a*)—jade set into the wooden back reminds us of the decorated bindings studded with semiprecious stones of Europe's Middle Ages. As in early European manuscripts, the pre-Columbian codex did not tend to individualize the human figure. The identity of a person was expressed by a name-sign, or glyph, and the gods were differentiated also by costume and their own special attributes. Since the entire life of the community was highly hieratic, little importance was attached to the individual. There are, however, a few codices in which lives of personages are related, such as Codex Colombino, which gives an account of the Zapotec or Mixtec warrior, "Eight Deer," to be discussed later in this chapter.[26]

The Maya, outstanding in their other arts, excelled also in the calligraphic work of codex illumination. It may be supposed that a great number of codices existed at the time of the Conquest. However, Diego de Landa, one of the first bishops of Yucatan, in his religious zeal ordered an *auto-da-fé* of all these works of the devil. Only three survive. Later in his life, he assembled a mass of material on the ancient culture of the Maya, which constitutes the main source of information from Conquest times. But the harm done was irreparable; the deciphering of Maya writing is greatly hampered by the scarcity of comparative material. To date less than one-third of the total glyphs known have been interpreted, including numerical symbols and those with astronomical significance.[92]

The numerals are expressed in two ways: by dots and bars and by characteristic heads. A bar-and-dot system for numbers was used also by the Zapotecs, but these were placed below, not above or beside, their glyphs.

After the Conquest several of the Maya-speaking tribes, among them the Quiché who dwelt near the shores of Lake Atitlán in Guatemala, wrote down the legends, mythology, and history of their people in their own dialect, inscribed phonetically in Latin characters. These books, the best known of which is called the *Popul-Vuh,* meaning "Book of the Community," have been translated into Spanish and reveal valuable details of the ancient beliefs and customs. However, since they do not contain pictorial and glyphic material, they furnish no clue to the hieroglyphs of pre-Columbian times.

Aztec writing had a more direct pictographic approach than the abstruse symbolism of the Maya. For example, the conquest of a town was indicated by a spear driven through a temple, above which the name-glyph was inscribed. The name-signs of personages developed into decorative appendages.

As fourteen medieval Mexican codices survive, a larger field is disclosed by the writings of these people. Besides religious and astronomical subjects, there are lists of the tribute exacted from vassal tribes, certain legal documents, and polychrome maps (see *Pl. 267, fig. c*). When Cortés landed on the coast of Mexico, Aztec scribes immediately painted pictures of the Spaniards, their horses, ships, equipment, and other novelties seen in their entourage to supplement the verbal report carried to Montezuma (see *Pl. 270*). Historical codices also exist, telling of the Aztec migrations and giving the general outline of their history. In these, tribal movements are shown by a line of painted footsteps passing from the glyph of one town to that of another, together with the date-signs. The codices were used in the schools of instruction and in the training of initiates for the priesthood. The number of persons, however, who could interpret the text was probably always quite small.[151]

In some civilizations, a symbol came to indicate a sound, and from there on writing and painting separated. Whether the pre-Columbian systems were standing on the brink of phonetics at the time of the Conquest is still a matter of discussion.

The fresco of medieval Europe was frequently a symbolical scene enlarged from manuscripts which the friars had illuminated. On walls, however, the condensed character of the compositions disappeared; the large surfaces called for and absorbed more and more decorative elements, until the spiritual content of the fresco tended to become of secondary importance and the main purpose came to lie in its decorative quality. Later the panel was placed on an easel and finally abandoned for canvas. Thus the manner which had been adapted to the static wall went through a great transformation and received at the same time considerable stimulus to further development. If a parallel could be drawn in medieval America, it might be found in the painted pottery vases of the Maya, where perhaps traditions of both mural and manuscript meet.

The mural in pre-Columbian America did not have the broad educational purpose as in medieval Europe, but rather was reserved for the initiate. It decorated the temple sanctuary and the palace, far from the walks of humble folk. The painter must have been a distinguished member of the artisan group, like the scribe who illuminated the codices, or the carver of jade, or the "jeweler," but it was apparently not the intention of any of these craftsmen to create art for art's sake, for the mere practice of virtuosity and the production of "beautiful" objects. The primary purpose of their work seems to have been to record or to invoke the power of magic, and the art never completely lost its symbolism to become purely decorative.

Pre-Columbian painting told its stories on the flat surface of a wall with the same pictorial language used on the page of a codex. Although on the walls, the figures were often enlarged, and the animal, plant, and building details frequently carried more minutiae, the modern eye will notice in both pictorial manifestations an absence of perspective. The lowest section of the picture is used to present that part of the scene nearest the spectator. Each level above it represents growing distance, although the figures are not necessarily reduced in size.

This manner of composing may appear strange to us, but we must not forget that in Europe, too, early painting denoted different distances by using different levels; with the exception of our western civilization, even today many cultures tell their stories without our studied use of perspective. The modern Russian icon does not employ it. Chinese scrolls, Japanese woodcuts, Persian miniatures all indicate it by working from the lower edge toward the top. The contrast of light and shade, one of the tricks of suggesting perspective, is not practiced by any of them. Figures are evenly lighted, without shadows; trees stand in the same tone of color in the foreground as in the background, and movements are conveyed mainly through the expressiveness of the lines. The surface to be painted is, as a rule, fully used—too crowded and too decorated for our eye. Yet, our own age shows the same symptoms, and our own illustrations, advertisements, moving pictures, and even more pretentious paintings are often crammed with people and detail.

If we keep all this in mind, the wall-paintings of pre-Columbian America may seem perhaps a little less strange. Unfortunately, far too few of them remain to allow a comprehensive study either of methods or development. The friable stucco wall of a temple or palace was the first part to disintegrate. Exposure to dampness, the growth of the jungle, whose rootlets spread like a web over the surfaces, have raised havoc among those wall-paintings that have survived the hands of man. Many must have been ruined in pre-Columbian times through the practice of filling in the lower rooms with rubble when a new building was superimposed. The ingenuity of the archaeologists, however, has rescued some buried murals. One at Chichen Itzá, revealed inch by inch on the crumbling plaster, was copied piecemeal by the artists, who did not perceive the full content until their work was fitted together.[94] Other paintings that did not disintegrate at the time of their discovery have since faded so badly that they are practically indecipherable; only the immediate copying in water color has saved their subject matter from being lost.

For this reason, most of the illustrations of murals shown here are necessarily copies, conscientiously executed, which give at least an impression even if lacking the weight of the original.

THE SOUTHWEST

The Indian in the Southwest carved human and animal figures on the rock walls of canyons and painted murals on the walls of his kiva. In some cases, the pictographs can be related to the wall-paintings and also, through certain ancient symbolic paraphernalia still surviving, to Indian designs of the present day. Some primitively painted figures in certain Southwestern sites have been known for a long time, but the recent excavations at Awatovi, in northeastern Arizona, and Kuaua, New Mexico, have considerably changed our ideas of the standard attained in this medium.

The section of wall-painting from Awatovi, reproduced on *Pl. 259, fig. a,* features human figures engaged in a ceremony. The geometrical shape at the extreme left doubtless has some symbolic significance. Note that the frontal figures are not full length: the central one is cut off below the waist and the second seems to stand elevated, with only the upper part of the body detailed. The two men in profile, on the other hand, are drawn in full, with the feet carefully executed. This may indicate that the first two are standing in the background, while the others are dancing in front of them, an impression borne out by their bended knees. The signs before their mouths may signify chanting. An elaborate object appears above the head of each—in the case of the largest figure, a bowl decorated with the step design, a favorite even today among the potters of the Southwest. Their ceremonial make-up shows great variety; even the patterns on the kilts of the two "dancers" are dissimilar. The lunar ornament at the throat of the chief celebrant shows not only excellent drawing but gives the impression that the piece itself must have been of delicate construction.

Fig. b shows another mural, 10 feet long and 4 feet 2 inches high, painted on a kiva wall at the same site. It presents an abstract design, highly complex and symbolic; but even though ignorant of its meaning, we are impressed with its stunning decorative character, the vigor in the layout, its play of line and color. Although the composition itself has complete equilibrium, the individual units are far from symmetrical, and it is this which gives the mural much of its interest and life. The birds on the lower edge differ in kind and color and few details are repeated in the right and left halves. Besides the white bands, which seem to embrace and connect the whole composition against its coral-red background, the color scheme includes blue, green, yellow, brown, and black. In contrast to the impression received from the abstraction of some modern paintings—which epitomize not so much an idea as a bid for attention and the will to be "different" —one is struck here with the integrity of purpose.

Another group of mural fragments was found on ancient kiva walls at a site called Kuaua, near Albuquerque, New Mexico. The preservation and removal of the crumbling adobe surfaces was a remarkable technical achievement for the University of New Mexico. In the painting (*fig. c*) a human figure is depicted holding a long slender staff bound with a tuft of feathers. The body is stylized into a long rectangular shape without proportion, but care is bestowed on the details of the skirt and the pendants or tassels on the belt. Execution of the face, especially the eyes, shows individual treatment when compared with the fragment in *fig. a,* although the painted design on the chin and the long hanging about the head make the expression remote for us.

The Indians in the Southwest never lost their talent for painting. Scenes picturing Spanish horsemen in a Christian procession were found on a cave wall, delineated in a style very similar to these kiva murals. The sand paintings of the present-day Navaho preserve many pre-Columbian characteristics, among them the angular elongated treatment of the human body. Even the splendid storytelling or decorative paintings of the young Indian artists at the United States School at Santa Fé display this atavistic trend.

MEXICAN AND MAYA AREAS

In medieval America the painter apparently had no intention of decorating a surface for the mere sake of beauty. His purpose was to commemorate an event, or, by applying magic symbols, to state an esoteric truth, or assure the benevolence of gods in whose honor a particular building had been erected. Therefore, if we, with our conscious esthetic approach, find our standards applicable to his work, it is purely fortuitous.

The fragment on *Pl. 260, fig. b* was painted on the base wall of a large altar in the Temple of Agriculture at Teotihuacan. This composition is among the very few in which accurate symmetry between the right and left halves can be observed. Even conceding a certain amount of simplification by the hand of the draughtsman who made this copy, we cannot escape the marks of intention in the use of two central units of glyphic significance—a stylized mask with feather headdress and a serpent scroll with stones and shells—as an axis from which wavelike motifs flow. These are chiefly floral and plant forms, rare in pre-Columbian art. In between, simple scalloped bands run across the surface, holding together the entire design.

In contrast to the horizontal linear conduct of this mural, there is in the second detail from this temple (*fig. a*) an outspoken tendency toward verticality. This results from an attempt to depict a complicated scene that for our eyes would demand a knowledge of perspective. Since the idea of foreshortening and the other devices for denoting distance were unknown to these people, the problem was solved by placing the figures on different levels. The picture supposedly represents a Toltec ceremony. The buildings at the right and left might be temples; their decorated character seems to support this impression. In front of each a fire is burning, the tall flame of it highly stylized. Men and women are making offerings—the symbols before their mouths denote speech or chanting. Care has been taken to differentiate the personages by costume and gesture. Particularly appealing is the figure seated at the right in the first row, holding a bird in his hands. On the third level, a man in dark raiment, his hand upraised, gives an idea of Toltec dress unlike any we have met before. The headdress also differs considerably from the elaborate ceremonial style with which we have become familiar. His necklace is emphasized, and his decorated shawl is an indication of an advanced textile art, even in that early period.

As in numerous early civilizations, the arts in medieval America were closely allied. Color was lavishly applied on masonry surfaces. Sculptured slabs, also painted, constituted structural parts in some of the temples and palaces. In certain cases a decorative effect similar to that of the mural was achieved by sculpturing the stone blocks of the walls themselves with a very shallow relief and painting the carving.

Pl. 261, fig. a shows a section of such a wall found in the small building at the base of the Temple of the Tigers in Chichen Itzá, called the Temple of the Bas-Relief. It pictures a ceremonial procession of priests and warriors moving toward an altar to do honor to their god Kukulcan. At the risk of seeming repetitious, we must call attention again to the fact that there is not the slightest sign of serializing the units which form the whole; no two of the elaborately dressed dignitaries, with their spears and spear-throwers, are exactly alike in attire or pose. Great differentiation in certain details is not evident; nevertheless the scene has none of the monotony of an Assyrian stone relief, though it may seem more remote to us because of its less familiar ideology. In other late structures of the same site the same technique is applied to square piers at entrances and in colonnades.

A comparison of the two illustrations on this plate shows the contrast in both composition and figure delineation between even the late Maya art and that of the Mexican high plateau. *Fig. b* presents a section from a mural painted on the sacrificial altar in Tizatlan near Tlaxcala. The Tlaxcalan people were kindred of the Aztecs and their name in Nahua means "land of maize." This tribe was the first to ally itself with the Spaniards and thus aided in the downfall of the whole pre-Columbian civilization.

In the fresco fragment here pictured, two figures face each other. The left, with a skull as head, represents the Death-god. Opposite him stands Tezcatlipoca, the God of Youth, who was believed invisible, omnipresent, and all-powerful.[151] Both were gods of primary importance, occurring frequently in codices. Death seems even more ferocious in his attack than the God of Youth, who shows a certain deliberation in his attitude. Both are dressed and ornamented with such a profusion of trappings that the outlines of their figures proper are virtually concealed. Their characteristic features, such as the open-mouthed skull and tufted headdress of the Death-god or the forward-thrust, clawlike right foot of Tezcatlipoca and the two painted streaks across his face, appear in every representation of them.[97] The skull of the Death-god is painted in white and his feet are white, otherwise the chief colors used in his costume are blue, red, and yellow. A darker scheme was employed for the God of Youth, with black and deep red predominating.

In technique and delineation, the frescoes were not far removed from the illumination of manuscripts. The ignorance of perspective or scale is noticeable whether the scene was painted on an immovable wall or a fragile sheet of animal or vegetable material. The medium did not affect to any great extent the composition or linear conduct; a closely related stylistic manner will be observed in either case.

The Maya offer an exception also in this field. They were so highly developed in their artistic sensitivity that they "felt" differently for a mural than a manuscript. This will be especially evident in the two plates that follow.

The ruins of Uaxactun in Guatemala have revealed the spectacular achievement of the early Maya people in architecture, pottery, and jade. Recently A. Ledyard Smith of Carnegie Institution of Washington uncovered a mural fragment which raises considerably the already high opinion held of their remarkable talent (*Pl. 262, fig. a*). A comparison of it with the murals of any other culture here presented will make clear why the art of the Maya has received the keenest interest and most favorable comment from outsiders.

The Teotihuacan painting (see *Pl. 260, fig. a*) is composed of small wooden units, and, while each figure has a certain animation in itself, the picture as a whole is flat and static. In contrast, the people in the Uaxactun scene are not detached from one another, as if introduced one after the other into the composition, but are blended into a rhythmic free-flowing procession. While in the Teotihuacan piece the figures are placed above each other, apparently as space afforded, in the Uaxactun mural use is made of two divided levels, exactly defined. Superior effectiveness must also be granted the delineation of dark figures on a light ground.

An evaluation of the drawing will also reveal the greater artistic talent of the Maya in the portrayal of such a diverse group of persons, no two quite alike in dress or deportment. The eye falls first on the three sitting inside a house; especially noteworthy is the one in white, admirably drawn. Outside, on the left, two elaborately dressed figures face each other, one in a commanding attitude, the other with his right hand on his left shoulder in sign of submission. At the right, taller and shorter persons are assembled in animated groups. Near the door, two are engaged in conversation, as are the two above them, but with what contrast in mood and appearance and how ingeniously spaced to bring out the difference in feeling. Above, one member is detaching himself from a loose group of four, apparently to join the others on the left—a clever connective in the composition. Below, a line of followers is massed behind a small seated figure with a scroll or drum. The variations in height, the uneven spacing of the feet express perfectly the shifting and straining as they await the result of their leader's discussion. It is difficult to realize that there is little overlapping of the figures, only the two on the extreme right being actually superimposed. There is no shading whatever; the highly differentiated poses and complicated drapery are communicated by outline alone. One more factor should be pointed out among the many real pictorial values of the piece, and that is the individual pose of all the feet. The clear fine glyphs may identify the event as well as the participants.

That the high standard of artistry shown here is not an isolated case is manifest from the free designs and rhythmic compositions painted on the extant polychrome vases discussed under pottery. But in this mural a more human atmosphere prevails when compared with the hieratic air usually dominant. A freedom from restriction is noticeable, perhaps resulting from an innate feeling for the broader surface.

Fig. b is a water color of a fragment found on a wall of Edifice 3 in Chacmultun, Yucatan. Although doubtless a less exact copy than the one above, enough of the composition is caught to give a good idea of the original. Its story takes place on one level. The ceremonial character of the scene is evident. In the upper half of the surface the lavish headdresses, standards, and canopies are distributed with considerable decorative feeling. Even if this mural has not the artistic finesse of the one from Uaxactun, it is still a whole world removed from the frozen friezes of Egyptian tomb frescoes and has nothing of the stiffness of early Christian mosaics and wall-paintings. The figures are light and varied, as they stand poised, step onto the platform, lean forward, or rest the hand on the hip; an adroit execution of details proves that the abundant artistic tradition of the Maya prevailed to a high degree also in the New Empire. In accordance with Dr. Spinden, we find the Maya spirit still predominant here.[137] When these illustrations are compared with those on the following plate, which seem to be of a later date, the transformation in Maya art due to Mexican influence becomes evident. The highly decorative pageant-like representation gives way to a less refined drawing with more agitation—one might say the key of the composition changes from minor to major.

A mural that originally covered a space 9 feet high and 12½ feet wide on one of the inner walls of the Temple of the Warriors at Chichen Itzá is reproduced from a water color on *Pl. 263, fig. a*. It was found in fragments in the débris of the temple. A scene of every-day life in a seacoast village of Yucatan is depicted. In the upper two-thirds of the picture land is represented, upon which stands the same type of whitewashed hut with a thatched roof that is built in that country today. The building on the right, with its greater size, more elaborate execution, and the serpent poised above it seems to be a palace or temple. The settlement is full of activity. A woman is seated by a cooking pot that stands over an open fire outside a door; men are starting off on a journey with staffs in their hands and burdens on their backs, held in place by straps around their foreheads. There are trees with spreading tops. A crane wings across the scene, and the fisherman's catch lies in a little heap on the shore. At the left, a figure is kneeling at the water's edge.[94]

The lower part of the painting is gray-blue water. Three canoes in a row move across it, each paddled by a standing rower and carrying two Indians in warrior's dress with shield and arrows. Fish and reptiles of various sizes, shapes, and colors swim through the waves.

The earth is painted a reddish brown, the color of the soil of Yucatan, the flying crane is a natural pearly gray, and the trees show variations of green. In the water large reddish crabs, white shells, and a turtle with brown head and legs and green striped back are recognizable. Here the same pictorial manner is applied as in the Teotihuacan mural, but with much more dash. The strange but appealing atmosphere conjures up something of the mood of Gauguin's Tahitian paintings, bringing with it an association that may help us come nearer to the vanished world depicted here.

Fig. b is a detail of the mural from the east wall of the inner chamber of the Temple of the Tigers at Chichen Itzá. Although not from the same building as the preceding illustration, it seems, nevertheless, to complement it. Stylistically both murals are related, although a comparison of the trees will show differences. Representations of plant and animal life predominate in the scene, with a jaguar pictured in the foreground, another clinging to a tree, three serpents, each differently posed, and a bird. The warrior at the lower edge and the figure at the right introduce the human element.

A detail of a wall-painting copied in water color from the west wall of the Temple of the Tigers at Chichen Itzá is shown in *fig. c,* depicting a battle in and around a town. The difference between this mural and the others lies not so much in its technical execution as in the subtle combination of figures in repose with those in highly agitated attitudes. Each of the four men seated in the center foreground is differently dressed and is drawn in a different posture. They might represent a war council; some have speech scrolls before their mouths. Note the woman in a relaxed position in the lower left corner, a figure that would not be out of place in any of the other scenes on this plate. The seated warrior in the opposite corner with his leg pulled up seems to be working on a weapon, while the five fighting men in the second plane are wielding darts or spear-throwers. Their costumes are worth study. Not only are all individually outfitted, but each reveals another fighting pose. Considering the crowded space, the variety and turbulence in the scene, the picture is beautifully composed. The presentation of the action is especially ingeniously solved: the quiet happenings take place on a horizontal line, while the vehemence of the fighting group is augmented by the oblique, upward trend of their movement.

The inclination of the Maya of the Great Period for calligraphy, apparent also in their other arts, is markedly present in the Uaxactun mural. It is noteworthy that, while here the figural composition is interspersed in several places with columns of glyphs, no writing appears in the later murals. On the other hand, the speech scroll, associated with Mexican cultures, is seen in *figs. b* and *c*. The Uaxactun fresco and, to a certain degree, that from Chacmultun represent an early and pure Maya art and the battle scene, with its companion pieces, a late period, permeated with alien influences. However, all radiate strong storytelling atmosphere. We can enrich ourselves with this pictorial symphony, from the *andante maestoso* of Uaxactun to the *allegro vivace* of this last illustration from Chichen Itzá.

Mural painting at Chichen Itzá does not seem to have been practiced continuously during the life of the city. At any rate, of the one hundred thirty-one coats of whitewash in the Temple of the Warriors, only one, the twenty-second from the wall, was so decorated. The pictures were sometimes executed ". . . on freshly applied stucco, still soft enough to groove beneath the stylus, with which, in such cases, the preliminary sketches were drawn, but more commonly upon hardened plaster where the sketch lines were done in red. After being outlined, the figures were filled in with the desired colors, then re-outlined in black. . . . Often there is marked divergence between the sketch and the finished painting. Sometimes the pose of a limb is changed, or the proportions of any feature may have been altered in size or relation, as revealed by the faint sketch lines to be found upon scrutiny beneath the later applied pigments.

"The nature of the colors that have so successfully resisted time is a matter of interest. The early colonists . . . enumerate various dyes of permanent color to be obtained from native trees and plants, and the Maya today affirm that the colors of the old paintings can be duplicated with vegetable dyes which could be made from growths in the neighboring bush. However, samples of every color found in the frescoes in the Warriors complex have been examined in the Geophysical Laboratory of Carnegie Institution and found without exception to be of mineral origin. Red clay, composed principally of iron oxide, is plentiful beneath the surface soil in depressions in the limestone everywhere about Chichen, but most of the greens, blues and yellows must have been drawn from far sources.

"Of the medium or media in which the pigments are mixed, nothing of a positive nature can be said. Commonly the wall paintings have the flat surface and clear transparency of water colors, but in some cases, notably on the benches in the buried temple, the different pigments, when applied, had a viscosity as of oil paint. Indubitably the medium used there was of syrupy consistence. Presumably it was some sap or other organic liquid, the dried residue of which has been so broken down by time that it is not recognizable to the chemists." [94]

Pl. 264 presents yet another style of wall-painting. Many of the tomb chambers explored recently at Monte Alban disclosed finds of gold, pearls, jade, turquoise, bone, and pottery, but Tomb 104 had something quite different to offer, though of equal importance. In this subterranean chamber the painted walls were in such a good state of preservation that they give a rare opportunity to study the original mural. The entrance to this tomb is now reconstructed so that the chamber proper can be closed off from the outside, thus preventing damage from exposure or defacement. The pottery figure above the outer doorway was seen on *Pl. 15, fig. d.*

In *fig. b,* a photograph taken from the door of the tomb is reproduced, showing the two side walls and the farther end. The general decorative effect of the mural is sensed at once. Pottery and offerings were found in the five niches in the walls and personal ornaments on the one skeleton—apparently that of a high priest—that lay outstretched on the floor.

As in some of the paintings at Chichen Itzá, the figures were first drawn on the smooth plaster in red, then the details filled in with red, blue, yellow, black, and gray. The white of the wall itself was also used in the design. A final touch was given by framing each detail with a black outline. An occasional divergence is noticeable between the original as sketched and its final execution. Dr. Caso remarks on the haste with which these walls were painted, caused apparently by the urgency of the interment. As a result, the red used in the two side figures is darker than that in the end wall, where the color seems to have been thinned to eke it out. Investigations show that all the pigments were derived from minerals. [24]

The figure on the left (*fig. a*) is supposed to represent Xipe-Totec, the God of the Spring and of the Flayed. On the end wall the great mask with ornaments extending at the sides and on top is a Zapotec god, not definitely identified, whose body seems part of the center niche. The figure on the right (*fig. c*) appears from its make-up to be a local version of the Maize-god. Smaller pictorial elements, such as the parrot on the left, the masks, and numerical glyphs, form connectives that bind the mural into one continuous unit (*fig. d*). The ceremonial attire of the two deities, quite specific in each case, can be studied on the unrolled aquarelle. Headdress, necklace, breechcloth, sandals are all executed in detail. Both figures hold a pouch in the hand nearer the spectator, while the other is extended. What orthodoxy governed this iconography is manifest in the different execution of the eyes: in the C-shaped eye of Xipe-Totec, the Mongol cut of the center mask, and the almond shape of the Maize-god. Note the use of jaguar tails in the costume of the last.

Such frescoed tombs seem to have been fairly common in Monte Alban, as others of the type have since then been discovered there. However, none so far has contained such well-preserved paintings.

The murals on this plate have a completely different pictorial atmosphere than those previously discussed. In the first place, they are not story-telling. In considering the design, it is noteworthy that it has elements of both wall-painting and the manuscript—neither realized to its full possibilities. A certain connection could perhaps be traced with the fragments of murals in Mitla (shown on the following plate), particularly in the glyphic units, but no similarity at all can be found to those of Teotihuacan. The great differences between the two cultures are apparent in this field also.

The same dual nature—with qualities of both mural and manuscript—is discernible in *Pl. 265, fig. a,* a section of a painted lintel at Mitla. Here, however, the leaning is more toward the manuscript, in which gods and other supernatural elements are presented with a condensation approaching glyphs. The total effect is that of a miniature, done in negative painting and applied on a large scale in combination with architecture. This same manner of decoration is also recognizable on pottery in the Mexican Area (see *Pl. 111, figs. d* and *f,* and *Pl. 116, fig. c*).

Fig. b is a detail of a painting on the Temple of the Frescoes at Tulum (see *Pl. 30*). The use of stylized serpent bodies to divide the surface recalls the painted relief at Chichen Itzá (see *Pl. 261, fig. a*). The Old Empire tradition of the manikin scepter is manifest in the figure in the lower right corner. In many of the figures, however, Mexican mythology seems to dominate; trends from as far as the Pacific coast of Nicaragua and northern Costa Rica have been recognized in certain details.[67] The condensed quality seen in the Mitla murals can be sensed also here.

While in Mexico, manuscript and mural remained close in their general aspect and pictorial quintessence, in a certain period of Maya art these two branches of painting found expression in divergent visual terms. A section of a page of the Maya Codex Dresdensis, or the Dresden Codex, presented in *fig. c,* will show the manuscript style. The fluent drawing that was apparent in the Maya murals and which is characteristic of all Maya art, here is raised to the quality of tinted copper engraving. Two rows of seated individuals are pictured, each of whom—with the exception of one raised on a dais—is apparently holding a smaller person in front of him or carrying one on his back. Some of the major figures are strikingly alike in appearance, even to pose, headdress, and ornament, and it is believed that they are different representations of the Moon-goddess.[155] Above each row a series of glyphs is drawn, which at a glance may seem fairly uniform but on closer inspection will reveal more individual differences than our Latin characters. When we consider that the section reproduced is less than 5 inches long, we can appreciate the skill required to execute so much design in such a small space.

Fig. d is a page from an Aztec codex (Borbonicus) which depicts the renewal of the sacred fire at the beginning of a 52-year cycle, a solemn ceremony in the Mexican Area. The year is indicated in a small square at the top of the page (left center). To the right of it, the tribal god of the Aztecs descends from his temple, above him the blue and white flag of the month. In the extreme right corner is the glyph of the place (Hill of the Star) where the new fire was lighted. A road, designated by footprints, leads down from the hill, passing in front of the houses, to the temple which the priests approach with their torches. Other dignitaries will be seen coming from the left carrying large fagots in their arms. The men, armed, await the result of the ceremony. In the houses of the village all the inhabitants, even the children, have their faces covered with masks made of maguey leaves, and, shut in a granary, a pregnant woman is guarded by a warrior, for according to their belief she may at this particular time turn into a beast.[21]

With this slight explanation, we find the page telling more of a story than is gathered at first glance, giving us a taste of the strange psychology of these people. It will be noted that in the frescoes the tendency was to fill up the surface with decoration or color, while in the manuscripts much of the background was left empty, in the natural color of the paper.

A full page of the Maya Dresden Codex is reproduced on *Pl. 266,* somewhat enlarged to show the miniature-like quality in the execution of the three figures. Interesting differences in the individual poses also led to the choice of this particular page for reproduction. The first two are believed to represent two manifestations of the god of the planet Venus, while below lies a prostrate victim.[155]

The seated figure at the top is strongly reminiscent of two jade pendants, both in costume and pose (compare *Pl. 240, figs. a* and *b*). He wears the same elaborate headdress, with the eye of the mask emphasized; his right hand holds a stylus-like tool, and the left lies unoccupied. This similarity between an early manuscript and jade pieces of rather late date—in all probability not even from the same region—offers further proof that the pantheon of the pre-Columbian peoples was settled and that a certain god had always certain irremissible iconographic paraphernalia.

The kneeling figure in the middle is the clearest; his whole attitude is that of a young and powerful warrior. His costume is minutely delineated, even to the fringe and tassels of his breechcloth and the ornaments which he had to wear on legs and wrists. The violent gesture of the right hand with the darts is so convincing that one fails to notice at first that the fingers are reversed. (In a naturalistic representation, the back of the hand would be seen.)

The recumbent figure at the bottom of the page wears a monster-mask. His position seems natural, if somewhat uncomfortable. Both feet are shown, giving the impression that one is looking at him from above. Particular finesse is evident in the drawing of the right arm, which appears actually to bear the body's weight. In its linear facility and the compactness of its execution, this figure recalls to a certain degree the great Initial Series glyphs carved in stone at Quiriguá (see *Pl. 71, fig. b*).

The combination of glyphs with such exquisite miniatures reminds us of the illuminated manuscripts of medieval Europe, with their finely painted initial letters always related in subject matter to the text. The writing here is fluent, almost cursive, with "air" provided by the numerical dot-and-bar symbols. Lively coloring is used in these three vignettes, and the outlines are brought out in dark brown which may originally have been black.

From the subtle and flowing delineation in the Maya codices, we turn to the more angular and static work of illumination found among the cultures of the Mexican high plateau.

On *Pl. 267, fig. a,* a section of an Aztec manuscript from pre-Conquest times, the Codex Vaticanus B, is opened to show the screenlike folding of the pages. Each carries a main figure supplemented with a number of subordinate details and is framed on the top and right sides with glyphs. Some of the codices were read horizontally from left to right across two pages, then down and back from right to left, the two pages in this way forming the unit. In other cases, the text follows a horizontal and vertical route, across and down, and still others are read by unfolding the screen, turning it in a vertical position, and following the glyphs from top to bottom in serpentine curves—a veritable puzzle to which only the initiate had the clue.

Although most of the pre-Columbian manuscripts are concerned with rituals and astrology, a few are devoted to genealogies and historical matters. In a scene from the Codex Colombino (*fig. b*) an individual, identified as Eight Deer, is pictured kindling the sacred fire in the presence of a high priest. The story of this hero seems to have been recorded in several codices. It is thought that he was a Zapotec or Mixtec king, named, as was usual, for the day of his birth.[26] Both figures are dressed in ceremonial garb. Beside the fire drill, flames are drawn. The temple at the left is ornate in its decoration, with the alternate stairs painted red and green. On the entrance platform is an altar with offerings.

A comprehensive idea of the type of map made by the Aztecs is given in *fig. c.* It shows a section of rather mountainous land, on which roads are marked by two parallel lines with footprints in between. Rivers (lower right corner and top left) are painted blue and designated by three parallel lines between wavy ones; the interspersed circles are abbreviations of the glyph for *atl,* meaning "water."[116] Towns are represented by cartouches with their name symbols, placed to show their relative positions to the road—different in every instance, just as the lay of the settlements doubtless differed. A glyph similar to the character in the lower left center—an open animal jaw—appears also as the name of a town in Montezuma's Tribute Roll (see *Pl. 269,* the center of the page). Mountains are painted dark green, representing the vegetation which covered them. On the left, a temple is found, drawn upside down, possibly to show that its entrance faced the crossroads. It is worth while to compare the trees in this map with those of the murals from Chichen Itzá. Maps of quite recent date from the Far East show a naïveté in cartography similar to this ancient example, perhaps as much as four hundred years old.

On *Pl. 268* drawings from pre-Columbian and post-Columbian times that use the same manner of delineation are placed side by side.

Fig. a was executed by a Mexican after the Conquest but retains much of the pre-Columbian spirit. It comes from the Codex Magliabecchiano, a pictorial series illustrating ancient Mexican feasts and deities. Judging from the bird-mask, the god Xochipilli is depicted here, taking part in a ceremony that occurred every seventh month of the Mexican year.[102] He is borne by two attendants and preceded by a musician blowing on a conch, whose dress is much more elaborate than that of the carriers. The three scrolls above the instrument denote the sound (compare *Pl. 294, fig. f*).

The Codex Mendoza, from which our next illustration is taken, was painted after the Conquest on the order of Don Antonio de Mendoza, the first and greatest of all Spanish viceroys of Mexico. He instigated the recording of the pre-Columbian history of the country. This manuscript, made on European paper and completed before 1550, incorporated a copy of an old Mexican chronicle, the original of which has since been lost, recounting the history from year to year of the kings of Tenochtitlan and their conquests, beginning with 1325 and ending with 1521. A copy of the Tribute Roll of Montezuma (see the following plate) was also included. The last portion, compiled by a Mexican scribe, is devoted to "life from year to year," and gives vignettes of the country as it was before the arrival of the Spaniards.

The adventures of this codex are typical of the century which produced it. The ship on which it was sent was captured, and the book was taken to Paris. Thirty years later, it was purchased by Richard Hakluyt, chaplain to the English ambassador, and brought to England, where an English translation was made soon after at the instance of Sir Walter Raleigh. It now rests in the Bodleian Library at Oxford.[27]

The drawing in *fig. b* shows a group of Aztec warriors in full regalia. All have a certain uniformity of make-up, but the feather ornaments fastened behind the neck show variety in execution, as do also the garments, necklaces, and spears. Note the insets, which were usually of obsidian, in their lances. The shields especially have individual patterns.

Fig. c, from the pre-Columbian Codex Borbonicus, pictures a fiesta of youths who have not yet graduated as warriors. They dance around a gaily decorated pole to the music of a drum (compare *Pl. 292*). In the lower right stands Otontecutli, the Otomi God of Fire, at the foot of his own temple stairs.[155] The celebration reminds us of the games of pole-climbing still to be seen in Mexico on certain feast days or of our own Maypole.

Pl. 269 shows one page of the original medieval Tribute Roll of Montezuma II, preserved in the Museo Nacional, Mexico. The reports of the *conquistadores* attest to the well-knit organization of the Aztec confederacy; this page, drawn in colors on maguey paper, is tangible evidence of it.

The Tribute Roll contains a list of more than four hundred tributary cities of the Empire, together with information on taxes in kind exacted from each. On the page illustrated, the names of the towns levied—in this instance, those of the "hot countries" or tropics—are placed in the bottom row and up the right side of the sheet. It is interesting to note the individuality that characterizes the glyph of each. The cone and flag-shaped designs above the articles listed denote the quantities required. Beginning in the upper left corner and moving right, the items are, row by row: varnished yellow gourd bowls, little pots of bees' honey; a large wooden pack full of grain (maize, sage, beans, and various seeds), baskets of white copal; balls of unrefined copal wrapped in palm leaves, five strings of jade beads; war dress—note the long legs, visible also in the preceding plate—in sets of yellow, blue, and green, respectively, with matching shields (the center type is reproduced on *Pl. 287, fig. a*); below these, white mantles of a specified size, and, next to them on the right, a number of copper axes; finally, quilted, striped, and richly embellished mantles and women's garments.[107]

Other pages list gold dust, small turquoises, diadems, and earplugs of gold, bags of cochineal, reams of maguey paper, salt in molds (for use of the nobility alone), loads of chocolate and small pottery vessels out of which it was drunk, cotton, scarlet feathers, and jaguar skins.[27]

Among the historians of the Conquest and of the pre-Columbian culture in Mexico, Bernardino Sahagun ranks as one of the greatest. This young Franciscan arrived in Mexico in 1529, before the cultural and artistic traditions of the country were completely shattered. He acted as Superior in several monasteries and finally settled in a college in the Mexican capital. Wherever he was, he tried to establish contact with the Indians, and later, after his research had received official sanction, he frequently assembled the most intelligent and best educated of the older natives who had grown up before the Conquest. He questioned them in friendly conversation about their ancient customs and beliefs and had the answers given him in the form of Aztec picture-writings. In this way, he compiled a manuscript of twelve books, containing, besides records of the religion, history, and social life of the Aztecs, a grammar and dictionary of the Nahua language.[57]

Sahagun wrote his volumes in this tongue and then translated parts of them into Spanish. The pictures which illustrate his work show a high degree of skill, combining the old Aztec tradition in picture-writing with much learned from the Europeans (*Pl. 270*). The evenly laid brick walls, for instance, the fore-shortening attempted in the interior (*fig. a*), and the landscape (*fig. f*) demonstrate familiarity with Spanish pictures, while certain primary forms, such as the mountains (*fig. h*) and the Indians themselves, retain their glyphic outlines. Their keen observation embraced all phases of life. *Figs. c, d,* and *e* are examples of their accurate depiction of animals.

Their botanical knowledge was no less thorough. In 1552, two Indians compiled an "Herbal" from Aztec lore, with illustrations and descriptions of one hundred eighty-five plants as well as their medicinal value. They divided the plants into classes, orders, families, and genera and presented them in color with remarkable clarity, showing leaves, flowers, and even roots.[37]

ANDEAN AREA

In the Andean Area, especially in the coastal region, walls were finished with plastered surfaces on which paintings were applied. The subject matter was generally similar to the stucco relief decoration of the walls (see *Pl. 43*) or reproductions of arabesque or animal patterns from their weaving and pottery. Fragments have been uncovered at Chan-Chan, Paramonga, Pachacamac, and elsewhere, but unfortunately none of these is well enough preserved to furnish any satisfactory impression.

There were no manuscripts in this area. Markham mentions pictures of past events painted on boards, but not a single such tablet has survived.[78] Various scenes appear on pottery, as has been shown. This type, however, becomes less frequent after the spread of the Inca Empire. Seemingly the subsequent stepping-up of production resulted in the abandonment of this naïve, sometimes virtuose, but always delightful manner of recording.

X

Miscellaneous Applied Arts

IN THE dark ages of Europe, when the continent was one vast battlefield of invading barbarians, applied arts, such as the fashioning of jewelry and horse trappings, weaving, and wood-carving, throve, laying the groundwork for stylistically independent national schools of later centuries.

If only the so-called "fine arts"—architecture, sculpture, and painting—are contemplated in medieval American civilization, the picture lacks the depth and color that the textiles, metal-work, pottery, and jades provide. But these people reached out even farther for raw materials and developed amazingly skillful techniques in carving wood, bone, and shell and in making mosaic and featherwork.

WOOD-CARVING

As common as stone and more easily worked, wood, next to clay, is the most obedient medium for the use of temple and palace. As it is more perishable than most other materials, little has survived unfortunately, even from less remote periods. Without question, the budding cultures of the Western Hemisphere used wood widely for articles of daily life as well as for the more obvious purposes of building. It is believed by some that the earliest glyphic writing was inscribed on it. Wood was generally a staple article of trade. Bernál Diaz, chronicler of the Conquest, describes a special precinct in the Aztec capital where boards, cradles, beams, blocks, and benches were sold, each commodity arranged separately. Even some of the tribute paid to Aztec rulers was in firewood, beams, and planks. Chairs, benches, thrones, and other furniture were made of wood. Montezuma is said to have had a wooden screen, brilliantly colored and gilded, which was set before him when he dined, for it was regarded as improper to see the ruler eat.

That there were objects of wood among the gifts which Cortés sent to Seville in 1519 is documented by the inventory that accompanied them. Among other things, suits of wooden armor, helmets, shields, bows, and *atlatls,* or spear-throwers, are mentioned.[126] Some of the *atlatls* now in European museums may date from that occasion. Besides the spear-thrower and wooden helmet, later discussed in more detail, the most unusual device is, perhaps, the slat armor, which was used in the Pacific section of the United States, also in the Southeast and possibly in the Mexican Area. Constructed of small ribs of wood held together with cords, it gave adequate protection against arrows and stone missiles, although not against bullets. Scarcely less important than the weapons were the images of the gods. Wooden statuary was common over a wide area at the time of the Conquest. Utilitarian objects were frequently made of wood. In the ruins of the Southwest, crutches were found which utilized the V-shaped crotch of a branch as arm support. Although household utensils for holding liquids and storing corn and seeds were generally fashioned of clay, they were also made of wood.

Even the simplest article nearly always carried on it some embellishment, if only a medallion. Wooden spoons or scoops, boxes, trays, and such small objects were decorated with carving in low relief or were sometimes painted, sometimes inlaid with turquoise, shell, and bone. Techniques related to lacquer were also applied. The artistic talent of the pre-Columbian Indian and his love for his craft are documented in these unimportant pieces as surely as in the more spectacular ones.

Mention should be made of the great trading boats, or *canoas,* sometimes capable of holding twenty-five to thirty passengers. The prow and, less frequently, the stern were ornamented with symbolic designs and human and animal shapes.

The great untapped forests of medieval America furnished in abundance the raw material. In Central America the chief wood for building was the extremely hard and durable *chico-sapote,* well adapted for structural purposes. Other woods commonly in use were cedar, cypress, pine, spruce, oak, laurel, mahogany, and other hard varieties peculiar to tropical and semitropical regions.[126]

The tools used in working the wood ranged from the primitive stone axe to —at late last—the copper hatchet and axes and adzes with copper blades. Large trees were probably felled by burning. Although the technique acquired in wood-carving may later have been applied to stone, it should be pointed out that finer and sharper implements are needed to sculpture wood without splintering it or raveling the long cross fibers. For this, the craftsman probably employed sharpened shells, bone, and obsidian.

The use of animal masks in ceremonies or for totemistic purposes was a wide-spread practice in medieval America. Two wooden masks from states outside our areas are presented on *Pl. 271* because of their remarkable workmanship. The first (*fig. a*) is about 11½ inches high and represents an antlered human head. Shell is set into the eyes and mouth, and it may have decorated the ear-plugs. The carving comes from the Spiro Mound in Oklahoma, which also yielded the embossed copper plaques shown on *Pl. 194,* as well as a large and important collection of stone pipes.

It is interesting to note how differently the same idea was expressed in a different culture. The masquette in *fig. b,* 10¾ inches over all, does not blend the human with animal features. It is the pure and beautifully naturalistic representation of a doe, executed with sculptural command. An amazing maturity, rare north of the Mexican Area, is manifest in this piece, unequaled in the delicacy of its linear conduct and full-blooded plasticity. It was found at Key Marcos in southern Florida and is said to have been carved about the 15th century by the Calusa Indians, a tribe now extinct. Besides the work illustrated, a number of masks, representing among other animals the deer, alligator, and wolf, were dug up from deposits of wet muck. All retain traces of paint and the eyes show inlay of shell. Parts of some, like the deer's ears in *fig. b,* had leather hinges so that they could be moved with strings.[31] Early Spanish reports mention a monumental art in wood in that region, all evidence of which is now lost.

The spear- or dart-thrower, called *atlatl* in Nahua, was for centuries the most effective weapon of pre-Columbian America. It was common to all areas here discussed and can still be found in use in remote districts. In certain regions the blowgun also was employed. The bow and arrow did not appear until late in medieval American history.

The butt of the spear or long dart rested against a peg or hook near the tip of the spear-thrower, which furnished, as it were, an extension of the throwing arm. With the aid of this contrivance the projectile was sped farther and with greater force than by hand alone. The sling, one of the earliest weapons of mankind, and one widely used in the Old World, is based on a similar principle.

Pl. 272 shows spear-throwers from three areas. The first (*fig. a*), a plain well-balanced piece, comes from the Southwest. Clearly visible at the top is the hollowed-out section with the hook to hold the spear; the grip at the other end resembles a saber hilt.

Fig. b is an elaborate specimen from the Mixtec region in Mexico. The length of the carved section is 13¾ inches and of the whole piece, 21⅜. The accompanying drawing (*fig. c*) gives the decoration in clearer detail. Four figures are depicted in various poses: the top one diving downward facing the left, the second standing with upturned face, the third facing right, and the fourth, like the second, looking upward. At the bottom is a finely executed mask with a glyph. The wood is very hard and highly polished. On the other side the groove, 19½ inches long, which held the spear, is bordered by a pattern of intertwining serpents.

The three weapons in *figs. d* and *e* come from the Andean Area and seem to be Ica in style. The first two, rounded and without a groove, have bone handles carved to represent heads, one animal and one human. The third carries a complete figure, also carved of bone, a little seated man only 3⅓ inches high playing a panpipe. Despite his oversize head and certain undeveloped details, the piece is as expressive in its modeling as the statuettes on *Pl. 258*.

The elaboration of the *atlatl* resulted in such magnificently carved pieces as those presented on *Pl. 273*. The very rare specimen covered with gold leaf (*fig. a*) was undoubtedly made for ceremonial use. Nine figural elements, one above the other, embellish it. As in *fig. b* on the opposite plate, a diving figure is at the top, here in frontal view. The carving is exquisitely wrought and would bear considerable enlargement to show the fine relief work employed—the same sculptural language as that used in stone on a much larger scale. The bone grip with its precise binding is additional evidence of remarkable workmanship.

The two *atlatls* in *fig. c,* also in a perfect state of preservation, were included to show that the decorative scheme was not always divided into small sections with mythological figures. In the one on the left the undulating body of a feathered serpent fills most of the ornamented space. At the top a human head can be discerned, emerging from the reptile's jaws—a motif often found in the late art of the Mexican Area (see *Pl. 234, fig. a*). The grooved face of the piece on the right carries two condensed motifs, geometric in effect. Both specimens bear traces of red and green paint.

In *fig. b* a part of a wooden ceremonial staff is shown. It is 11¼ inches long and was recovered from the Sacred Well at Chichen Itzá during the dredging operations there. The larger figure wears a tall headdress, while the smaller head below is sculptured within a serpent's jaws. In both cases, tiny arms and legs on the sides, more clearly seen in the lower figure, suggest a condensed body in a diving attitude. The character of the carving differs completely from that on the *atlatls*.

Some authorities believe that the forerunners of the Maya stone stelae were of wood. At any rate, a number of the early monuments show a shallow rounded style better adapted to the softer material than to stone (see *Pl. 236, fig. a,* dated 677). Later the art of wood-carving attained such heights as that reproduced on *Pl. 274.*

As a composition, this piece, taken from Temple IV at Tikal, Guatemala, and dated 741, is completely in harmony with the severe and awe-inspiring style of this religious center. The precision of outline and the softly rounded surfaces show complete mastery over the medium. The lintel measures about 5 by 7 feet. Its central theme is a standing dignitary and the feeling of ceremonial pomp is well conveyed. His face, turned toward the left, is typically Maya in feature. The spreading headdress is a study in small elements of decoration, pressed one beside the other. Shoulders and chest are also covered with dense ornament. His apron-like hanging in front and the befeathered shield and staff which he carries should be noted.

He stands within a loop formed by a great feathered serpent (compare *Pl. 9*), one head of which, with half a masked figure emerging from the jaws, can be seen at the left in the photograph. The stylized elements of a second head, discernible on the extreme right, are similar in line to the fret-scrolls on the marble vases from the Ulua Valley (see *Pls. 94* and *95*).

This relief is not only the largest extant wood-carving of the Maya, but it embodies the essence of their greatest period in art. The fine differentiation between the larger motifs that make up the serpent body, flowing and less dense in arrangement, and the compact smaller elements of the main figure successfully throws the emphasis on the human, despite the wealth of detail. It required great skill to separate such ornate units, practically superimposed, in such shallow relief. The Serpent Bird at the top center, which also appears at Palenque, Piedras Negras, and Copan, should be mentioned. Tablets of glyphs fill the upper corners.

This flamboyant manner of presentation—almost overornate for our taste—is evident also in Chinese, Hindu, and Tibetan art, where there is so much detail that the main subject often seems submerged in the surrounding embellishment. Although the Maya's preference for extravagant decoration remained a characteristic until the Conquest, in later centuries it lost its exuberance to give way to a more loosely composed and more conventionalized style.

The great thickness of the walls at Tikal accounts for the large size of the lintel. Several of this type were removed by Dr. Gustave Bernoulli in 1877 and are now in the Museum für Völkerkunde at Basle, Switzerland. Maler's account explains in great measure their damaged condition. The problem of dismantling them was a difficult one, as Indians do not use the saw. Consequently, the natives frequently resorted to burning off the beams at both ends to save the cutting edges of their *machetes*. As this was a slow process, they often left the fire to go for their meals or a drink, heedless of the damage done to "a pair of sacerdotal feet, the plume of a helmet, or some interesting hieroglyphs." Furthermore, unless watched, they were apt to throw away one piece or another of the heavy wood to lighten their loads on the long journey back through the jungle.[75]

The arid climate that prevailed along the coastal strip in the Andean Area preserved in excellent condition wooden objects that escaped vandalism. *Fig. a* on *Pl. 275* shows the decorated top of a long pole which has a flattened section at the opposite end. In the rows of lacy carving below the sextette of stiff little wooden men, one feels the influence of woven patterns. Even the human figures are pattern-like in their uniformity. This type of work seems to have been practiced in the Ica Valley and its vicinity. The purpose of such pieces is unclear. According to some they served as tomb markers, while others would have them steering paddles.

Fig. b is allegedly the decorative pendant which hung from a woven coca-bag and is also Ica in style. Coca leaves, from which we derive cocaine, were mixed with lime and chewed, especially on long journeys, to provide extraordinary endurance. On the wooden section alternating rows of two motifs are carved in low relief, the top one similar to the perforated "star" pattern in *fig. a*. The center of each unit was inlaid with shell, and four rows of silver bands ornamented the heavy strands of the fringe. This piece was probably not of great importance, nevertheless the good taste and skill shown in combining the materials reflect the high quality of this culture.

In *fig. c* are four wooden spoons with figures on the handles. The larger two are about 4 inches high. There is a flat two-dimensional quality in the carving. In the third from the left the material below the design was not even cut away. Nevertheless, the figures, even though sketchy, have considerable liveliness when compared with *fig. a.* The pattern build-up and technique of execution are characteristically Coast Tiahuanaco, and the figures are reminiscent of Viracocha's two types of attendants on the Gateway of the Sun. All show the kneeling or running posture seen on this monument and "starred" heels which appear on the pottery. Note the ceremonial staff with a human head carried by the one on the right and the small bent figure at the feet of the one beside him.

The art of applying a lacquer-like finish to wood or calabash was known in the Andean as well as the Mexican Area. This pre-Columbian accomplishment is one of the few that continued into post-Conquest times. On *Pl. 276* a group of wooden cups is shown treated in this manner, called by the Quechua name, *kero*. All date from late Inca, some even from post-Columbian times, and many have been handed down in families. The wood was first covered with a clear varnish, then the surface to be colored was lightly engraved, and finally the pigments were applied.

The decoration on *fig. a* is especially delightful because of its spacing, with widely separated human figures in the upper section and, in the center, a tight geometric pattern recalling textile motifs (see *Pl. 191*). Flowers at the base, harmonizing with those just below the rim, serve to unify and balance the composition.

Fig. b shows a goblet, about 7 inches high, decorated with encircling bands of geometric and stylized bird elements. (Compare *Pl. 192, fig. b.*) Variety is furnished by the vertical incised lines on the body of the vessel and the striking zigzag on the rim against a cross-hatched background.

Nearest to our esthetic standards is the beaker in *fig. c*, 6½ inches high, with its pleasing row of birds carved in low relief. A plastic band, suggestive of a snake, encircles it like a cord, and is, with its series of mushroom-shaped ornaments, a rare feature; unusual skill was necessary to execute it on the curving side of the vessel.

In *fig. d* an interesting division of figural and geometric themes is again apparent. The handles here are particularly noteworthy, carved in the shape of animals—probably pumas—holding tenaciously to the edge of the beaker. Although the creatures are not too naturalistic, the clinging position, especially of the forepaws, is distinctly conveyed.

The *kero* in *fig. e* is shaped like a puma head. Flat story-telling pictures in brilliant hues cover the plastic representation—an example of the composite language of decoration in the Andean Area.

Fig. f presents an unusual shape: a shallow bowl standing on three curving legs set on a rounded base. In this piece the inlay-like appearance of the finish is particularly clear. The geometric patterns, the serpent on one leg, and the other motifs taken from nature on the base furnish indeed a miscellany of designs. The "fortress" with banners carries a cross at the top—an indication probably of post-Conquest inspiration.

In the coloring of these *keros,* glowing red predominates; buff and yellow, blue-green, brown, olive, black, and salmon also occur. It is believed that the cups were used for the native beer.

A wooden seat from late Inca times is illustrated on *Pl. 277, fig. a.* Compare it with the Late Maya jaguar throne on *Pl. 92.* The piece is over 11 inches high, 14 long, and 11 wide. The two animals, each on its own oblong base, face in opposite directions, connected only by the hollowed-out seat which they support. They are painted a greenish black with yellow spots and have scarlet tongues and grass-green eyes. The use of much cream and white lightens the general effect. Note the elaborate designs everywhere along the edge.

Fig. b shows a wooden beam of a scale, 7 inches long and probably Chimu in style (see *Pl. 299, fig a*). In the balanced combination of human, animal, and geometric designs the characteristic charm of Chimu art is perceptible.

TURQUOISE MOSAIC

An original and very skillfully handled technique was that of mosaic-work, by means of which objects of various sizes and shapes were incrusted with turquoise and other semiprecious stones. Just as jade was revered in the Maya and Mexican areas, turquoise was highly prized in many regions for its symbolic meaning. In the soft blue of the stone was envisioned the spirit of the vaulted heavens or of an expanse of life-giving water.

Examples of mosaic-work have been found in the Southwest, the Mexican, Maya, and Andean areas. The Incas, however, although expert lapidary workers, do not appear to have engaged in this craft; at any rate, no specimens are known. It would seem that not only the greatest number but the greatest variety has been found in the Mexican Area, but even here they are comparatively rare, with less than fifty known at the present time. Seventeen were uncovered in one cave in the Puebla region, where they had been treasured by the natives for years after the Conquest, probably revered as precious relics of a lost but not forgotten epoch.[125] Still more recently in the Maya Area at Chichen Itzá a number of objects incrusted with mosaic were dredged from the bottom of the Sacred Well, among them, staff heads and masks. During the reconstruction of the Temple of the Warriors, a beautiful mosaic plaque was uncovered, composed of more than three thousand bits of stone,[93] and another was found in the throne buried in the Castillo (see *Pl. 92, fig. b*), embedded in the back of the jaguar.

Unworked turquoise as well as finished mosaics was exacted in the annual tribute of the Aztecs; on the Tribute Roll eleven towns were assessed for it and five more for *piedras ricas de azul*. According to the description of Cortés, in the great market of Tenochtitlan the merchants who sold gold and the venders of precious stones displayed their wares side by side.

One of the earliest expeditions from Cuba toward the mainland, made in 1518 under Grijalva, received presents of mosaic-work with stones resembling turquoise, and between 1519 and 1525 Cortés obtained on various occasions, either as gifts or loot, a number of articles mentioned in his letters or in the writings of early chroniclers. A glance at a partial list of these will reveal not only the wide application made of this art, but its importance as decoration. The stone was used with feathers in a very original combination. According to one description, there was a large feather-work box "lined with leather and ornamented with a large disk of gold and a design in blue stones; a sceptre with inlaid stone mosaic with two golden rings and feather decoration; an armlet of stone inlaid with mosaic; a mirror placed in a piece of blue and red stone mosaic with feather-work stuck to it; sixteen shields of stone mosaic with colored feathers hanging from the edge; a piece of colored feather-work which the lords of the land wore on their heads and from which dangled two ear ornaments of stone mosaic work with bells and golden beads; a bracelet of gold with ten pieces of blue and two of green stone; a butterfly of gold with wings of scallop shell and body and head of green stone." [125]

The development of the art of the lapidaries and mosaic workers in Mexico, like that of the goldsmiths, is attributed by Sahagun to the Toltecs. He describes the elaborate technique of preparing the turquoise, mentioning also the working of pearls, amber, and amethyst and their incorporation into jewelry. Walter Lehmann, however, believes that the art became known to the Aztecs by way of the Zapotec culture.[64]

The materials most commonly used in mosaics were turquoise, jade, malachite, quartz, beryl, garnet, obsidian, pyrites, and shell. Wood generally constituted the base, but stone, bone, gold, silver, and perhaps even vegetable paper were also used. Turquoise of good quality is not very hard and can be easily worked. In Sahagun's description of the technique, it was shaped by an instrument of tempered copper and scraped with sharpened flints. Facets were cut and the piece polished with great care, sometimes with bamboo, which gave it a special luster. Stones were carefully sorted for color and shade. The inlay was built up, bit by bit, often into a highly complicated pattern, and glued to the foundation by a vegetable pitch or gum.

The principle of mosaic-work may be said to appear also in the composite stone ornaments on buildings. The ruins at Mitla (*Pls. 16 to 18*) show the idea, enlarged on a grand scale. Also, according to tradition, the inner walls of certain edifices at Tula, on the Mexican high plateau, were ornamented with colored jasper and shell set off by plaques of gold and silver.

The turquoise mosaic mask in *Pl. 278, fig. a*, 6½ inches high, is one of the best preserved pieces extant. The base is of cedar and painted red on the inside. The turquoise used in the incrustation is rather pale, except for the minute particles which rim the eyes with brilliant hue. Cabochon stones stud the face, ingeniously breaking the monotony of the even surface. Eyes, nostrils, and mouth are pierced through, and the eyeballs are designated by pieces of iridescent pearl shell with holes bored in the centers for iris. Shell teeth are inserted between the parted lips, and the gum which holds the shell in place is gilded.[125] The rows of small stones are tellingly placed to bring out the lines of the features. A black-and-white photograph can only slightly convey the vibrant color scheme of any of these mosaics.

Fig. b is a sacrificial knife about a foot long, the blade of which is fashioned of light-colored waxy chalcedony chipped to a leaf shape. Its carved wooden handle, overlaid with mosaic, represents a crouching human wearing an eagle headdress and a feather cloak falling over his shoulders and back (compare *Pl. 286*). The figure, grasping the blade in both hands, is so firmly bound to it with cord that he seems to be pushing it with his whole body—a conception singularly appropriate to an instrument of a savage rite.

The large double-headed serpent of mosaic in *fig. c*—interpreted as the monster that carries the sun[153]—was probably a breast ornament. It is 17½ inches long and 8 high, with the foundation again of wood, hollowed out at the back and painted red. The teeth and fangs are of white shell, while the gums are indicated by a strip of pink shell. A raised band of turquoise and deep red shell is laid across each nose. The sparing contrast of coral-pink and rich red on the heads gives a dazzling effect. Turquoise of the finest quality was used throughout, shading deepest toward the edges to bring out the rounded body.

The helmet, 7½ inches high (*Pl. 279, fig. a*), is hollowed out to fit the head and painted green inside. In spite of whole sections of missing inlay, the composition is striking, both in color and shape. Two gaping serpent heads can be distinguished at the base of the two crests, picked out in iridescent shell. It is possible that the main surface of the helmet was covered with a design denoting their intertwining bodies.

Because of its decoration and its almost perfect state of preservation, the shield shown in *fig. b* is one of the most important examples of aboriginal American mosaic. It is 12¾ inches in diameter with an average thickness of ¾ of an inch. The holes in the margin indicate that it was either applied to another piece or was rimmed with another material, perhaps an edging of feathers. The wood of its base is probably cedar. For the most part, this splendid mosaic consists of minute circular pieces of sky-blue turquoise, and the pattern is brought out by the fine gradations of color as well as by the use of larger pieces in outlining. It has been estimated that nearly fourteen thousand stones went into the composition.

A sun disk is represented, with eight points extending across the wide outer circle. In the upper center the sun appears again, inclosed by the "celestial band," with a female figure, probably a goddess, plunging head downward from it. Two other persons stand holding objects somewhat similar to those borne by the deity. An irregular shape, probably a speech scroll, emerges from their mouths. All these figures are composed of larger pieces of turquoise shaped and often incised to represent details of features and costume. The earplugs protrude above the surface of the piece, as do a number of other rounded elements, somewhat in the manner of the cabochons of *Pl. 278, fig. a*. At the bottom of the inner circle, very distinct against the darker background, is the glyph for Colhuacan, an important town in the Valley of Mexico in medieval times. The string of four dots at either side of this is believed to have calendrical meaning. Saville is of the opinion that the scene relates to the worship of the planet Venus and reads the date as 1461 or 1513.[125]

Two types of shields were in use by the Aztecs: one for war, the other ceremonial. The shield of the common soldier was probably plain, that of a man of rank was often painted. Shields used on festive occasions were very ornate.

Most of the hundred and fifty listed among the booty of Cortés carried feather-work, twenty-five were ornamented with mosaic, and some were adorned with gold (see *Pl. 287*).

In addition to the examples illustrated here, earplugs, idols, and animal figures studded with mosaic-work or inlaid with stones and shell should also be mentioned. The artistry in this work was appreciated quite soon in Europe, and as early as the middle of the 17th century a book was published in Italy, describing and illustrating this Mexican craft.[125]

SHELL-WORK

To the pre-Columbian peoples, who put their hand to all the gifts of nature in their arts, shells offered still another medium. Sea shells, naturally highly prized in the interior, were valued as ornaments and for inlay also by the inhabitants of coastal regions.

As in numerous early cultures, shell played a multiple rôle in the Western Hemisphere. In Alaska, among certain tribes of California, and widely among the aborigines of eastern and central United States, it constituted a medium of exchange. Its most general use, however, was as jewelry, either in combination or alone. Quetzalcoatl, the tribal god of the Toltecs—Kukulcan in Maya mythology—is traditionally depicted with a section of conch as breast ornament. Small shells were used as pendants on the mantles of young men of the military school in several highland tribes of Mexico,[151] and among the coastal people of the Andean Area the material was cut into shapes of small animals, birds, and fish and sewed onto garments.

Although five of the shell ornaments illustrated on the next two plates do not belong to the areas presented in this survey, they are included because of certain technical and iconographic affinities they have to late works from the Mexican Area.

On *Pl. 280, fig. a,* a shell gorget from Tennessee is pictured, nearly 4 inches in diameter. A human figure is incised on it in a half-kneeling or leaping pose. In his right hand he holds a human head or mask, in the left, a short club or ceremonial staff. His head is drawn in sharp profile, turned right. Noteworthy are the copper head ornament, which is like a double-bladed axe (see *Pl. 194, fig. a*), and the leaf-shaped "apron" or breechcloth that also appears in the next illustration, a piece from a distant region. The thick necklace may be a twisted rope of shell beads, such as has been found in many burials. Concentric incised circles form both frame and background, serving almost as a lens to focus attention on the figure.

Fig. b presents an incised conch, 13 inches long, from Spiro Mound, Oklahoma. The unrolled pattern appears beside it, showing more clearly the mythological bird-man with outspread wings and tail. As ingeniously as the design is arranged, the shape of the shell itself is not utilized to bring out any plastic effect of the subject.

The gorget with the scalloped edge (*fig. c*), 5 inches in diameter, comes from the same site in Oklahoma. The attitude of the figure is quite similar to that in *fig. a,* but has more dash; the static quality of design in the Tennessee piece is here replaced by vigorous drawing, which gives the figure a rushing, leaping, almost flying appearance. A certain emancipation is also shown in the liberty with which the incised right hand and both feet trespass into the plastic border, and a more articulate artistry is manifest in the combination of incised design with a raised and evenly "beaded" frame. Note the eyes on the elbows.

From the subject matter of these pieces contact with Mexico is hypothesized, believed to date after the 15th century, probably in the spread of a cult.[108]

The examples on *Pl. 281* show a certain development in that the background is cut away, producing an openwork effect. The gorgets in *figs. a* and *c* also belong to the Mound Builder culture and were excavated from the Etowah Group in Georgia. A motif common among the Etowah people, the pileated woodpecker, is featured in the first (*fig. a*). The two birds, standing on a perfect cross (inverted) are as pleasing in their stylization as a Byzantine design. There is a certain heraldic and outspokenly decorative quality in the ornament that reaches beyond the culture group which produced it.

In contrast, *fig. c* is characteristically pre-Columbian. It shows a warrior-like figure wearing a headdress of deer antlers and a breechcloth tied with a large loop. Except that the profile is turned to the left instead of the right, the subject is in linear conduct quite like that of *fig. a* on the opposite page. At the same time, there is an interesting similarity of design to the bird-man on that plate: the barred section at the right resolves itself into a wing resembling those incised on the conch. Both figures have an aquiline nose and paint around the mouth; even the necklaces appear to be of the same type. The clawlike right hand of the Georgia piece supports the idea that an eagle-man is represented.

Fig. b speaks a different language. This pendant, highly articulate in both concept and execution, comes from the Huaxtec region of the Mexican Area. It is about 7 inches high. The subject seems to be of a sacrificial character. On the left, leaning forward, a male deity is shown holding a tube which leads down to a broad shallow vessel in the center of the piece. At the right is seated a female deity who carries two darts or arrows bound together. Both figures rest on the open jaws of two feathered serpents, whose intertwined bodies support the bowl mentioned above. The lozenge-shaped section below the group signifies water. Although the lower frame is lacking, a recumbent figure with upraised knee and arm can be discerned at the bottom.[11]

An interpretation of this mythical scene would lead too far afield and is unnecessary for an appreciation of the art in the piece. The general impression is highly decorative. Openwork alternates with solid surfaces in perfect balance, and the graceful loop in the center breaks any monotony that may be felt in the build-up. Various incised elements are introduced, not only in the execution of the two main figures, their jewelry, teeth, even fingernails, but also in the free-flowing lines of the snake heads and plumes. The serpents themselves are differentiated and the shift of their individual markings can easily be followed.

The small finger ring (*Pl. 282, fig. a*), scarcely three-quarters of an inch in diameter, comes from a Hohokam village in the Gila Valley in southern Arizona. The material is glycimeris shell, common in the region but originating in the Gulf of California, a distance of nine days' journey on foot. The perforations appear to have been made by deepening an incision with a sharp-edged sandstone tool until the core could be broken out by tapping, for the use of a drill would doubtless have shattered the brittle material. Piles of such cores have been found in the district. This technique is similar to that employed by the Alaskan and British Columbian natives in the manufacture of jade implements.[170]

The enlargement in the photograph shows the details—considerably more than one would expect to find in such a diminutive piece and in a material so fragile. Two birds perched back to back constitute the face of the ring, each holding the head of a serpent in its beak and clutching the rattles in its claws. The twined bodies of the reptiles form the hoop of the piece. We may assume that the eyeholes were originally inlaid, and paint may have contributed to the effect. Within these lilliputian dimensions, material and composition are brought together in a solution that would have never occurred to the white man.

The miniature head in *fig. b*, 2½ inches high, is fashioned in the round from a solid ball of yellowish-red shell. Objects made of reddish shell are listed among the treasures which Cortés received from Montezuma. The general absence of contours in the features and the double mouth show this to be another representation of Xipe-Totec, the God of the Flayed. So realistic is the execution that we can sense the god's eyes and nose beneath the sagging skin. Remarkable detail work is noticeable in the headdress, earplugs, the hair pulled back toward the side, and the collar that frames the face. Here a round drill must have been extensively used, a highly difficult operation in this medium.

The beautifully opalescent mother-of-pearl, 3¾ inches high (*fig. c*), was allegedly found at Tula, Hidalgo, a site fifty miles north of Mexico, D.F., and believed to be one of the earliest cities on the Mexican high plateau. Toltecs, Chichimecas, and Aztecs occupied it in turn and left the marks of their respective cultures there. Certain similarities between sculptures at Tula and those of Maya sites would indicate an exchange of cultural ideas, and trade might account for this piece turning up here, for its stylistic characteristics are strongly Maya.

The use of this medium for such a representation is very rare. A chief is shown, seated cross-legged, wearing an elaborate headdress. His placement and posture remind us of figures on jade pendants; but, though the subject is handled in the manner of a jade carving, the softness of the shell and the high lights bring out more sensuous qualities in the figure, well caught in the photograph. His headdress has received much attention, with the extraneous material at the side cut away. The left hand with its closed fingers is a particularly fine detail that deserves mention. The ornament is quiet in atmosphere and superb in execution. It has four glyphs on the back, and was bored for suspension.

On this plate, three areas with markedly different styles are represented, as well as three different ways of working the same material: openwork technique, three-dimensional carving, and relief—a variety which should be noted.

Three examples of the skillful and appealing work in shell from the Andean Area are presented on *Pl. 283*. The two earplugs (*figs. a* and *c*) are about 2½ inches in diameter, and both show human figures pieced together out of many small colored bits of shell. The task of fitting and setting the small units, one beside the other, required much dexterity, and the effect is naïve and toylike. In *fig. c,* the little man stands in a static pose, with feet turned outward and arms outstretched, holding objects in both hands. In the other (*fig. a*), movement may be expressed; the feet, both pointing to the right, and the floating line of the mantle suggest motion. The rim in each case is of iridescent shell and the background a deep lavender; tones of orange-tan and jade-green are used, and the inlaid eyes of the figure on the right seem to be turquoise. From their style, the earplugs are thought to belong to the Chimu culture.

Still greater patience, as well as a marvelous color sense, was required to produce the central piece (*fig. b*), a shell cup with an inlaid base, fashioned in an interesting hour-glass effect. It is nearly 9½ inches high, Chimu in style, and comes from Lambayeque. The cup is admirably proportioned and sophisticated in conception. Unfortunately in a black and white reproduction the refinement of the color combination is lost. The cup proper consists of four slightly curving sections of translucent white shell, evenly cut and polished, which are ingeniously held together with metal clasps concealed by four inlaid panels. It blends smoothly into the main body of the piece, which is made of wood and inlaid with shell. The bulk of the fish in the center is eased by the tapering lines of its head and the brilliant pink stripes of the fins and tail. Its head is a solid piece of the same bright tone. Inlay of milky color in the body also serves to lighten the effect and makes a good connection with the translucent white above it. Inlaid fish motifs of pearl and darker iridescent shell enliven the dark brown of the wooden stem.

BONE-CARVING

In early medieval times, ivory—rather neglected today—was much valued in the Eastern Hemisphere. The pre-Columbian carver of our areas did not have this material at his disposal but utilized to good advantage the bones and teeth of smaller trophies of the hunt, among them peccary, jaguar, deer, and mountain sheep.

The skull of a wild boar was used for the carving, or rather engraving, shown on *Pl. 284, figs. a* and *d,* a piece found in a tomb at Copan. The main subject, incised on the top of the skull (*fig. a*), depicts two men seated within a quatrefoil medallion, facing each other in a conversational attitude. More unusual is a detail from the side (*fig. d*), where a group of running boars is pictured with considerable verve. Animal representation in such a realistic manner as this is quite rare in Maya art. The problem of superimposing one body on the other seemingly did not hamper the carver. Smaller animated figures of a jaguar, monkey, deer, and a flying bird appear on the same piece. It is interesting that peccaries are drawn on peccary bone.

In addition to its treasures of gold, jade, and rock crystal, Tomb 7 at Monte

Alban yielded more than thirty pieces of carved jaguar and deer bones similar to those shown in *figs. b* and *c,* some studded with turquoise. They range between 6 and 8½ inches in length and their use has yet to be definitely settled. It has been suggested that they were nose ornaments, knife handles, or ceremonial daggers.

In the compositions, gods are represented in human and animal form, some of which have been described as having calendrical significance. A discussion of the glyphic meanings of the carvings is not necessary, however, to enjoy the full extent of the carver's mastery, especially when we consider the limited surface upon which the complicated and condensed subjects had to be placed. The diversity of the design arrangements—now horizontal, now vertical in tendency, and in others, separated by oblique bands—makes an interesting study under a magnifying glass.

A small tool, only about 2 inches high, from the Hohokam culture of the Southwest is presented on *Pl. 285, fig. a.* It was made from the leg bone of a mountain sheep or a deer and used as the handle of a bone awl. Its relationship to the bird ring cut from shell (see *Pl. 282, fig. a*) can be sensed. The piece was calcined in a crematory fire, but was saved after excavation by ingenious chemical treatment. A mountain sheep stands above entwined rattlesnakes, combining favorite motifs of the region. The carving is simple but cleanly executed and somewhat reminiscent of early Near Eastern statuary. The tubular formation of the bone was utilized for the shaft of the implement and the natural contour of the end, for the sheep's horn.[171] Although it expresses a totally different and much simpler artistic concept than the companion figure on this plate, it holds its own beside it through its power and sincerity.

Among the masterpieces of Maya art—perhaps the smallest in size but by no means the least in importance—is the diminutive figure, 2¾ inches high, carved from the femur of a jaguar (*fig. b*). Its provenience is unknown. It has been suggested that it was used as ornament for the top of a scepter or ceremonial staff; holes in the base would indicate some such application.

As the figure carries no weapons, it is thought that he represents a priest.[25] His unbending and stoic expression is emphasized by the arms akimbo. He is clothed in the skin of a jaguar and the large fan-shaped headdress doubtless was made of quetzal feathers. Its lines are carved with such variety that it avoids ungainliness. The hole above the forehead was very likely for a jade or turquoise inlay, and a carved pendant in the shape of a monkey head hangs on the breast. Remnants of red paint are visible, which may have caused the roughened surface noticeable in the front. Maya glyphs, probably of chronological significance, are carved both on the front and rear of the narrow pedestal.

In *fig. c* is seen the back of the statuette. The jaguar pelt wrapped about the hips shows clearly, with its spots and hanging tail. The back of the headdress was worked into an inverted jaguar mask. Another stone was doubtless set in the depression at the waist as ornament for the broad belt.

Even were bone sculptures from the Maya Area less rare than they are, this little piece would demand especial attention for the monumental qualities embodied within its small dimensions.

FEATHER-WORK

Mankind on all continents has been fascinated by the birds. Their secret of flight, their gorgeous plumage have made them the subject of many stories and legends, from Daedalus and Icarus of Greek mythology to the naïve couple, Papageno and Papagena, in Mozart's *Magic Flute*. All civilizations have appreciated the decorative value of their feathers and perhaps even attributed some symbolic significance to them, as is shown by the ostrich-plumed helmets of knights and warriors, the colorful regalia of savage dancers, and the splendid standards which appear at a festival Papal Mass. But no one has used them more ingeniously than the peoples of medieval America.

Before advancing modern civilization disturbed the belt extending from the southern border of Mexico to Colombia, this region abounded in birds of real paradisiacal appearance, and even today in the more remote sections some of them survive, a delight to the traveler and a reward for all the discomfort and fatigue endured on his journey.

The most renowned, and justly so, is the quetzal, a bird about the size of a turtle dove. Its feathers are a deep iridescent green, turning at an angle to midnight blue, above a flaming scarlet breast. The tail of the male develops three plumes, which measure about three and a half feet long, emerald-green in color with a golden shimmer. The bird is further remarkable for the absence of down and the large size of its contour feathers, which are extremely soft and so loose that they come off easily in the hand. Before the Conquest, the gorgeous plumage of the quetzal was reserved for the chiefs alone, a symbol of their rank. Eagle and turkey feathers were also used in the Indian's regalia.

Among numerous other birds resplendent in color were the various humming birds of different hues, one species of which had a brilliant turquoise breast that was used with exquisite effect. Throughout pre-Columbian America the parrot also plays a rôle in some form; its likeness is found in Mound Builder remains as well as in the carvings of Copan. Members of this family were quite common as far north as Lake Erie and Lake Ontario and as far south as the Strait of Magellan. In the Andean Area, feathers of the duck and hen were used, as well as those of the rhea, or American ostrich, which was domesticated not only for its meat but also for its plumage. Father Cobo, the chronicler, writes of a humming bird upon whose breast was a tiny gold-green spot, highly prized for decoration.

Birds were hunted with bird lime, traps, or slings, and were not necessarily killed when robbed of their feathers. According to the early writers, Montezuma had an aviary where richly colored birds were plucked once a year and their feathers carefully classified as to shade and texture.

The plumage was used to embellish headdresses, shields, standards, garments, bands, and other accessories. The technique of applying feather beside feather —called, rather inaccurately, "feather mosaic"—was developed to a fine art. A few specimens from the Mexican Area and many from the Andean survive. The elaborate plumed headdresses of the Maya dignitaries depicted on stelae, pottery, and carved medallions, as well as the occasional fans of honor (see *Pl. 129, fig. c*), attest to the skill of these people, too, in feather-work, although probably due to the unfavorable climate, no examples survive.

For pieces intended as wearing apparel, a fine woolen or cotton cloth was first woven, then feathers were laid on a row at a time, each quill hooked over a thread and secured by a knot in a second thread running parallel to the first. The subsequent rows were completed in like manner, one after another, each sewed to the cloth in such a way as to conceal the quills of the row below, leaving only the colored portions visible. Thus row by row the design was built up. In the arrangement of a pattern the position of the feathers of each tint had to be carefully calculated beforehand. When fixed in place, the tips were clipped to give a sharper contour to the design.[84]

For headdresses, standards, and similar articles, an ingenious light-weight construction of reeds and small sticks held the showy parts together. After the pattern arrangement was made, the colorful material was glued to a base of hide or dried plant fiber with a sticky juice. When the piece was completely dry, it achieved considerable durability—as is proved by the specimens which were sent to Europe at the time of the Conquest and are still on display, showing even today not only a veritable kaleidoscope of color but a fairly well-preserved and sound inner structure.

Pl. 286 features the magnificent feather headdress or cloak presented by Montezuma to Cortés as a gift for his sovereign. Passed on by Charles V to Archduke Ferdinand of Tirol, it was preserved in a Habsburg castle at Ambras, Austria, where it was discovered toward the end of the last century and transferred to the Museum für Völkerkunde, Vienna.

The feather-work symbolizes a gigantic settling bird, and as such once had a golden head and beak, probably a casque, which was mentioned in the early inventories of the collection at Ambras but disappeared during the 18th century. Well over 4 feet high, the piece is divided roughly into three zones. Four different kinds of feathers are used. The gathered furry section at the bottom is of brilliant turquoise-blue, decorated with twenty-eight crescents and fifteen step-shaped plaques of gold. A fluffy band of crimson separates this from the second zone, where a few short uneven quetzal plumes are laid against a ground of rich cocoa-brown feathers, so placed that their white tips form an edge for the band. Three rows of small gold disks, one hundred eighty-seven in all, decorate its border. Beyond spread the iridescent tail feathers of the quetzal, shimmering gold and emerald-green. The protruding center is built up on a similar scheme.

The number of gold disks, crescents, and plaques has been explained as of calendrical significance. The blue, brown, and white of the composition are said to symbolize the sky, earth, and water, and thus the wearer of the headdress may have personified the power of these three elements of nature.[115]

The sketch at the right (*fig. b*) is another illustration from the Sahagun Codex, showing craftsmen engaged in making a large piece of feather-work, while at the left a merchant brings in the raw material from the "hot lands."

For the Aztec shield in *Pl. 287, fig. a,* about 2 feet in diameter, feathers were mounted on an animal pelt, apparently from a jaguar, stretched over a wooden frame. Long tufted plumes trailed from the lower edge like a fringe. A shield of this pattern is specified on the Tribute Roll (see *Pl. 269*) and also appears in the Codex Mendoza (see *Pl. 268, fig. b*), carried by one of the warriors.

In better condition and displaying a far more impressive pattern is the feather shield in *fig. b,* another gift from Montezuma to Cortés's king. On it is emblazoned the figure of a coyote rampant in turquoise-blue with a purple belly against a background of mottled red feathers. A weblike frame of thin narrow strips of pure gold marks the outline of the animal and delineates its claws, teeth, eye, and fur. The coyote is one version of the Fire-god of the Aztecs, and its lashing tongue, as well as the tufts of yellow and red shaded feathers around the rim, signifies flame. Mouth, claws, eye, and the ragged back and tail display excellent observation and sprightly talent for the decorative. The technical execution in such an unusual medium is astonishingly inventive.

Fig. c shows a princely standard which was worn on the back, rising like a colored aureole behind the head. The standard proper is about 18 inches in diameter and made up of a ten-spoked wheel with an outer rim of stiff feathers radiating in a fanlike fashion. In the center of this side the "fire-flower" is represented; the "fire-butterfly" is depicted on the reverse. A band of twenty-eight chevrons, worked in various colors, encircles the medallion, giving a rotating effect to the pattern. Note that this design moves from left to right, a convention observed in the chevron bands seen in Maya Chamá pottery (see *Pls. 130* and *131*). This is inclosed and set off by a frame of purple, beyond which come the unclipped feathers of the rim. The handle is of a light reedlike wood with a finely woven scaly cover.

It is interesting to speculate whether Mozart's librettist had not seen some of these pre-Columbian garments and objects of feather-work when he clothed his Papageno and Papagena in the unprecedented feathered raiment frequently commented upon by both contemporary and later critics. In mid-18th century such pieces probably existed in greater number than today, for, as we know, the art of feather working was not abandoned immediately after the Conquest. Mitres, stoles, and holy pictures were made of feathers during the Spanish viceregal period, some of which are still preserved.

The mitre and infula illustrated (*Pl. 288*) were made in the first decades of Spanish dominance and present an achievement well worth consideration—a proof of the Indian artist's remarkable ability in this medium, even though the subject was alien to him. Steeped in the concepts of his own religion and art, which had been formulated for centuries, he was confronted almost overnight with a specialized technical civilization and a religious iconography completely different from his own. These pieces also show the far greater talent of the Indian in reproducing a Christian scene than that of the contemporary Spaniard when depicting the Indian.

The details of minor scenes, such as the Last Supper at the bottom of the mitre or the Resurrection on the infula (left), as well as the main subject, are well worth study under a magnifying glass for their story-telling quality. They reflect unmistakably the ecstatic pictorial mannerism of the 16th-century Spanish paintings that were placed before the workers to be copied. Scrutiny will reveal that the same method was applied here that went into the construction of medieval American feather-work. The technique of outlining seen on the coyote shield in the preceding plate was used, not only on the figures but also for the floral garland which meanders between the individual scenes.

The general background is a deep iridescent purplish blue, against which the fiery dots scattered here and there seem actually luminous. All the colors are rich in tone. The figure of Christ is executed in every instance with especial care—even the eyelashes are depicted with an infinitesimal feather tip, shimmering gold.

Only a few colonial specimens of this unique art remain. Besides churchly objects of the sort illustrated, holy pictures have been seen in Vienna, London, and Madrid. In the last city there is an arresting feather-work shield, fashioned for Philip II. It carries four complete battle scenes on its surface, showing the greatest triumphs of the Spaniards over the Moslems.[33]

With *Pl. 289* we return to medieval times and enter the Andean Area. The fan or headdress in *fig. a,* about 10 inches high, probably came from the Central Coast of Peru. A woven framework holds the feathers firmly in the arc. White tips are most effectively used as edging. The depth of color, the richness and density of the plumage are remarkable after so many centuries.

A pair of earplugs, a little more than 2½ inches in diameter, are shown in *fig. b.* These are Ica in style, and bear the ∽ motif already familiar from the pottery of the region. Even on such small pieces, contrasting colors and a divided pattern were applied, rendering them lively and appealing.

The fondness for striking colors and designs observed in the textile art of this area expresses itself with increasing brilliance when woven materials were covered with feathers. The poncho in *fig. c* came from a Chimu grave. A rich canary-yellow is the color of the body of the piece; the two bands are brown. In between them flows a scroll in black, a sharp and well applied contrast.

A different build-up of design is seen in the Ica poncho with animals (*Pl. 290, fig. a*), showing strong affiliation to the textiles of this culture. Here the dark subjects stand free against a white background. Neat clipping of the feathers makes the figural and geometric decoration clear and precise.

The large feather poncho in *fig. b,* 51 inches long by 42 wide, is Chimu in style. The body is a yellowish red, and yellow and black alternate in the small circles, the centers of which are turquoise-blue. This brilliant hue is repeated in the yoke at the neck and the bands on the lower edge. The fantasy play of shades is most subtle and effective.

Such gorgeous pieces of ingenious craftsmanship—feather mantles, ponchos, and ornaments—help one to visualize the pomp that dazzled the Spaniards when they first met the dignitaries of medieval America. The high standard of this civilization is confirmed by those small pieces of the applied arts which belonged to and beautified the life of its people. In addition to objects for ceremonial use, we have seen articles of lesser importance—all bearing the stamp of artistic talent.

XI

Facets of Daily Life

PEOPLE who had such varied and ingenious impulses in the arts as the natives of medieval America could not help but manifest their talent in the ordinary walk of life. There are a number of accurate and colorful books describing their customs in detail and, therefore, we shall give in the following plates only random aspects of the field, which may be pursued further by any one who takes an interest in one or another. The illustrations bring up material that falls outside a rigorous interpretation of the arts, showing either some lesser known or spectacular facet of their daily life. In the broader picture thus presented we gain a deeper appreciation of their achievement.

AGRICULTURE

Medieval America never knew the plow. The chief implement was the planting stick, and, as corn is planted a few kernels at a time—not sown broadcast like wheat—it served its purpose very well. In some regions ancient agricultural methods are still in operation, each adapted to a specific climate.

Pl. 291, fig. b shows Sahagun's illustration of the planting stick from the Codex Florentino. A remarkable parallel appears in the picture beside it (*fig. c*), taken after the turn of the century in our Southwest, where the Indian methods of dry-farming still prevail.

Remnants of irrigation canals have been found in all our areas, and the use of fertilizers seems also to have been fairly general. Frequently a small fish was deposited with the seed, and in certain parts of the Andean Area guano was used. In the Maya and Mexican areas land was prepared for cultivation by burning it over—a wasteful method, producing a steadily diminishing crop, as is often pointed out.

Agriculture in the Andean Area, also pursued under especially great handicaps, shows marvelous organization. In the coastal regions, systems of aqueducts made the arid valleys bloom, while in the highlands, terraces were laid out with arduous labor along the precipitous shoulders of their mountains. The magnitude of this task can be judged from the photograph reproduced in *fig. a,* showing a site recently excavated in southeastern Peru. The terraces average from 20 to 24 feet in height.[35] Note the almost endless system of stairways, cutting directly across them or leading from one level to the next. The expert contour farming of these people is also evident in the terraces seen on *Pl. 51, fig. a,* and *Pl. 55, fig. c.* The irrigation water was guided in at the top and flowed from one section to the other.

It might be of interest to mention here that the metabolism of the corn-eating Indians of the lowlands in Yucatan differs from that of those living in the extremely high altitudes of the Andean highlands and both are found to be quite different from ours.

In many ways the fare of the aboriginal American was superior to that of his European contemporary, although he did not use milk or its products. We have only to list the food and medicinal plants of American origin that have been adopted into our civilization to make this clear. The most important are maize, potatoes, sweet potatoes, tomatoes, pumpkins, squash, beans (lima, kidney, and others), peppers, cocoa, pineapples, and peanuts as foods; quinine and cocaine as drugs; henequen (sisal) as fiber, and rubber and chicle as gums.

MUSICAL INSTRUMENTS

No one who has ever witnessed an Indian dance can doubt the remarkable sense of rhythm of these people. They have subtle changes, variations, and crescendi, which we distinctly feel but try to analyze without satisfaction.

In medieval times, their instruments were drums, rattles, whistles, trumpets, panpipes, and flutes. All of these point to a very early stage of musical development. We should not forget, however, that music as we know it came late even to Western Europe. The lack of fixed tonality and any system of musical notation made the medieval festivals even of that continent noisy and unmelodious affairs.

A detail from the Codex Florentino (*Pl. 292, fig. c*) pictures a festival scene in medieval Mexico. Two drums are shown in use, the smaller, a slit one tapped with sticks, the larger, covered with stretched jaguar skin, beaten with the hands. The other participants in the ceremony are apparently chanters carrying rattles.

An example of the larger type of drum—carved of wood and remarkably fine in its detail—is reproduced in *fig. b.* An eagle, the symbolic bird of the Aztecs, stands probably on the double-bodied serpent of Aztec mythology. The sign near the beak has been interpreted as the glyph of the war cry it utters.

The Aztec slit drum (*fig. a*), called *teponaztli,* is about 28 inches long and made of basaltic rock. It has a clear bell-like tone. The figure Macuilxochitl, or Five Flower, is represented, his own weird features spelling out his name. Note the effective expressionistic manner of denoting the eyes. Jaguar skin is carved on the ends of the drum.

The *teponaztli* had two tones of different pitch. It varied in size from the larger type set on a stand, seen in the Sahagun sketch, to those about 12 inches in length which were suspended on a cord around the neck. These are said to have been used to tap out signals on the battlefield.[126]

Two pottery flutes from Mexico, each with four finger holes, are seen in *fig. d,* the longer about 7 inches. A gaping monster or a snake mouth forms the end of the smaller instrument. Both have a fine red polish, very well preserved.

Fig. e shows a group of pottery figurines from Monte Alban Period III. Three of the little men in front, each about 4½ inches tall, are blowing trumpets, while the fourth, on the left, appears to direct them. Small as they are, one feels they fill the air with their blasts, and the dignitaries arranged behind them seem to swell to the sound.

Pl. 293 presents examples of drums which are masterpieces of the wood carver's art. The composition of ornately costumed figures in the lower piece of *fig. a* is carried out with deep precise incisions, but the bland surfaces and shallow carving of the single figure on the one above it is far more fluent and effective, seeming almost winged with its smooth contours and plain background. The drumsticks were padded or tipped with rubber.

Different styles are pictured in *figs. b* and *c,* one carved in human and the other in animal form. *Fig. b* is unusually plastic and has inlaid eyes and teeth of shell. The arms and legs, awkwardly placed, add a certain strangeness to the piece, but the carving is concise and shows assurance. Far more decorative is the drum shaped into an animal body (*fig. c*), which was also further embellished with inlay. The curling motifs are excellently applied and the treatment of the fringed legs and plumed tail is highly ornamental.

More melodic possibilities are offered by the instruments of the Andean Area (*Pl. 294*). The various lengths in the panpipes—which were made of reed and stone (*figs. a* and *c*) and even of clay—produced a variety of notes. Their music has a melancholy pastoral quality, and the five-tone scale is used. (See also *Pl. 258, fig. b,* and *Pl. 272, fig. e.*) The panpipe is still played in the region, as is evidenced by the scene in *fig. b,* taken on Lake Titicaca, which shows a group of Indians in a *balsa,* or reed boat, with a sail of the same material.

The bulbous clay flute, or ocarina (*fig. e*), fashioned in the semblance of an animal, came from Costa Rica, but the type was widespread, and human as well as various animal figures are found. The instrument has a dull hollow note, not shrill. It is interesting to note that in Europe the ocarina cannot be traced farther back than mid-19th century.[119]

The Mochica, excellent observers of details in other phases of their daily life, also left records of musicians in their pottery. The two in *fig. d* are playing flute and drum. Mention also should be made of the whistle jars of the area. These were double vessels that, when half full of liquid, made a whistling sound if blown into at one end.

In *fig. f* a conch trumpet, wooden flute, and clay trumpet are shown, all from the coast of Peru. Together, these instruments were capable of producing a considerable range of sound because of the variety in their materials.

The recitation of dramatic legends and the many types of dances and festive performances cannot be taken up here. There is too little authentic information concerning them to form a definite picture, but there is no doubt that such performances occurred everywhere and were elaborate affairs. The text used was polished and flowery; it would seem that it resembled in style more the poetry of a Li T'ai-po or a Rabindranath Tagore than the classics of Europe. There was no rhyming in the composition, but it was held together by an inner rhythm of thought and cadence.

There were even puppet shows. Sahagun describes one presented by a "necromancer" who made a tiny figure dance on the palm of his hand. There is evidence that medieval America had string-operated marionettes, used by the medicine men.[62] A suggestion of this art is found in the deer mask with movable ears (see *Pl. 271, fig. b*) as well as the silver doll from Peru with hinged arms (see *Pl. 202, fig. c*).

PIPES

On the next three plates, pipes from the Mound Builder culture and the Mexican Area are illustrated. Because of their plastic qualities, they could have been included under sculpture and pottery, but since they add to the picture of daily life, they are shown here instead of among the more imposing works of stone carving or modeling. As is known, tobacco is a plant indigenous to America and smoking was a ceremonial act. The stem apparently was not held between the teeth but only between the lips and the pipe puffed through a reed.

On *Pl. 295, fig. a,* we see the most universal type, undecorated—except for the one in the upper right, with its charming little squirrel—and absolutely modern. The two smaller ones are made of stone and come from Georgia, while the larger piece, 9½ inches long, is of pottery shaped like a corncob and was found in Mexico.

In *fig. b* the human figure appears. This example, 8 inches high, comes from a Mound Builder site in Ohio, but has plastic characteristics that recall the art of the Mexican Area. Note the large circular earplugs. The mouthpiece of the pipe is in the top of the head.

Although the pipes of the Mound Builders were sometimes carved in human shape, they were generally fashioned into animals, chosen with amazing variety. *Fig. c* shows an owl effigy from Illinois, 7 inches high. The eyes were inlaid. Here attention should be called to a certain sculptural relationship to Totonac work (see *Pl. 65, fig. a*). Influence from Mexico can be discerned also in *fig. e,* a limestone carving from Carthage, Alabama. However, considerable originality is embodied in the piece. The duck figure with an owl's head on its tail (*fig. f*) comes from Virginia. It is 10 inches long, and the dark mottled stone is polished to a high degree. The realistic portrayal of the duck is not in the least influenced by the unexpected addition of the other bird's head. As a sculpture, the composition is singularly well knit. In *fig. d,* from the Tremper Mound, Ohio, a squirrel stands on a curving base, 3¼ inches long. Gray with red marbling, its color adds to the naturalness of its appearance.

Three examples on *Pl. 296* (*figs. a, b,* and *d*) were found at the same site as the squirrel, Tremper Mound, Ohio. All have the same curving base, and are made of local pipestone, an indurated material much valued by the Indians for pipes. Its wide variety of colors was used to advantage for realistic effects. *Fig. a* is the only dog effigy found in the many Ohio mounds, although bones of dogs have been excavated.[130] Compare his pose with that of the mythical animal from Puebla (see *Pl. 60, fig. c*). *Fig. b* represents an otter carrying a fish. In *fig. d* a hawk is carved in greater detail. The claws especially are faithfully portrayed. Its eyes are inlaid with copper.

In *fig. c* a duck is strikingly caught in the movement of swimming. Its placement on the tubular pipe shows admirable balance. The pipe in *fig. f,* from Ohio, showing a spoonbill duck on the back of a fish or amphibian, is a more elaborate variation of a similar theme. Despite the fantastic coupling of the two creatures, it gives a highly realistic impression. Note the shiny uniform quality of the stone.

Perhaps the greatest artistic courage is manifest in the crane effigy (*fig. e*), a red clay pipe, 5½ inches long, also from Ohio. The daring line of the long neck produces an unusually beautiful effect. Besides the reaching head of the bird, the terse but expressive outline of the wing and leg is noteworthy.

The portrayal of the various animals on Mound Builder pipes is generally so naturalistic that they can be identified by species within the genus.

The pottery pipe on *Pl. 297, fig. a,* a little over 5 inches long, comes from Mexico. The human figure is excellently employed and the elongation of the left leg to serve as the pipe stem is resourceful and original. Especially noteworthy are the elaborate headdress with its flower-like decoration and the large round ornament on the chin. The bow at the belt is executed with the ease typical of this area.

Fashioned in a somewhat similar attitude is the figure on the effigy pipe from Oaxaca (*fig. c*), about 6½ inches long. The face, here half turned away, seems to have a beardlike appendage, and the small pellets of clay covering the head are unusual. Glyphs characteristic of the region appear on the back and around the bowl of the pipe. (Compare *Pl. 125, fig. a.*)

Glyphs also ornament the tripod incense burner from Oaxaca (*fig. b*), a little over 12 inches long, which is included for the sake of comparison. Here the human figure is used only for decoration on a utilitarian vessel; he lies along the handle in a comfortable pose, while a snake is shown crawling toward him from the opposite end. The facial features have definite Oaxaca traits (see *Pl. 123*).

MIRRORS

Before the mirror with mercury was invented, it was a universal custom to use the polished surface of metals and hard shining stones. On *Pl. 298, fig. a,* we find a rounded slab of obsidian employed, placed within a carved and gilded wooden frame. It is said to come from Vera Cruz. How well it reflected is shown by the image of a small effigy vessel that was placed before it but which is not visible in the photograph (see *Pl. 118, fig. a*). The frame, similar on both sides, with its alternating elements of the double-headed serpent and a four-leaf-clover pattern, still retains enough of its gilding to form an excellent contrast to the black volcanic glass.

In the hand mirror from the Andean Area (*fig. b*), pyrite is used as the reflecting surface. Though broken and dulled today, it must have served its purpose well when new. The three alert heads on top of the wooden frame lend the piece a certain piquancy. It allegedly came from the coast of Peru and might be Chimu.

The wooden frame for a hand mirror, the back of which is shown in *fig. c*, is said to have come from Lambayeque. It is 9½ inches high, including the handle. The small figure standing under a roof is characteristically Chimu. This panel must have been carved separately and set in, for the grain of the wood differs from that in the frame. The upper rounded molding is well worked out and the section above it, now broken off, also probably carried some kind of decoration. Adorned with painted patterns in various colors, this small utilitarian object again bespeaks an originality and talent that left its mark on anything it touched.

COUNTING AND MEASURING

The markets of medieval America aroused the enthusiasm of the *conquistadores* wherever they saw them. They were held several times a month and surplus products of garden plots and labor were exchanged by barter, for there was no money as we know it. Controllers were present to check on weights and measures and the quality of the merchandise.

The balance scale with its beam of bone and finely netted bags (*Pl. 299, fig. a*) is an unpretentious but *éclatant* example of the great Chimu culture which produced it. Note the tiny birds carved on top.

Various ingenious methods of counting and recording were devised in the different regions. Grains of maize, beans, or pebbles were used, and still are, in calculating addition and subtraction. Among the highland Maya, accounts were kept by means of counted kernels set aside in separate boxes or bags. In certain regions of medieval America there are indications of the existence of a type of primitive abacus.

In the Andean Area private trade was confined within narrow limits. Commerce was in the hands of the state, which managed it according to its own rules. There was heavy traffic in the interchange of regional products. Into the highland warehouses flowed cotton, peppers, fruits, and fish from the coast, and wood, coca, feathers, and dye stuffs from the eastern forests. In return, wool, meat, potatoes, and metal were sent down from the mountains.[95]

Although the inhabitants of the Andean Area never developed the glyph, they had nevertheless a system of numeration and invented an ingenious device upon which they did their counting and kept certain records. This is the *quipu* (*fig. b*), a series of knotted strings of different colors and lengths, sometimes a yard long. The one illustrated here was found at Chancay, on the Central Coast of Peru. Each color referred to a separate subject or category. The knots denoted numbers and those designating the same number were tied in a horizontal line, the same distance from the top on all the strings. On the six strings tending upward from the heavy twined base in this illustration, units, tens, hundreds, and thousands are registered, while in the lower groups units, tens, and hundreds are shown.[82] Those who know the system give remarkably parallel readings.

By this means the complicated business of the great Empire was transacted, a census of the people and animals recorded, and an inventory made of grain, cloth, and other produce. The device is still in use today among the Peruvian shepherds. In China and Tibet, knot records are said to have preceded the invention of writing.

Among the Incas, the accounts were in charge of officials trained for the service. Youths were prepared for these positions in schools, where they learned the traditions, history, and even geography of their land. Relief maps, modeled in clay, were used to help them visualize certain topographical features. Traditions were preserved by memorizing past events. Here the *quipus* were of assistance, suggesting facts and figures, in the reconstruction of the great panorama of the past. As is known from other civilizations without written signs, those who do not write generally have prodigious memories.

ROADS

It is not surprising that the splendid cities of medieval America were joined by roads or that the highways were constructed with the same thoroughness that characterized other phases of this civilization, even though there were no carriages and wheeled vehicles, no beasts of burden, except the llama in the Andes, to make use of them. They were built for travelers and carriers on foot, for men bearing palanquins with chiefs and priests going from one city to another with pompous suites. So wide were they that four files of men with their loads could easily pass. Relay runners even carried sea fish alive in salt-water containers from the shore to the palaces of Aztec and Inca rulers.

Most of the roads, however, are now buried in jungle growth or obliterated by the shifting sands of the Pacific coast. A study of them has only just begun. Flights over the jungle of northeastern Yucatan have resulted in such photographs as that reproduced on *Pl. 300, fig. a.* It shows the intersecting of two ancient Maya highways, now buried in the bush, on the outskirts of Cobá. One of them led to a village a short distance from Chichen Itzá, sixty-five miles away. The fresh-water lakes and ponds that dot the scene made living possible here in earlier times. Investigations by the Carnegie Institution of Washington reveal that a network of roads was laid out between the once-flourishing Maya cities.

Maya highways were constructed no less carefully than the causeways of medieval Europe. The ancient road builders began by digging down to hardpan and erecting on either side retaining walls of roughly dressed limestone set in mortar, sometimes to a height of eight feet. A foundation of heavy boulders was then laid and the spaces filled with smaller stones. The surface may have been leveled with stone rollers. One such stone, 13 feet long, $2\frac{1}{4}$ in diameter, and weighing about five tons, was discovered near the section shown here. It has been suggested that the roads were surfaced with cement; if so, they must have been dazzling in the tropical sunshine. From the material found in connection with them, they are believed to have been constructed between the 4th and 7th centuries.[19] A few years ago the writer saw the same method of road building in practice on the border of Guatemala and El Salvador.

To facilitate travel, bridges had to be erected and rest houses built for the traveler. Simple thatched-roof shelters stand today in the highlands of Central America, sometimes on passes from 12,000 to 14,000 feet above sea level, at a distance of one day's journey on foot. Here the tired Indian finds protection against the icy chill of the night and prepares his warm meal—a wise custom which he follows at least once a day even in his "hot country." In the morning a few fresh pieces of straw and the dying embers of a carefully covered fire are all the evidence left by the nightly visitor, already well on his road.

In the Andean Area under Inca rule these wayside stations, or *tambos,* grew into veritable hostelries, born as they were of the same need as the romantic caravanseries of the Orient. They were built of stone and had blankets, firewood, food, utensils, and, in many cases, a caretaker; in the absence of an attendant, it is recorded that the travelers showed considerable responsibility for the welfare of those who would come after them. One squadron of *conquistadores* lived for weeks on such supplies during a reconnoitering trip into remote parts of the Andes.

Many chroniclers consider the Inca roads the most outstanding achievement of this remarkable people. For the stretch that passes over the great mountain plateau from Cuzco to Quito, galleries were cut through solid rock, rivers spanned by swinging bridges, ravines filled up, and precipices scaled by steps cut into their sides.[82]

When a new land was conquered, part of the inhabitants were moved over these highways to other parts of the Empire, while loyal subjects were brought in to take their places, a precautionary measure taken against rebellion and for the dissemination of the Quechua tongue (the language of the Incas) over the subjugated territory.[29]

But even before the Inca organization stretched out its fingers after distant provinces, there were roads on the coastal plain. *Fig. b* shows one that led to Talara through the Chicama Valley, near the great Chimu center of Chan-Chan. As straight as if laid out by a surveyor, broad and comfortable, it still gives one a profound respect for the culture that flourished here before the Incas rose to power. The ruin with its walls and high fortress-like base was probably a station.

Equal to the roads as an achievement were the aqueducts which brought water from the mountains and distributed it over large tracts in the coastal districts that otherwise would have been uninhabitable desert. The very engineering skill of the people, however, contributed to their own overthrow. Many aqueducts were too long to be adequately defended, and as soon as the upper channels were in the hands of the enemy, the whole region was faced with starvation or surrender.[54] Now everything that man built here is going back to the sand from which it was made, but if desolation and decay can speak, these ruins are indeed eloquent.

CITY-PLANNING

The views on *Pls. 301* and *302* present different sites from the air, showing well-planned layouts that are little suspected from the ground.

The Southwest, frequently overshadowed by the other areas, furnishes brilliant examples of organized city-planning. One case in point is Pueblo Bonito, already shown on *Pl. 4;* another is Aztec Ruin in New Mexico (*Pl. 301, fig. a*).

This is a rectangular walled-in complex, with the largest kiva near the center, the interior of which was illustrated earlier (see *Pl. 5, fig. b*). Smaller kivas, recognizable by their circular outlines, can be singled out, set among the living quarters and storage rooms. It is a clearly conceived and evenly walled construction.

A bird's-eye view of Tulum (*fig. b*) gives a broad picture of the defense wall and the cliffs which protected this Maya town (see also *Pls. 29* and *30*). Though crumbling before the aggressive growth of the jungle, the barrier still has enough stones left in place to make an impression. At the corner the ruins of a watch tower are distinguishable. The grouping of the buildings is clear in the photograph, some concentrated around the center, others scattered farther away and now completely overgrown.

Teotihuacan and Chan-Chan stand among the most venerated of the numerous sites of medieval America. An airview of the former has already displayed to advantage the impressive layout of this early Toltec ceremonial center (see *Pl. 7, fig. b*). Here a more comprehensive view of the Citadel is presented (*Pl. 302, fig. a*). It faces the broad Avenue of the Dead (right) that leads directly to the Pyramid of the Moon and on that side a wide stair mounts the embankment. Within the square of the rampart rises the solid pile of the Temple of Quetzalcoatl, only partly reconstructed (see *Pl. 8*). The centuries have greatly changed the aspect of this place, but the regular lines of the square, the even level of the platforms still show a precision of workmanship that could not be improved upon today.

Chan-Chan also has been discussed under architecture. Its ruins as seen from the air (*fig. b*), showing the beautifully planned construction of the vast Chimu capital, need little elucidation. Approximately 250,000 people are estimated to have lived on the site amidst palaces, temples, and sunken gardens. Remnants of walls are evident everywhere—walls that once supported the roofs of dwellings, walls that separated one palace or one section of the city from another. Details of the splendid stucco decoration lavished on them were shown on *Pl. 43*. The dark oblong in the center of the photograph was probably a reservoir, overgrown with vegetation since the city was abandoned. Although Chan-Chan was overshadowed by Inca grandeur, the site even in ruins still remains a most impressive monument of one of those great cultures from which the Incas drew strength for an empire.

BATHS AND RESERVOIRS

The display of clear water in fountains, pools, and basins, as well as the use of hot and mineral springs for medicinal purposes, was revived in medieval Europe by the Moors and Turks. The people of pre-Columbian America made these discoveries for themselves.

Near Texcotzingo in the Mexican highlands, some thirty miles from the former Aztec capital, the king of Texcoco built a royal retreat. Here a large basin was hewn from the solid rock, with steps leading down into it, stone seats, and a fountain. The bath is still in relatively good condition.

Medicinal bathing was practiced in all areas, and even today ceremonial baths persist in many regions. Many Indians in the tropical and semitropical countries preserve their ancient tradition of cleanliness, bathing and changing their meager garments every evening upon returning to their thatched huts from work.

At Chichen Itzá a sweat bath of the Maya was excavated. The building (*Pl. 303, figs. a* and *b*) is in the late style of this site, plain except for flaring cornices. The vault of the spacious antechamber has not been fully reconstructed (*fig. a*), and reveals the built-in dais and a small square door opening into the bath proper. Here, within a low chamber, water was poured over heated stones, producing somewhat the same effect as our Turkish steam bath. The superfluous vapor passed out through a small round opening in the wall that can be seen in *fig. b*. It is interesting to note that another such sweat bath was discovered at Piedras Negras.

Mention has already been made of the involved irrigation works of various arid regions. In *fig. c* we see the remnants of a distributing plant at Sacsahuaman in the Andes. A section of narrow channel lined with massive stones (right foreground) gives an idea of the thoroughness that extended to even the smallest detail in the construction. The carefully plotted layout of the whole system is again an impressive example of Inca genius for organization.

STAIRWAYS

Stairways are among the most grandiose features of Maya, Mexican, and Andean architecture and deserve separate consideration. Inviting as the idea would be to present a series of them, only a few can be included here. It is noteworthy that they were generally in the open, like those of ancient cultures in the Eastern Hemisphere and early Christianity.

El Castillo at Chichen Itzá has already been described (see *Pl. 41*). The main stairway of the four that mount this symmetrical temple-base is shown on *Pl. 304, fig. a*. As was mentioned in an earlier chapter, it is two feet wider at the top, which exaggerates its monumentality. The sharp incline of the steps and the narrow treads are apparent at first glance.

In contrast, the Southwest made little use of stairs. People here employed ladders, which, in case of attack, could be pulled up into the building. These were of the same primitive type as seen in the inset—a tree trimmed of its branches with footholds hewn along its length. This particular example was found and photographed by us quite recently; it was in use by a road gang of Indians on the border of Guatemala and El Salvador. The two pictures, side by side, demonstrate the unbelievable contrasts in the civilization of medieval America. From what lowly beginning did the grand stairways spring.

On *Pl. 305, fig. a* we see the Temple of the Dwarf at Uxmal from the southeast, photographed before any preservation work was undertaken (see also *Pl. 35, fig. a*). The tapering artificial mound upon which the temple stood is imposing in itself, much more so if we try to visualize its whole great bulk covered with regularly laid stone facing broken with sculptural decoration. Up the side of this pile of masonry leads the stairway, steep and broad, crumbling from age so that in this photograph the single steps look like ripples on its surface. The climbing quality, however, is still in them and a certain detachment from the structure can be sensed.

Although some of the mounds in the coastal districts of the Andean Area reached two hundred feet in height, no stairways survive. The mass of sun-baked clay could not withstand the rare but devastating rain storms. In the highlands, however, many striking examples remain, made of stone. In the detail from Machu Picchu (*fig. b*) the completely different position they held in Inca architecture is evident. They are not dramatic decorative features. Neither so steep nor so thoroughly digested into the structure as in the Mexican and Maya areas, they are here purely functional.

The stairway of each people reflects the particular civilization which produced it. Pre-Columbian America developed its own, uninfluenced by the achievements of other continents. They have little in common with the broad steps of Egypt, the heroic lines of those of Greece, or the luxuriously sweeping stairs of Rome. They were adapted to the use of the ancient red man with his agile wildcat tread and his clinging sandals. How much so, we realized when we saw modern Maya waveringly making their way up the stairway of their ancestors.

ENVOI

The site pictured on *Pl. 306* was very recently discovered in southeastern Peru by Paul Fejös. It lies at an altitude of 12,000 feet about one day's distance by mule from Machu Picchu and was named by the natives Phuyu Pata Marka, "the city above the clouds." Approximately five and one-half acres were cleared and surveyed.[35]

In *fig. a* we see the northeastern part of the settlement. The masonry is of polygonal white granite blocks and the ground is squared off with characteristic precision into evenly laid terraces, cut through by two breath-taking flights of steps. The large white granite boulder in the foreground of the picture is carved with two couchlike depressions on the east side and two seats, like armchairs, on the west. Their similarity to the better-known Throne of the Inca at Sacsahuaman (see *Pl. 49, fig. b*) would point to some ceremonial use for such monuments.

Immediately above it is a row of five cubicles. These are water basins or baths, all connected by subterranean channels and fed from the main canal, visible at the left though not entirely excavated when the picture was taken. Apparently this aqueduct supplied the water for both household purposes and the irrigation of the terraces farther down the slope. A sixth cubicle can be seen to the left nearer the foreground. This outlying section is connected with the city by a monolithic bridge.

The other side of this site (*fig. b*) gives an even better idea of the immense and precipitous mountain slope to which it clings. The whole ground is shaped into rounded terraces, the outcroppings of ledge apparently taken into account and neatly skirted. Flights of steps, like flexible bands, follow the slope, slanting now mildly, now steeply. The houses, too, conform to the contours of the terrain. Nothing is incidental or casual; each building has a well-laid plan and even the bedrock was carved to receive the masonry. Seemingly constructional difficulties did not deter these ancient builders—witness the house at the left, poised so skillfully above the precipice; probably the tillable land was so precious that every bit of it had to be reserved for the terrace fields.

Phuyu Pata Marka, the City above the Clouds, is the last of our illustrations. After the dazzling array of the more famous sites in this survey—all generals— it lies, an unknown soldier, appealing through its very obscurity for more effort, greater understanding, deeper homage.

XII

Evolution or Influence

SINCE the discovery of America, the civilization of its aborigines has been the subject of fantastic conjectures. In the 16th, 17th, and 18th centuries, the study of human races was haphazard and weakly organized. The comparisons and allusions of travelers in the service of Spain concerning the American natives were accepted at their face value. Accurate information was almost impossible to obtain. The hardships of travel, the constant battle with diseases of a most deadly character, the despotism of local "little kings," as well as the overwhelming vastness and foreign aspect of the land, all weighed upon the visitors and made it difficult for them to form objective opinions. At the same time, most could not see beyond the conceptions of their day.

In addition, a strict control and censorship were exercised over the Spanish colonies of the New World until the movement for independence at the beginning of the 19th century. With the exception of a few cases—such as that of the English priest, Thomas Gage, who, after twelve years in Mexico and Central America, returned to his native land—all descriptions and reports had to pass the scrutiny of the Council of the Indies in Seville. Carloads of unpublished material on the colonial empire and its past lie even today in the stately Renaissance building there which was its headquarters. As late as the beginning of the 19th century, the scientist Alexander von Humboldt, sent to investigate the mineral resources of New Spain, with personal letters of recommendation from the king himself, met the barriers maintained by the Inquisition. He writes that in the Mexican capital he obtained permission to dig up and study a gigantic Aztec statue, buried since the Conquest in the patio of a monastery, on the express condition that it be re-interred before sundown of the same day.[50]

The study of man developed slowly in the early centuries of our age even with reference to the European nations and their immediate neighbors. The Turkish domination of a large part of Europe, the religious struggles among the

Christians themselves permitted little time or inclination for the study of savages on distant continents. However, with the Renaissance a certain interest in other great civilizations was aroused. The cultures of China, of ancient Egypt, and Mesopotamia began to be extolled and interpreted for the European and the arts and customs of these countries described and illustrated. By the early 19th century, a fairly well established basis of art appreciation already existed, and the framework of what later became art-history and archaeology was laid down. The humanistic writers of this post-revolutionary age consolidated certain principles of esthetics, guiding the taste and interest of the rising middle class. At that time, the cultures of the Near and Far East were looked upon as mere forerunners of our European civilization, and whatever we had adopted from them —from gunpowder and printing to the making of porcelain—we took unto ourselves for our own glory, giving little credit to the country of its origin.

In such a set-up there was no place for pre-Columbian America. Although shortly after the Conquest it was conceded that the American Indian had a soul (which it behooved the white man to bring within the realm of Christ), he was too far from Europe to be considered seriously as a humanistic problem. America was for centuries only a land of the present: El Dorado for the Spaniard, the land of golden opportunity for the Anglo-Saxon settler and the other colonists. When its amazing early civilization, overgrown with the destructive tropical plants of the jungle or buried beneath the shifting sands of deserts, finally demanded attention, the science of the day made elaborate endeavors to file it in the pigeonholes already existing.

Thus, regardless of striking differences, the remnants of medieval American art were coupled with every possible culture of the Eastern Hemisphere by savants who had never visited the scene or studied any great number of pre-Columbian objects. Kinship with the lost tribes of Israel and the Egyptians of the Pharaohs was thrust upon the native American. Scientists in general had already built their structure of classifications and were unwilling to make any drastic change in it.

But with the opening of better transportation facilities and the consequent freedom of movement in Latin America, the accounts of these regions became more enlightened. As the 19th century neared its close, all America began to receive greater attention from the rest of the world, not only because of its industrial and social achievements but also for its scientific activities. In the short span of about seventy years, travelers and scientists, for the most part unknown to the general reader, have put together piece by piece the picture of pre-

Columbian America. Although still far from complete, the elements in general are assembled and, within the last fifteen to twenty years, many details have been worked out.

At the same time, research in early civilizations in the rest of the world has also advanced, so that the characteristics of both hemispheres are much more clearly defined and better differentiated than in the last century. Today we have a greater knowledge and a more efficient method of procedure to help us form conclusions on the origin and development of the pre-Columbian peoples.

Remnants of human skeletons have been found in America in proximity to extinct mammals, and arrowheads, fashioned by the hands of man, have been excavated alongside skeletal parts of the ground sloth and three-toed horse, animals which disappeared from the Western Hemisphere long ago.[114] Experts who reckon cautiously declare this era to be some fifteen to twenty thousand years ago. More and more support is being given the theory that as America had a developed plant and animal life in such early times, the presence of man also may be assumed. The abundance of fish, fowl, and wild game, the richness of the primeval forests and the plains with their edible plants, wild grains, and berries, and, toward the south, a climate well suited for the beginnings of agriculture, argue for this thesis.

For our purpose, however, the indisputable date of the earliest habitation of the Western Hemisphere is not of primary importance; our concern in this chapter is whether medieval American art is the result of autochthonous evolution or of influence from another continent. It has been noted that everything here of high artistic value, in a universal sense, is coincident in time with the appearance of Christianity in Europe and the centuries after. But it does not follow that this date marks the beginning of great art in the Western Hemisphere. While it is true that the earliest stelae of the Maya Area are contemporary with the first Christian centuries, they cannot be taken as products of a budding culture; they and the art surrounding them are too mature not to have a longer past behind them. However, the remnants of the beginning phases of pre-Columbian civilization are lost, just as children's clothing disappears from the wardrobe as a boy grows to a man; it is doubtful if they will ever be found to any great extent.

In examining the problem of evolution or influence, let us first consider the date and type of the earliest veritable arts in the Eastern Hemisphere. Investigations in China, in the Mohenjo-daro Valley in India, in the Ur Valley of

Mesopotamia, and in Egypt enable us to look back as far as 3800 to 4500 B.C., and, since the architectural or minor-art discoveries from that time show so much expression and skill in technique, we can assume that a formative period preceded them. Thus, considering the slow movement of prehistoric development, the so-called "horizon" of the cultures there can be pushed back well beyond the fourth millennium before Christ.

The prehistory of less civilized regions, on the other hand, is more uncertain. Various findings suggest movement of peoples and very early intercourse over long distances. As early as the Middle Stone Age, pottery types of the Danube Basin turned up in India. Nor was the spread of culture prevented by strips of water: as early as 7000 B.C. small geometric flint implements, known to have occurred previously only in eastern and northern Europe, had crossed over Gibraltar into North Africa.[106]

The greater migrations of some of the Mongolian peoples into Europe since the Christian era are familiar to us from history. The Huns, Avars, Magyars, Tatars all started in central Asia and in some cases reached as far as France. These waves, accelerated by the use of the horse and wheeled cart, brought numerous innovations from the nomad peoples that enriched European civilization—the stirrup, trousers, the cup with handles, among others.

It is possible, however, that even before the great migration took place in the direction of Europe, there were drifts toward the east into America. Most migrations seem to start from the need of new hunting and fishing grounds, or, with a pastoral people, for more adequate grazing land; the push of successful warlike tribes often drove before them a more peaceful population. These martial forces were doubtless at work also before history was recorded. Primitive peoples, as hunters and fishers, mobile and with few possessions, would follow first the forest and the water, and only later, as herders of domesticated cattle, more numerous and ponderous in movement, would they search the plains.

As such hunters and fishers, the early inhabitants of pre-Columbian America are believed to have crossed the Bering Strait. They came in bands, clad in animal skins, possibly over a land bridge or perhaps in boats, using the islands as stepping-stones. Probably they never amounted to any great number; this hemisphere was populated not by them but by their descendants. Certainly they were not conscious of the fact that they were treading the soil of another continent. The distance today from one mainland to the other is fifty-six miles. The stretch is broken by three islands, one of them four miles in length, so that the longest section of open water is twenty-five miles, across which one can see even in moderately clear weather. The embracing line of the Aleutian Islands marks off a sort of basin—the Bering Sea with its shores in both Siberia and Alaska. Even with crude water craft it would not require too much courage to cross to a land clearly visible with islands breaking the way. It has been pointed out that travel on foot would also have been possible during the time when the region was covered with ice.[134]

The case for the land bridge is also good. Where the two continents approach, like two animal profiles facing each other across the strait, the present depth of the water is less than one hundred eighty feet. This shallowness might indicate that a land bridge, now submerged, existed before cosmic upheavals produced the present topography. Excavations thirty feet below the present water level have revealed old beach deposits.

The Mongolian and the American Indian have some physical characteristics in common. Their head measurements are close. Both have scanty beard growth and little body hair in contrast to the Caucasian. Their hair is generally straight, while that of the white race is wavy and of the black, woolly.

Dr. Ewing, as quoted by Hans Zinsser in the following excerpt, introduces the head louse of the pre-Columbian peoples as evidence from another angle. "The scalps of hair samples from twenty prehistoric American Indian mummies were secured. It was found that the insects from Peruvian mummies were slightly different from those taken in the Southwestern United States, and that all the lice from prehistoric mummy scalps showed differences from some of the lice obtained from a living Indian. The louse adapts its color to that of the host, so that we have the black louse of Africa, the smoky louse of the Hindu, the yellowish brown of the Japanese, the dark brown one of the North American Indian, the pale brown one of the Eskimo, and the dirty gray one of the European. This prehistoric American louse has been described as quite similar to the Chinese head louse and to the lice found upon Aleutian Eskimos—another argument for the 'Migration' across the Bering Straits." [173]

Thus, there is evidence of relationship between the pre-Columbian American and the Mongolian or proto-Mongolian; but contact must have ceased early, as there are a number of basic Old World inventions and cultural achievements that are not found in the New. Early archaeological finds in Asia, dated approximately 4000 B.C., reveal an established and well-developed agriculture. On a cylinder seal of the fourth millennium B.C. from the Ur Valley in Mesopotamia the Sumerian type of plow is depicted, with a plowshare and two handles, a long curved pole, and two tackles for yokes over a pair of oxen.[172] The same subject, an animal-drawn plow, appears in a wall-painting from the 12th Dynasty in Egypt, about 2800 B.C. Terra-cotta models of chariots with disk wheels are also found in Mesopotamia from a very early Sumerian period. Certain Chinese ceramic pieces show the use of the potter's wheel before 1800 B.C.

On the other hand, the principle of the wheel, the use of the plow, and the domestication of beasts of burden (except the llama) were all unknown to pre-Columbian America. The agricultural implement here was the planting stick (see *Pl. 291, figs. b* and *c*). The only domesticated animals were the dog, the turkey, some other forms of poultry (ducks and hens) in certain regions, and, in addition, in the Andean Area, the llama and related groups. The case of the llama, herded locally for its wool and sometimes for its meat, serves to strengthen the argument for the early isolation of the continents, for this member of the camel family must itself have branched off at a very early period to have developed into an animal so unlike its Asiatic relatives.

The domesticated horse figures in the prehistoric civilizations of Asia from at least 3000 B.C.,[113] but the pre-Columbian peoples were overwhelmed at the sight of the horses ridden by the *conquistadores*. They thought at first that rider and horse were one, a superhuman creature. Even later, in one isolated stronghold of the Maya, an incapacitated animal left behind by the Spaniards was treated with reverence and awe, as if it were a living god; offerings of maize, flowers, and copal were made to it. At its death, a statue was erected to the new deity. A population so ignorant of the use of the horse could certainly not have had much intercourse with Asia, where for millennia the movement and migrations of nations had been based increasingly on that animal.

Rice, wheat, rye, and barley, the staple grains of the Near and Far East from prehistoric times were alien to the Western Hemisphere, while maize, beans, squash, tomatoes, potatoes, peanuts, and tobacco were New World discoveries to the Spaniards. The early Americans used the spear-thrower and blowgun, much more primitive weapons than the bow and arrow which appear late, relatively a short time before the Conquest and only in some sections. Bronze was unknown except in parts of South America. To all intents and purposes, the people remained within the neolithic phase. Furthermore, no satisfactory evidence has been found to identify a New World language with an Old World stock, except for the idiom of the Eskimos, who are a group by themselves.[169]

The great variety of Indian tongues indicates that numerous waves of different peoples, perhaps originating in diverse regions of the Old World, found habitation here. The difference in quality of the various pre-Columbian cultures, as well as the various burial customs, substantiates this theory. That the American Indians are, however, closely related to one another in racial stock is shown by the fact that a very high percentage (80 to 90) of pure-blooded Indians, whether from Peru, Yucatan, or Baffin Bay, belongs to the blood-group O.[173]

Musicology adds its own findings to the problem. It is interesting that all relatives of pre-Columbian musical instruments, aside from a few universal ones, are found exclusively in China, India, the Malay Archipelago, and the Pacific Islands. Outside of America, the notched flute is said to be confined to the Far East, including Mongolia. The absolute pitches and the scales of pre-Columbian, Melanesian, and eastern Asiatic panpipes have been found to be alike. Against these findings stands the complete absence of stringed instruments in the aboriginal cultures of America. In Asia as well as the Near East, the lute and lyre were known in legendary times. They were not only recorded on reliefs and in minor sculptures, but remnants of actual instruments have been excavated in several sites, in connection with cultures older than 3000 B.C. In China the long zither is mentioned in an ode written about 1100 B.C.; in due time it spread to the Malay Archipelago and most of the larger Pacific Islands. In pre-Columbian America all the instruments belonged to a groping stage of musical development. If those regions in the Old World had any influence on the cultures here, it must have been in very early prehistoric times.[119]

All this evidence would indicate that migrations of any importance must have ceased before the Old World achievements mentioned had been acquired or, at any rate, before they had reached that part of Asia from which the early Americans came. It does not, however, preclude a drift of Arctic tribes back and forth, relaying locally certain cultural traits. Bone and wood carvings of the northwest coast of British Columbia and Alaska point to this and are frequently referred to in discussion of similarities between the pre-Columbian and Asiatic arts. These cultures unquestionably profited from the rich and established form-world of the northeast coast of Asia. But in concept and execution their work is strongly differentiated from the art of the various pre-Columbian areas presented here. The specimens offered are mostly of post-Columbian date and prove only that local contacts had been made from Asiatic to American shores even before the Russians came with their ships as far as San Francisco Bay.

The thesis that there was also a prehistoric migration to America across the Pacific Ocean cannot be accepted so far. Accumulating facts point more and more to the relative lateness of the movement which populated Polynesia.[17] The early Maya and Andean cultures were already past their zenith when the Pacific Islands were being settled by the races who dwell there today. The migrations to the Polynesian Islands from the Asiatic mainland required considerable seamanship and knowledge of navigation, and the people of this region still retain their nautical skill. At the time of the Conquest, however, in America, there was not the slightest evidence of a seafaring tradition such as would surely have survived among a people able to cross the vast Pacific.

Today when the synthesis of Eurasian cultures has been achieved to a considerable extent, it is tempting to formulate conclusions in a similar vein for the pre-Columbian civilization. However, before our knowledge will be adequate for the task, much further investigation will first be necessary—not only in the Western Hemisphere but in the northeastern regions of Asia, where the Stone Age lasted longer than in what we know as China.

On the whole, the arts of most early cultures seem nearest alike when they first express their ideas unhesitatingly and, to our eyes, artistically, although without the sharp regional characteristics which later serve to separate them. We must not forget that in primitive art parallel solutions for parallel problems were often worked out with similar neolithic tools. On the other hand, we ourselves are doubtless frequently at fault in failing to see greater differences in the various manifestations. All of them have an alien radiation for us; we are deceived by their "primitiveness" and their strangeness and class them all together, unable to distinguish with finesse the unrealistic, the stylized, and the symbolic. Our eyes and minds are still inadequate for the full appraisal and we find ourselves trying to measure incommensurables.

There are some semblances between the mature arts of medieval America and the higher civilizations of the Eastern Hemisphere that have led to attempts to establish a definite connection between these, too. Careful cool-headed comparison of specimens from both regions, however, will show that such similarities are optical illusions.

The scholars indulging in such theorizing all too frequently are primarily Sinologists, Egyptologists, or others from remote fields, who would not venture into far-fetched deductions in dealing with early civilizations of the East. Their methods show from the start several defects. They have seldom been in any of the regions where pre-Columbian art originated. Their conclusions are based on second-hand reports and are the result of preconceived ideas, not of a careful and impersonal survey of the entire field. In the absence of the actual objects, they have hunted out illustrations to substantiate their theories that are too often retouched photographs or inaccurate drawings, thus betraying a lack of discrimination in a most important factor in any discussion of the arts. It requires great skill and thorough occupation with the pre-Columbian cultures to make adequate copies of their specimens. Pre-Columbian art was created and developed by a mentality totally alien to ours. An artist trained to our beauty ideals and technical mannerisms will unconsciously approach the pre-Columbian subject biased by his preconceptions. The writer was furnished startling proof of this during the preparation of this survey, when a friend, an anthropologist steeped in the study of primitive art, failed to identify a small sculpture from a new photograph, although he was familiar with a drawing of the same piece as published in an authoritative book. He admitted that the subject was identical but maintained that both spirit and linear conduct in the two reproductions were dissimilar.

Photography and the making of plaster casts are methods in which our function is purely administrative and not creative. A clear photograph, a precise cast, remaining neutral, at least will not guide us onto false trails, as sketches, retouched plates, and the like, unavoidably do. It is for this reason that we have included very few drawings and models, even though occasionally a photograph is not entirely satisfactory.

One of the comparisons most frequently presented to link medieval American and Oriental art places Ulua marble vases (see *Pls. 94* and *95*) beside Chinese bronze vessels from the Shang or Chou dynasties. At first glance, even to one familiar with the two styles, a certain pattern will show a superficial similarity, but sober scrutiny will dispel this impression. The group which advocates direct Asiatic influence in this instance bases their argument on one particular element. This is the curving "dragon" motif of the Chinese vessels, which they consider to have influenced the fret-scroll pattern, the main decorative theme, of the Ulua vases.

As we have seen in the chapter on sculpture, the Ulua vases are a localized product from one valley in Honduras and are believed to date around the 10th century of our era, or later. They do not show great variety of form and are, upon inspection, quite simple—generally cylindrical, varying from deep to shallow, and almost without exception with handles in the shape of animals. The greater part of the surface is carved with fret-scrolls and with animal-masks made up of the same elements. Gnashing teeth are always features.

‹ 378 ›

Compare these with the ceremonial bronzes of the Shang (1766–1122 B.C.) and Chou (1122–249 B.C.) dynasties. The many hundreds of these beautiful specimens of cast metal fall into twenty-eight general types, with complicated and often unsymmetrical shapes, many with deep spouts, movable handles, and especially fitted and ornamented covers. There are square canisters and gourd-shaped wine vessels. The horned animal—not the toothed—is featured and some are stamped with the Chinese character for "ox." The mask-panels of the Chinese pieces are executed in high relief and embellished with intricate ornament, while the backgrounds are filled with subordinate designs. Bernard Karlgren, who made an intensive study of the ancient Chinese vessels, proves that in the earliest examples every curve had a dragon head, and analyzes the permutations of the figure through the centuries until it became more and more a conventional coil.[111] A vertical tendency is apparent in the pieces.

In contrast, the decoration of the Ulua vases presents a horizontal trend. Their relief is low, the design linear, the masks are unemphasized, and there is an absence of secondary pattern. It is evident that the fleeting similarity between the fret-scrolls of the Ulua vases and the Chinese bronzes is most marked when the Chou design loses its realistic meaning and becomes a facile stylized pattern.

If there had been intercourse between China and pre-Columbian America, then the art of complicated bronze casting also should have reached the Western Hemisphere; as we know, it was only approximated here millennia later, within a limited area, and with small objects. One would expect writing in characters also to have been transmitted or the use of coins adopted—current in China since the third millennium B.C.—to take the place of the woven blankets, cocoa, and the like, which served as a medium of exchange among the Indians. In other words, China had many more important cultural advantages to pass on to the rising pre-Columbian peoples than a mere square-cornered spiral motif.

If, as has been suggested, contact was only sporadic, one asks why the precious vessel was not more accurately "copied." If nothing even approaching the shape or general design of the Chinese bronzes is visible in the Ulua vases, why should we accept as an indication of influence the application of one reminiscent detail-motif of a scroll, used as a stereotyped "fill-in"—one of the least obtrusive features of the bronzes. How did it happen that a Shang or Chou vessel, dating from three hundred to eighteen hundred years before Christ, should have reached the Ulua Valley, not one more nearly contemporary to the period of "copying," for instance, a vessel from the Han or T'ang dynasties, very different in character.

The greatest argument, however, for the independence of the Ulua vases from Chinese influence lies in the fact that they are completely integrated with the artistic scheme of indigenous Middle American cultures. They show some relation to the Chorotegan pottery with animal handles from the south and to certain other pottery types of the neighborhood. The fret-scroll motif runs throughout Middle American art, from the early wood lintel at Tikal to the stone relief at Tajin. As individual and localized as the marble vases are, they nevertheless speak an autochthonous language to those who are familiar with it and do not require a far-fetched theory to explain their presence here.

Where similarity to the Oriental motif exists, it is in examples from both continents in which the pattern has become degenerate. Peru offers another case in point. Here the art became much more stylized and condensed than in Middle America and its geometric character lends itself still more easily to generalization.

There is and probably always will be a school of archaeologists and art-historians—"insectologists" of the humanities—who value the detail above the whole. For them, sections of a design will always carry more weight than the spirit of the entire piece. They start from a spiral, a step pattern, a repeated square, knowing already where they intend to arrive. The specimen is important for them only because it carries the motif upon which their theory is based. What does not fit their picture is disregarded. The ambition to bring parallels and to show influences becomes a working method, so that in the end not the essence of a civilization is taken into consideration but rather the best examples obtainable for a series of comparisons.

To pursue pattern details that are only superficially similar brings one to a dead end. The invention of patterns is technically limited and many of them are universal; the dash, circle, square, oblong, spiral, star or cross, swastika—all were invented and used by several civilizations independently during long centuries of development. The models for most of them can be found in nature. Even similarity in ideology is not necessarily to be explained by contact, for it may be the result of parallel development—very possible in races that branched from the same family tree in an early time, at present undeterminable.

The problems facing research in the civilization of medieval America are far from solved. Because of the mystery which surrounds most of its phases and because the approach can be made through different branches of the humanities —exploring new ground—the field is all the more fascinating. But its greatest attraction lies in its imposing body of art, unique in its psychological apartness. When finally, in decades to come, the chronology of pre-Columbian cultures has been established in greater detail and the various styles are more precisely defined, it will still remain for our perception to read from the reconstructed picture the living impulses that created on this continent in isolation the admirable material for a new chapter in the history of art.

CHRONOLOGICAL CHART OF TENTATIVE DATES

compiled on the basis of latest publications

	SOUTHWEST AREA	MEXICAN AREA	MAYA AREA	INTERLYING AREA	ANDEAN AREA
	ARCHAIC	ARCHAIC	ARCHAIC	ARCHAIC	ARCHAIC
B.C.					
A.D.					
100	BASKET MAKER	EARLY ZACATENCO			? — EARLY TIAHUANACO; ? — CHAVIN
200		COPILCO; MONTE ALBAN I (ZAPOTEC)	OLD (FIRST) EMPIRE		
300	HOHOKAM ?				
400		CUICUILCO; MONTE ALBAN II	EARLIEST STELA (UAXACTUN) STELA PERIOD		NAZCA PARACAS ? → CLASSIC TIAHUANACO
500		TEOTIHUACAN (TOLTEC)	(UAXACTUN, TIKAL, COPAN, PALENQUE, PIEDRAS NEGRAS, YAXCHILAN, QUIRIGUÁ, EARLY KAMINALJUYÚ, EARLY CHICHEN ITZÁ, EARLY TULUM, ETC.)		MOCHICA → COAST TIAHUANACO
600	(PEAK)	MONTE ALBAN III			
700	(EARLY PUEBLO)				COAST DECADENT TIAHUANACO
800	PUEBLO I	HUAXTEC	889—LAST DATE ON STELAE; NEW (SECOND) EMPIRE; MEXICAN PERIOD; TOLTECS IN CHICHEN ITZÁ; LEAGUE OF MAYAPAN		
900	PUEBLO II	TARASCAN; TOTONAC			
1000		TOLTEC EXPANSION; MONTE ALBAN IV			ICA LATE NAZCA; CHIMU; INCA (HIGHLANDS)
1100	PUEBLO BONITO (GOLDEN AGE); CLIFF PALACE; PUEBLO III; MIMBRES	AZTEC	SACK OF CHICHEN ITZÁ; DECLINE OF NEW EMPIRE; LATE TULUM	? →	(INCAS CONQUER SOUTH COAST)
1200	GREAT DROUGHT, 1276–1299			PIPIL, GUETAR, CHOROTEGA, CHIRIQUI, COCLÉ, CHIBCHA, QUIMBAYA, ETC.	(INCAS CONQUER NORTH COAST)
1300	PUEBLO IV	(TENOCHTITLAN) (AZTEC EMPIRE); MONTE ALBAN V (MIXTEC)			
1400			OVERTHROW OF MAYAPAN; INDEPENDENT SMALL PROVINCES		INCA EMPIRE
1500	SPANIARDS, 1540; ESTABLISHED, 1598	SPANIARDS, 1519, 1521	SPANIARDS, IN GUATEMALA, 1524; IN YUCATAN, 1540	SPANIARDS, 1510, 1538	SPANIARDS, 1532, 1535

INTERLYING AREA: UNDETERMINED AND UNCLASSIFIED CULTURES

Bibliography

The literature dealing with pre-Columbian civilization is extremely voluminous. Eyewitnesses and early chroniclers of the Conquest treated it mostly from a historical point of view, but their works are full of important observations which give a clue to the archaeology and ethnology of the various regions. During the viceregal period, a long line of commentators and historians, many of them influenced by preconceived theories or prejudices, occupied themselves with the past of the Indians. With the 19th century, the study of man began to be permeated with an enlightened spirit, and the literature of this period shows a tendency toward objective approach and accuracy. In the last thirty years, the field of research has divided itself more and more into particular branches of the subject.

Lack of space prevents us from giving a full list of these books as well as the names of various scientific and museum periodicals and publications in Europe, Latin America, and the United States, which are full of valuable notes and papers. Our modern and admirably organized libraries can furnish comprehensive bibliographies. Only those titles are included here which were used as source works or may be suggestive to the general reader for further pursuit of the subject. Books which have an extensive or valuable bibliography are marked with a dagger; the numbers denote text references.

Ackerman, Phyllis
    Tapestry, the Mirror of Civilization. London, 1933.
    [1] Handwoven Textiles. Pasadena, 1935.

Adam, L.
    Primitive Art. London, 1940.

Alexander, Herbert J., and Reiter, Paul
    [2] Report on the Excavations of Jemez Cave, N.M. Albuquerque, 1935.

Amsden, Charles Avery
    Navaho Weaving. Los Angeles, 1934.

Andrews, E. Wyllys
    A Group of Related Sculptures from Yucatan in *CIW Contrib. to Am. Anthro. and Hist.* Washington, 1939.
    Chronology and Astronomy in the Maya Area in "The Maya and their Neighbors," *q.v.*

[3] "Archeological Monuments of Mexico." 150 pages of illustrations. New York, 1933.

Baessler, Arthur
    Altperuanische Kunst. Berlin, 1902–03.

Baldwin, G. C.
Further Notes on Basket Maker III Sandals from Northeastern Arizona in *American Anthropologist,* 1939.

Baltimore Museum of Art
The Art of the Maya. Catalogue. Baltimore, 1937.

Bandelier, Adolph F.
The Islands of Titicaca and Koati. New York, 1910.

Bandelier, Adolph F., and Hewett, Edgar L.
4 Indians of the Rio Grande Valley. Albuquerque, 1937.

Bartle, Ira B., San Luis Obispo, Calif.
5 Correspondence on diseases of pre-Columbian times.

Basler, Adolphe, and Brummer, Ernest
L'Art Précolombien. Paris, 1928.

Bennett, Wendell C.
Peruvian Gold in *Natural History,* 1932.
Excavations at Tiahuanaco. New York, 1934.
6 Machu Picchu in *Natural History,* 1935.
7 Weaving in the Land of the Incas in *Natural History,* 1935.
Excavations at La Mata, Maracay, Venezuela. New York, 1937.
Chimu Archeology in *Scientific Monthly,* 1937.
Archaeology of the North Coast of Peru. New York, 1939.
Chavin Stone Carving. New Haven, 1942.
8 Critical review and correspondence on this survey.

Bergsoe, Paul
9 The Metallurgy and Technology of Gold and Platinum among the Pre-Columbian Indians. Copenhagen, 1937.
10 The Gilding Process and the Metallurgy of Copper and Lead among the Pre-Columbian Indians. Copenhagen, 1938.

Bevan, Bernard
The Chinantec. Mexico, 1938.

Beyer, Hermann
The Stylistic History of the Maya Hieroglyphs. New Orleans, 1932.
11 Shell Ornament Sets. New Orleans, 1933.

Bingham, Hiram
12 The Discovery of Machu Picchu in *Harper's Magazine,* 1913.
13 Inca Land. Boston, 1922.
Machu Picchu, a Citadel of the Incas. New Haven, 1930.

Blom, Frans
Commerce, Trade and Monetary Units of the Maya in *Middle American Papers.* New Orleans, 1932.
The Maya Ball-game in *Middle American Papers.* New Orleans, 1932.
L'Art Maya in *Gazette des Beaux-Arts,* 1933.
The Conquest of Yucatan. Boston, 1936.
14 Unpublished manuscript on Maya pottery flasks (with H. Beyer).

BIBLIOGRAPHY

Blom, Frans, and La Farge, Oliver
    [15] Tribes and Temples. New Orleans, 1926.

Boas, Franz
    Album de Colecciónes Arqueológicas. Mexico, 1911–12.
    Primitive Art. Oslo, 1927.

Boyle, Mary E.
    In Search of Our Ancestors. London, 1927.

Brand, Donald D., and Harvey, Fred E.
    Editors, So Live the Works of Men. Albuquerque, 1939.

Braunholtz, H. J.
    [16] A Gold Pendant from Ancient Colombia in *The British Museum Quarterly,*
        1939.

Brenner, Anita
    Idols behind Altars. New York, 1929.

Brown, F. Martin
    America's Yesterday. Philadelphia, 1937.

Brummer, Ernest. *See* Basler, Adolphe

Bryan, Kirk
    Geologic Antiquity of Man in America in *Science,* 1941.

Buck, Peter H.
    [17] †Vikings of the Sunrise. New York, 1938.

Butler, Mary
    A Pottery Sequence from the Alta Verapaz, Guatemala, in "The Maya and
        their Neighbors," *q.v.*

Byers, D. S., and La Farge, Oliver
    The Yearbearer's People. New Orleans, 1931.

Cahill, Holger
    American Sources of Modern Art. Catalogue. Museum of Modern Art, New
        York, 1933.

Carbrera, Paul Felix
    [18] Description of the Ruins near Palenque. London, 1822.

Carnegie Institution of Washington
    [19] The Great "White Ways" of the Maya in *News Service Bulletin,* Sept. 24, 1933.

Caso, Alfonso
    [20] Las Estelas Zapotecas. Mexico, 1928.
    [21] The Use of Masks among the Ancient Mexicans in *Mexican Folkways,* 1929.
    [22] Las Exploraciónes en Monte Alban. Mexico, 1932.
    [23] Reading the Riddle of Ancient Jewels in *Natural History,* 1932.
    The Religion of the Aztecs. Mexico, 1937.
    [24] Exploraciónes en Oaxaca. Mexico, 1938.
    [25] Thirteen Masterpieces of Mexican Archaeology. *Tr.* by Edith Mackie and
        Jorge R. Acosta. Mexico, 1938.

Pre-Spanish Art in "Twenty Centuries of Mexican Art," Museum of Modern Art (N.Y.) Catalogue. 1940.

Casson, Stanley
Progress of Archaeology. London, 1934.

Catherwood, Frederick
Views of Ancient Monuments in Central America, Chiapas and Yucatan. London, 1844.

"The Changing Indian." *Ed.* by Oliver La Farge. Norman, Okla., 1942.

Chapman, Kenneth M.
Pueblo Indian Pottery. Nice, France, 1933 and 1936.
The Pottery of Santo Domingo Pueblo. Santa Fé, 1939.

Charlot, Jean
Mayan Art in *American Magazine of Art,* 1935.
See also Morris, Earl H.

Charnay, Désiré, and Viollet-le-Duc, E. E.
Cités et Ruines Américaines. Paris, 1863.

Clark, J. Cooper
[26] The Story of "Eight Deer." London, 1912.
[27] *Editor* and *translator,* Codex Mendoza, the Mexican Manuscript known as the Collection of Mendoza and preserved in the Bodleian Library, Oxford. London, 1938.

Cobo, Bernabé
[28] Historia del Nuevo Mundo. Seville, 1890–93.

Colton, Harold Sellers
Prehistoric Trade in the Southwest in *Scientific Monthly,* 1941.

Cordry, Donald B. and Dorothy M.
Costumes and Textiles of the Aztec Indians of the Cuetzalán Region, Puebla, Mexico. Los Angeles, 1940.

Cortés, Hernando
Five Letters. *Tr.* by J. Bayard Morris. London, 1928.

Cossío-Pijoán
Summa Artis. Madrid, 1931.

Crawford, Morris De Camp
Peruvian Textiles. New York, 1915.
Peruvian Fabrics. New York, 1916.
The Heritage of Cotton. New York, 1924.
The Conquest of Culture. New York, 1938.

Cunow, Heinrich
[29] Geschichte und Kultur des Inkareiches. Amsterdam, 1937.

Davis, Emily C.
[30] Ancient Americans. New York, 1931.

Densmore, Frances
Cheyenne and Arapaho Music. Los Angeles, 1936.

BIBLIOGRAPHY

Diaz, Bernál, del Castillo
  The Discovery and Conquest of Mexico. *Tr.* by A. P. Maudslay. London, 1928.
Doering, Heinrich. *See* Lehmann, Walter
Dorsey, George
  Archaeological Investigations on the Islands of La Plata, Ecuador. Chicago, 1898.
Douglas, Frederic H.
  Numerous articles on Indian art in *Denver Art Museum Leaflets.*
Douglas, Frederic H., and d'Harnoncourt, René
  [31] †Indian Art of the United States. New York, 1941.
Douglass, E. A.
  [32] Dating Pueblo Bonito and Other Ruins of the Southwest. Washington, 1935.
Dupaix, Guillelmo
  Antiquités Mexicaines. Paris, 1834.

"Early Man." A compilation. *Ed.* by George Grant MacCurdy. Philadelphia, 1937.
Ekholm, Gordon F.
  The Archaeology of Northern and Western Mexico in "The Maya and their Neighbors," *q.v.*
Emmons, George T.
  Jade in British Columbia and Alaska. New York, 1923.
"Essays in Anthropology." A compilation. *Ed.* by Robert H. Lowie. Berkeley, 1936.
Estrada, Genaro
  [33] El Arte Mexicano en España. Mexico, 1937.
"Exposición de Escultura Mexicana Antigua." Catalogue. Mexico, 1934.

Farabee, W. C.
  Ancient American Gold in *The Museum Journal*, Philadelphia, 1920.
  [34] A Golden Hoard from Ecuador in *The Museum Journal*, 1921.
Fejös, Paul
  [35] Correspondence concerning excavations in Andean highlands.
Ferdon, Edwin N., Jr.
  Reconnaissance in Esmeraldas in *El Palacio*, 1940.
  Preliminary Notes on Artifacts from La Libertad, Ecuador, in *El Palacio*, 1941.
Fergusson, Harvey
  [36] Rio Grande. New York, 1933.
Fewkes, Jesse Walter
  Two Summers' Work in Pueblo Ruins. Washington, 1904.
  Antiquities of Mesa Verde National Park. Washington, 1911.
  Designs on Prehistoric Pottery from the Mimbres Valley, New Mexico. Washington, 1924.
Fleure, Herbert John. *See* Peake, Harold

Fogg Art Museum
  † An Exhibition of Pre-Columbian Art. Catalogue. Cambridge, 1940.
Fry, Roger
  Last Lectures. New York, 1939.

Gage, Thomas
  The English-American. A New Survey of the West Indies, 1648. *Ed.* by
    A. P. Newton. London, 1928.
Gallop, Rodney
  Mexican Mosaic. London, 1939.
Gamio, Manuel
  Las Excavaciónes del Pedregal de San Angel y la Cultura Arcáica del Valle de
    México. Mexico, 1920.
  La Población del Valle de Teotihuacan. Mexico, 1922.
Gann, T.
  Mounds in Northern Honduras. Washington, 1900.
Gann, T., and Thompson, J. Eric
  The History of the Maya. New York, 1931.
Gates, William, *editor* and *translator*
  Yucatan by Friar Diego de Landa. Baltimore, 1937.
  [37] The de la Cruz—Badiano Aztec Herbal of 1552. Baltimore, 1939.
Gladwin, Harold S., and associates
  Excavations at Snaketown. Globe, Ariz., 1937.
Goddard, Pliny Earle
  [38] Indians of the Southwest. New York, 1931.
Golden Gate International Exposition
  Pacific Cultures. Catalogue. San Francisco, 1939.
  Aboriginal Cultures of the Western Hemisphere. Catalogue. San Francisco,
    1940.
Gordon, G. B.
  [39] Pre-Historic Ruins of Copan. Cambridge, 1896.
  [40] Caverns of Copan. Cambridge, 1898.
  [41] Researches in the Ulua Valley. Cambridge, 1898.
  Examples of Maya Pottery in the Museum and other Collections. *Ed.* by J. A.
    Mason. Philadelphia, 1925 and 1928.

Halle, Louis J., Jr.
  [42] River of Ruins. New York, 1941.
Hammond, Harriet
  [43] Maya Art in *Fogg Art Museum Notes*. Cambridge, 1930.
Hamy, E. T.
  Galérie Américaine du Musée d'Ethnographie du Trocadéro. Paris, 1897.
  [44] Note sur Une Statuette Mexicaine in *Journal de la Société des Américanistes*,
    1906.

BIBLIOGRAPHY

d'Harcourt, Raoul
>Les Textiles Anciens du Pérou et leurs Techniques. Paris, 1924.
>L'Ocarina à Cinq Sons dans l'Amérique Préhispanique in *Journal de la Société des Américanistes*, 1930.

d'Harnoncourt, René
>North American Indian Arts in *Magazine of Art*, 1939.
>Living Arts of the Indians in *Magazine of Art*, 1941.
>Indian Arts and Crafts and their Place in the Modern World in "The Changing Indian," *q.v.*
>*See also* Douglas, Frederic H.

Harrington, M. R.
>Certain Caddo Sites in Arkansas. New York, 1920.

Hartman, C. V.
>Archaeological Researches in Costa-Rica. Stockholm, 1901.

Harvey, Fred E. *See* Brand, Donald D.

Haury, Emil W.
>The Age of Lead Glaze Decorated Pottery in the Southwest in *American Anthropologist*, 1932.
>The Mogollon Culture of Southwestern New Mexico. Gila Pueblo, 1936.

Hay, Clarence L.
>[45] A Contribution to Maya Architecture in *Natural History*, 1935.

Hewett, Edgar Lee
>[46] Ancient Life in the American Southwest. Indianapolis, 1930.
>[47] The Chaco Canyon and its Monuments. Albuquerque, 1936.
>[48] Ancient Andean Life. Indianapolis, 1939.

Hodge, Frederick Webb
>Circular Kivas near Hawikuh, New Mexico. New York, 1923.
>*Co-editor,* "Introduction to American Indian Art," *q.v.*

Hollenbach, Marion
>Pre-Columbian Art. Catalogue. Los Angeles County Museum, 1940.

Holmes, William H.
>The Use of Gold and Other Metals among the Ancient Inhabitants of Chiriquí, Isthmus of Darien. Washington, 1887.
>[49] Archaeological Studies among the Ancient Cities of Mexico. Chicago, 1895 and 1897.

Hooton, Ernest A.
>The Indians of Pecos Pueblo. Cambridge, 1930.

Humboldt, Alexander von
>[50] Vue des Cordillères et Monuments des Peuples Indigènes de l'Amérique. Paris, 1810.
>Essai Politique sur le Royaume de la Nouvelle-Espagne. Paris, 1811.

"Introduction to American Indian Art." *Ed.* by Frederick Webb Hodge, Herbert J. Spinden, and Oliver La Farge. New York, 1931.

Izikowitz, Karl Gustav
Musical and Other Sound Instruments of the South American Indians. Göteborg, 1935.

[51] Jade, correspondence on, with Harvard Geological Museum, Cambridge, and J. L. Kraft, Chicago.

Jenness, D.
Editor, The American Aborigines. A compilation. Toronto, 1933.

Jockelson, W.
Archaeological Investigations in the Aleutian Islands. Washington, 1925.

Johnson, Frederick
[52] Linguistic Map of Mexico and Central America in "The Maya and their Neighbors," *q.v.*

[53] *Journal de la Société des Américanistes,* 1916, miscellaneous short notes in.

Joyce, Thomas Athol
[54] South American Archaeology. London, 1912.
Ancient American Mosaic in *Burlington Magazine,* 1914.
Mexican Archaeology. New York and London, 1914.
Central American and West Indian Archaeology. London, 1916.
Guide to the Maudslay Collection of Maya Sculptures. London, 1923.
[55] An Example of Cast Goldwork Discovered at Palenque by Waldeck. *Proc. 25th Internat. Cong. of Americanists,* The Hague, 1924.
Maya and Mexican Art. London, 1927.
A Maya Jadeite Carving from Central America in *The British Museum Quarterly,* 1929.
[56] The Gann Jades in *The British Museum Quarterly,* 1938.

Judd, Neil M.
Dating Our Prehistoric Pueblo Ruins. Washington, 1930.
The Excavation and Repair of Betatakin. Washington, 1930.

Kelemen, Pál
[57] Battlefield of the Gods. London, 1937.
Pre-Columbian Jades in *Parnassus,* 1939.
Some pre-Columbian Gold Pieces in *Parnassus,* 1940.
[58] The Stephens Centenary in *El Palacio,* 1941.

Kelly, Eoghan John
Pedro de Alvarado Conquistador. Princeton, 1932.

Kelsey, Vera, and Osborne, Lilly deJongh
[59] Four Keys to Guatemala. New York, 1939.

Kidder, Alfred, II
[60] South American Penetrations in Middle America in "The Maya and their Neighbors," *q.v.*
See also Strong, William Duncan

Kidder, Alfred V.
[61] An Introduction to the Study of Southwestern Archaeology. New Haven, 1924.
The Pottery of Pecos. Vol. I. Andover, Mass., 1931.
Archaeological Problems of the Highland Maya in "The Maya and their Neighbors," q.v.

Kidder, Alfred V., and Shepard, Anna O.
The Pottery of Pecos. Vol. II. New Haven, 1936.

Kidder, Alfred V., and Thompson, J. Eric
The Correlation of Maya and Christian Chronologies. Washington, 1938.

Kluckhohn, Clyde
The Conceptual Structure in Middle American Studies in "The Maya and their Neighbors," q.v.

Krickeberg, Walter
Die Totonaken. Berlin, 1925.

Kroeber, A. L.
Archaeological Explorations in Peru. Chicago, 1926.
Culture Stratifications in Peru in *American Anthropologist*, 1926.
Coast and Highland in Prehistoric Peru in *American Anthropologist*, 1927.
Conclusions: The Present Status of Americanistic Problems in "The Maya and their Neighbors," q.v.
See also O'Neale, Lila M.

La Farge, Oliver
Maya Ethnology: The Sequence of Cultures in "The Maya and their Neighbors," q.v.
Editor, "The Changing Indian," q.v.
Co-editor, "Introduction to American Indian Art," q.v.
See also Blom, Frans, and Byers, D. S.

Lago, Roberto, and Cueto, Lola
[62] Mexican Folk Puppets. Birmingham, Mich., 1941.

Landa, Diego de. *See* Gates, William, and Tozzer, Alfred M.

Larsen, Helge
[63] The Monolithic Rock Temple of Malinalco in *Ethnos,* 1938.

Las Casas, Bartolomé de
Historia de las Indias. Mexico, 1877.

Lehmann, Heinz
Les Styles des Vases de Nazca in *Journal de la Société des Américanistes,* 1934.

Lehmann, Walter
[64] Ergebnisse und Aufgaben der Mexikanistischen Forschung. Braunschweig, 1907.
Die Sprachen Zentralamerikas. Berlin, 1920.

Lehmann, Walter, and Doering, Heinrich
Kunstgeschichte des Alten Peru. Berlin, 1924.

Lilly, Eli
    Prehistoric Antiquities of Indiana. Indianapolis, 1937.
Lincoln, J. Steward
    The Maya Calendar of the Ixil of Guatemala in *CIW Contrib. to Am. Anthro. and Hist.* Washington, 1942.
Lines, Jorge A.
    Una Huaca en Zapandi. San José, Costa Rica, 1936.
    [65] Notes on the Archaeology of Costa Rica. San José, Costa Rica, 1939.
Linné, S.
    †Archaeological Researches at Teotihuacan, Mexico. London, 1934.
    †Zapotecan Antiquities. Stockholm, 1938.
Linton, Ralph L.
    North American Maize Culture in *American Anthropology*, 1924.
    Use of Tobacco among North American Indians. Chicago, 1924.
    Study of Man. New York, 1936.
    [66] Crops, Soils, and Culture in America in "The Maya and their Neighbors," *q.v.*
    Primitive Art in *The Kenyon Review*, 1941.
    Land Tenure in Aboriginal America in "The Changing Indian," *q.v.*
Los Angeles County Museum
    Pre-Columbian Art. Catalogue. 1940.
Lothrop, Samuel Kirkland
    [67] Tulum, an Archaeological Study of the East Coast of Yucatan. Washington, 1924.
    Pottery of Costa Rica and Nicaragua. New York, 1926.
    Pottery Types and their Sequence in El Salvador. New York, 1927.
    [68] Sculptured Fragments from Palenque in *Journal of the Royal Anthropological Institute*, 1929.
    Sculptured Pottery of the Maya and Pipil in *Maya Research*, 1936.
    [69] Zacualpa. Washington, 1936.
    [70] †Coclé. Cambridge, 1937.
    Gold and Silver from Southern Peru and Bolivia in *Journal of the Royal Anthropological Institute*, 1937.
    [71] Inca Treasure as Depicted by Spanish Historians. Los Angeles, 1938.
    The Southeastern Frontier of the Maya in *American Anthropologist*, 1939.
    South America as Seen from Middle America in "The Maya and their Neighbors," *q.v.*
Lowie, Robert H.
    American Culture History in *American Anthropologist*, 1940.
    Editor, "Essays in Anthropology," *q.v.*
Lummis, Charles F.
    [72] Mesa, Cañon and Pueblo. New York and London, 1925.

MacCurdy, George Grant
    A Study of Chiriquian Antiquities. New Haven, 1911.
    Editor, "Early Man," *q.v.*

McGregor, John C.
 [73] †Southwestern Archaeology. New York, 1941.

Madariaga, Salvador de
  Christopher Columbus. New York, 1940.

Maler, Teobert
 [74] Researches in the Central Portion of the Usumatsintla Valley. Cambridge, 1901.
 [75] Explorations in the Department of Peten, Guatemala. Tikal. Cambridge, 1908–11.

Marett, R. H. K.
 [76] Archaeological Tours from Mexico City. New York, 1934.

Markham, Clements R.
 [77] A History of Peru. Chicago, 1892.
 [78] The Incas of Peru. London, 1910.
  Translator and *editor,* Reports of the Discovery of Peru. London, 1872.
  See also Vega, Garcilaso de la

Marquina, Ignacio
  Estudio Arquitectónico Comparativo de los Monumentos Arqueológicos de México. Mexico, 1928.

Marshall, J.
  Mohenjo-Daro and the Indus Civilization. London, 1931.

Martin, Paul S.
  Archaeology of North America. Chicago, 1933.
  Lowry Ruin in Southwestern Colorado. Chicago, 1936.

Mason, J. Alden
  Use of Tobacco in Mexico and South America. Chicago, 1924.
  Turquoise Mosaics from Northern Mexico in *The Museum Journal,* Philadelphia, 1929.
 [79] A Maya Carved Stone Lintel from Guatemala in *The University Museum Bulletin,* Philadelphia, 1931.
 [80] Collections from Santarem in *The University Museum Bulletin,* 1935.
  Three Inca Wood Cups in *The University Museum Bulletin,* 1935.
  Observations on the Present Status and Problems of Middle American Archaeology in *American Antiquity,* 1938.
  See also Gordon, G. B.

Maudslay, Alfred Percival
 [81] Biologia Centrali-Americana. London, 1889–1902.

Maudslay, Alfred P., and Maudslay, Anne Cary
  A Glimpse at Guatemala. London, 1899.

†"The Maya and their Neighbors." A compilation. New York, 1940. *Ed.* by Clarence L. Hay, Ralph L. Linton, Samuel K. Lothrop, Harry L. Shapiro, and George C. Vaillant.

Mead, Charles W.
 [82] Old Civilizations of Inca Land. New York, 1932.

Means, Philip Ainsworth
Some Comments on the Inedited Manuscript of Poma de Ayala in *American Anthropologist,* 1923.
[83] Peruvian Textiles. Metropolitan Museum of Art, New York, 1930.
[84] †Ancient Civilizations of the Andes. New York, 1931.
[85] A Study of Peruvian Textiles. Museum of Fine Arts, Boston, 1932.
Fall of the Inca Empire. New York, 1932.
The Philosophic Interrelationship between Middle American and Andean Religions in "The Maya and their Neighbors," *q.v.*
†Pre-Columbian Art and Culture in the Andean Area in *Bulletin of the Museum of Art,* Providence, R.I., 1940.
Pre-Columbian Andean Art in *Magazine of Art,* 1940–41.
Mena, Ramón
[86] Catálogo de la Colección de Objetos de Jade. Museo Nacional, Mexico, 1927.
Mera, H. P.
Observations on the Archaeology of the Petrified Forest National Monument. Santa Fé, 1934.
The "Rain Bird." Santa Fé, 1937.
Merrill, E. D.
[87] Domesticated Plants in Relation to the Diffusion of Culture in "Early Man," *q.v.*
Merwin, Raymond E., and Vaillant, G. C.
The Ruins of Holmul, Guatemala. Cambridge, 1932.
Michigan, University of
Latin-American and Pre-Columbian Art. Catalogue. Ann Arbor, Mich., 1939.
Mills, C. William
Certain Mounds and Village Sites in Ohio. Columbus, 1916.
Mimenza Castillo, Ricardo
La Civilización Maya. Barcelona, 1929.
Minnesota, University of
Primitive Art. Catalogue. Minneapolis, 1940.
Montell, Gösta
Dress and Ornaments in Ancient Peru. Göteborg, 1929.
Moorehead, Warren K.
Explorations of the Etowah Site in Georgia. New Haven, 1932.
Morant, George S. de
[88] A History of Chinese Art. London, 1931.
Morgadanes, Dolores
[89] Similarity between Mixco and the Yalalag Costumes in *American Anthropologist,* 1940.
Morison, Samuel Eliot
Admiral of the Ocean Sea. Boston, 1942.

BIBLIOGRAPHY

Morley, Frances R., and Sylvanus G.
> [90] The Age and Provenience of the Leyden Plate in *CIW Contrib. to Am. Anthro. and Hist.* Washington, 1939.

Morley, Sylvanus Griswold
> An Introduction to the Study of Maya Hieroglyphs. Washington, 1920.
> The Inscriptions at Copan. Washington, 1920.
> Unearthing America's Ancient History in *The National Geographic Magazine,* 1931.
> [91] Guide Book to the Ruins of Quiriguá. Washington, 1935.
> The Inscriptions of Peten. Washington, 1937–38.
> [92] Maya Epigraphy in "The Maya and their Neighbors," *q.v.*
> *See also* Smith, A. Ledyard

Morris, Earl H.
> [93] The Temple of the Warriors. New York, 1931.

Morris, Earl H., with Charlot, J., and Morris, Ann A.
> [94] The Temple of the Warriors at Chichen Itza, Yucatan. 2 vols. Washington, 1931.

Murdock, George Peter
> [95] Our Primitive Contemporaries. New York, 1934.

Museum of Modern Art
> Twenty Centuries of Mexican Art. Catalogue. New York, 1940.
> *See also* Cahill, Holger

Nash, Ruth Cutter
> [96] Calendrical Interpretation of a Golden Breastplate from Peru. New York, 1939.

Noguera, Eduardo
> [97] Ruinas de Tizatlan, Tlaxcala. Mexico, 1927.
> Algunas Características de la Cerámica de México in *Journal de la Société des Américanistes,* 1930.
> Ruinas Arqueológicas del Norte de México. Mexico, 1930.
> Extensiónes Cronológico—Culturales y Geográficas de las Cerámicas de México. Mexico, 1932.
> [98] Importancia Arqueológica del Descubrimiento en Texmilincan, Guerrero, in *Boletín del Museo Nacional.* Mexico, 1933.
> [99] Guia Morelos. Mexico, 1934.
> [100] Guidebook to the National Museum. Mexico, 1938.
> Excavations at Tehuacan in "The Maya and their Neighbors," *q.v.*

Nordenskiöld, Erland
> The Copper and Bronze Age in South America. Göteborg, 1921.
> The American Indian as an Inventor in *The Journal of the Royal Anthropological Institute,* 1929.

Nordenskiöld, G.
> The Cliff-dwellers of the Mesa Verde. Stockholm, 1893.

Norman, Daniel, and Johnson, W. W. A.
[101] Note on a Spectrographic Study of Central American and Asiatic Jades in *Journal of the Optical Society of America,* 1941.
Nuttall, Zelia
Ancient Mexican Feather Work at the Columbian Historical Exposition at Madrid. Washington, 1895.
The Fundamental Principles of Old and New World Civilizations. Cambridge, 1901.
[102] The Book of Life of the Ancient Mexicans. Berkeley, 1903.
A Penitential Rite of the Ancient Mexicans. Cambridge, 1904.

Olsen, R. L.
[103] The Indians of the Northwest Coast in *Natural History,* 1935.
O'Neale, Lila M.
[104] Wide-Loom Fabrics of the Early Nazca Period in "Essays in Anthropology," *q.v.*
Textiles of the Early Nazca Period. Chicago, 1937.
O'Neale, Lila M., and Kroeber, A. L.
[105] Textile Periods in Ancient Peru. Berkeley, 1930.
Orchard, William C.
Peruvian Gold and Gold Plating. New York, 1930.
Osborne, Lilly deJongh
Guatemala Textiles. New Orleans, 1935.
See also Kelsey, Vera
Osgood, Cornelius
The Archaeological Problem of Chiriqui in *American Anthropologist,* 1935.

Palacios, Enrique Juan
Arqueología de México. Mexico, 1937.
Mas Gemas del Arte Maya en Palenque. Mexico, 1937.
Paul, A. J. Drexel, Jr. *See* Strong, William Duncan
Peabody Museum of Archaeology and Ethnology, Harvard University
Prehistoric Ruins of Copan, Honduras. Cambridge, 1896.
†An Exhibition of Pre-Columbian Art. Catalogue. Fogg Art Museum, Cambridge, 1940.
Peake, Harold
Early Steps in Human Progress. London.
Peake, Harold, and Fleure, Herbert John
[106] Hunters and Artists. Oxford, 1927.
The Horse and the Sword. Oxford, 1933.
Peñafiel, Antonio
[107] Monumentos del Arte Mexicano Antiguo. Mexico and Berlin, 1890.
Phillips, Phillip
[108] Middle American Influences on the Archaeology of the Southeastern United States in "The Maya and their Neighbors," *q.v.*

Pijoán. *See* Cossío-Pijoán

Pleasants, Frederick R.
> Pre-Columbian Art at the Fogg in *Magazine of Art,* 1940.

Pollock, H. E. D.
> [109] Round Structures of Aboriginal Middle America. Washington, 1936.
> Sources and Methods in the Study of Maya Architecture in "The Maya and their Neighbors," *q.v.*

Posnansky, Arthur
> Una Metropolí en la América del Sud. Berlin, 1914.

Prescott, William H.
> Conquest of Mexico. New York, 1855.
> [110] Conquest of Peru. New York, 1855.

Preuss, K. Th.
> Monumentale Vorgeschichtliche Kunst. Göttingen, 1929.

Priest, Alan
> [111] Chinese Bronzes. Catalogue. Metropolitan Museum of Art, New York, 1938.

Radin, Paul
> Histoire de la Civilisation Indienne. *Tr.* by Eva Métraux. Paris, 1935.

Redfield, Robert
> The Folk Culture of Yucatan. Chicago, 1941.

Reiss, W., and Stuebel, A.
> Das Totenfeld von Ancon in Peru. Berlin, 1880–87.

Reiter, Paul. *See* Alexander, Herbert J.

Richardson, Francis B.
> Non-Maya Monumental Sculpture of Central America in "The Maya and their Neighbors," *q.v.*

Rickards, Constantine George
> The Ruins of Mexico. London, 1910.
> Monograph on Ornaments on Zapotec Funerary Urns in *Journal de la Société des Américanistes,* 1938.

Ricketson, O. G.
> [112] Report on the Excavations at Uaxactun. Washington, 1925.

Ries, Maurice
> Stamping: A Mass-production Printing Method 2000 Years Old in *Middle American Papers*. New Orleans, 1932.
> Ancient American Art. Catalogue. Santa Barbara, Calif., 1942.

Riggs, Arthur Stanley
> [113] The Romance of Human Progress. Indianapolis, 1938.

Riggs, Elmer S.
> [114] The Geological History and Evolution of the Horse. Chicago, 1932.

Rivero, Mariano Eduardo de, and Tschudi, Juan Diego de
> Antigüedades Peruanas. Text and map. Vienna, 1851.

Rivet, Paul, and Verneau, R.
    Ethnographie Ancienne de l'Equateur. Paris, 1912.
Röck, Fritz
    Ein Altindianisches Bilderbuch. Vienna, 1935.
    Kalenderkreise und Kalenderschichten im alten Mexiko und Mittelamerika. Vienna.
    Kunstgewerbe von Mexiko, Mittelamerika und Westindien. Berlin.
    [115] Feder Kopfschmuck des Gottes Quetzalcoatl. Manuscript. Museum für Völkerkunde, Vienna.
Rosny, Leon de
    [116] Les Documents Écrits de l'Antiquité Américaine. Paris, 1882.
Ruppert, Karl
    [117] The Caracol. Washington, 1935.
    A Special Assemblage of Maya Structures in "The Maya and their Neighbors," q.v.
Ruskin, John
    [118] Stones of Venice. London, 1853.

Sachs, Curt
    [119] The History of Musical Instruments. New York, 1940.
Sahagun, Fray Bernardino de
    A History of Ancient Mexico. Tr. by Fanny R. Bandelier. Fisk University, Nashville, 1932.
Salaman, R. N.
    Deformities and Mutilations of the Face as Depicted in the Chimu Pottery of Peru in The Journal of the Royal Anthropological Institute, 1939.
Sapper, Carl
    Altindianische Ansiedelungen in Guatemala und Chiapas. Berlin, 1895.
Satterthwaite, L., Jr.
    [120] Notes on the Work of the Fourth and Fifth University Museum Expeditions to Piedras Negras, Peten, Guatemala, in Maya Research, 1936, and in The University Museum Bulletin, Philadelphia, 1933, 1936, 1937.
    Identification of Maya Temple Buildings at Piedras Negras in Twenty-fifth Anniversary Studies. Philadelphia Anthropological Society, 1937.
Saville, Marshall H.
    Cruciform Structures near Mitla in Bulletin, American Museum of Natural History, 1900.
    The Antiquities of Manabí, Ecuador. New York, 1907 and 1910.
    A Sculptured Vase from Guatemala. New York, 1919.
    [121] The Goldsmith's Art in Ancient Mexico. New York, 1920.
    [122] Editor, The Earliest Notices Concerning the Conquest of Mexico by Cortes in 1519. New York, 1920.
    [123] A Golden Breastplate from Cuzco, Peru. New York, 1921.
    [124] Bibliographic Notes on Uxmal. New York, 1921.
    Editor, Reports on the Maya Indians of Yucatan. New York, 1921.

[125] Turquoise Mosaic Art in Ancient Mexico. New York, 1922.
   The Gold Treasure of Sigsig, Ecuador. New York, 1924.
[126] The Wood-Carver's Art in Mexico. New York, 1925.
[127] Bibliographic Notes on Palenque, Chiapas. New York, 1928.
   Bibliographic Notes on Xochicalco, Mexico. New York, 1928.
[128] Tizoc, Great Lord of the Aztecs. New York, 1929.

Schmidt, Max
   Kunst und Kultur von Peru. Berlin, 1929.

Seler, Edward
[129] Gesammelte Abhandlungen zur Amerikanischen Sprach- und Altertumskunde.
   Berlin, 1902–23.

Shapiro, Harry L.
   World Migrations in *Natural History,* 1942.
   The Mixed-Blood Indian in "The Changing Indian," *q.v.*

Shepard, Anna O. *See* Kidder, Alfred V.

Shetrone, H. C.
[130] The Mound-Builders. New York, 1930.

Smith, A. Ledyard
   Report on the Investigation of Stelae. Washington, 1929.
   Excavations at Uaxactun. Washington, 1933.
   Uaxactun. Washington, 1935.
[131] The Corbeled Arch in the New World in "The Maya and their Neighbors,"
   q.v.

Smith, A. Ledyard, and Morley, Sylvanus G.
[132] Report on Some Excavations at Uaxactun. Washington, 1932.

Smith, Howell
[133] Brief Guide to the Peruvian Textiles. Catalogue. Victoria and Albert
   Museum. London, 1926.

Smith, Philip S.
[134] Certain Relations between Northwest America and Northeast Asia in "Early
   Man," *q.v.*

Smith, Robert E.
[135] A Study of Structure A-1 Complex at Uaxactun, Peten, Guatemala, in *CIW
   Contrib. to Am. Anthro. and Hist.* Washington, 1937.
   Ceramics of the Peten in "The Maya and their Neighbors," *q.v.*

Spinden, Ellen S.
[136] Place of Tajin in Totonac Archaeology in *American Anthropologist,* 1933.

Spinden, Herbert J.
[137] †A Study of Maya Art. Cambridge, 1913.
   Notes on the Archaeology of Salvador in *American Anthropologist,* 1915.
   The Origin and Distribution of Agriculture in America. *Proc. 19th Internat.
   Cong. of Americanists,* Washington, 1917.
   The Reduction of Mayan Dates. Cambridge, 1924.

The Chorotegan Culture Area. *Proc. 21st Internat. Cong. of Americanists.* Göteborg, 1925.

Ancient Civilizations of Mexico and Central America. New York, 1928.

Indian Manuscripts of Southern Mexico. Washington, 1935.

Huaxtec Sculptures and Apotheosis in *The Brooklyn Museum Quarterly,* 1937.

[138] Diffusion of Maya Astronomy in "The Maya and their Neighbors," *q.v.*

Co-editor, "Introduction to American Indian Art," *q.v.*

Squier, E. G.

Nicaragua, its People, Scenery, Monuments and the Proposed Interoceanic Canal. With numerous original maps and illustrations. New York, 1852.

The States of Central America. New York, 1858.

[139] Peru, Incidents of Travel and Exploration in the Land of the Incas. New York, 1877.

Stafford, Cora E.

Paracas Embroideries. New York, 1941.

Stallings, W. S., Jr.

Dating Prehistoric Ruins by Tree-Rings. Santa Fé, 1939.

Stephens, John L.

Incidents of Travel in Central America, Chiapas, and Yucatan. New York, 1841.

[140] Incidents of Travel in Yucatan. New York, 1843.

Stirling, Matthew W.

An Initial Series from Tres Zapotes, Vera Cruz, Mexico. Washington, 1940.

[141] Expedition Unearths Buried Masterpieces in *The National Geographic Magazine,* 1941.

Stirling, Matthew W., and Marion

Finding Jewels of Jade in a Mexican Swamp in *The National Geographic Magazine,* 1942.

Stone, Doris

[142] Masters in Marble. New Orleans.

The Ulua Valley and Lake Yojoa in "The Maya and their Neighbors," *q.v.*

Archaeology of the North Coast of Honduras. Cambridge, 1941.

Strómsvik, Gustav

[143] Substela Caches and Stela Foundations at Copan and Quiriguá in *CIW Contrib. to Am. Anthro. and Hist.* Washington, 1942.

Strong, William Duncan

Anthropological Problems in Central America in "The Maya and their Neighbors," *q.v.*

Indian Religion in the Modern World in "The Changing Indian," *q.v.*

Strong, William Duncan, Kidder, Alfred, II, and Paul, A. J. Drexel, Jr.

Preliminary Report on the Smithsonian Institution-Harvard University Archaeological Expedition to Northwestern Honduras, 1936. Washington, 1938.

BIBLIOGRAPHY

Stuebel, A., and Uhle, Max
Die Ruinenstätte von Tiahuanaco im Hochlande des Alten Peru. Leipzig, 1892.

[144] "A Survey of Persian Art." *Ed.* by Arthur Upham Pope. London and New York, 1939.

Sydow, Eckart von
Die Kunst der Naturvölker und der Vorzeit. Berlin, 1923.

Tello, Julio C.
Introducción a la Historia Antigua del Perú. Lima, 1921.
[145] Los Descubrimientos del Museo de Arqueología Peruana en la Peninsula de Paracas. Rome, 1928.
Antiguo Perú. Lima, 1929.

[146] Tenayuca. A compilation. Mexico, 1935.

Terry, T. Philip
[147] Terry's Guide to Mexico. Boston, 1931.

Textile Museum of the District of Columbia
Correspondence and data concerning Peruvian fabrics.

Thausing, M.
[148] Quellenschriften für Kunstgeschichte—Dürers Briefe, Tagebücher und Reime. Wien, 1888.

Thompson, Edward Herbert
Archaeological Researches in Yucatan. Cambridge, 1904.
[149] People of the Serpent. Boston, 1932.

Thompson, J. Eric S.
[150] The Civilization of the Mayas. Chicago, 1927 and 1942.
A Correlation of the Mayan and European Calendars. Chicago, 1927.
[151] Mexico before Cortez. New York, 1933.
Archaeology of South America. Chicago, 1936.
An Eccentric Flint from Quintana Roo, Mexico, in *Maya Research,* 1936.
[152] Excavations at San José, British Honduras. Washington, 1939.
[153] The Moon Goddess in Middle America in *CIW Contrib. to Am. Anthro. and Hist.* Washington, 1939.
Archaeological Problems of the Lowland Maya in "The Maya and their Neighbors," *q.v.*
[154] Dating of Certain Inscriptions of non-Maya Origin. Washington, 1941.
Maya Arithmetic. Washington, 1941.
[155] Critical review and correspondence in reference to this survey.
See also Kidder, Alfred V., and Gann, T. W.

Totten, George Oakley
Maya Architecture. Washington, 1926.

Tovey, Donald Francis
The Integrity of Music: A Musician Talks. London, 1941.

Tozzer, Alfred M.
A Comparative Study of the Mayas and the Lacandones. New York, 1907.
[156] A Preliminary Study of the Prehistoric Ruins of Tikal, Guatemala. Cambridge, 1911.
[157] A Preliminary Study of the Prehistoric Ruins of Nakum, Guatemala. Cambridge, 1913.
Social Origins and Social Continuities. New York, 1925.
Time and American Archaeology in *Natural History,* 1927.
Maya and Toltec Figures at Chichen Itzá. *Proc. 23rd Internat. Cong. of Americanists.* New York, 1930.
Maya Research in *Maya Research,* 1934.
Stephens, Prescott, Bancroft and Others in *Los Mayas Antiguos.* Mexico, 1941.
[158] †*Editor,* Landa's Relación de las Cosas de Yucatan. Cambridge, 1941.

Tozzer, Alfred M., and Allen, G. M.
Animal Figures in the Maya Codices. Cambridge, 1910.

Trik, Aubrey S.
[159] Temple XXII at Copan in *CIW Contrib. to Am. Anthro. and Hist.* Washington, 1939.

Tschudi, Juan Diego de. *See* Rivero, Mariano Eduardo de

Tucker, Mary
†Books of the Southwest. A General Bibliography. New York.

Uhle, Max
[160] Pachacamac. Philadelphia, 1903.
[161] Explorations at Chincha. Berkeley, 1924.
See also Stuebel, A.

Vaillant, George C.
[162] Excavations at Zacatenco. New York, 1930.
[163] Artists and Craftsmen in Ancient Central America. New York, 1935.
Indian Arts in North America. New York, 1939.
Patterns in Middle American Archaeology in "The Maya and their Neighbors," *q.v.*
†Aztecs of Mexico. New York, 1941.
See also Merwin, Raymond E.

Valcárcel, Luís E.
El Cuzco Precolombino. Cuzco, 1924.
Ancient Peruvian Art. Lima, 1937.
[164] The Latest Archaeological Discoveries in Peru. Lima, 1938.
Muestrario de Arte Peruano Precolombino. Lima, 1938.

Vega, Garcilaso de la
The First Part of the Royal Commentaries of the Yncas. *Tr.* and *ed.* by Clements R. Markham. London, 1871.

BIBLIOGRAPHY

Vignaud, Henry
> Toscanelli and Columbus. London, 1902.

Villacorta B., Carlos A.
> Vaso de Guastatoya. Guatemala, 1941.

Villacorta C., J. Antonio
> Arqueología Guatemalteca. Guatemala, 1927.
> [165] Prehistoria e Historia Antigua de Guatemala. Guatemala, 1938.

Waldeck, Frédéric de
> [166] Voyage Pittoresque et Archéologique dans la Province d'Yucatan, pendant les Années 1834 et 1836. Paris, 1838.

Waldeck, Frédéric de, and Brasseur de Bourbourg, C. E.
> Monuments Anciens du Mexique. Paris, 1866.

Wardle, H. Newell
> [167] Guetar Art in Stone in *The University Museum Bulletin,* Philadelphia, 1939.
> [168] Correspondence and data furnished for this survey.

Wauchope, Robert
> Zacualpa. Washington, 1936.

Wiener, Charles
> Pérou et Bolivie. Paris, 1880.

Willard, T. A.
> The City of the Sacred Well. London.

Wissler, Clark
> [169] †The American Indian. New York, 1922.

Woodward, Arthur
> [170] A Shell Bracelet Manufactory in *American Antiquity,* 1936.
> [171] Notes on the Archaeological Specimens from the Grewe Site, Gila Valley, Arizona. Typescript. Los Angeles, 1936.

Wooley, C. Leonard
> [172] Ur Excavations. London and New York, 1934.

Zinsser, Hans
> [173] Rats, Lice and History. New York, 1934.

Zweig, Stefan
> Amerigo. New York, 1942.

Index

Italic numbers refer to plates

INDEX

Painting, codex, 178, 313-315, 320, 327-332; in Andean Area, 332; mural or wall, 315-327; on stucco or sculptured surfaces, 66, 319; technique, 324-325; vase, 177, 315

Palace, Labná (Structure I), 75-76, *32b;* Sayil, 74, *31a*

Palace Group, Palenque, 66, *26;* 130, *79;* 132, *81a;* 142, *91a*

Palace of the Five Stories, Tikal, 62, *25*

Palace (House) of the Governor, Uxmal, 80, *35b, 36a*

Palace of the Six Columns (Palace II), Mitla, 49-50, *16, 17*

Palace I, Kabah, 77, *34*

Palaces, distinguished from temples, 51, 62

Palenque, architecture, 64-68, *26, 27;* Early Maya city, 18; pottery, 182, *133b;* sculpture, 66; 125, *75;* 129-132, *79, 81a;* 136, *86a;* 142, *91a;* water-lily associated with style of, 186

Palmas, 106-107, 115-116, *67*

Panpipes, 357-358, *294a, b, c*

Papantla, 42

Paracas, architecture, 94; grave finds, 224, 235; weaving, 224-227, *175a, 176b, 177a, b;* 233-235, *187, 188, 190b*

Paramonga, architecture, 91-92, *44;* painting, 332

Peabody Museum of Harvard University, 69, 194

Pennsylvania, University of, 68, 174, 194

Périgny, Maurice de, 69

Phuyu Pata Marka, 369, *306*

Piedras Negras, architecture, 68-69; Early Maya city, 18; jade head, 304, *251a;* sculpture, 121-124, *72a, b, 73, 74;* 127-129, *77, 78a;* 134-135, *83a;* 137, *86b;* sweat bath, 367

Pipes, 107, 359-361, *295-297*

Pipils, 88

Pisac, 100-102, *51, 52*

Pizarro, Francisco, 11, 21, 23, 90, 239-240; Hernando, 99; Juan, 99

Plants, indigenous, 10-11, 357

Ponchos, Chimu, 230, *182a;* 232, *185a;* 235, *189b, c;* 354-355, *289c, 290b;* Ica, 234, *189a;* 354, *290a;* Inca, 236-237, *191, 192b;* Paracas, 235, *190b;* Tiahuanaco, 227, *178a;* 235, *190a*

Popul-Vuh, 314

Portrait vessels, Mochica, 205-206, *159, 160*

Post-Columbian weaving, 222-223, *172b, 173c. See also* Spanish colonial weaving.

Pottery, 153-212; Andean Area, 200-212; identified at Malinalco, 38, and Calixtlahuaca, 40; incised, 162-163, *108c, 109b, d, 110c;* 184, *135;* 188, *139b,* 192-193, *143b, c,* (199-200), *150c, d;* Interlying Area, 193-200; "killing" of, 154; Maya Area, 174-193; Mexican Area, 47, *15d;* 163-174, 358; miscellaneous U.S.A., 161-162; relief, (176), *127c;* 184-190, *136-140f;* Southwest, 154-161; stuccoed, 163, *110b;* 177-178, *128;* value to archaeology, 153

Pre-Columbian art, scope of, x

Prescott, William H., 4, 21, 32

Pseudo-glyphs, 189-191

Puebla, lapidary-work (298), *243b;* 304-(305), *251b, 252a;* mosaic, 340; pottery, 164, *111c;* 174, *125a*

Pueblo architecture, 26-30, *1b, 2-6;* 365, *301a;* culture,

Pueblo (*Continued*) 12, 30; pottery, 154-159, *101a, b, c, d, 102-105c;* weaving, 220-222, *170a, b, 171a*

Pueblo I basket, 219-220, *169c*

Pueblo III basket "cradle," 220, *169a;* kiva jars, 158, *105b;* textile fragment, 221, *171b*

Pueblo IV textile fragment, (221), *171c*

Pueblo Bonito, 14, 28-29, 365, *4*

Pueblos, 13, 221; basket-work of, 219; decline of, 30

Puppet shows, 359

Pyramid, defined, 31, 44

Pyramid of the Moon, Teotihuacan, 32, 366

Pyramid of the Sun, Teotihuacan, 31, *7b*

Pyrite figure, 306, *253b;* used in mirrors, 362, *298b*

Quechua, language of the Incas, 365

Quetzal, 350

Quetzalcoatl, Mexican Wind-god, 32; conch symbol of, 32, 344; mask of, (342), *278a;* round structures associated with, 84; step-fret sign of, 50. *See also* Temple of Quetzalcoatl.

Quiché region, effigy jar, 190, *141b*

Quimbaya culture, 21, 259; gold work, (258)-261, *214-216;* 263-265, *218b-220;* 271, *226b;* pottery, 199, *150b*

Quipu, use of, 313, 363, *299b*

Quiriguá, 18; jade, 290, *236c;* pottery, 182; *132a;* 187, *138a;* sculpture, 120-122, *71b, c, 72c;* 138, *88b*

Quito, 23, 255

Rain-god, Maya, 72; masks of, 80, *36b;* 88, *42b;* well sacred to, 82, 281. Mexican, *see* Tlaloc.

Red House, Chichen Itzá, 77, 82, *33c, d*

Red Tiger. *See* Chacmool.

Reservoirs, 367

Reviewing Stand, Copan, 59, *20c*

Rings, copper, 273, *228b;* gold, 273-274, *228a, c, d, e;* shell, 346, *282a*

Rio, Antonio del, 65

Rio Bec, 69-71, *28*

Rito de los Frijoles. *See* Frijoles Canyon.

Roads, 363-365, *300*

Roof-comb, Chichen Itzá, 77; evolution of, 64; Palenque, 67; Rio Bec B, 70; Tikal, 64; Uxmal, 81

Rosny, Leon de, 131-132, 308

Round structures, associated with Wind-god, 84; Calixtlahuaca, 39; Caracol, Chichen Itzá, 84; *chulpas,* 96; Malinalco, 37; Mayapan, 78; Ocmulgee Earth Lodge, 39

Ruskin, John, 104

Sabacche, 77, *33b*

Sacerdotal Palace, Tikal, 63, *25*

Sacred Well, Chichen Itzá, 82, 281, 295; jades, 295-296, *240e, f, 241d;* mask, 281-282, *234b;* mosaic-work, 341; textiles, 213; wooden staff, 336, *273b*

Sacsahuaman, 98-99, *49;* 367, *303c*

Sahagun, Bernardino, 154, 331-332, 341-342, 359. *See also* Codex Florentino.

San Andres Tuxtla, 288

San Augustín, Colombia, sculpture, 149

San Bartolo Tenayuca. *See* Tenayuca.

INDEX

San Martín, José de, 24
Santa Lucia Cotzumalhuapa. *See* Cotzumalhuapa.
Santarem bottle, 198-199, *149d*
Sarcophagus, clay, 191, *141d*
Saville, Marshall H., 131, 280, 343
Sayil, 74-75, *31a*
Sculpture, 105-152, 289, 358-361; Andean Area, 149-151; characteristics of, 106-107, 151-152; Interlying Area, 147-149; material used in, 106; Maya Area, 119-147, 289; Mexican Area, 108-118, 151, 358; Mound Builder, 107, 359-361; Southeast, 107, 360; Southwest, 107
Seler, Edward, 308
Serpent Bird, 122, 337
Serpentine, 106, 283; mask, 304, *250d;* plaque, 292, *238a;* statuette, (297), *243a*
Shell-work, 344-348, *280-283;* in mosaic, 341
Shields, 343; Aztec feather, 352, *287a, b;* mosaic, 343, *279b;* Spanish colonial feather, 354
Shoshonean stock, 14
Sillustani, 97, *47b*
"Singing Girl," 140
Sitio Conte gold cuff, 269, *224b. See also* Coclé.
Slat armor, 334
Smith, A. Ledyard, 176, 297, 321
South Coast (Peru), 22, 92
Southeast pottery, 161-162, *108c, d;* sculpture, 107, 360, *295;* shell gorgets, 345, *281a, c;* slat armor, 334; wood-carving, 335, *271b. See also* Mound Builder.
Southwest, altitude, 10; architecture, 25-30, 365; area defined, 9; bone figure, 349; cotton introduced into, 12, 221; history, 11-13; maize introduced into, 10; painting, 317-318; pottery, 154-161; sculpture, 107; shell ring, 346; spear-thrower, 335; tree-ring calendar, 13; turquoise, 283, 340; weaving, 219-222
Southwest Museum, 220
Spanish colonial feather-work, 353-354, *288;* weaving, 236-238, *192;* wooden bowl, 340, *276f. See also* Codex Florentino, Magliabecchiano, and Mendoza.
Spear-throwers, 334-336, *272, 273a, c;* used by Basket Makers, 11
Spinden, Herbert J., 17, 54, 120, 132, 322
Spindles, Andean Area, 224-225, *174b*
Spiro, Temple Mound, metal-work, 242-243, *194b, c, d;* shell-carving, 345, *280b, c;* wood-carving, 335, *271a*
Spruce Tree House, Mesa Verde, (26), *1b*
Square Tower Ruin, Mesa Verde, 27, *2c*
Squier, E. George, 100, 102
Staff heads, bone, 349-350, *285b, c;* bronze, (252), *206e;* gold, 264-265, *219;* wood, 244-245, *196c*
Stairways, 43, 45, 367-368
Stelae, 17, 119; Copan, 120, *71a;* 289, *236a;* 293; Piedras Negras, 121, *72a, b;* 123-124, *73, 74;* Quiriguá, 121-122, *71b, c, 72c;* Raimondi, 150, *99b;* Tenam, 118-120, *69c;* Tikal, 119-120, *70a;* Totonac, 117-118, *69a;* Xultun, 119-120, *70b*
Stephens, John L., 56, 72-73, 75-78, 81
Stirrup-spout vessels, Chimu, 253, *207b;* Mochica, 200-206, *152, 153c, d, 154a, b, 156, 157a, 158a, 159a;* 244, *196b*
Stone, Doris, 146

Stucco heads, 136-137, *86;* relief, 129-131, *79, 80;* 142, *91c. See also* Pottery, stuccoed vases.
Sundials, in Andean Area, 101-102

Tajin, 42-44, *12;* sculpture, 112, *63a;* 134-135, *83c*
Talus-houses, 25, *1a*
Tampumachay ruins, 98, *48b*
Taos, 30, *6b*
Tarascan clay figures, 164-166, *112, 113a, 115a, b;* 168, *117c;* 183, *134d;* copper mask, 272, *227a*
Tarascans, 15, 164
Tehuantepec region, 277
Temple Group, Pisac, 101, *51b*
Temple of the Bas-Relief, Chichen Itzá, carved wall, 319, *261a*
Temple of the Chacmool, Chichen Itzá, mural, 143, *92a*
Temple of the Cross, Palenque, 67-68, *27;* pottery, 182, *133b;* tablet, 125
Temple (House) of the Dwarf, Uxmal, 78, *35a;* 368, *305a*
Temple of the Foliated Cross, Palenque, 67, 125
Temple of the Flying Façade, Sabacche, 77, *33b*
Temple of the Frescoes, Tulum, 72-74, *30;* mural, 326, *265b*
Temple of Kukulcan, Chichen Itzá, *see* Castillo; Uxmal, *see* Temple of the Dwarf.
Temple of Quetzalcoatl, Calixtlahuaca, 39, *10d;* Teotihuacan, 32-33, *8;* 366, *302a*
Temple of the Sculptured Doorway (Structure 22), Copan, 59-61, *22, 23;* Maize-god, 140, *90*
Temple of the Sun, Cuzco, 98; Palenque, 67, 125, *75*
Temple (House) of the Three Lintels, Chichen Viejo, 82-84, *39b*
Temple of the Tiger, Monte Alban, (46), *15a*
Temple of the Tigers, Chichen Itzá, 85-86, *40a;* murals, 323, *263b, c*
Temple of the Warriors, Chichen Itzá, 87-88, *42;* carving, 142, *91d;* mosaic, 341; mural, 322, 324, *263a*
Temple-base, 31, 43; obsidian, 308, *256c*
Temples, distinguished from palaces, 51, 62; rebuilding of, 32, 41, 45, 55, 83, 87-88
Tenam stela, 117-120, *69c*
Tenayuca, 40-42, *11*
Tenochtitlan, Aztec capital, 15-16, 40; history in Codex Mendoza, 330; market of, 15, 272, 333, 341
Teopanzolco, 35
Teotihuacan, architecture, 14, 30-34, *7, 8;* 366, *302a;* jade pendant, 292, *238b;* painting, 319, 321, *260a, b;* pottery, 163, *110b, c*
Texcoco, Lake, 14, 40; metal-work, 275-276, *230b, 231b*
Texcotzingo, 38, 366
Texmilincan disk, 280-282, *234a*
Textiles. *See* Weaving.
Tezcatlipoca, God of Youth, 320, *261b*
Thompson, E. H., 82, 281
Thompson, J. Eric S., xi, 18, 50, 298
Throne of the Inca, 99, 369, *49b*
Tiahuanaco, architecture, 89, 94-96, 100, *46;* bronze worked in, 251; metal-work, 244, *196a;* 247, *200a, b;* 255, *209d;* pottery, 208-211, *163a, c, 164a, 165a, b, 166-167b;* sculpture, 151, *99c;* weaving, 224-233,